REVEL, RIOT, AND REBELLION

REVEL, RIOT, AND REBELLION

Popular Politics and Culture
in England
1603–1660

DAVID UNDERDOWN

CLARENDON PRESS · OXFORD
1985

Oxford University Press, Walton Street, Oxford OX2 6DP

Oxford New York Toronto
Delhi Bombay Calcutta Madras Karachi
Kuala Lumpur Singapore Hong Kong Tokyo
Nairobi Dar es Salaam Cape Town
Melbourne Auckland
and associated companies in
Beirut Berlin Ibadan Nicosia

Oxford is a trade mark of Oxford University Press

Published in the United States
by Oxford University Press, New York

British Library Cataloguing in Publication Data
Underdown, David
Revel riot and rebellion: popular politics and
culture in England 1603–1660.
1. West Country (England)—Politics and
government 2. West Country (England)—Social
conditions 3. Great Britain—Politics and
government—1603–1649 4. Great Britain—
Politics and government—1649–1660 5. England
—Social conditions—17th century
I. Title
306'.2'09423   DA670.W49
ISBN 0-19-822795-7

Library of Congress Cataloging in Publication Data
Underdown, David.
Revel, riot, and rebellion.
Bibliography: p.
Includes index.
1. Great Britain—History—Puritan Revolution,
1642–1660—Causes. 2. Dorset—History. 3. Somerset—
History. 4. Wiltshire—History. I. Title.
DA406.U53 1985 941.06 85-5027
ISBN 0-19-822795-7

Set by Butler & Tanner Ltd
Printed and bound in Great Britain by
Biddles Ltd, Guildford and King's Lynn

For
SUSAN

Preface

THIS book addresses two simple and straightforward questions: first, how did the English common people (that is to say, people below the gentry rank) behave during the civil wars and revolutions of 1640–60; and second, how can we explain that behaviour? The questions emerge naturally out of the whole working life of an historian trying in vain to grasp the complex realities of the English Revolution. I can recall two particularly decisive moments in my formulation of them. The first occurred when I was working out the civil war history of my native county of Somerset and grasped the full implications of the simple, obvious fact that the gentry and commons of that county had followed different paths in the conflict. The other occurred in the tea-room at the Institute of Historical Research when I rashly assured John Morrill that regional variations of allegiance could best be understood as a product of cultural differences between the regions in question. Dr Morrill sensibly asked for some evidence of those cultural differences and for their alleged impact on the civil war. At that time, I confess, I was unable to answer so challenging a question; this book is an attempt to do so.

We shall return to the matter of regional cultural contrasts in due time, but let us for the present confine ourselves to the two original questions about popular allegiance. They seem straightforward enough, yet they immediately raise a whole series of related questions. *Did* the people in fact take sides in the civil war, or did they try to stay out of it? Did those who took sides do so of their own free will, or were they coerced by their landlords or employers, or by irresistible military pressures? To the extent that an element or free choice was involved, what variables—ideological, social, geographical—influenced their alignment with King or Parliament? Since 'the people' cannot be treated as a single, monolithic mass, were there differences of outlook and behaviour between people of different status, wealth, and occupation, between those in different regions or different types of community? What were the aspirations and expectations of these various subsets of 'the people', and how far did the revolution implement or disappoint them? Finally, was the revolution, as far as the common people were concerned, an isolated episode, or had it some relation to their history before and afterwards?

These and many other questions will be repeatedly raised in the course of this study. Before the tentative answers that will be proposed in this book can be achieved, some daunting problems of evidence have to be overcome. Even if we restrict ourselves to the original questions about

civil war allegiance (which we shall find it impossible to do) we immediately encounter formidable difficulties. Surviving seventeenth-century
sources make it relatively easy to study the lives of the élite, the literate
minority who left estate papers, correspondence, and in a few cases diaries
or memoirs; who read and occasionally wrote books, sermons, and
pamphlets; whose careers can be traced in the records of kingdom and
shire, diocese, university, and Inn of Court. But the further down the
social scale we penetrate the more often our subjects appear only as a
faceless, depersonalized mass, as mere names in a parish register, in lists
of communicants or of subscribers to an oath of loyalty; as tenants in a
manorial survey or rent-roll; as taxpayers in a rating list or (if we are
looking at the poorest levels of society) as people exempt from taxation
because of poverty.

The records of local courts, both civil and ecclesiastical, form the one
great exception to this general silence of the sources on the personal lives
(and not merely the criminal behaviour) of the lower orders. Obviously
the people who appear in them are not a representative sample of the
entire population, but they are the best we can do, and they have been
used extensively in this work. Without them, unless we are fortunate
enough to encounter such a village as Myddle, Shropshire, of which
Richard Gough wrote a marvellously personal anecdotal account, we are
left with only an occasional will or inventory to break the silence.

The military events of the civil war, one might suppose, are better
documented. It is true that sources such as memoirs and correspondence
give some clues to popular behaviour during the fighting, but they raise
almost as many problems as they solve. Accounts written long afterwards,
like those of the royalist Earl of Clarendon and the parliamentarian
Edmund Ludlow, often tell us more about the presuppositions of their
authors than about the events they describe. The correspondence of
military commanders is little more useful, usually betraying no interest in
the civilian population except as a source of money, men, and supplies, or
as an obstructive nuisance. Accounts of campaigns in printed pamphlets
and newsbooks sometimes provide clues about popular involvement, but
are inevitably coloured by propagandist purposes; both sides always tried
to demonstrate that they had popular support, their enemies that of only a
few factious or immoral individuals. Petitions, regularly proclaimed as
evidence of popular feeling by their organizers, often prove no such thing
and have always to be viewed with the gravest suspicion. Statements about
their neighbours by frightened constables to the authorities of one side or
the other are more likely to reflect the instinct for self-preservation than
an assessment of real opinion. And finally, to compound the historian's
frustration, in the confusion of civil war many kinds of records simply
disappeared or were kept even more imperfectly than in peacetime.

The wisest course for the historian confronted by such problems might well be to abandon the enterprise and consign questions about popular allegiance to the extensive category of the interesting but unanswerable. Happily, the situation is not quite as bleak as it might seem, and in fact the historian equipped with the conventional tools of the craft—among them common sense and a critical approach to the sources—can obtain some general impressions of group behaviour in the civil war, and of the complex social and cultural forces which helped to shape it. The apparent silence of the sources can sometimes be penetrated by reading between the lines; the biases of memoirs, letters, and newsbook accounts compared and allowed for. When we find a given area described as royalist or parliamentarian in sources stemming from opposite sides of the political divide we are entitled to conclude that such was indeed its general outlook. And a few sources exist which provide evidence about the allegiance of quite large numbers of people—lists of suspected royalist sympathizers in 1656, of former soldiers who received pensions after the Restoration. These sources too are not without their problems, but they will enable us in a later chapter to analyse the distribution of support for the two sides in some areas. The problems of evidence in the end prove less fearsome than at first sight.

In a perfect world, in which historians had unlimited time, unlimited funds, and armies of research assistants at their disposal, it might be possible to investigate the patterns of civil war allegiance throughout the whole of England. In a necessarily imperfect world in which these requirements are lacking, a more modest approach, concentrating on one region, has to be adopted. The region which is the primary focus of this study—the three-county area of Dorset, Somerset, and Wiltshire—has been chosen for a number of reasons. First, it contains a wide selection of topographical and agricultural zones, economies, and settlement types. Secondly, it offers a variety of different local responses to the civil war. The region was a fiercely contested one, experiencing several periods of intense fighting in which choices had to be made, even by the reluctant. An area such as East Anglia, which remained firmly in Parliament's grasp throughout the war, offers fewer opportunities for such a study. Finally, it produced in the risings of Clubmen in 1645 the most extensive popular movement of the entire civil war period.

This does not mean, however, that our study of popular allegiance, or of the social and cultural forces which help to explain it, can be absolutely confined to the three western counties. Large urban centres, particularly London, have been, to be sure, for the most part avoided. Their economic and social structures, the sheer scale of their existence, and the nature of their political experience were all so totally different from those of small towns and villages in which the overwhelming majority of the English people lived, that their history demands separate attention. Even Bristol, on the edge of the three-county region, and with a population of only some 15,000, but nevertheless the nearest thing to a metropolitan centre in the region, presents problems of such complexity and with so little similarity to those of its rural hinterland, that it has to be excluded, except peripherally, from this study. However, events in London, Bristol, and in a wide variety of towns and regions outside the western counties will occasionally be discussed when they are necessary to illuminate particular points, or when they provide useful comparative perspectives. To do this may appear to involve an element of inconsistency, but may perhaps have the value of showing that the social and political forces affecting the western counties did not exist in a vacuum. Cross-regional comparison, in turn, may also have the value of suggesting how the experience of the western counties was typical of, or different from, that of the kingdom at large.

A great deal of this book—indeed, almost half of it—will deal not with the civil war, but with developments during the half-century or so that preceded it. There are two reasons for this. One is probably fairly obvious: that in order to answer Dr Morrill's question about regional cultures and their impact on the war, we need to observe English social and cultural development over a longer period of time than the twenty years of the revolution. The second is perhaps less obvious but equally important. I do not regard the English Revolution as a fortuitous accident, unrelated to fundamental political and social processes—as having been caused by the ineptitude of Charles I, the personal ambition of John Pym and other opposition leaders, or accidents like the untimely death of the fourth Earl of Bedford. The civil war occurred at the end of a long period of social, political, and religious instability. That it occurred when it did may have been a coincidence, but this strikes me as unlikely. I believe that if we are to understand the revolution, we must first try to uncover its causes by paying some attention to the history of the preceding period. That, as well as answering Dr Morrill's question, is what this book attempts to do, focusing primarily upon the popular dimension of that history. Having obtained some understanding of the social, cultural, and political experience of the English people in the years before the revolution, we shall be in a better position to analyse their divided allegiance in the civil war itself.

ACKNOWLEDGEMENTS

Research for this book was greatly assisted by the award of fellowships by the American Council of Learned Societies and the National Endowment for the Humanities; I am happy to acknowledge the generosity of both the Council and the Endowment. Parts of several chapters have previously appeared in my essays 'The Chalk and the Cheese: Contrasts among the English Clubmen', 'The Problem of Popular Allegiance in the English Civil War', and 'The Taming of the Scold: The Enforcement of Patriarchal Authority in Early Modern England': I am grateful to the Editor of *Past and Present*, the Council of the Royal Historical Society, and Cambridge University Press respectively for permission to reprint these pages. Even more than most scholars at the end of their researches, I am deeply conscious of the courtesy and helpfulness of the staffs of the libraries and archives which I have used: the British Library; the libraries of Brown, London, and Yale Universities; the Bodleian Library; the Institute of Historical Research; the Public Record Office; and the Record Offices of Dorset, Gloucestershire, Somerset, and Wiltshire.

In writing this book I have been influenced by a large number of friends and colleagues, not always, I suspect, in ways that they will recognize. Among the many from whose understanding of the seventeenth century I have benefited, both through their publications and through numerous discussions with them, Anthony Fletcher, Christopher Hill, Clive Holmes, William Hunt, Martin Ingram, Joyce Malcolm, Conrad Russell, Lawrence Stone, and Keith Wrightson should be particularly mentioned. I also wish to thank my colleagues and students (both graduate and undergraduate) at Brown for so patiently enduring many long digressions on the culture of the English fields and forests. Earlier versions of parts of the book were read at the seminar on popular culture at the Institute of Historical Research led by Robert Scribner and Michael Hunter, at the Cambridge Seminar in Early Modern History at Harvard, the Yale Concilium on International and Area Studies, the Western Societies Program at Cornell University, the Pembroke Center for Teaching and Research on Women (Brown University), and the Shelby Cullom Davis Center for Historical Studies (Princeton University). I am grateful to all who participated in those discussions and helped me to clarify my arguments. The kindness of other scholars who allowed me to consult theses and other unpublished work is acknowledged in many of the footnotes below; I especially wish to thank Patricia Croot, Richard Cust, Martin Ingram, and Margaret Stieg. Richard Wall of the Cambridge Group on the History of Population and Social Structure helpfully supplied parish register tabulations, and Geoffrey Quaife provided other useful references. William Hunt, Joan Scott, Donald Spaeth, and Jack Thomas read parts of the book in manuscript and made many valuable suggestions. Cynthia Boutin was an unfailingly prompt, efficient, and uncomplaining typist.

Two obligations demand special acknowledgement, both of them being impressive reminders of the fact that friendship and occasional creative disagreement are not incompatible. The first is to John Morrill, whose questions over the tea-cups set in motion the whole enterprise, and whose warm encouragement, wise criticism, and careful reading of every chapter have given me repeated examples of scholarly co-operation which I shall always hope to emulate. The other is to Susan Amussen, who in both her written work and conversation has forced me to confront some of the central themes of this book far more clearly than I should otherwise have done. The historical insights that she has contributed will be less obvious to the reader than the many references to Norfolk sources that I owe to her, but they have been crucial ones.

Throughout the book spelling and punctuation in quotations have been modernized. Dates in the text follow the 'old style' usage, except that the year is regarded as beginning on 1 January; in footnote citations both the old and new style year are given when appropriate.

Providence, Rhode Island
February 1985

Contents

	List of Illustrations	xiv
	List of Maps	xv
	List of Abbreviations	xvi
1	Theories of Allegiance	1
2	Order and Disorder	9
3	Cultural Conflict	44
4	Regional Cultures	73
5	Popular Politics before the Civil War	106
6	The Civil War and the People	146
7	The Geographical Distribution of Allegiance	183
8	Popular Politics, 1646–1660	208
9	Culture and Politics, 1646–1660	239
10	The Restoration and English Political Culture	271
	Appendix I Population Estimates	293
	Appendix II Tables	295
	Bibliography	300
	Index	315

Illustrations

Between pages 160 *and* 161

1. *The World Turned Upside Down:* title-page of a 1647 pamphlet
2. Disorders in London, 1640–1
    A. Rioters outside Lambeth Palace, 1 May 1640
    B. Riot in Westminster Hall, 27 Dec. 1641
3. The Protestation
    A. A minister and his parishioners take the oath
    B. Procession of the Buckinghamshire petitioners, 11 Jan. 1642
4. Civil War
    A. Soldiers on the march
    B. Roundhead soldiers burn 'popish' images, 1643
5. Cultural conflict
    A. Demolition of Cheapside Cross, 2 May 1643
    B. Burning of the Book of Sports, 10 May 1643
6. Popular stereotypes
    A. Roundhead and Cavalier
    B. The Exciseman
7. The threat to patriarchal order
    A. The war as an opportunity for cuckoldry
    B. Skimmington beats her husband
    C. The Parliament of Women
8. Charivari
    A. The 'riding' of a monopolist, 1641
    B. The charivari theme used in political caricature, 1647

Acknowledgements: all photographs except 7B are from the Thomason Tracts, and are reproduced by permission of the Trustees of the British Library. 7B, from John Taylor's *Divers Crabtree Lectures* (1639), is reproduced by permission of Bodley's Librarian.

Maps

I   The three counties   6

II   Wiltshire regions and popular festivals, 1603–1640   74

III   Somerset regions and popular festivals, 1603–1640   87

IV   Dorset regions and popular festivals, 1603–1640   92

Abbreviations

BIHR	*Bulletin of the Institute of Historical Research*
BL	British Library
CCC	*Calendar of the Proceedings of the Committee for Compounding,* ed. M. A. E. Green, 1889–92
CJ	*Journals of the House of Commons*
CSPD	*Calendar of State Papers, Domestic*
DNB	*Dictionary of National Biography*
DNHP	*Dorset Natural History and Archaeological Society Proceedings* (under various titles)
DRO	Dorset Record Office
Ec. H.R.	*Economic History Review*
Eng. H.R.	*English Historical Review*
GRO	Gloucestershire Record Office
HJ	*Historical Journal*
HMC	Historical Manuscripts Commission
JBS	*Journal of British Studies*
JSH	*Journal of Social History*
LJ	*Journals of the House of Lords*
N & Q	*Notes and Queries*
NRO	Norfolk Record Office
P & P	*Past and Present*
PRO	Public Record Office
QS	Quarter Sessions
RO	Record Office
RS	Record Society, or Records Society
SDNQ	*Somerset and Dorset Notes and Queries*
SQSR	*Quarter Sessions Records for the County of Somerset* (1603–60), ed. E. H. Bates [Harbin], SRS xxiii, xxiv, xxviii, 1907–12
SRO	Somerset Record Office
SRS	Somerset Record Society
TRHS	*Transactions of the Royal Historical Society*
TT	Thomason Tracts
VCH	*Victoria County History*
WAM	*Wiltshire Archaeological Magazine* (under various titles)
WRO	Wiltshire Record Office

Place of publication is London, unless otherwise stated.

1

Theories of Allegiance

SEVERAL different hypotheses about popular behaviour in the civil war have been advanced by previous students of the conflict. Perhaps the most familiar one is that the English common people had no real allegiance to either side—that they were mere cannon-fodder, targets for plunder, at best deferential pawns who did as they were told. This belief has a long and respectable ancestry.[1] Many of the combatants themselves believed it, regularly noting the automatic changes in local attitudes when news arrived of distant victories or defeats. In post-war political disputes the people were often regarded as no more independent: 'they know it is safest to be in favour with the strongest side', a newsbook commented.[2] When they fought, in this view, it was because they had no alternative. How often, Anthony Ascham lamented, 'ambitious or angry men form subtleties and pretences, and afterwards the poor people (who understand them not) are taken out of their houses . . . to fight and maintain them at the perils of one another's lives'.[3] Looking back after 1660, men as various as Thomas Hobbes and Richard Baxter took the same line. 'There were very few of the common people that cared much for either of the causes, but would have taken any side for pay or plunder', Hobbes tells us. Baxter has been often quoted: 'The poor ploughmen understood but little of these matters; but a little would stir up their discontent when money was demanded'.[4]

Hobbes and Baxter might well appear to be supported by the massive illiteracy of the English population. Male illiteracy averaged about 70 per cent in the rural areas; women were even less likely to be literate. People who could not read, it might be supposed, could have had no real interest in the great issues dividing King and Parliament.[5] A logical deduction is

---

[1] For recent expressions of this view see Lawrence Stone, *The Causes of the English Revolution*, 1972, p. 145; Robert Ashton, *The English Civil War*, 1978, p. 174; Perez Zagorin, *Rebels and Rulers, 1500–1660*, Cambridge, 1982, ii. 155.

[2] BL TT, E. 346 (10): *Scotish Dove*, no. 144 (22–31 July 1646). For local reactions to changing military fortunes, see, for example, *The Letter Books 1644–45 of Sir Samuel Luke*, ed. H. G. Tibbutt, 1963, pp. 304, 306.

[3] Anthony Ascham, *Of the Confusion and Revolutions of Government*, 1649 edn., p. 144.

[4] Thomas Hobbes, *Behemoth or the Long Parliament*, ed. F. Tönnies and M. M. Goldsmith, 1969, p. 2. *Reliquiae Baxterianae*, ed. M. Sylvester, 1696, p. 17.

[5] David Cressy, *Literacy and the Social Order: Reading and writing in Tudor and Stuart England*, Cambridge, 1980, esp. pp. 72–3. Peter Laslett, *The World We Have Lost*, 2nd edn., 1973, pp. 20, 68, 209.

that the armies of both sides must have been composed largely of mercenaries hired for 'pay or plunder', or of levies who went to war with varying degrees of reluctance, either because they were the tenants or dependents of men who had power over them, or because they were simply conscripted. If this was indeed the case, patterns of military recruitment will tell us nothing about the actual sympathies of either the men involved or the communities from which they came. If we accept this 'deference hypothesis' we can understand the civil war by analysing the politics of the gentry, and need look no further.

A second, and recently popular view of the civil war may be labelled the 'neutralist' hypothesis. The first priority of the lower orders, it is argued, was to protect their homes, families, and communities from the armies of both sides: the wider issues of the civil war did not touch them. Recent scholars have done much to illuminate the strength of neutralism and localism at all levels of English society during the civil wars, and it would be a rash historian who neglected them.[6] Even the gentry, with their broader horizons and closer involvement in a national political culture, often tried to stay out of the conflict. Both sides had sworn to uphold the Protestant religion, the Shropshire gentleman Jonathan Langley remarked, 'what reason have I therefore to fall out with either?'[7] If the gentry regarded disputed national issues as less pressing than the preservation of good order and community, it would be absurd to expect their inferiors to view the situation differently. A Wiltshire countryman earlier in the century neatly expressed the hopeless detachment from great public issues felt by many of the rural population: 'It were no matter if the King and Queen and all were hanged unless the price of corn do fall'. The 1640s abound with similar outbursts of popular agnosticism.[8]

Besides the 'deference' and 'neutralist' hypotheses there is a third, equally familiar theory about popular allegiance. This rests on a very different set of assumptions: that many of the common people *did* take an active part in the civil war, *did* have real preferences for one side or the other, and that the side they overwhelmingly preferred was that of Parliament. Like the others, this interpretation has a venerable ancestry. Born in the war itself, it echoes constantly through the pages of Clarendon's *History of the Rebellion*. The people, Clarendon notes, were solidly parliamentarian, largely through envy of the rich and, in the towns

---

[6] The pioneering work in a genre that includes many other important county studies is Alan Everitt, *The Community of Kent and the Great Rebellion*, Leicester, 1966. See also J. S. Morrill, *The Revolt of the Provinces*, 1976. For a critical discussion of the localist interpretation, see Clive Holmes, 'The County Community in Stuart Historiography', *JBS* xix, no. 2 (1980), 54–73.

[7] 'The Ottley Papers relating to the Civil War', ed. W. Phillips, *Shropshire Archaeological and Natural History Society Transactions*, 2nd Ser. vii (1895), 264.

[8] 'Extracts from the Records of the Wiltshire Quarter Sessions: Reign of King James the First', ed. R. W. Merriman, *WAM* xxii (1885), 33.

especially, out of a 'natural malignity' born of hatred of authority: 'the fury and license of the common people', inflamed by demagogic preachers, burst forth in 'barbarity and rage against the nobility and gentry'.[9]

It is important to note that neither Clarendon nor many of the other writers previously quoted were always very precise about what they meant by 'the people'. The ambiguities of the term, then as always, were limitless, but at the cost of some over-simplification two broadly contrasting positions can be distinguished. On the one hand was the view that 'the people' consisted of all adult males (the universal acceptance of patriarchal authority excluded women by definition); on the other was the application of the term only to propertied heads of households—to freeholders, masters, independent craftsmen, the 'middling sort' as the common phrase went—with the rest of the population unceremoniously relegated to the categories of 'the poor' or 'the rabble'.[10] For our purposes both groups, as well as the vast numbers who occupied indeterminate positions between the middling sort and the poor, must be included within the undifferentiated term, 'the people'. But the distinction between them must always be kept in mind.

Competing civil war propagandists might differ on the motives underlying popular support for Parliament, but most agreed that it existed among 'the people' of all social levels. Royalists pointed to their enemies' dependence on the poorer element, the mutinous rabble intent only on lining their pockets at the expense of the rich. Parliamentarians naturally emphasized their support among the respectable and propertied. Again Baxter provides a typical example: a civil war which ranges the sober, godly 'middling sort' against the corrupt gentry and the godless mercenary poor. The theme is echoed by countless parliamentarian propagandists.[11] The underlying assumption is that Parliament's cause is that of reason and religion, and that its typical supporters (yeomen, freeholders, and independent craftsmen) are literate, rational, and religious. The modern expression of this equation between Parliament and people is the 'class' interpretation of the civil war. The 'middling sort', it is suggested, had reached the degree of consciousness of common identity necessary to define them as a class. The labouring poor had not, and therefore had no independent role to play. They provided, however, a

---

[9] Edward, Earl of Clarendon, *The History of the Rebellion and Civil Wars in England*, ed. W. D. Macray, Oxford, 1888, ii. 226, 318 (the work contains many other examples). See also Christopher Hill, *Puritanism and Revolution*, 1958, pp. 199–214.

[10] Christopher Hill, 'The Poor and the People in Seventeenth-Century England', William F. Church Memorial Lecture, Brown University, 1981.

[11] *Reliquiae Baxterianae*, pp. 30–3. For other examples, see John Corbet, 'A True and Impartial History of the Military Government of the Citie of Gloucester', in *Somers Tracts*, ed. Sir W. Scott, 1809–15, v. 302–7; and Thomas May, *The History of the Parliament of England which began November 3, 1640*, Oxford, 1854.

constant reservoir from which both sides could draw recruits either by material inducements or by conscription.[12]

We have, then, three alternative hypotheses which deserve to be tested against the evidence: that allegiance was primarily determined by deference, localism, or class. At first sight none of the three is entirely convincing. The first two—deference and localism—require us to believe that both sides in the war relied on impressed men, half-hearted militia forces, and the reluctant dependents of peers and gentlemen, supplemented in Parliament's case by a few zealous Puritans, mainly from London and the eastern counties, and in the King's by levies from Ireland, Wales, and the 'dark corners of the land'. The third—middling-sort parliamentarianism—at least explains how Parliament got an army and the degree of popular support necessary to sustain it, but not how the King managed to do so.[13] Yet the fact is that the Royalists controlled large areas of the country for considerable periods of time—the Welsh border counties, much of the north, and more pertinently for the present study, at various times the counties of Dorset, Somerset, and Wiltshire. It seems unlikely that a unanimously hostile population over such wide areas could have been held down for long periods solely by force, especially during a civil war in which there often were friendly forces nearby to assist them. On the other side of the conflict some nominally parliamentarian counties showed a conspicuous lack of enthusiasm for their cause: Kent is a well-known example.[14] Some parts of England were obviously more parliamentarian, some more royalist, than others, and as the case of Somerset reminds us, these differences did not always coincide with the loyalties of the local élites. It appears, therefore, that there was such a thing as 'popular royalism' as well as neutralism and 'popular parliamentarianism'. While paying due attention to the deference, neutralism, and class hypotheses (all of which, as we shall see, have some explanatory validity at certain times and places), we can, therefore, propose a fourth hypothesis: that contrasts in popular allegiance had a regional basis, and were related to local differences in social structure, economic development and culture.

*

The most useful analytical tool for exploring regional differences in early modern England is the typology of rural communities and economies

[12] The most uncompromising recent advocate of this argument is Brian Manning, *The English People and the English Revolution*, 1976.

[13] See, for example, Joyce L. Malcolm, *Caesar's Due: Loyalty and King Charles 1642–1646*, Royal Hist. Soc. Studies in History, xxxviii, 1983; and 'A King in Search of Soldiers: Charles I in 1642', *HJ* xxi (1978), 251–73.

[14] Everitt, *Community of Kent*. A similar lack of enthusiasm has been observed in other 'parliamentarian' counties: Clive Holmes, *The Eastern Association in the English Civil War*, Cambridge, 1974, chs. 1–4.

proposed by agricultural historians, emphasizing the social differences between the arable farming and woodland or pasture areas.[15] In the 'field' or 'champion' country—the regions of arable cultivation covering much of southern and eastern England—the age-old pattern of largely unenclosed common fields still prevailed. It was, to be sure, being slowly transformed by the trend to capitalist farming, which in many places spawned an occasional bigger, enclosed farm producing a surplus for the market. But even where this was happening the older settlement pattern was not much changed: the arable village was nucleated, tightly packed around church and manor-house (often with a resident squire), the whole structure firmly bound by neighbourhood and custom, and by powerful mechanisms of social control.

In the dairying and cattle-grazing districts, and in the still extensive woodland tracts, there was a very different pattern of settlement. Parishes tended to be larger, the inhabitants scattered in small hamlets or isolated farms, often far from the watchful eye of parson or squire. The Elizabethan writer William Harrison conveniently summarizes the two settlement types:

> Our soil being divided into champaign ground and woodland, the houses of the first lie uniformly builded in every town together, with streets and lanes, whereas in the woodland countries (except here and there in great market towns) they stand scattered abroad, each one dwelling in the midst of his own occupying.[16]

Working small enclosed family farms, the people here were likely to be more individualistic, less circumscribed by ancient custom. Lacking strong manorial institutions, the villages were often unable to prevent immigration by outsiders. They thus tended to grow more rapidly than the more controlled arable parishes, and to be more unstable, more vulnerable to high prices in bad harvest years. In many such places there were industrial by-employments to attract newcomers, further exposing them to economic fluctuations from which the more stable arable villages were largely shielded.

The field–pasture dichotomy of course grossly over-simplifies the complex realities of English regional and village structures. Still, it provides a convenient introduction to a brief topographical survey of the three western counties, in which the distinctions are clearly recognizable. The heartland of arable cultivation was the 'sheep-corn' region of the Wiltshire and Dorset downlands, stretching from the Hampshire border in the east and the Marlborough Downs in the north, across Salisbury Plain and into Dorset, to their final western escarpment north-east of

[15] The typology is conveniently described in Joan Thirsk, 'The Farming Regions of England', and Alan Everitt, 'Farm Labourers', in *The Agrarian History of England and Wales*, iv, ed. Joan Thirsk, Cambridge, 1967, pp. 1–15, 109–12, 462–5.

[16] William Harrison, *The Description of England*, ed. Georges Edelen, Ithaca, 1968, p. 217.

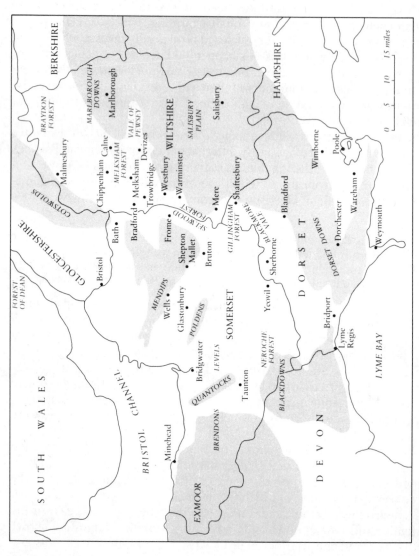

I The three counties

Bridport. Here are the small compact parishes, the nucleated villages, the strong manorial structures. In the extreme north of Wiltshire, along the edge of the Cotswolds, a similar pattern prevailed, though with a greater admixture of pastureland and somewhat less strikingly nucleated village centres than was common in the downlands. Over the rest of the three counties various types of pasture economy were the rule. In north-west Wiltshire, from Westbury across the plain to Chippenham, Calne, and beyond, lay the 'cheese country', devoted to dairy farming—and also the manufacture of cloth, often by the same families. Parishes of larger area, patterns of scattered settlement rather than nucleated villages, extensive tracts of woodland in Braydon, Chippenham, and Melksham forests, and weaker manorial controls—John Aubrey notes that the 'destroying of petty manors' had already begun by 1500, and that as it became common 'the mean people lived lawless, nobody to govern them'—these were the prevailing characteristics of the Wiltshire 'cheese country'.[17]

Somerset north of the Mendips and along the Wiltshire border to the north of Bruton was very similar. Dairy farming and cloth production dominated the local economy, and again there were extensive woodlands along the eastern border of the county, in Selwood Forest near Frome. In south-eastern Somerset, from Bruton south to Yeovil and west towards Ilminster, and in north Dorset in the Blackmore Vale region, there was another kind of pasture area, in which dairy farming and cattle-raising were less frequently combined with cloth manufacturing. This region was also characterized by a settlement pattern which contained elements of both the nucleated and the scattered types: villages established in woodlands that had been partly cleared in the middle ages, with nucleated cores and open fields (though these were fast disappearing by the sixteenth century), but also with outlying areas of more scattered settlement which resulted from later clearance of woods further from the village centre.[18] West Dorset, especially in the Marshwood Vale area north and north-west of Bridport, was a pasture region of almost classically scattered settlement, with few compact village centres, but again one in which the cloth industry was of less consequence than in north Somerset and north-west Wiltshire.[19] Central Somerset contained the only extensive area of fenland in the three counties, stretching from Langport and

[17] *Topographical Collections of John Aubrey*, ed. J. E. Jackson, Devizes, 1862, p. 9. My description of Wiltshire agricultural regions is based on E. Kerridge, 'Agriculture c.1500–c.1793', *VCH, Wiltshire*, iv. 43–64. For a typical scattered settlement, see Maude F. Davies, *Life in an English Village: An Economic and Historical Survey of the Parish of Corsley in Wiltshire*, 1909, pp. 6–10.

[18] Thirsk, 'Farming Regions', pp. 71–80. Eric Kerridge, *The Agricultural Revolution*, 1967, pp. 117–20. Christopher Taylor, *The Making of the English Landscape: Dorset*, 1970, pp. 95–7, 120.

[19] Barbara Kerr, *Bound to the Soil: A Social History of Dorset, 1750–1918*, 1968, pp. 8–11, 50–1, and note esp. Plate 22. For much further information I am indebted to J. H. Bettey, 'Agriculture and Rural Society in Dorset, 1570–1670', Ph.D. thesis, University of Bristol, 1977.

Ilchester in the south, to the low-lying shores of the Bristol Channel east and north of Bridgwater. Here the villages hugged the intervening or surrounding upland ridges, being relatively nucleated along the Poldens and at the foot of the Mendips, but with extensive tracts of pastureland running down into the levels, on which elaborate intercommoning arrangements provided fair access for neighbouring villages.[20] Finally, in the west and south-west of Somerset, there were large areas of infertile uplands in Exmoor and Blackdown, where the villages were small and widely dispersed, and again, as in Blackmore Vale, contained both nucleated and scattered characteristics.

This hurried survey far from exhausts the variety of agricultural economies and settlement types that existed in the three western counties. One could add the barren heathlands of south-east Dorset, the almost equally barren Mendip mining region, and at the other extreme the magnificently fertile Vale of Taunton Deane, with its mixed economy of pasture, grain, and fruit-growing. But it is enough to show something of the variety that existed, and to introduce the contrast that will recur many times in this book between the 'traditional' areas of open-field, sheep-corn husbandry in the nucleated villages of the chalk downlands, and the more individualistic economies and settlement patterns of the north Somerset and Wiltshire cheese and cloth-making country; with the less industrially developed pasture region in south-east Somerset and Black-more Vale representing an intermediate type in respect of both economic and settlement patterns.

We should not exaggerate the contrasts or expect to discover that the inhabitants of the three zones inhabited totally different mental worlds. They held many common assumptions about family and community, church and state, shared in a large common stock of culture. But by 1600 these regions were beginning to diverge both economically and socially. Roland Mousnier and other historians have noted that in France similar regional contrasts were related to different levels of rural unrest. The peasant revolts of the seventeenth century occurred mainly to the west and south-west of a line from Normandy to Dauphiné, in areas of small enclosed farms, dispersed settlements and woodlands. In the still largely common-field north-east of France, village society was more cohesive and major outbreaks of violence rare.[21] Has this insight, we may ask, any relevance to the divided allegiance of the English common people in the civil war? Before that question can be answered, a more careful exam-ination of the behaviour of the common people in the early seventeenth century—their social, cultural, religious, and political development—must be attempted.

---

[20] Michael Williams, *The Draining of the Somerset Levels*, Cambridge, 1970, pp. 89–91.

[21] Roland Mousnier, *Peasant Uprisings in Seventeenth-Century France, Russia, and China*, trans. Brian Pearce, New York, 1972, chs. 2–6. See also C. S. L. Davies, 'Peasant Revolt in France and England: a Comparison', *Agricultural History Review*, xxi (1973), 122–34.

2

Order and Disorder

IT is not uncommon for a society to be torn between ideal and reality, and the people of early seventeenth-century England experienced this tension to an unusual degree. In the century before 1640 the country had undergone a social and economic transformation while retaining a static theory of society to which the changes could not be accommodated. Sir Thomas Smith, William Harrison, and countless other Elizabethans expressed notions which may have been challenged in theory by a handful of religious dissidents, and were certainly being undermined in practice, but which remained the accepted consensus of all sorts and conditions of Englishmen. Belief in a divinely-ordained cosmic order, linking the entire universe from inanimate matter to God himself, provided every individual with a natural place or degree. A chain of reciprocal authority and obedience joined King to humblest labourer in a series of interlocking hierarchies: the hierarchy of the family and household, ruled by benevolent father or master; the hierarchy of the village or urban community, presided over by squire and parson, mayor and aldermen; the hierarchy of the county community, directed by the Lord Lieutenant and his deputies, by High Sheriff and JPs; the hierarchy of the community of the realm, surmounted by King and lords. To tamper with any one of these hierarchies was to threaten them all, to invite confusion and social disintegration.[1]

At the heart of this conception of order was the patriarchal family. The authority of husbands over wives, of parents over children, of the patriarchal head over subordinate members of the household—servants and apprentices as well as blood-relations—was the central axiom on which all else depended. Its divine origin justified, by analogy, the authority of clergy over laity, of gentry over dependents, of kings over subjects. The sonorous message of the Elizabethan Homily on Obedience, incessantly reiterated in the teaching and catechizing of the young and in sermons to their elders, was sustained by the whole majesty of church, law, and government. 'As it is a thing required by law and reason', declared Thomas Beard, 'that children bear the honour and reverence to their

---

[1] For the underlying intellectual system, see E. M. W. Tillyard, *The Elizabethan World Picture*, 1943. For its political expression, Gordon J. Schochet, *Patriarchalism in Political Thought*, New York, 1975, esp. chs. 2, 3.

natural parents which is commanded; so it is necessary . . . that all subjects perform that duty of honour and obedience to their Lords, Princes, and Kings'.[2] And in return there was the reciprocal responsibility of rulers for ruled. 'As the father over one family,' intoned Sir Robert Filmer, 'so the King, as father over many families, extends his care to preserve, feed, clothe, instruct and defend the whole commonwealth'.[3] Virtually unquestioned and all-pervasive, the notion of patriarchal authority was the ultimate foundation of both domestic and civil order.

The King was at the summit of this pyramid of degree; beneath him the heads of independent households made up the effective members of the commonwealth. They were, however, of far from equal status. Sir Thomas Smith provides the conventional four-part analysis of Elizabethan society: nobility; gentry; burgesses (urban) and yeoman (rural); and 'the fourth sort of men which do not rule'. Later writers indulged in further elaboration, but Smith's scheme of classification remained the basis for most other versions. Gentlemen, yeomen (usually defined as farmers worth over £40 a year), husbandmen, craftsmen, labourers, and paupers: apart from some uncertainty about the position of clergy and other professional men, the status hierarchy of rural England was in theory clear enough.[4] Each rank had its public function. The major gentry ruled their shires as JPs and Deputy-Lieutenants; the lesser gentry (whose lands and influence did not extend beyond their own parishes) shared with the yeomen such offices as high constables of hundreds, served on grand juries, and voted when opportunity occurred in parliamentary elections. Even the husbandmen and craftsmen, of 'no voice nor authority . . . but only to be ruled' in Smith's account, nevertheless had their modest responsibilities, being 'commonly made churchwardens, aleconners, and many times constables'.[5] They also played a vital role in village self-government through participation in the manor court and, whatever their condition, enjoyed the protection of the King's laws. Even labourers, noted the Devonian Thomas Westcote, 'though the most inferior, are yet, notwithstanding, *liberi homines*—free-men of state and conditions: no slaves'.[6]

[2] Thomas Beard, *The Theatre of Gods Judgements* (1597), 4th edn., 1648, p. 160.

[3] *Patriarcha and Other Political Works of Sir Robert Filmer*, ed. Peter Laslett, Oxford, 1949, p. 63; and see also intro., pp. 11–13.

[4] Sir Thomas Smith, *De Republica Anglorum*, ed. L. Alston, Cambridge, 1906, pp. 31–46. Later versions of the hierarchy include Thomas Westcote, *A View of Devonshire in MDCXXX*, ed. G. Oliver and P. Jones, Exeter, 1845, pp. 45–54; and George Snell, *The Right Teaching of Useful Knowledge*, 1649, pp. 89–93. See also Lawrence Stone, 'Social Mobility in England, 1500–1700', *P & P* no. 33 (Apr 1966), 16–55.

[5] Smith, *De Republica Anglorum*, p. 46, quoted in Laslett, *World We Have Lost*, p. 32. Joan Kent, 'The English Village Constable, 1580–1642', *JBS* xx, no. 2 (1981), 28–9, argues that constables were usually of higher status.

[6] Westcote, *View of Devonshire*, p. 54.

But active participation in this hierarchy of rank and status involved only the propertied heads of households. The rights of wives, children, and servants were subsumed within those of their husbands, parents, and employers. Married women had few rights to property of their own, and their roles in household governance and the family economy were always subject to the authority of their husbands. Widows had more independence, and had the same obligations as other property-owners in such matters as taxation and the performance of public duties. In villages where the offices of constable or churchwarden were held in rotation they usually, though not always, hired male substitutes.[7] Obviously the wives and children of people of rank enjoyed greater respect than those below them, but that respect depended on the status of their husbands or fathers. However, theirs was a very different case from that of the unattached vagrant. 'They that are not listed within the orders aforementioned', wrote George Snell at the end of a survey of the status hierarchy, 'are in the eye of the law as vagabonds and wanderers, as being of no family, of no parish church, of no town, of no shire'.[8] The member of even the poorest household inhabited a completely different world from that of the 'masterless' man or woman.

*

Order was maintained by the functioning of hierarchy in family and kingdom, but also by the fact that the English people lived in communities—in towns and villages. The village had its own hierarchy, ranging from the gentry (though not all villages had resident squires) and other 'parish notables' at the summit to the landless poor at the base. Ideally it was a community in which territorial identity was reinforced by shared values of harmony, co-operation, and 'good neighbourhood'.[9] Villagers knew well enough that they differed in wealth and status, but in theory at least these inequalities were transcended by the reciprocal ties that bound them: the enduring ties of kinship, neighbourhood, the common experience of the stable certainties of the church calendar and the agricultural year. Like all such ideals, the harmony may have been more honoured in the breach than in the observance, but if it was a myth, it was a powerful one.

As is the common way with myths, the notion of the idyllically stable community was most poignantly celebrated when it was already losing

[7] Lawrence Stone, *The Family, Sex and Marriage in England 1500–1800*, abridged edn., Harmondsworth, 1979, pp. 136–7. But see also Pearl Hogrefe, 'Legal Rights of Tudor Women and their Circumvention by Men and Women', *Sixteenth Century Journal*, iii (1972), 97–105. For examples of women churchwardens and the appointment of substitutes, see *Accounts of the Wardens of the Parish of Morebath, Devon, 1520–1573*, ed. J. E. Binney, Exeter, 1904, pp. 200, 209, 217, 241.

[8] Snell, *Useful Knowledge*, p. 93.

[9] For a typical expression of the ideal, see the passage from a 1608 Star Chamber case quoted in Clive Holmes, *Seventeenth-Century Lincolnshire*, Lincoln, 1980, p. 29.

touch with reality. Almost a century before Goldsmith, descriptions of
village life such as that of Great Cheverell, Wiltshire, by its rector
Nathaniel Shute show the continuing strength of the ideal. The inhabitants, Shute declared, were 'industrious in their husbandry', living
'friendly and neighbourly . . . ready to assist each other upon occasion'. It
was a quiet, sober community (there were no alehouses and for almost
forty years not a single bastard had been born in the parish), in which the
preferred diversions of the young men were 'those masculine and innocent exercises of football and ringing'. Such few paupers as existed were
well supported by the poor rate and by private charities, so begging was
unknown. It is of course too good to be true, but whatever may have been
the real truth about Great Cheverell, Shute's account is a convenient
summary of what many people thought village life ought to be.[10]

Great Cheverell was a nucleated village, still in the late seventeenth
century retaining its common fields. Such indeed was the ideal type of the
'traditional' rural community. In spite of the slow, continuing transition
from subsistence to market-oriented farming, in the chalk downlands of
Wiltshire and Dorset, as in many other parts of England, open-field
husbandry still remained widespread.[11] Its very nature demanded a co-
operative community. In reaching collective decisions on crop-rotation,
pasturing, and drainage, on routine matters such as the marking of
boundaries and the control of straying beasts, villagers were constantly
acting together. The village provided essential public services: the sheep-
fold, the rook nets, the common cowherd, the mole catcher. Management
of the common pasture required just as much co-operation as that of the
arable fields, especially in places adjacent to large grazing areas, such as
the villages of the Somerset levels, where elaborate intercommoning
arrangements existed.[12]

Village identity was institutionalized in the manor and the parish. The
manor courts were declining during the seventeenth century as indi-
vidualist farming eroded the open-field system, and as other order-
enforcing mechanisms grew in strength. But in the years before the civil
war they were still in many places an essential forum of community

[10] 'A Document from Great Cheverell', ed. H. C. Brentnall, *WAM* liii (1949–50), 430–40. There
is a similar description of Brightwell, Oxon., in Robert Plot, *The Natural History of Oxfordshire*,
Oxford, 1677, pp. 203–4.

[11] Thirsk, 'Farming Regions', pp. 6–7, 32–4, 41–5, 64–7, 81–92. Kerridge, *Agricultural Revolution*,
esp. pp. 23–4; 'Agriculture c.1500–c.1793', pp. 45–6. Bettey, 'Agriculture and Rural Society in
Dorset', chs. 3, 5. M. A. Havinden, 'Agricultural Progress in Open-field Oxfordshire', in *Essays in
Agrarian History*, ed. W. E. Minchinton, Newton Abbot, 1968, i. 150–5. W. G. Hoskins, *The Midland
Peasant*, 1957, pp. 90–5, 152–66, provides a useful description of the survival of open-field agriculture
at Wigston Magna, Leicestershire.

[12] Bettey, 'Agriculture and Rural Society in Dorset', pp. 23–4, 57, 62–3, 154, 162. Williams,
Somerset Levels, pp. 89–91. For similar arrangements in Lincolnshire, see Joan Thirsk, *English Peasant
Farming*, 1957, pp. 25–8, 84–90, 118.

self-government. In the manor court the landholding tenants ran their own affairs, regulated their own economy, and rotated the necessary offices such as hayward and aleconner among themselves.[13] How far this self-government extended depended on the amount of control a lord of the manor chose to exert, directly or through his steward, and this varied greatly from place to place. But even if there were limits to the tenantry's independence, the age-old process of presentment was no mere formality: when their interests were threatened jurors were often ready enough to resist their lord or steward.[14] Where manorial institutions had collapsed, as at Wigston Magna in Leicestershire, village meetings cutting across manorial boundaries took over the function of agricultural regulation.[15] But it was usually in the manor court that villagers enforced local customs of tenure and inheritance, modes of husbandry, the collection of wood, turf, and stone, and an infinite variety of day-to-day affairs. The historian of Castle Combe, Wiltshire, describes it as 'a community to a great extent self-governed'. It was far from unique.[16]

A random example is enough to show the kind of regulative routine performed by a manor court. Not far from Castle Combe, on the edge of the Cotswolds, lay the manor of Nettleton. It seems to have been a tranquil enough place, rarely disturbed by anything more serious than a brawl between two strangers at the inn or some exchanges of invective between scolding women. The business recorded in the Nettleton court book for 1615 is typical of a thousand such places. Tenants are presented for not keeping houses, stables, hedges, ditches, and boundaries between tenements in repair; for allowing cattle to stray; for killing pigs in the street 'to the annoyance of the people'; for grazing excessive numbers of sheep on the common; and there is a significant concern about controlling migration into the village. There is little sign of interference by the lord, or his steward: order is maintained collectively by the tenants.[17]

But Nettleton was a parish as well as a manor. If the manor was the civil expression of the community, the parish was its spiritual expression. The church—and the parish as an institution—encompassed, however, far

[13] Coke's distinction between the 'two natures' of the Court Baron (as a court of freeholders and as a court of copyholders) was rarely enforced in practice: John P. Dawson, *A History of Lay Judges*, Cambridge, Mass., 1960, p. 211.

[14] Dawson, *Lay Judges*, pp. 225–7. See also William B. Willcox, *Gloucestershire: A Study in Local Government, 1590–1640*, New Haven, 1940, ch. 10, esp. pp. 292–7; and the many examples in R. H. Tawney, *The Agrarian Problem in the Sixteenth Century*, 1912.

[15] Hoskins, *Midland Peasant*, pp. 93–8.

[16] G. P. Scrope, *History of the Manor and Ancient Baronage of Castle Combe*, 1852, p. 347.

[17] BL Add. MS 23151 (Nettleton Court Book, 1600–62), ff. 54–5. Lawrence Stone notes the parallel between the regulation of economic life by manor courts and of personal life by ecclesiastical courts. Both forms of regulation expressed the essentially co-operative nature of the village community: *Family, Sex and Marriage*, p. 76.

more than the religious life of the village as we should understand it.[18] The parish church was automatically the site of the formal gatherings in which the unity of the village and its hierarchical order were symbolically affirmed. Parishioners of all ranks and conditions sat weekly in the same church, participated in the same rituals, responded to the same visible and verbal imagery. The church calendar mirrored the agricultural calendar in its comforting rhythmic certainty, marking the annual cycle of birth, growth, death, and resurrection. Christmas, Plough Monday, Easter, the Whitsun revel, the perambulation of the bounds, the harvest home: the church was at the heart of the community's affirmations of both social and territorial identity. Herrick's songs of 'maypoles, hock-carts, wassails, wakes' of course idealize the innocence of the country scene, but once again they show the surviving strength of the ideal—the ideal of a parish in which overlapping religious and festive rituals jointly express the inhabitants' aspirations to neighbourly amity and co-operation. As in the larger commonwealth, each member had his or her appointed place: some high, to provide governance, employment, and hospitality; others low, to respond with obedience, hard work, and gratitude. The church's seating arrangements were a constant reminder of these differences, with the village dignitaries at the front, the servants and the poor at the back, men and women appropriately segregated in their separate hierarchies. Yet family and status hierarchies were fused: all were within one church, one community.

Village communities sometimes had to confront situations more difficult than the routine supervision of an unchanging open-field economy. Decisions to enclose, alter crop rotation patterns, or introduce new irrigation systems, all involved action in the courts. Sometimes, as we shall see, they led to disputes undermining the harmony that was the ideal. But at least as often manor court books reveal villagers harnessing their resources to cope with change. After some enclosures at Puddletown, Dorset, in 1625, a road was built 'over Broadmoor in the new lanes and droves there made'. The court appointed collectors to raise money by a rate, named four men to help the steward hire day-labourers, and laid down rules requiring tenants to send carts and men or come themselves with pickaxes and spades.[19]

Like the communities they served, however, village institutions were better fitted to cope with continuity. The stubborn conservatism of the rural commons was notorious. Before the civil war, says John Aubrey, it

---

[18] The parish was becoming a civil as much as an ecclesiastical institution. See Sedley L. Ware, 'The Elizabethan Parish in its Ecclesiastical and Financial Aspects', *Johns Hopkins University Studies in Historical and Political Science*, Ser. xxvi, nos. 7–8, Baltimore, 1908; Carl Bridenbaugh, *Vexed and Troubled Englishmen 1590–1642*, New York, 1968, pp. 243–7; Christopher Hill, *Society and Puritanism in Pre-Revolutionary England*, 1964, ch. 12.

[19] DRO D 39/H2 (Puddletown Court Book, 1624–38), ff. 8–9.

was thought wrong if a man was 'more knowing than his neighbours and forefathers. Even to attempt an improvement in husbandry, though it succeeded with profit, was looked upon with an ill eye.' Gervase Markham put it more bluntly, despising 'the rude, simple and ignorant clown, who only knoweth how to do his labour, but cannot give a reason why . . . more than the instruction of his parents, or the custom of the country'.[20] The age worshipped precedent, prescriptive right, custom 'whereof the memory of man runneth not to the contrary'. Custom could be a double-edged weapon, used by lords bent on exploiting every profitable loophole as well as by tenants defending ancient rights. Yet manorial custom often served the tenants well enough. At Wigston the lords were worn down by twenty years of lawsuits to protect copyholds by inheritance; in the end they sold out to the inhabitants. The tenants of Beaminster Secunda, Dorset, followed well-worn practice in raising a common fund to fight their lord in Chancery, accusing him of innovating 'a new and strange custom to the Manor . . . for private lucre and gain, and to the great prejudice of the customary tenants and their ancient customs'.[21]

It was not only in economic activities that villagers demanded neighbourly conduct and respect for custom. Social relations were governed by the same expectations. Brawls and quarrels, breaches of accepted standards of sexual or familial behaviour were equally to be watched, restrained by a variety of unofficial sanctions, and in the last resort denounced to the authorities. The alacrity of early modern villagers to pry and eavesdrop has been often remarked on. There are some similarities (as well as many differences) between these and the Mediterranean communities whose codes of 'honour and shame' have received attention from modern scholars: 'small scale, exclusive societies where face to face personal . . . relations are of paramount importance'.[22] The essential thing was not to be different. A reluctant Gillingham copyholder signed an enclosure agreement in 1626, he said, only because everyone else did so, in order that 'he might not be singular'.[23] Pressures to conform were likely to be even stronger in nucleated arable villages, where people lived at close quarters and organized their agriculture co-operatively. But throughout the kingdom villagers assumed their right to know everything about their neighbours' family, sexual, and working lives, and to take

---

[20] John Aubrey, *The Natural History of Wiltshire*, ed. John Britton, 1847, pref. Gervase Markham, *The English Husbandman* (1635), quoted in Thirsk, *Peasant Farming*, p. 179.

[21] Quoted in Bettey, 'Agriculture and Rural Society in Dorset', p. 234. A list of precedents at the beginning of the Court Book of the Manor of Afpuddle, 1589–1612 (DRO D 29/M1) was obviously drawn up for the benefit of the lord. See also Hoskins, *Midland Peasant*, pp. 103–14.

[22] *Honour and Shame: The Values of Mediterranean Society*, ed. J. G. Peristiany, 1966, intro., p. 11. See also Peter Burke, *Popular Culture in Early Modern Europe*, 1978, p. 57.

[23] J. H. Bettey, 'The Revolts over the Enclosure of the Royal Forest at Gillingham 1626–1630', *DNHP* xcvii (1975), 22.

appropriate action if community norms were violated. Often indeed, if local people rather than outsiders were involved, it might be appropriate to do nothing, as a Wiltshire man thought was the case when he refused to denounce a thief, 'for neighbourhood sake'.[24]

Pressures for conformity may have been strongest in the very communities in which they are worst recorded. Informal methods of dealing with misbehaviour or resolving disputes were more readily available in the close-knit arable villages than in the more scattered, fragmented wood-pasture settlements: wood-pasture disputes were the ones most likely to end in the courts.[25] But the differences should not be exaggerated. People everywhere were concerned by the disruptive effects of litigation and resorted to their natural leaders—clergy, gentry, and other parish notables—to try to prevent it.[26] The ideal of quiet, neighbourly living was the same in town and countryside. 'It is most necessary in all places, and namely in boroughs and towns corporate, to provide that amity, love and quietness may be continued', the corporation of Devizes declared in 1560 when they stripped two offenders of their burgess-ships. For once mediation had failed, but more often the mayor and his brethren persuaded the contending parties to agree, after which, in a typical case, they took 'each other by the hands, and went to the Hart and drank together'.[27]

Nettleton provides a rare glimpse of the mediation process at work in a 'traditional' rural parish, and of the resort to unofficial community action when it failed. In 1612 and 1613 two village women, Agnes and Margaret Davis, were presented at the court leet for scolding. The parson was asking to 'examine the matter' and persuade the offenders to reform themselves, and for a time he seems to have been successful. In 1614, however, the pair were again accused of scolding, and a cucking-stool (the usual expedient for punishing unruly women) had to be hastily improvised. It may be significant that Nettleton had not previously felt the

[24] M. J. Ingram, 'Communities and Courts: Law and Disorder in Early-Seventeenth-Century Wiltshire', in *Crime in England 1550–1800*, ed. J. S. Cockburn, Princeton, 1977, p. 128. Ingram notes the high proportion of 'outsiders' among people indicted for theft, and shows that they were more likely to be convicted than local suspects were: pp. 132–3. Ingram's 'Ecclesiastical Justice in Wiltshire 1600–1640', D.Phil. thesis, University of Oxford, 1976, is an impressively detailed treatment of the subject of community regulation. For briefer ones, see Anthony Fletcher, *A County Community in Peace and War: Sussex 1600–1660*, 1975, pp. 159–63; and Keith Thomas, *Religion and the Decline of Magic*, New York 1971, esp. pp. 526–30.

[25] Aubrey suggests that the pasture country of north Wiltshire produced twice as many lawsuits as the arable southern part of the county: *Nat. Hist. Wilts.*, pp. 11–12.

[26] On informal mediation see Ingram, 'Communities and Courts', pp. 110, 125–7; T. C. Curtis, 'Quarter Sessions Appearances and their Background', in *Crime in England*, ed. Cockburn, pp. 142–3; Carol Z. Wiener, 'Sex Roles and Crime in Late Elizabethan Hertfordshire', *JSH* viii, no. 4 (1975), 45–6; and Holmes, *Lincolnshire*, pp. 52, 61. George Herbert's 'Priest To the Temple' stresses the parson's mediating role: *The Works of George Herbert*, ed. F. E. Hutchinson, Oxford, 1941, pp. 259–60.

[27] *Some Annals of the Borough of Devizes*, ed. B. H. Cunnington, Devizes, 1925–6, i. pt. i, 28–9, 44.

need to own one of these devices, whereas in towns and wood-pasture villages they were, as we shall see, in common use. The sentence in the court leet did not end the matter. Margaret Davis was duly ducked, but Agnes (supported by some of her neighbours) appealed to the steward and got her own sentence suspended. Another group of villagers resented this favouritism and tried to duck Agnes on her way to church; the parson, however, managed to stop them. Only after several hours of feasting at Christmas were the vigilantes sufficiently emboldened to put the protesting Agnes Davis in the pond. The incident exemplifies attitudes to order typical of many traditional communities: a preference for persuasion rather than legal process; informal mediation by the clergy; official connivance (in this case by the steward) at failure to punish a law-breaker; finally a resort to direct action to counter the authorities' neglect of community feelings.[28]

We should not sentimentalize the pre-capitalist village community as Goldsmith's idyllic Auburn, untouched by greed, selfishness, and inhumanity. John Aubrey's nostalgia for the good old days of genial hospitality and good-fellowship evokes a past that never really existed.[29] But even after the polarization of many villages into a handful of wealthy yeomen at one extreme and a mass of small peasants and labourers at the other, important unifying bonds remained. Sir Thomas Overbury well expressed an ideal of yeomanly behaviour that was not totally removed from reality: 'Though he be master, he says not to his servants "Go to field", but "Let us go"'. Rich and poor continued to be linked by a common relationship to the environment.[30] Subject to rapid population turnover and increasing social stress they may have been, yet many seventeenth-century arable villages were still functioning communities.

*

The preceding discussion has attempted to construct a model or idealtype of the traditional village community. Like any usable model, it has some correspondence with historical reality. But again like most such models, it represents men's aspirations rather than their behaviour. During the sixteenth century reality came increasingly to diverge from ideal. England was subjected to a series of interlocking, dimly understood

[28] BL Add. MS 23151 (Nettleton Court Book), ff. 50, 52. PRO STAC 8/123/16 (*Davis* v. *Bishop*, 1615). For similar behaviour by officers in Lancashire and Essex, see Keith Wrightson, 'Two Concepts of Order: Justices, Constables and Jurymen in Seventeenth-Century England', in *An Ungovernable People*, ed. John Brewer and John Styles, 1980, pp. 31–2.
[29] For Aubrey's nostalgia, see Michael Hunter, *John Aubrey and the Realm of Learning*, New York, 1975, p. 186, and ch. 4.
[30] Overbury, 'Characters' (1614–16), in *The "Conceited Newes" of Sir Thomas Overbury and His Friends*, ed. James E. Savage, Gainesville, 1968, p. 212. Cf. the later comments of George Bourne on the farmers of his Surrey village, quoted in Hoskins, *Midland Peasant*, p. 199.

yet profoundly unsettling social and economic changes, which affected some parts of the country more severely than others. By 1600 we can, at the cost of some over-simplification, detect two Englands. In one, roughly coterminous with the surviving areas of open-field arable husbandry, the old conception of the stable, harmonious village community based on deference and good neighbourhood retained some vitality. In the other, comprising many of the towns, the pasture and woodland areas linked to an expanding market economy, and the industrializing regions devoted to cloth-making, mining, and metal-working, the ideal was increasingly threatened.

First among the destabilizing forces was demographic growth. Between 1540 and 1600 the population of England and Wales increased by roughly 45 per cent, from under three million to over four million. By 1650 there had been a further increase to around 5,250,000. The chronology of this growth varied from village to village, and it was most marked in the industrializing wood-pasture regions, but all areas were to some extent affected.[31] Such unprecedented population expansion had profound social and economic effects. It led to land shortage, to the subdivision of holdings, to attempts to expand the cultivated area by reclaiming wastes and woodlands. It led to greater geographical mobility, to constant migration by people in search of work or land: even relatively stable arable villages such as Wigston Magna and Galby, Leicestershire, witnessed a considerable turnover of population.[32] It led to inflation of grain prices, as population growth was not accompanied by a corresponding increase of food production, and to a prolonged and disastrous decline in real wages for the labouring poor.[33] The swollen populations of towns and industrializing rural areas deficient in food production stimulated the growth of capitalist agriculture. The economy of the open-field village was originally one of subsistence: production for the market encouraged different methods of land-use. The result was the increasing tendency of wealthy villagers to engross the farms of less successful ones struggling against adversity.[34]

Enclosure often followed, or accompanied, engrossing. Enclosure is a complicated subject, for the gradual replacement of open fields by individually-farmed holdings was not quite the ruthless process of expropriation that Tawney's seminal work depicted. Much enclosure was

[31] E. A. Wrigley and R. S. Schofield, *The Population History of England 1541–1871*, 1981, p. 528. For local variations see W. G. Hoskins, *Provincial England*, 1963, pp. 185–200, 206–7; and Margaret Spufford, *Contrasting Communities: English Villagers in the Sixteenth and Seventeenth Centuries*, Cambridge, 1974, pp. 12–28.

[32] Hoskins, *Provincial England*, pp. 190–3; *Essays in Leicestershire History*, Liverpool, 1950, p. 36.

[33] Everitt, 'Farm Labourers', p. 435 and n. 3 summarizes the evidence.

[34] Spufford, *Contrasting Communities*, chs. 2–4.

piecemeal, by the exchange or consolidation of holdings, as often under-taken by yeomen and husbandmen as by rich landlords depopulating whole villages.[35] It was, however, a process which reflected the gradual transformation of the economic ideology of the propertied. Governments and local officials still strove to curb the excesses of competitive acquisi-tiveness, especially at times of dearth, and the consuming poor retained their protective notions of a 'moral economy', but influential opinion was changing fast. Agricultural writers from Tusser to Markham and beyond proclaimed the virtues of enclosure and improvement, and they found willing listeners.[36] During the 1631 dearth the Norfolk JPs openly rejected the older regulative philosophy and questioned a Council order to enforce traditional market procedures. Appealing, inevitably in a precedent-minded age, to ancient custom however doubtful the evidence for its antiquity, they spoke approvingly of 'the old way that hath been in use to this day, for every man to sell and deliver his corn at the place most convenient for him'.[37] The interests of rich and poor alike would be served by allowing the economy to be regulated only by the dictates of the free market.

If the market economy was making headway in the arable regions in the early seventeenth century, it is not surprising to find it also doing so in the pasturelands. An extreme case was the drainage of the fens: the big schemes in the eastern counties, the smaller ones in the Somerset levels. Both provoked much local opposition that will be discussed in a later chapter. They reflected the improving acquisitiveness of wealthy projec-tors and aristocrats such as the Earl of Bedford and his associates, but also the willingness of local gentlemen and yeomen to exploit the opportunities for profit that would follow the disappearance of the old fenland economy. 'Rich men', complained Thomas Fuller, 'to make room for themselves, would jostle the poor people out of their commons.'[38] A similar replace-ment of farming for use by farming for the market was stimulated by Charles I's sale of forest lands in Wiltshire and Dorset to favoured courtiers. Again there was much resulting disorder which will receive further attention. Common grazing did not disappear from the pasture-lands, but the trend was clearly against it. Everywhere, but more rapidly in

[35] Joan Thirsk, 'Enclosing and Engrossing', in *Agrarian History*, iv. ch. 4, provides a balanced view of the subject. For a more extreme rejection of Tawney, see Eric Kerridge, *Agrarian Problems in the Sixteenth Century and After*, 1969.

[36] For the agricultural writers see G. E. Fussell, *Old English Farming Books from Fitzherbert to Tull*, 1947. For attitudes to economic regulation, see E. P. Thompson, 'The Moral Economy of the English Crowd in the Eighteenth Century', *P & P* no. 50 (Feb. 1971), 76–136; John Walter and Keith Wrightson, 'Dearth and the Social Order in Early Modern England', *P & P* no. 71 (May 1976), 22–42.

[37] 'Reasons agst a General Sending of Corne to ye Marketts in ye Champion parte of Norfolke', ed. T. S. Cogswell, *Norfolk Archaeology*, xx (1921), 17.

[38] Quoted in Thirsk, *Peasant Farming*, p. 37; and cf. also ibid. pp. 19–21, 68–9, 111–12, 124–5, 148.

the pasture than the arable regions, a new kind of economy was taking root.

*

Population growth, inflation, and the changing agricultural economy had profound social consequences. Put simply, the conditions of the century before 1640 favoured people whose incomes were elastic while their expenditures were inelastic: those who could take advantage of a fluid land market, or produce a surplus at a time of rising prices. People in the opposite situation—those with reduced access to land, or with incomes that failed to keep up with inflation—suffered correspondingly. The result was a heightened polarization of society which makes this period an important stage in the long process of class formation. England was still very far from being a class society, but the lines were beginning to sharpen, the horizontal ties linking the 'respectable' and dividing them from the poor to cut across the vertical ones of local identity. The process did not begin in the seventeenth century, and it was not to be completed until the nineteenth; but it was under way.[39]

One social group which enhanced its economic position and became more assertive of its status during the period 1540–1640 was the gentry. Vast quantities of historical ink and effort have been expended in the debate over the 'rise of the gentry', and this is not the place to reopen the argument.[40] But when all is said, admitting all the statistical uncertainties, the problems of definition, and the bewilderingly varied fortunes of particular families, it is hard to resist the conclusion that the gentry as a group were profiting. For one thing, there were simply more of them, their increasing influence reflected in the much larger numbers of men named to the commissions of the peace. By 1640 in almost every county a larger group of governing families existed than had been the case before the profits of Tudor office, the plunder of the church, and the redistributive consequences of inflation had worked their way into the social system. They were often less subject to the authority of the great noblemen whose ancestors had governed the shires through their clients. Somerset, with its oligarchy of Hoptons and Horners, Pouletts, and Phelipses, is a conspicuous example of a gentry-ruled county.[41]

[39] Keith Wrightson, 'Aspects of Social Differentiation in rural England, c.1580–1660', *Journal of Peasant Studies*, v (1977–8), 33–47, provides a thoughtful discussion of this subject. C. H. George, 'The Making of the English Bourgeoisie, 1500–1750', *Science and Society*, xxxv (1971), 385–414, exaggerates the degree of middle-class consciousness attained in the seventeenth century; John Langton, 'Residential patterns in pre-industrial cities', *Institute of British Geographers Transactions*, lxv (1975), 22, underestimates it.

[40] The debate is summarized in *Social Change and Revolution in England, 1540–1640*, ed. Lawrence Stone, 1965, with selections from most of the major contributions.

[41] J. H. Gleason, *The Justices of Peace in England 1558 to 1640*, Oxford, 1969. Thomas G. Barnes, *Somerset 1625–1640*, Cambridge, Mass., 1961, chs. 2, 3.

There were also many more lesser gentry—people who may have owned no more than parts of a manor or two, but whose presence in their villages was more visible than that of their more powerful, but also more remote, superiors. In the early sixteenth century fewer than half of all English villages had resident gentry; by the later seventeenth century about three-quarters had them. Often these parochial gentry emerged from the ranks of the more successful yeomen, by incremental accumulation over several generations. The process has been observed in Leicestershire villages such as Wigston Magna, in Cambridgeshire villages such as Chippenham and Orwell, in Essex villages such as Terling, and in Norfolk villages such as Cawston.[42] The pattern is a universal one.

The division between rulers and ruled, between the gentry and the rest, had always been at the heart of the ideology of hierarchy and order. It generated sporadic outbursts of hostility which bear many of the hallmarks of class feeling. This was especially evident in the risings of 1549, but recurrent mutterings of popular sedition continued to surface during Elizabeth's reign, especially in times of dearth. 'Why should one man have all and another nothing?' a Somerset rioter demanded in 1549, and the angry question was repeated often enough to give us pause before we assume a total acceptance of the doctrines of order and obedience.[43] The lessons for the gentry were plain: order must be enforced, status asserted.

Even in the quieter times which followed 1549 the English gentry remained obsessed with their status, and the preoccupation increased by the end of the century. They eagerly collaborated in the racket by which the College of Heralds legitimized the distinctions raising them above the common herd. The distinctions had to be easily recognizable. In 1621 a Hampshire MP opposed sumptuary legislation that would have required gentry families to wear broadcloth in winter: there would be 'so little left betwixt us and our servants as betwixt October and May a gentleman should not know his wife from his chambermaid'. Such attitudes were not new. Nor were the ones underlying the insistence that gentlemen ought not to be shamed by 'slavish' punishments like whipping or the stocks.[44]

[42] Keith Wrightson, *English Society 1580–1680*, 1982, pp. 26–7, 134–6. Hoskins, *Midland Peasant*, pp. 133–40, 196–7; *Essays in Leics. History*, pp. 41–4, 50–1, 62–3, 156–9. Spufford, *Contrasting Communities*, pp. 108–11. Keith Wrightson and David Levine, *Poverty and Piety in an English Village: Terling, 1525–1700*, 1979, pp. 73–4. Susan D. Amussen, 'Governors and Governed: Class and Gender Relations in English Villages, 1590–1725', Ph.D. thesis, Brown University, 1982, pp. 51–2.

[43] HMC, *Bath*, iv. 109. For the general subject of Tudor disorder, see Anthony Fletcher, *Tudor Rebellions*, 2nd edn., 1973. The 1549 risings have been recently treated by Barrett L. Beer, *Rebellion and Riot: Popular Disorder in England during the reign of Edward VI*, [Kent, Ohio], 1982; and Diarmaid MacCulloch, 'Kett's Rebellion in Context', *P & P* no. 84 (Aug. 1979), 36–59. For Elizabeth's reign see J. Samaha, 'Gleanings from Local Criminal-Court Records: Sedition Amongst the "Inarticulate" in Elizabethan Essex', *JSH* viii, no. 4 (1975), 61–79; William Hunt, *The Puritan Moment: The Coming of Revolution in an English County*, Cambridge, Mass., 1983, pp. 58–63; and Peter Clark, *English Provincial Society from the Reformation to the Revolution*, Hassocks, Sussex, 1977, pp. 249–51.

[44] Quoted in Joan Kent, 'Attitudes of Members of the House of Commons to the Regulation of "Personal Conduct" in Late Elizabethan and Early Stuart England', *BIHR* xlvi (1973), 51.

They were, however, being uttered with particular urgency in the early seventeenth century.

Gentlemen expected, and usually received, deferential obedience from their tenants. 'You that are my friends get you out of the church, as many as depend upon me', shouted Sir George Ivie in the course of a dispute with the parson of West Kington, Wiltshire.[45] Contempt by inferiors was sometimes met by violence, as when Sir Samuel Sandys of Ombersley, Worcestershire, ordered his servants to beat up a tithingman who had provokingly kept his hat on in Sandys's presence and had spoken insulting words.[46] Status assertion by the gentry was often reflected in conflicts over church seats, placement in church being so visible an affirmation of status. Thomas Fraunceis of Gerberstone, Somerset, was enraged when his claim to the whole north aisle of West Buckland church was challenged by a minor bureaucrat named Charles Ley and his brother, a clothier; men 'of mean and obscure parentage', Fraunceis sneered, their mother 'by birth, marriage and estate very poor, mean and worthless . . . the daughter of one James Bowerman a tanner'. At Lullington, near Frome, there was a brawl in the church when the clothier Richard Wallis was ejected from a disputed pew by clients of John Champneys, squire of the neighbouring village of Orchardleigh. At Maiden Bradley in 1626 Sir Henry Ludlow preferred insult to violence, sending his scullion, 'all in a black greasy suit of clothes', to sit next to the wife of George Nosse, a minor gentleman who was disputing Ludlow's claim to a pew; there was 'great laughter' in the congregation.[47]

Insistence on status was accompanied by insistence on property rights as land came increasingly to be viewed as a source of profit rather than responsibility. The old tolerance of hunting by inferiors, for example, began to diminish as gentlemen adopted an attitude of proprietary exclusiveness towards the game they controlled under rights granted by the King.[48] So with manorial custom: if agricultural improvement dictated enclosing or interfering with customary rights, it would have to be done. This was true for some lords of manors even in the more paternalist arable regions. The Dorset village of Puddletown had survived the partial enclosures of the mid-1620s without a total breakdown of harmony. Its owner, Henry Hastings, appears in Ashley Cooper's recollections as an

[45] PRO STAC 8/253/12 (*Russell* v. *Ivie*, 1613).
[46] PRO STAC 8/255/14 (*Sandys* v. *Jones*, 1608).
[47] PRO STAC 8/141/13 (*Fraunceis* v. *Ley*, 1612); STAC 8/196/20 (*Ley* v. *Fraunceis*, 1612); STAC 8/99/9 (*Champneys* v. *Wallis*, 1606); STAC 8/303/30 (*Wallis* v. *Champneys*, 1606). SRO D/D/Cd 37 (Diocesan Court Depositions, 1606). WRO AS/ABO 14 (Act Book, 1624–30), fo. 125ᵛ. The Ludlows had a short way with people who challenged their status: G. M. Young, 'Some Wiltshire Cases in Star Chamber', *WAM* l (1942–4), 451.
[48] P. B. Munsche, 'The Gamekeeper and English Rural Society, 1660–1830', *JBS* xx, no. 2 (1981), 84–6.

archetype of this old-fashioned squire—benevolent, generous, hospitable. In 1629, however, his conduct was far from paternalistic. He personally bulldozed an elaborate water-meadows scheme through the manor court, overcoming 'great debate' and 'questions moved by some of the tenants'. His steward bore the brunt of the poorer copyholders' resentment, but Hastings was convinced that their 'many vehement complaints . . . divers calumnies and slanders' were really directed against himself. After various efforts to 'avoid their clamours' he referred the grievances to two local gentlemen, who not surprisingly concluded that it was all the tenants' fault.[49]

Hastings was not the only landlord to fall short of the paternalist ideal. There were others who rack-rented their tenants or whose conduct as JPs showed more concern for self-interest than for good governance: 'basket-justices', a 1601 MP described them. Maurice Gilbert of Wincanton was one such, if his enemies are to be believed; a man 'of small living and not set above three pounds in the subsidy book and much indebted besides', who took bribes, sold alehouse licences, and engaged in other corrupt practices.[50] However, just as Gilbert does not represent the general standard of county magistracy, so Puddletown is not necessarily typical of arable Dorset. There were still many local gentry who tried to protect the interests of their poorer tenants, and believed that improved estate management was not worth the price it exacted in strained tenurial relations. When in 1624 the Earl of Salisbury heard allegations about the oppressive behaviour of his deputy-steward at Cranborne, the Puritan Richard Sherfield, he too asked some of the neighbouring gentry to investigate. They found that Sherfield had imposed 'such strict penalties and law quirks that he hath justly drawn on him the hate and ill opinion of that part of the country'. Salisbury promptly dismissed him.[51] The contrast between the outcomes at Puddletown and Cranborne suggests that although the lure of profit was eroding the older paternalism, in some parts of the chalk country it continued to function. In spite of Henry Hastings, Ashley Cooper's admiring picture of the downland gentry may not be totally without foundation.

*

[49] DRO D 39/H2 (Puddletown Court Book), ff. 114–20. W. D. Christie, *A Life of Anthony Ashley Cooper, First Earl of Shaftesbury*, 1871, i. App., pp. xiv–xvii. Bettey, 'Agriculture and Rural Society in Dorset', pp. 137–8, describes the conflict. See also J. H. Bettey, 'Sheep, Enclosures and Watermeadows in Dorset agriculture in the Sixteenth and Seventeenth Centuries', in *Husbandry and Marketing in the South-west 1500–1800*, ed. Michael Havinden, Exeter, 1973, pp. 9–18.

[50] PRO STAC 8/43/3 (*Adams v. Gilbert*, 1603). The term 'basket-justices' is quoted by Kent, 'Attitudes of Members', p. 52.

[51] Lawrence Stone, *Family and Fortune: Studies in Aristocratic Finance in the Sixteenth and Seventeenth Centuries*, Oxford, 1973, pp. 126–7. For paternalist examples in other counties, see Everitt, *Community of Kent*, pp. 48, 51; and Willcox, *Gloucestershire*, pp. 281–2.

The other major rural beneficiaries of the great inflation were the
yeomen. Again we encounter problems of definition, for neither tenure
nor wealth consistently defined yeomen status. A yeoman was not
necessarily a freeholder, and an occupant of thirty acres might be a
yeoman in one area but only a husbandman in another.[52] But for our
purposes a loose definition is enough: a yeoman was usually a substantial
farmer concentrating primarily on the market rather than on subsistence
agriculture. Yeomen were men of standing in their communities; men
who sometimes, like Robert Loder of Harwell, Berkshire, had incomes
greater than many of the poorer gentry; men whose accounts and
inventories reflect their comfortable prosperity. Like the gentry, the
yeomen had benefited from a century of rising agricultural prices, and for
much the same reasons. Their increasing acceptance of the ethos of the
market justified the pursuit of individual profit, sometimes at the expense
of the traditional ideal of the co-operative community. Yeomen were
the villagers most able to take advantage of a lord's sale of demesne
lands, profit from piecemeal enclosure by agreement, or buy out poorer
neighbours driven to the wall by a run of bad harvests. Everywhere
there were open-field farmers who by the early seventeenth century
had built up large enough holdings to prosper in the new economic
climate.[53]

In the pasture regions the demographic and economic pressures had
somewhat different effects. In fen and woodland areas subjected to
large-scale drainage or disafforestation schemes the outcome was an even
more marked polarization than in the arable regions: a relatively egalitarian society was replaced by one in which a handful of people controlled
the land, while the majority were reduced to landlessness and wage
labour. In more stable pasture regions, however, the trend was in the
opposite direction, as population growth led to the division of holdings
and thus an increase in the number of small landholders. Even in places of
this kind, however, as the experience of the fen-edge village of Willingham, Cambridgeshire, demonstrates, there might be more middling
yeomen, farming over thirty acres, after the bad years of the 1590s than
there had been earlier. Terling, in the Essex mixed farming country,
witnessed no increase in the number of small farmers, but no absolute
decline either, even after the difficult years between 1590 and 1620; there
was, though, as in many other such places, a marked increase in the

[52] Mildred Campbell, *The English Yeoman Under Elizabeth and the Early Stuarts*, 2nd edn., New
York, 1960, ch. 2.
[53] *Robert Loder's Farm Accounts 1610–1620*, ed. G. E. Fussell, Camden 3rd Ser., liii, 1936. For a
Wiltshire example, see 'The Note Book of a Wiltshire Farmer in the Early Seventeeth Century', ed.
Eric Kerridge, *WAM* liv (1951–2), 416–28. For the subject in general see Thirsk, 'Enclosing and
Engrossing'; and Campbell, *English Yeoman*, chs. 3–5.

number of landless poor.[54] The situation of many Wiltshire cheese country villages was closer to that of Willingham. Before 1590 about half the holdings in this area were of less than twenty acres; by 1640 the proportion was nearly three-quarters. The Dorset pasturelands, on the other hand, were less affected by these changes: in Blackmore Vale copyholders had unusual security of tenure, there was still no clear correspondence between wealth and status, and the emergence of a few big farmers was delayed until after the civil war.[55] The greater socio-economic stability of this region was reflected, we shall find, in both its culture and its politics.

Population growth and inflation had equally significant effects in the towns and the rural industrial areas. As in agriculture, sixteenth-century developments favoured the larger producer or entrepreneur. In the towns this led to further concentration of power in the hands of wealthy oligarchies.[56] In rural areas where the chief industry, cloth-making, was located—south Gloucestershire, north-west Wiltshire, and north Somerset, for example—the situation was compounded by the broadcloth industry's chronic sluggishness after the depression of the 1550s. There were still plenty of independent producers and small employers, as a 1608 Gloucestershire muster-roll reveals. But both agricultural and industrial conditions made it harder for families who combined small-scale farming and cloth-making to survive. The clothing region was also a wood-pasture area in which population pressure and land shortage were most marked, and its inhabitants suffered severely when even worse depression descended in the 1620s. Employers who diversified, like the Ashes of Freshford, making a timely switch to new, lighter fabrics, showed that there were still large profits to be made in the cloth industry. But they were profits for the few.[57]

In communities of all types demographic and economic forces were widening the gap between the few, the parish élites of wealthy yeomen and

---

[54] Spufford, *Contrasting Communities*, ch. 5, esp. pp. 134–40. Wrightson and Levine, *Poverty and Piety*, pp. 33–6, 108.

[55] Anthony Salerno, 'The Social Background of Seventeeth-Century Emigration to America', *JBS* xix, no. 1 (1979), 47. J. H. Bettey, 'Marriages of Convenience by Copyholders in Dorset during the Seventeenth Century', *DNHP* xcviii (1976), 1; 'Agriculture and Rural Society in Dorset', ch. 8, esp. pp. 197, 200. *Probate Inventories and Manorial Excepts of Chetnole, Leigh and Yetminster*, ed. R. Machin, Bristol, 1976, pp. 20–4.

[56] *Crisis and Order in English Towns 1500–1700*, ed. Peter Clark and Paul Slack, 1972, intro., pp. 21–3. For some examples, see Roger Howell, Jr., *Newcastle Upon Tyne and the Puritan Revolution*, Oxford, 1967, ch. 2, esp. pp. 39–43; W. G. Hoskins, *Old Devon*, Newton Abbot, 1966, pp. 74–97; and Peter Clark, '"The Ramoth-Gilead of the Good": Urban Change and Political Radicalism at Gloucester 1540–1640', in *The English Commonwealth 1547–1640: Essays in Politics and Society*, ed. Peter Clark, Alan G. R. Smith, and Nicholas Tyacke, Leicester, 1979, pp. 173–4.

[57] G. D. Ramsay, *The Wiltshire Woollen Industry in the Sixteenth and Seventeenth Centuries*, Oxford, 1943, chs. 3, 7. Julia de L. Mann, *The Cloth Industry in the West of England from 1640 to 1880*, Oxford, 1971, pp. 89–91, 94–6. Barry E. Supple, *Commercial Crisis and Change in England 1600–1642*, Cambridge, 1959, chs. 2, 3, 5–7. Willcox, *Gloucestershire*, pp. 171–7. Clark, 'Ramoth-Gilead', pp. 170–6.

clothiers, and the many, the small landholders and landless poor. The polarizing process had been under way long before 1600: even in medieval times some arable villages had contained relatively small numbers of landholders and large numbers of landless labourers.[58] The seventeenth-century pattern is one of often confusing diversity, but through the local variations some common features can be detected. Whether by partial enclosure in the arable areas—enclosure of demesne lands by one or two big farmers, for example, leaving the rest of the common fields intact—or the influx of landless poor into the less stable, cloth-making pasturelands, gradations of wealth and status were becoming more sharply defined.[59] There were, to be sure, many arable villages where this did not happen, and even some pasture regions, like Blackmore Vale and the Somerset levels, where a broader distribution of wealth was still the norm. But the pattern elsewhere is clear enough.

It is a commonplace that by 1640 more villages had resident squires than had been the case a century earlier. But such people were often remote from the day-to-day functioning of their communities. It was the consolidation of the yeomen oligarchies that decisively changed the realities of village life. This development has recently been traced at Terling before 1640, as prosperous farmers such as John Green and his son Robert moved into the group of parish notables who monopolized local offices. 'In many parishes', Gerrard Winstanley was soon to complain, 'two or three of the great ones bear all the sway.'[60] A fortunate few, as we have seen, moved steadily upwards to gentility. Usually, though, the parish notables remained enclosed in their own social networks, content like the Furses of Devonshire with their yeoman ancestry, or like the Gasts of Chetnole, Dorset, with the wealth and influence their own efforts had earned them.[61] Their clothier counterparts are typified by men such as John Noyes of Calne, prominent enough to be MP for the town, yet still living 'over the shop', his wife running the family business when he was away.[62] Such too were the Martock yeomen of whom the Somerset topographer Thomas Gerard spoke admiringly: 'Wealthy and substantial men though none of the best bred, which is the cause their neighbours about them are apt enough to slander them with the title of clowns; but they care not much for that, knowing they have money in their purses to make them gentlemen when they are fit for the degree'.[63]

[58] Alan Macfarlane, *The Origins of English Individualism*, New York, 1979, pp. 148–9.

[59] For examples see Bettey, 'Agriculture and Rural Society in Dorset', ch. 5, esp. pp. 116–19.

[60] Quoted by Hill, 'The Poor and the People'. For Terling, see Wrightson and Levine, *Poverty and Piety*, pp. 73–4, 104–6. Cf. the situation at Kelvedon Easterford: J. A. Sharpe, 'Crime and Delinquency in an Essex Parish 1600–1640', in *Crime in England*, ed. Cockburn, pp. 93–5.

[61] Campbell, *English Yeoman*, pp. 50–2. *Probate Inventories*, ed. Machin, pp. 23–4.

[62] A. S. M., 'John Noyes, of Calne', *Wiltshire N & Q* iv (1902–4), 421–2.

[63] *The Particular Description of the County of Somerset . . . by Thomas Gerard of Trent, 1633*, ed. E. H. Bates, SRS xv, 1900, p. 125.

Gerard's description implies that the yeomen were not only prospering, but were also developing a stronger sense of their own identity. The yeomen were, they knew, men of the best 'credit and reputation' in their communities, automatically entitled to leadership. 'Credit and reputation': the phrase is among many similar ones that made up the vocabulary of social differentiation. Henry Collins, a clothier at Winsham, Somerset, deposed that in his village overseers of the poor were invariably 'persons of the best note, conversation and credit'. Churchwardens were appointed at parish meetings, normally after evensong on Sunday, in which the wealthier inhabitants naturally had the strongest voice. At Creech St. Michael in 1631 the election was by 'the major part of the substantial parishioners', including an esquire and a minor gentleman, but also a yeoman, a husbandman, and a carpenter. In this case the parish élite was still fairly inclusive, but times were changing.[64]

Office-holding was not the only matter in which the opinions of people of credit were decisive. These were the people who decided whether prosecutions should be brought against unlicensed alehouse-keepers and offenders of every other possible kind. At Bathampton, as in many other places, presentments to the ecclesiastical courts were made on the basis of 'a common fame in our parish amongst the substantial parishioners'.[65] People lacking in wealth and status also lacked 'credit'. In a typical suit, against the Frome lawyer James Cottington, witnesses were variously dismissed as 'no subsidy man . . . hath no means in Frome Selwood'; 'a man of little or no credit or reputation'; 'by the common report and estimation of his neighbours of a far meaner estate' and thus liable to be suborned by Cottington.[66] Such interested statements of course tell us nothing about the actual circumstances or reputations of the witnesses. But they reveal a whole world of assumptions about the operation of a system of power, in which local governance was increasingly becoming the preserve of the few. From a national perspective these men might appear to have little influence, but in the eyes of their poorer neighbours their power could loom very large indeed.[67]

For many of those poorer neighbours—the 85 per cent of the English population below the yeoman rank—the sixteenth century had a less

[64] PRO STAC 8/88/7 (*Collins* v. *Hawkes*, 1623). SRO D/D/Cd 71 (Depositions, 1631–5), *Callow* v. *Gill*, 11 May 1631.
[65] SRO D/D/Ca 220 (Diocesan Court, Comperta, 1620), Batheaston presentment, 11 Sept.
[66] SRO D/D/Cd 76 (Depositions, 1633–4), *Powell and Yearburie* v. *Cottington*, 18 Dec. 1633. For the whole subject of credit and reputation I am greatly indebted to Amussen, 'Governors and Governed', ch. 7.
[67] This point is made by G. E. Aylmer, 'Crisis and Regrouping in the Political Elites: England from the 1630s to the 1660s', in *Three British Revolutions: 1641, 1688, 1776*, ed. J. G. A. Pocock, Princeton, 1980, p. 147.

happy outcome.[68] Small husbandmen survived in large numbers in many open-field arable villages, though their ability to do so depended greatly on the strength of local customary rights. If they grew enough for their families' subsistence they were partly shielded from the inflation, and a small surplus would cover their necessary outlays. Even so, they were often in dire trouble during the bleak years of the 1590s and a good many were gobbled up. Excessive population growth thus contributed to the increasing numbers of the landless, driven from the ranks of the independent producer to those of the day-labourer, the cottager, the squatter on the waste, or the vagrant migrating in search of work. The level of poverty and unemployment in the depression-racked clothing districts was particularly acute, and none of the elaborate mechanisms of Tudor social legislation was ever able to reduce it. Yet people still drifted into the clothing industry, for anything was preferable to the grinding toil, the monotonous poverty, of agricultural employment. Thomas Westcote noted how many west-country people preferred to apprentice their children to 'mechanical trades' rather than condemn them to the life of the farm labourer.[69]

By the early seventeenth century, therefore, the orderly, vertically integrated society assumed by Tudor theorists was seriously diverging from reality. Rural society was dividing, with a minority of middling property-owners acquiring a sense of identity which detached them from the previously relatively homogenous village community, and led them to devise new mechanisms for imposing their own conception of order on those below them. The social consequences of this development varied from place to place, from region to region, and were by no means entirely determined by economic interest. In many arable villages where economic polarization was most marked, the sense of communal identity survived, as we shall see, more strongly than it did in some of the pasture regions where small landholders existed in larger numbers, but where the forces of disorder in the shape of landless vagrants and underemployed clothworkers were more threatening.[70]

*

The authority of the new parish élites was not established without opposition and acrimony. Some of the issues around which the conflicts

---

[68] My estimates of the social distribution of the population are based on Gregory King's table, printed in Laslett, *World We Have Lost*, pp. 36–7.

[69] Westcote, *View of Devonshire*, p. 62. James Howell also remarks on the sacrifices humble people often made in order that their children might be educated: *Epistolae Ho-Elianae: The Familiar Letters of James Howell*, ed. Joseph Jacobs, 1892, ii. 523–4. On depression in the clothing districts, See Ramsay, *Wiltshire Woollen Industry*, ch. 5.

[70] For an excellent synthesis of the subject, taking due account of regional variations, see Wrightson, *English Society*, pp. 125–45.

revolved—moral reformation and the treatment of the poor—will merit our attention later in this book. Struggles of the kind recently described at Burnham-on-Crouch, Essex, were fairly common. Between 1637 and 1640, after the arrival of a zealous new Puritan minister, Burnham's leading parishioners began prosecuting each other for drunkenness, fornication, and other offences, each group retaliating against the other's adherents. Such contentions were especially frequent in the towns: the Devizes corporation's appeals for 'amity, love, and quietness', for example, were repeatedly put to test in the years after 1570.[71]

Competition for status was a regular source of local conflict. A period of rapid social change is obviously liable to produce anxiety about status, especially on the part of *nouveaux riches* or recent arrivals in their communities. Verses circulating in the Wiltshire parish of Crudwell in 1617 derogating 'the upstart and his wife' quickly goaded Jeffrey Portlock into a libel action.[72] We have already noted that the gentry were often preoccupied with status to the point of obsession. But so too were people of lower rank. 'Neighbour Bond, am I a stone picker or a day labourer?' exclaimed Richard Berrie one Sunday in 1617 when the Chippenham parish clerk called on the congregation to perform their duty of working on the highways.[73] And clergymen were often equally worried about their status, perhaps because it was socially ambiguous. The parson demanded respect by virtue of his office and calling. But he was often an outsider in his village, coming from social origins no more exalted than many of his parishioners. Distanced from their flocks by a higher level of learning than had often been the case in earlier days, many ministers were nevertheless worse off financially than their predecessors. The poet George Herbert's experience in his Wiltshire parish led him to reflect on 'the general ignominy which is cast upon the profession', partly because of its low financial rewards. The minister at Maiden Bradley, a disgruntled resident declared, 'was but a ten pound priest'.[74]

As Richard Berrie reminds us, the performance of highway service in person rather than by a paid substitute was demeaning. Far worse was to be denied, Sunday after Sunday, one's rightful place in the parish church. If the images and stained glass of the old religion had been the poor man's bible, the seating-plan of the church was his guide to the status system, a weekly reminder of the realities of local precedence. Customs by which

---

[71] Wrightson, 'Two Concepts of Order', pp. 41–3. *Annals of Devizes*, i, pt. i, 70–9; pt. ii, 3–5.

[72] WRO QS Rolls, Michaelmas 1617, nos. 107, 156–8. In this and the following discussion of church seating I am further indebted to Amussen, 'Governors and Governed', esp. ch. 8.

[73] WRO AW/ABO 5 (Act Book, 1616–22), fo. 23.

[74] Herbert, quoted in Christopher Hill, *Economic Problems of the Church from Archbishop Whitgift to the Long Parliament*, Oxford, 1956, p. 209 (and ch. 9 for the subject in general). WRO AS/ABO 13 (Act Book, 1620–4), fo. 209.

pews were allocated varied widely, however, so some observations on previous developments are in order.

Before the Reformation in most rural churches seats had been assigned not to individuals or families, but to tenements—to farms or houses. The practice survived in many places in the seventeenth century. One of them was Myddle, Shropshire, where Richard Gough's account shows that although there was a rough correspondence between status and seating (since inhabitants of the bigger farms sat near the front) it was not an absolute one.[75] But in Myddle as elsewhere a transition from this customary system to one based directly on status and wealth was under way. It had started in the towns. The practice of reserving pews in return for payment (in the form either of rent or the purchase of a life-interest) began even before the Reformation in places like Salisbury and Sherborne. At Reading payment for seats was at first limited to those for elderly women, but by the middle of the sixteenth century possession of a seat had become a mark of a woman's status rather than of her age. Finally in 1607 the whole church was parcelled out and all propertied parishioners, men as well as women, had to pay for their seats. In such places a large proportion of the church's income came from the sale or renting of seats, though this did not necessarily preclude the continued use of other, more communitarian methods of fund-raising. Payment for church seats clearly bespeaks a socially divided community, and it is not surprising to find this emerging earliest in the towns.[76]

A similar transition can be observed in rural parishes, for all their diversity. The trend was clearly towards modification of the old customary system by permitting the wealthier parishioners to pay for, and thus control, their seats. At East Coker most seats were still assigned to tenements in 1634. Towards the end of the sixteenth century, however, population growth had led to the construction of additional pews in which the churchwardens were empowered to sell life interests. In another Somerset parish, Spaxton, the process appears to have had two stages: distinctions were made between customary seats linked to tenements, 'ancient non customary seats' let for a year at a time, and newer ones in which people bought life interests. By the early seventeenth century reserved seats were beginning to appear in parishes all over the west country.[77]

---

[75] Richard Gough, *This History of Myddle*, ed. David Hey, Harmondsworth, 1981, from p. 77, *passim.*

[76] Hill, *Economic Problems*, pp. 175–82. J. Charles Cox, *Churchwardens Accounts from the Fourteenth Century to the Close of the Seventeenth Century*, 1913, pp. 187–8. 'Sherborne All Hallows Church Wardens' Accounts', *SDNQ* xxiii (1939–42), 229 ff. At Tewkesbury a large income from church seats was still occasionally supplemented by receipts from plays: GRO P 329, CW/2/1 (Tewkesbury Churchwardens accounts, 1563–1703).

[77] SRO D/D/Cd 76; 71 (Depositions, 1633–4; 1631–5), *Pennie* v. *Giles*, 7 and 30 May 1634; D/D/Cd 81 (Depositions, 1635), *Leave* v. *Kebbie*, 30 Sept. The sale or rental of seats was already the practice at Axbridge by 1570: SRO D/P/ax, 4/1/1 (Axbridge Churchwardens accounts). At Minchinhampton,

The assignment of seats gave added power to people at the top of the parish hierarchies. In theory seats were at the disposal of the incumbent, and in some places this was so in practice—though at Longborough, Gloucestershire, the vicar shared the privilege with the lord of the manor.[78] But effective decisions nearly everywhere were made by the churchwardens. Where customary seats had disappeared, church rate assessments provided a guide to appropriate ranking. The conclusion was obvious: no church rate, no seat (and some parishioners drew the corresponding deduction: no seat, no church rate).[79] Inevitably there were accusations of abuse or favouritism. A man who had promised to buy a life-interest in a seat at Spaxton failed to pay up, so the churchwarden, Barnabas Leave, announced that he would put the seat up for auction. When the 'substantial parishioners' gathered after evening prayer they were outraged to find that the auction was off because Leave had already sold the seat to his son.[80]

Whatever the system of allocation, the church's seating was supposed to mirror the social order of the community: the squire, if any, and the substantial inhabitants at the front, the rest in descending order of status to the servants and poor at the back, with parallel, segregated arrangements for the women. Theory, as always, often failed to correspond with reality, especially in the eyes of those anxious to emphasize the distance between the respectable and the poor. This was the case at Myddle by the 1650s. A parish meeting was called to reassign the seats because, says Gough, 'it was held a thing unseemly and undecent that a company of young boys, and of persons that paid no leawans, should sit . . . above those of the best of the parish'.[81] There were similar outcries in Wiltshire parishes. At Sherston Magna there had been a general reseating some years earlier, but in 1614 the churchwardens complained of 'a row of seats or boards unseemly set up, wherein the meanest of the parish have for some time sat, and divers more substantial men . . . do want seats': they were told to seat the poor people elsewhere and build a 'comely' row of seats for their betters. Two decades later the Heytesbury churchwardens declared that 'many poor people who pay nothing to the church are placed in most of the best seats', whereas others who contributed had none. Again the remedy was obvious.[82]

Glos., however, it appears to have begun only in 1634: 'Extracts from Accounts of the Churchwardens of Minchinhampton', ed. John Bruce, *Archaeologia*, xxxv (1853), 443.

[78] Gough, *Myddle*, p. 77. GRO GDR 148 (Depositions, 1622–5), *Matthews* v. *Colling*, 9 Apr. 1628.
[79] As did Robert Moore of Donhead St. Mary: WRO AS/ABO 13 (Act Book, 1620–4), fo. 83.
[80] SRO D/D/Cd 81 (Depositions, 1635), *Leave* v. *Kebbie*, 30 Sept.
[81] Gough, *Myddle*, p. 117.
[82] WRO B/ABO 7 (Act Book, 1613–15), fo. 43; Dean's Peculiar, Presentments 1635, no. 102. For a similar incident in Warwickshire, see *Warwick County Records*, iii: *Quarter Sessions Order Book, Easter, 1650, to Epiphany, 1657*, ed. S. C. Ratcliff and H. C. Johnson, Warwick, 1937, p. 162.

Systematic reseating schemes to deal with problems of this kind were fairly common in the first half of the seventeenth century, as parishes confirmed the new pattern of social relations. Some of them were provoked by special circumstances, as at Holy Trinity, Dorchester, where the new seating-plan of 1615 came two years after a disastrous fire had consumed much of the town.[83] But quite often they reflect social transition. At Corsley, Wiltshire, where a general reseating was ordered in 1635, and at Tarrant Crawford, Dorset, where there is a 1637 list 'of all the seats newly erected in their said church', the same mixture of customary and private seats is visible as at East Coker and Spaxton.[84] Cumulatively, these and other examples suggest that by 1600 changes had occurred that made it necessary to redraw the social map that the church seating-plan provided. Reseatings were usually undertaken on the initiative of the more substantial parishioners and approved by the diocesan authorities without question. But villagers were often reluctant to undergo the costly and divisive business of general reseating except in extreme necessity. 'About the placing of seats', a Chardstock minister warned an officer of the peculiar, 'there will be no agreement between the parishioners themselves.'[85]

That some parishes were willing to confront the matter is sufficient testimony to the recent changes. Many of them, though, were content to muddle through, trusting to informal mediation as disputes arose and going to the ecclesiastical courts only as a last resort. The number of seating cases reaching the courts increased in the early seventeenth century, and some of them dramatically reveal the intensity of status competition. 'Oh Mr. Devenish, you do not see her', said a Bridgwater woman to the vicar of a certain Alice Garvin, 'she comes into the church like a lion staring . . . it was good her pride was taken down.'[86] The gentry, as we have seen, were often involved, but the many disputes between people of lower rank also indicate the tensions that redefinition of the local status hierarchy could produce. Some of them suggest particularly severe stresses in pastoral villages, which lacked the mechanisms of informal mediation available in the more cohesive arable parishes. A case at Sherston Magna has many typical features. Two of the inhabitants were charged with refusing to pay their shares of the cost of the 1602 reseating, 'to show themselves contrary to the good proceedings of the substantial inhabitants'. They replied that they had been denied 'their ancient places', the customary seats 'belonging to their houses', and that they

[83] DRO P 173, CW/1 (Dorchester, Holy Trinity, Churchwardens accounts, 1613–41).

[84] Davies, *Life in an English Village*, pp. 295–8. 'Tarrant Crawford Churchwardens' Account Book, 1637', *SDNQ* xvii (1921–3), 162–3. See also C. H. Mayo, 'Seats in Gillingham Church, 1615', *SDNQ* xiv (1914–15), 158–62.

[85] WRO, Dean's Peculiar, Presentments 1635, no. 8, John Pytt to John Johnson, 14 Nov. 1635.

[86] SRO D/D/Cd 71 (Depositions, 1631–5), *Bale alias Gulliford v. Garvin*, 1634.

would contribute only if 'every household may have his place there as before'.[87] Defence of traditional seating arrangements implied defence of threatened community traditions.

Many disputes were in fact simply defensive actions by the poor and marginal. Women were especially vulnerable to symbolic reductions of their status and doubtless often suffered in silence. At Tisbury in 1637, however, some of them protested. The diocesan chancellor had authorized the churchwardens to accommodate a growing population by reseating the congregation 'according to ranks, qualities, and conditions'. Two women stoutly declared that 'they would sit in no other seats than what pleased them', one of them exploding in court, 'blessed are they that do comfort the widows, but cursed are they that do them wrong'. She was of course promptly excommunicated.[88] Protests of this kind were easily dealt with by both ecclesiastical and civil authorities, who invariably upheld the hierarchies of rank and gender.[89]

The change in seating arrangements in so many early seventeenth-century parish churches, from systems based on custom and residence to systems based on ability to pay, was clearly related to the concurrent process of social differentiation. Population growth and social mobility had undermined the correspondence between the customary arrangements and the realities of the status hierarchy. When the process of social change had gone far enough, a visible affirmation of the new parish élites' leadership and hence a reorganization of church seating became necessary. The resulting disputes both reflected and intensified the competition for power and status. By 1640 their placement in church was more than ever likely to remind parishioners of the social distance between those in authority and the rest.

*

That assertion of social distance was made all the more necessary by the parish notables' sense of being a beleaguered minority in a world beset by chaos and disorder. Themselves propertied, respectable, and inclined to a religion which valued hard work, household discipline, individual responsibility, and sobriety, they reacted with alarm to the large segment of the population who valued none of these things.[90] The growing fears of a

---

[87] WRO B/ABO 5 (Act Book, 1600–6), fo. 20.

[88] WRO AS/ABO 15 (Act Book, 1636–40), fo. 48; quoted in Ingram, 'Ecclesiastical Justice in Wiltshire', pp. 94–5. For another case involving the displacement of poor women, see SRO D/D/Cd 71 (Depositions, 1631–5), *White* v. *Crosse*, 14 May 1634.

[89] For Somerset examples, see *SQSR* i. 30–1, 55; and for a striking case at Wells, SRO D/D/Cd 65 (Depositions, 1628–30), *Smith* v. *Meade*, 26 Apr. 1630.

[90] The English parish élites of this period strongly resemble the economically innovative groups observed by Clifford Geertz in modern Indonesia, seeing themselves as 'the main vehicle of religious and moral excellence within a generally wayward, unenlightened, or heedless community': Geertz, *Peddlers and Princes: Social Change and Economic Modernization in Two Indonesian Towns*, Chicago, 1963, p. 50. I owe this reference to Naomi Lamoreaux.

'crisis of order' were most evident in the towns and the clothing parishes, and contributed to their increasing social polarization. There were similar stresses in arable villages, but they were less acute and the resulting polarization correspondingly less serious.

The overwhelming public preoccupation of the 'substantial men' of these threatened parishes was the ever-increasing number of the poor. The scale of Elizabethan and early Stuart poverty is well known. There were no great subsistence crises in southern England like those still occurring in continental Europe, but shortages and high prices still demanded constant attention by government in all but the most fruitful years. Depression in the cloth industry, which reached disastrous proportions after the outbreak of European war in 1618, fuelled the numbers of vagrants and unemployed, a threat to property and order as well as a heavy burden on the poor rates.[91]

The high incidence of poverty and disorder in woodland areas such as Selwood, along the Wiltshire–Somerset border, was notorious. Forest dwellers were generally believed to be addicted to crime and violence— 'all rogues', a man from the more stable village of Cheddar alleged.[92] In the early seventeenth century regions such as the Forest of Arden in Warwickshire experienced a marked increase in the numbers of landless poor, squatting on commons and wastes. It is surely no coincidence that between 1590 and 1620 the Henley-in-Arden court leet regularly presented people for engaging in violent affrays, in numbers out of all proportion to the population.[93] Suggested remedies, including forced emigration, were legion. In 1624 the Somerset vicar Richard Eburne proposed Newfoundland as an outlet for 'the excessive multitude' of poor people. Naturally nothing came of it, but modern studies show that emigrants to other colonies were drawn heavily from the wood-pasture and clothing districts.[94]

The complex migration patterns within England itself have also recently been intensively studied. The general direction was from the poorer north-western highland region towards the relatively prosperous

[91] On the depression-crime relationship see J. S. Cockburn, 'The Nature and the Incidence of Crime in England 1559–1625', in *Crime in England,* ed. Cockburn, pp. 49–71.

[92] SRO CQ 3/1/98 (2) (Sessions Rolls, 1658–9), no. 18. A draft bill proposed restrictions on the use of 'bypaths and foot ways in woodland countries' because of the outrages committed by vagrants: BL Add. MS 29 975 (Pitt MSS), ff. 156–7.

[93] V. H. T. Skipp, 'Economic and Social Change in the Forest of Arden, 1530–1649', in *Land, Church and People: Essays Presented to Professor H. P. R. Finberg,* ed. Joan Thirsk, Reading, 1970, pp. 107–9; see also Skipp, *Crisis and Development: An Ecological Case Study of the Forest of Arden 1570–1674* New York, 1978. *Records of the Manor of Henley in Arden,* ed. F. C. Wellstood, Stratford-Upon-Avon, 1919, pp. 27–85.

[94] Eburne, quoted in David Underdown, *Somerset in the Civil War and Interregnum,* Newton Abbot, 1973, pp. 17–18. See also Salerno, 'Seventeenth-Century Emigration'; and David Souden, ' "Rogues, whores and vagabonds"? Indentured Servant Emigrants to North America, and the case of mid-seventeenth-century Bristol', *Social History,* iii (1978), 23–38.

south and east, and into the towns, London above all. In the rural southland, the villages and small towns of the wood-pasture regions had the heaviest in-migration, both because they lacked the means to prevent it and because of the opportunities for industrial employment they offered.[95] These places in turn generated a further flow into the bigger towns, especially in times of depression. Thus Salisbury had to contend with growing swarms of vagrants in the 1620s, many of them from the wood-pasture districts of Wiltshire and the adjacent counties.[96] Most were young adults, single men and women escaping from covenanted service. But unemployed craftsmen and other casualties of the economic dislocation also wandered in search of work. Their explanations tended to be greeted with scepticism: to the propertied householder vagrants and paupers were by definition idle and dishonest.[97]

The assumption that refusal to work denoted laziness and immorality was as common in Stuart as in later times. When the inhabitants of Ashwell, Hertfordshire, denounced Robert Willson as 'a fellow of unreformed willfulness', who stole corn and flouted authority, they also noted that he would 'follow no lawful occupation but at excessive wages'. William Wheate, squire of Glympton, Oxfordshire, dismissed a petition for relief with the observation that the man's wife was 'able to work, but will not . . . unless she may have as good wages as the ablest young woman'.[98] But something had to be done about the poor, and of course it was done: the impersonal parish rate replaced the older personal duty of charitable giving. Bequests of bread for the poor had once been common in the wills of Leicestershire yeomen; by 1600 they had virtually disappeared.[99] The deserving (the aged and impotent) were now to be taken care of by the regular provisions of statute, the rest disciplined and put to work. The victims constituted a vast, disorganized reservoir of discontent, as well as a source of guilt for those who ignored or coerced them. A tendency to look for scapegoats among the vulnerable—to indulge in accusations of witchcraft, for example—was a natural result.[100] There were other methods of imposing social discipline, but for the vagrant the whip, the stocks, and the

[95] Paul Slack, 'Vagrants and Vagrancy in England, 1598–1664', *Ec.H. R.* 2nd Ser., xxvii (1974), 374–5. John Patten, *Rural-Urban Migration in Pre-Industrial England*, Oxford, 1973, pp. 23–4, 30. See also Joan Thirsk, 'Industries in the Countryside', in *Essays in the Economic and Social History of Tudor and Stuart England*, ed. F. J. Fisher, Cambridge, 1961, pp. 70–88.

[96] Slack, 'Vagrants', pp. 360–1, 369–70, 375. Slack, 'Poverty and Politics in Salisbury 1597–1666', in *Crisis and Order*, ed. Clark and Slack, pp. 170–3.

[97] Slack, 'Vagrants', pp. 364–6. A Cornishman apprehended as a vagrant in Somerset gave a typical answer, saying that for two years he had gone 'up and down in the country working here and there a month or six weeks in a place as he could find a master': SRO CQ3/1/23 (Sessions Rolls, 1616), no. 95.

[98] *Hertford County Records*, i: *Notes and Extracts from the Sessions Rolls, 1581 to 1698*, ed. W. J. Hardy, Hertford, 1905, p. 82. Oxfordshire VCH Office, Glympton papers, Memo. by W. Wheate, 1651.

[99] Hoskins, *Midland Peasant*, p. 182.

[100] Thomas, *Religion and the Decline of Magic*, pp. 526–34, 552–67.

House of Correction were the preferred solutions. Yet there were significant contrasts between different regions. In Essex in the 1630s even aged
paupers and vagrants were whipped or put in the stocks; in more 'backward' Westmorland they were still objects of charity.[101]

Poverty was not an exclusively urban problem, but it was more visible
and threatening in the towns, and urban efforts to combat it were likely to
be correspondingly energetic. Dr Slack has described the programme of
the Puritan reformers at Salisbury; there was a similar campaign at
Dorchester. Both places embarked on elaborate schemes combining
discipline with relief (for the able-bodied as well as the impotent),
financed by the profits of municipal breweries which also helped to
control the drink trade. Similar, if less ambitious, efforts were made at
Weymouth, Devizes, and other towns.[102] At Southampton in 1616 the
court leet lamented the 'continual and great increase of poor people', and
recommended the establishment of a House of Correction. Excessive
generosity, it was believed, only compounded the problem by attracting
paupers from other places: thus Chippenham, for example, in 1633
imposed stringent eligibility requirements for grants from a private
endowment.[103]

The vagrant was the extreme case of that much-feared menace, the
'masterless' man or woman. A society held together by the cement of the
household required that everyone have a parent or master. Seventeenth-
century court records are littered with orders to masterless individuals,
frequently women, to put themselves into service.[104] As always, the
problem was most conspicuous in the towns. The Dorchester authorities
busily hunted down masterless persons of both sexes, often finding, as did
their counterparts elsewhere, that the offence was combined with other
moral failings. Sarah Cosh, for instance, was both 'a slack comer to
church, and a masterless person'.[105] Masterlessness did not necessarily
mean idleness, but attempts by people of lower status to work inde-
pendently were just as alarming. From around 1580 there was much
concern in Southampton about 'young women and maidens which keep

[101] Slack, 'Vagrants', p. 366.
[102] Slack, 'Poverty and Politics', pp. 181–9. *Poverty in Early Stuart Salisbury*, ed. Paul Slack, Wilts.
RS, xxxi, 1975. *Municipal Records of the Borough of Dorchester*, ed. C. H. Mayo, Exeter, 1908, pp. 525–6.
*Descriptive Catalogue of the Charters, Minute Books and other Documents of the Borough of Weymouth and
Melcombe Regis*, ed. H. J. Moule, Weymouth, 1883, p. 110. *Annals of Devizes*, i, pt. ii. 81.
[103] [*Southampton*] *Court Leet Records*, i: *1550–1624*, ed. F. J. C. and D. M. Hearnshaw, Southampton
RS, 1905–8, pp. 514–15 (and see also pp. 533, 536, 550, 568). *Records of Chippenham*, ed. Frederick H.
Goldney, 1889, p. 55.
[104] For example, orders by the Dorset JPs, 1625–6, regarding four Winterborne Steepleton women:
DRO, QS Order Book, 1625–37, ff. 12, 52.
[105] DRO B2/8/1 (Dorchester Court Book, 1629–37),fo. 161 (and many other examples in this volume).
Hugh Farrington of Stoke St. Gregory, Somerset, was similarly accused of 'living out of service' and
of obstinately being absent from church: SRO D/D/Ca 187 (Act Book, 1615–16), 5 Oct. 1616.

themselves out of service and work for themselves in divers men's houses', women whose offence was to 'take chambers and so live by themselves masterless'. They were a potential burden on the poor rates, but their conduct was the more serious because it also defied conventional assumptions about women's dependence.[106]

Many of these 'charmaids' were newcomers to Southampton, part of the urban migrant stream. They also belonged to another undesirable category: that of 'inmates', people living in households without proper ties of kinship or service. Even in arable villages constant vigilance was necessary to exclude such people. The Nettleton manor court followed up many individual orders with a general one in 1613: no one was to take 'any under-tenant or inmate into his house but such as are town-born children'.[107] Once again, larger towns were the worst affected. In 1603 the Southampton jury complained about a recent influx of inmates, and ordered landlords to accept only 'such as are subsidy men or women' or who would give security against becoming a charge upon the town.[108]

Another symptom of disorder was the proliferation of landless cottagers. A 1589 statute prohibited the building of cottages without at least four acres of land, but enforcement was sporadic. At Cerne Abbas, for example, there was much subletting to 'base people, mere mendicants' in the early seventeenth century: 60 per cent of the landholders had less than five acres, subsisting on casual employment in the brewing and tanning industries. Market towns like Mere and Shaftesbury were similarly afflicted.[109] Poor cottagers were especially numerous, as we might expect, in the depressed clothing districts, where their presence was sometimes encouraged by people with a vested interest in providing cheap labour for the industry. At both Frome and Lacock manorial lords were among the culprits.[110]

Poverty, vagrancy, masterlessness, landlessness: all seemed to strike at the very foundations of order. No longer could it be assumed that all Englishmen and women were bound together in that interlocking network of households and communities on which stability depended. Even the

---

[106] *Southampton Court Leet Records*, i. 186, 236, 511. *The Assembly Books of Southampton*, i: 1602–1608, ed. J. W. Horrocks, Southampton RS xix, 1917, pp. xxxiii, 53, 70–1, 97–8, 102. *The Southampton Mayor's Book of 1606–1608*, ed. W. J. Connor, Southampton Record Series, xxi, 1978, pp. 50, 53.

[107] BL Add. MS 23151 (Nettleton Court Book), ff. 50ᵛ, 55. Similar measures were taken at Compton Abdale, Glos.: BL Add. MS 23150 (Compton Abdale Court Book, 1608–48), ff. 11, 14ᵛ, 15ᵛ, 21. See also Willcox, *Gloucestershire*, pp. 256–7.

[108] *Southampton Court Leet Records*, i. 386–7; other examples at pp. 486, 511, and in *Southampton Mayor's Book*, 1606–8, pp. 44–113.

[109] J. H. Bettey, *Dorset*, Newton Abbot, 1974, pp. 127–8; 'Agriculture and Rural Society in Dorset', pp. 348–50.

[110] PRO STAC 8/88/18 (*Coker v. Leversage*, 1603). *Records of the County of Wilts. . . . Extracts from the Quarter Sessions Great Rolls of the Seventeenth Century*, ed. B. H. Cunnington, Devizes, 1932, p. 31. For further discussion see Ingram, 'Ecclesiastical Justice in Wiltshire', pp. 375–6.

patriarchal family—the lynch-pin of the entire structure—appeared to be threatened. Whether early seventeenth-century Englishwomen were in fact more inclined than their forebears to independence and self-asser-tion, children and servants to disobedience and rebelliousness, is a matter on which two views are possible. But as is so often the case in history, reality is less important than perception. The flood of Jacobean anti-feminist literature and the concurrent public obsession with scolding, domineering, and unfaithful wives indicate widespread fears that in familial as well as in community relations the world was badly out of joint. Such fears were an important component of the 'crisis of order'.

By itself, the literary evidence that this was a period of unusual strain in gender relations is not conclusive. The misogynist tradition in literature is a long one, the battle of the sexes an eternally popular theme. But late Elizabethan and Jacobean writers were unusually preoccupied with themes of female independence and resolve.[111] They were particular favourites of dramatists: men, of course, so it is not strange that the plays reflect the patriarchal consensus. Beatrice and Rosalind might have their brief hour of independence, but both Shakespeare and his audience knew that in the end they must submit to their proper wifely roles. In the theatre, as in carnival, sexual inversion temporarily turns the world upside down, but only to reinforce, not subvert, the traditional order.[112] As for that extreme case of the assertive woman, the shrew or scold, the most celebrated instance may contain some ambiguities, for Kate's creator well appreciated the tension between ideal and reality. Still, the play was clearly aimed at an audience with conventional notions about proper relations between the sexes.[113] Even more significant of the concern for familial order is Heywood and Brome's *The Lancashire Witches* (1634), in which a whole community is thrown into chaos by its absence. Wives rule their husbands, children their parents, servants their employers. 'This is quite upside down', a bewildered character exclaims, '... sure they are all bewitched'. He is right, of course: Satan's minions have inverted the natural order.[114]

A fascination with rebellious women is even more obvious in popular literature. Titles like *The Cruell Shrew* and *Hic Mulier, or, the Man-Woman* show what Grub Street thought was on people's minds. Joseph Swet-

[111] For fuller consideration of the matters covered in this and the four following paragraphs, see David Underdown, 'The Taming of the Scold: The Enforcement of Patriarchal Authority in Early Modern England', in *Order and Disorder in Early Modern England*, ed. Anthony Fletcher and John Stevenson, Cambridge, 1985, ch. 4.

[112] Burke, *Popular Culture*, pp. 199–204, discusses the ambiguities of ritual inversion, with appropriate references.

[113] Ian Donaldson, *The World Upside Down: Comedy from Jonson to Fielding*, Oxford, 1970, p. 10. On 'The Taming of the Shrew' see also Juliet S. Dusinberre, *Shakespeare and the Nature of Women*, 1975, pp. 105–8.

[114] Thomas Heywood, *Dramatic Works*, 1874, iv. 183.

nam's *Arraignment of lewd, idle, froward and inconstant women* ran through ten editions between 1615 and 1634, and other hacks also exploited the theme. The conventional message is typified by one of John Taylor's efforts:[115]

> Ill fares the hapless family that shows
> A cock that's silent, and a hen that crows.
> I know not which live more unnatural lives,
> Obedient husbands, or commanding wives.

The endless reiteration, surely, would have been unnecessary if there had not been uneasy feelings that too many such families existed. Concern spilled over into parliamentary debate, an MP in 1601 declaring that 'every man can tame a shrew but he that hath her'.[116] Traditional worries about sexually aggressive women were compounded by fears of the subversive notions others might pick up in their leisure time. 'Do you come from an alehouse bench', bawls one of Taylor's henpecked husbands, 'from amongst the rest of your talking gossips, to tell me what I have to do?'[117]

Anxiety about patriarchal order was more than a literary phenomenon. Between 1560 and 1640 local court records show an intense concern about unruly women. Women scolding and brawling with neighbours, defying or even beating their husbands, seem to be distinctly more common than in the periods before and afterwards. In some regions, as we shall see in a later chapter, couples in which the natural order was inverted by the wife's dominance or infidelity were the targets of charivari processions, to shame them into reforming themselves or leaving the village. As for scolds, a Southampton complaint is typical. In 1603 a jury noted 'the manifold number of scolding women that be in this town'; the mayor, it was lamented a year later, was 'daily troubled with such brawls'.[118] There had always been scolds, of course, but by now more places felt the need for drastic shaming rituals, to replace the hitherto customary penances or small fines.[119] Hence the widespread resort to cucking-stools for ceremonially ducking scolds, whores, and other female offenders. They appear in the later sixteenth century at Southampton, Marlborough, Devizes, Shrewsbury, and many other places.[120]

---

[115] [John Taylor], *Divers Crabtree Lectures, Expressing the Severall Languages that Shrews read to their Husbands*, 1639, pp. 73–4. The literature on this theme is surveyed by Carroll Camden, *The Elizabethan Woman*, Houston, 1952, pp. 255–71; and Louis B. Wright, *Middle-Class Culture in Elizabethan England*, Chapel Hill, 1935, pp. 481–506.

[116] Quoted by Kent, 'Attitudes of Members', p. 55.

[117] [Taylor], *Divers Crabtree Lectures*, p. 71.

[118] *Southampton Court Leet Records*, i. 381, 401.

[119] See 'Taming of the Scold', for further discussion.

[120] The best introduction to the subject is John W. Spargo, *Juridical Folklore in England Illustrated by the Cucking-Stool*, Durham, NC, 1944.

One final point: it is well known that this was the period in which accusations of witchcraft, almost always against women, reached their peak. It may seem odd to place the witch in the category of independent women, the typical suspect being usually old and powerless. But witchcraft fantasies were often a response of the powerless to isolation and oppression that were both social and sexual in origin. Parallels between witchcraft and scolding were not lost on contemporaries: the chief fault of witches, Reginald Scot observed, 'is that they are scolds'.[121] The scold who cursed a more fortunate neighbour and the witch who cast a spell were both rebelling against their assigned places in the social and gender hierarchies.[122] The chronology of the two offences is roughly similar, each reaching its peak in the later sixteenth century and declining to virtual insignificance a century or so later. Literary and popular evidence thus combine to suggest that a perceived threat to patriarchal authority in the years around 1600 was a major feature of the 'crisis of order'.

*

The social tensions we have been surveying may seem remote from the central theme of this book, the popular response to the revolution of the 1640s. There is, though, a real connection. The division in the English body politic which erupted in civil war in 1642 can be traced in part to the earlier emergence of two quite different constellations of social, political, and cultural forces, involving diametrically opposite responses to the problems of the time. On the one side stood those who put their trust in the traditional conception of the harmonious, vertically-integrated society—a society in which the old bonds of paternalism, deference, and good neighbourliness were expressed in familiar religious and communal rituals—and wished to strengthen and preserve it. On the other stood those—mostly among the gentry and middling sort of the new parish élites—who wished to emphasize the moral and cultural distinctions which marked them off from their poorer, less disciplined neighbours, and to use their power to reform society according to their own principles of order and godliness. These two socio-cultural constellations can be observed in all parts of England, but in varied strengths in different geographical areas: the former more conspicuously in the arable regions, the latter in the cloth-making wood-pasture districts. Two alternative societies existed side by side, both increasingly polarized between rich and poor, but one relatively stable and reciprocally paternalistic and

---

[121] Quoted by Thomas, *Religion and the Decline of Magic*, p. 530.
[122] The two accusations were sometimes explicitly combined: see Underdown, 'Taming of the Scold', pp. 120–1.

deferential, the other more unstable, less harmonious, more individual-istic.

In unsettling times people are prone to look for new ways of formulating their beliefs about society and the universe, and it is not surprising that in the seventeenth century they did so in religious terms. The familiar certainties of traditional religion—Catholicism, or the moderate Protestantism of the Elizabethan compromise—were well suited to close-knit arable communities. The division between literate clergy and illiter-ate, and thus dependent, laity; the emphasis on ritual and imagery; the regular invocations of unity in parish feasts and processions: all were appropriate to this older kind of society. But in communities more subject to the disorders of population growth, inflation, and the market economy, such beliefs and rituals had less meaning. The parish élites needed a more systematic, more disciplined way of ordering their and their neighbours' lives. They found it in the cluster of beliefs which for want of a better word we can only label Puritanism.

Puritanism was of course much more than simply a response to dis-order, much more than simply a means of enabling its adherents to integrate themselves into a different kind of community. The term is impossible to define with precision, can mean almost anything its users want it to mean, and there are modern historians who would like to abandon it altogether.[123] Yet if we were to adopt this heroic remedy we should have to put some other, probably clumsier, term in its place, for no discussion of religion in early modern England can do without it. Throughout this book, 'Puritanism' is used loosely to mean the set of beliefs held by people who wished to emphasize more strongly the Calvinist heritage of the Church of England; to elevate preaching and scripture above sacraments and rituals, the notions of the calling, the elect, the 'saint', the distinctive virtue of the divinely predestined minority, above the equal worth of all sinful Christians. Among much else, Puritanism was indeed a response to social instability.[126] It gave its adherents the comforting belief that they were entrusted by God with the special duty of resisting the tide of sin and disorder that surged around them. Through preaching, prayer, the study of scripture, and regular self-examination, it provided a strategy for cultivating the personal qualities necessary to these ends. And in the concept of the elect it provided the basis for a new kind of community, united by belief and mission, sometimes formally by covenant in a 'gathered church', as a

---

[123] Hill, *Society and Puritanism*, ch. 1. C. H. George, 'Puritanism as History and Historiography', *P & P* no. 41 (Dec. 1968), 77–104.

[124] Alan Everitt has suggested a possible link between Puritanism and economic insecurity, e.g. in areas subject to grain shortage: Everitt, *Change in the Provinces: the Seventeenth Century*, University of Leicester, Dept. of English Local History Occasional papers, 2nd Ser. i (1969), p. 36.

substitute for the territorial parish community that was now disintegrating. In doing so it gave further impetus to that disintegration.[125]

There were Puritans at all levels of English society, from great noblemen like the Elizabethan Earl of Huntington to the humble weavers and labourers who were drawn into separatist congregations and sometimes went with them into exile.[126] Puritan preachers thundered quite as fiercely as their less Calvinist colleagues against usury and material greed. Yet though they condemned the sinful abuse of acquisitive values, they spoke with particular resonance to those of the middling sort who were adopting these values and abandoning the more traditional communal ones. Their listeners had risen above their neighbours by sobriety, diligence, and godliness, and only by imposing those values on those around them could their position be protected.[127] But the Puritan was not inspired merely, or even primarily, by selfish materialism. Like many others in this period of religious conflict, he was inspired by the sense of participating in a universal moral drama, a fundamental conflict between great cosmic forces of good and evil. Every dispute—over foreign policy, episcopal or ministerial authority, church ritual, the erection of a maypole, the licensing of an alehouse—reflected a crucial moral conflict about the whole nature of the community. Given a different set of circumstances, such as prevailed in the Massachusetts of the 1690s, Puritan moral passion might turn as fiercely against the representatives of a new capitalist order as against its opponents.[128] But in early Stuart England Puritanism spoke most plainly to those who were profiting from, and contributing to, the onset of that new order.

Puritans still shared many of the prevailing values of their times. Their beliefs might threaten the stability of the traditional parish community, but they did not directly challenge the even more fundamental unit of society, the family. The Puritan household might be inspired, ideally, by greater mutual affection—husbands and wives, said Daniel Rogers, should be 'as two sweet friends'—and wives given greater responsibility for the spiritual education of their children, but the family was still a 'little

---

[125] This paragraph relies heavily on Michael Walzer, *The Revolution of the Saints*, Cambridge, Mass., 1965.

[126] The differences between separatists and mainstream 'church-type' Puritans are of course huge and fundamental. But both stemmed from a common Protestant tradition, and to exclude separatists from the loose definition of 'Puritan' adopted in this book would create unnecessary complications.

[127] The old, unresolved issue of the appeal of Protestant teaching to the commercial classes has recently been thoughtfully discussed by Hunt, *The Puritan Moment*, esp. pp. 124–9. See also Hill, *Society and Puritanism*, chs. 4, 5, 7. Keith Wrightson, 'The Puritan Reformation of Manners with special reference to the counties of Lancashire and Essex', Ph.D. thesis, University of Cambridge, 1973, is an extremely valuable comparative study of its impact in two very different regions.

[128] Paul Boyer and Stephen Nissenbaum, *Salem Possessed: The Social Origins of Witchcraft*, Cambridge, Mass., 1974, pp. 102–7.

commonwealth' in which the husband was the natural head.[129] Yet the Puritans' ideal community was very different from the traditional one. Their determination to reshape their world provoked in the England of James I a cultural and religious conflict that foreshadowed, and contributed to, the later divisions of the civil war.

[129] Rogers, quoted by Stone, *Family, Sex and Marriage*, p. 102. See also Roberta Hamilton, *The Liberation of Women: A Study of Patriarchy and Capitalism*, 1978, ch. 3.

3

Cultural Conflict

By the early seventeenth century important social differences were emerging between English pasture and arable regions. These in turn were reflected in cultural differences which help to explain the varying responses of those regions to civil war. Political attitudes are a part of culture, part of that 'historically transmitted pattern of meanings embodied in symbols . . . by means of which men communicate, perpetuate and develop their knowledge about and attitude towards life'.[1] The use of ritual to affirm community values in non-literate societies has been a favourite theme of modern anthropologists. 'Ritual', says R. A. Rappaport, may 'validate and intensify the relationships which integrate the social unit, or symbolize the relationships which bind the social unit to its environment'. Or, as Victor Turner has put it, 'in hierarchical social structures *communitas* is symbolically affirmed by periodic rituals, not infrequently calendrical or tied in with the agricultural cycle'.[2] Historians cannot be direct observers of the rituals they analyse, cannot sit, as it were, at the ringside of the Balinese cock-fight. But they too are increasingly aware that a civic or parish ritual—a mystery play, a Rogationtide procession—or a festive gathering—a midsummer revel, a football match, an election riot—may reveal important features of the social and religious, and even perhaps the political, identity of a community.[3]

There were noticeable differences, as we shall discover, between the cultures of English regions, even within as small an area as the three south-western counties we are chiefly concerned with. Before they can be fully understood, however, it is necessary to review more generally the chronology of cultural conflict during the period, and to explore some of its social and ideological dimensions. We must of course first accept that English people of all regions and types of communities had much in common, many shared assumptions about church and state, family and

---

[1] Clifford Geertz, *The Interpretation of Cultures*, New York, 1973, p. 89.

[2] R. A. Rappaport, 'Ritual Regulation of Environmental Relations among a New Guinea People', in *Environment and Cultural Behavior: Ecological Studies in Cultural Anthropology*, ed. Andrew P. Vayda, Austin, 1969, p. 182. Victor Turner, *Dramas, Fields, and Metaphors: Symbolic Action in Human Society*, Ithaca, 1974, p. 53.

[3] Many recent studies are synthesized in Burke, *Popular Culture*. For an example covering an earlier period see Charles Phythian-Adams, 'Ceremony and the Citizen: The communal year at Coventry 1450–1550', in *Crisis and Order*, ed. Clark and Slack, ch. 2.

locality. Regional cultural differences are likely to be, at most, marginal. We should also bear in mind that cultural conflict did not erupt suddenly in the early Stuart reigns, but had a long earlier history. The old culture of the lower orders had been under attack from magistrates and clergy ever since the Reformation. And the campaign was not limited to England—it was a European-wide phenomenon, visible in Catholic and Protestant countries alike.[4]

It is all too easy to look back on late medieval popular culture through a haze of antiquarian nostalgia. People were already beginning to do this even in the seventeenth century. John Aubrey's lament for the passing of the old days of hospitality and neighbourliness is a typical example:

There were no rates for the poor even in my grandfather's days: but for Kington St. Michael (no small parish) the church ale at Whitsuntide did their business. In every parish is, or was, a church house, to which belonged spits, crocks, etc., utensils for dressing provision. Here the housekeepers met, and were merry and gave their charity: the young people came there too, and had dancing, bowling, shooting at butts, etc., the ancients sitting gravely by, looking on.

'Such joy and merriment was every holiday', Aubrey concludes, and he is echoed by many other admirers of the country feasts.[5] No doubt they exaggerated the charm and tranquility of it all. Yet there is also no doubt that fifteenth-century England had produced a popular culture of quite remarkable richness. Larger towns like Chester, Coventry, and York had their cycles of religious plays, their St. George's Day or midsummer civic processions, all accompanied with colourful pageantry. In the villages similar, if less elaborate, customs abounded. Celebrations such as Plough Monday and the perambulation of the bounds at Rogationtide brought welcome relief from toil; they also brought neighbours together and affirmed the links that bound them to each other and to the world of nature. They too had their simple pageantry, their ritualized processions. In Cornwall and other counties miracle plays still flourished, and even the small Somerset village of Croscombe could promote an annual cycle of plays and revels, complete with Robin Hood and other folk heroes.[6]

In many towns civic pride (and also the fact that they were good for trade) ensured the survival of these traditions long after the Reformation.

---

[4] Burke, *Popular Culture*, pp. 207–22, 229–34.

[5] *Top. Coll. John Aubrey*, pp. 10–11. Cf. Richard Carew, *The Survey of Cornwall*, ed. F. E. Halliday, 1953, p. 141; and Nicholas Breton, 'The Court and Country' (1618), p. 7, in *Works in Verse and Prose of Nicholas Breton*, ed. A. B. Grosart, 1879, ii.

[6] E. K. Chambers, *The Mediaeval Stage*, Oxford, 1903, i. 118–19. Phythian-Adams, 'Ceremony and the Citizen'. *Church-Wardens' Accounts of Croscombe, Pilton, Yatton . . . 1349 to 1560*, ed. Bishop Hobhouse, SRS iv, 1890, pp. 1–31. For an Essex example, see 'The Dunmow Parish Accounts', ed. L. A. Majendie, *Essex Archaeological Soc. Transactions*, ii (1863), 230–2. For an account of the rural festive year see George C. Homans, *English Villagers of the Thirteenth Century*, Cambridge, Mass., 1941, chs. 23–4.

At Marlborough in 1578 the chamberlain still laid out 13*s*. 8*d*. 'for a gallon of wine and gunpowder at the Lord of Misrule's coming'. The inhabitants of Burford still paraded their giant and dragon through the streets at midsummer well into the seventeenth century. There were still morris dancers at Plymouth on May Day, 1605; the Florists' Feasts still gladdened the hearts of Norwich citizens in the 1630s. Sherborne, Tewkesbury, Yeovil—the list could be endlessly extended—all held elaborate plays annually until about the middle of Elizabeth's reign, and occasionally thereafter.[7]

In the villages too, as antiquaries like Aubrey and Robert Plot attest, many traditional festivals still lingered, though it is not always clear how well they survived official disapproval. Aubrey is a mine of information on Wiltshire revel feasts, as well as on wassailings, midsummer bonfires, harvest homes, and sheep-shearings, always kept with 'good rustic cheer'. Plot describes the famous Abbotts Bromley hobby-horse dance, which certainly lasted into the Interregnum, and other Staffordshire festivals like the annual 'Court of Music' and bull-running at Tutbury. Church ales and perambulations survived here and there right down to the civil war.[8] Many places were naturally reticent about their merry-makings, but they occasionally surface even in Puritan East Anglia: at Seething, Norfolk, for instance, there was a Christmas 'masque or mummery' in 1590. And harvest songs still echoed through the summer nights in Suffolk in 1603, as grateful labourers serenaded 'the gentlemen or chief men of every parish'.[9] Festivities involving dancing were naturally especially popular among young people, for whom they provided convenient courting opportunities. In Wiltshire in 1604, there was a gathering on the Sunday after Twelfth Night 'of the youth of the parish of All Cannings, at the parsonage house . . . and after supper many then and there present went to dance'. A man planning to attend 'some dancing or other sports' at Maddington, Wiltshire, at Whitsun 1608 said that he was 'going a-wooing, or to get him a wife'.[10] The church itself was often the

---

[7] *Historical Records of Marlborough*, ed. B. H. Cunnington, 1928–30, p. 4. Plot, *Nat. Hist. Oxfordshire*, p. 349. John T. Murray, *English Dramatic Companies 1588–1642*, 1910, ii. 384 and n. R. W. Ketton-Cremer, *Forty Norfolk Essays*, Norwich, 1961, pp. 14–16.

[8] *Top. Coll. John Aubrey*, pp. 139, 146, 185, 198, 272–4. Aubrey, 'Remaines of Gentilisme and Judaisme', in Aubrey, *Three Prose Works*, ed. John Buchanan-Brown, Carbondale, Illinois, 1972, pp. 137–8, 143, 212. Robert Plot, *Natural History of Staffordshire*, Oxford, 1686, pp. 434–40. Chambers, *Mediaeval Stage*, i. 173, n. M. H. A. Stapleton, *Three Oxfordshire Parishes*, Oxford Hist. Soc., xxiv, 1893, pp. 252–3. J. Brand, *Observations on the Popular Antiquities of Great Britain*, ed. Sir Henry Ellis, 1848–9, i. 280–1.

[9] NRO DEP/25 (Consistory Court Deposition Book, 1590–1), fo. 107ᵛ (I am indebted to Susan Amussen for this reference). PRO STAC 8/176/14 (*Hall* v. *Wolverston*, 1603). For harvest dinners in Cornwall, see Carew, *Cornwall*, p. 141.

[10] WRO, Bishop's Deposition Book 22b (1603–4), ff. 49ᵛ–50; Dean's Deposition Book 6 (1608), fo. 87. Aubrey notes the important role of young people in the preservation of ancient customs: 'Remaines', pp. 137–8.

scene of youthful merriment. Bell-ringing at unauthorized hours was a common pastime: at Braunton, Devon, some of the parishioners admitted ringing the bells at Whitsuntide and on other summer Sundays in 1614 'somewhat late in the evening'.[11]

*

Disapproval of these diversions was not, as we have already noted, confined to Protestants. But Protestants' association of such things as saints' days and mystery plays with the old days of 'popery and superstition' gave their campaigns against popular festivals a peculiar intensity.[12] Many saints' days and celebrations such as Plough Monday were banned in the 1540s, and church dedication feasts (common pretexts for village revels) officially restricted to a single Sunday in October.[13] Other opportunities for popular recreation were also curtailed. An act of 1541 repeated earlier prohibitions against 'tables, tennis, dice, cards, bowls' and other 'unlawful games', except for people of at least yeomen status; archery (defence-related, of course) was the only plebeian sport encouraged. Status distinctions were further defined in the Injunctions of 1559, which limited Rogationtide processions to property-owners (perambulating the parish bounds also confirmed property-rights) and prohibited the customary bells, banners, and feastings.[14]

As Elizabeth's reign wore on, Puritan writers and preachers thundered with increasing ferocity against what remained of the 'heathenish' and popish revellings. When the returned Marian exile William Kethe came as rector to the Dorset village of Childe Okeford he was scandalized at the tide of popery and sinful merry-making that engulfed the region. His faith fortified by a spell as preacher with the army sent against the northern rebels in 1569, he bitterly denounced profaners of the sabbath in a sermon before the JPs at Blandford Sessions. 'Where God calleth it his holy sabbath', he lamented, 'the multitude call it their revelling day, which day is spent in bull-baitings, bear-baitings, bowlings, dicing, carding, dancings, drunkenness and whoredom'. Revels, declared Kethe, were a threat to household order; when a neighbouring parish had held a church

[11] They also admitted encouraging the organist to give informal recitals after evensong: PRO STAC 8/69/5 (*Browning* v. *Stone*, 1614). For other examples of festive bell-ringing see Willcox, *Gloucestershire*, p. 237; and Henry Burton, *A Divine Tragedie Lately Acted, or A Collection of Sundrie Memorable Examples of Gods Judgements upon Sabbath-breakers*, 1641, pp. 14–15, 22.

[12] Thomas, *Religion and the Decline of Magic*, pp. 64–7. Burke, *Popular Culture*, ch. 8.

[13] *Visitation Articles and Injunctions of the Period of the Reformation*, ed. W. H. Frere and W. M. Kennedy, 1910, ii. 126, 175.

[14] 33 Hen. VIII, c.9: *Statutes at Large*, ed. Danby Pickering, v (Cambridge, 1763), 85. *Visitation Articles*, iii, 164, 264, F. J. C. Hearnshaw, *Leet Jurisdiction in England, Especially as Illustrated by the Records of the Court Leet of Southampton*, Southampton, 1908, p. 124.

ale, 'men could not keep their servants from lying out of their own houses
. . . at night'.[15]

Anxieties about collapsing familial discipline were central to the whole
crisis of order. Revels were an obvious scapegoat. They permitted women
an unacceptable degree of sexual freedom, particularly through mixed
dancing—'most unseemly and intolerable', John Northbrooke groaned,
'the storehouse and nursery of bastardy'. They undermined parental
authority by encouraging young people to associate freely, with inevitably
sinful results, and to the neglect of their work and religious duties. Attacks
on festive customs by moral crusaders like Northbrooke had a gen-
erational character: they were in part an offensive against a youth culture.
The Puritan Philip Stubbes made the point explicitly: 'Are not unlawful
games, plays, interludes and the like everywhere frequented? . . . Was
there ever seen less obedience in youth of all sorts, both menkind and
womenkind, towards their superiors, parents, masters and governors?'[16]

To be sure, the concern for order was not unique to Puritans, but was a
product of the widening gulf between the substantial people 'of credit and
reputation' and the disorderly poor. The preoccupation with social discipline is visible at all levels of English life. The bleak economic conditions of the 1590s provoked a marked increase in the number of
parliamentary bills concerned with moral reformation. In the sessions of
1601, 1604, and 1606, for example, twenty-five bills for the regulation
of alehouses were introduced (in no other three consecutive sessions
between 1576 and 1629 were there anything like half as many), and there
was a similar increase in the number of bills to enforce sabbath
observance. Puritan members such as Francis Hastings and Sir Francis
Barrington were in the forefront, but the obsession with moral order was
shared by virtually all their colleagues.[17]

The gentry's preoccupations as MPs mirrored their concern as county
magistrates. Besides encouraging idlers and vagrants, the Cheshire
magnate Sir Richard Grosvenor declared, alehouses directly undermined
familial order: 'Here are you deprived of the obedience of your sons, of
the duty of your servants'.[18] The regulation of alehouses, enforcement of
church-attendance laws and a host of other disciplinary measures

[15] William Kethe, *A Sermon made at Blandford Forum, in the Countie of Dorset*, 1571, pp. 8, 15—16,
19—20. For Kethe, see *DNB*. There was a marked intensification of the campaign in the 1570s, for
example in the diocese of York: *Records of Early English Drama: York*, ed. Alexandra F. Johnston and
Margaret Rogerson, Toronto, 1979, i, 358, 369. For the campaign in general see Hill, *Society and
Puritanism*, pp. 168—76, 188—9.
[16] J. Northbrooke, *Distractions of the Sabbath*, 1579, pp. 175—6. Philip Stubbes, *The Anatomie of
Abuses*, 4th edn., 1595, Epistle Dedicatory and pp. 109—10. Northbrooke (p. 12) blames it all on
parental permissiveness.
[17] Kent, 'Attitudes of Members', pp. 41—8, 64—71. See also Hill, *Society and Puritanism*, pp. 160—1.
[18] Richard Cust and Peter G. Lake, 'Sir Richard Grosvenor and the Rhetoric of Magistracy', *BIHR*
liv (1981), 45.

dominated the work of many county magistracies by the end of James I's reign. But there were significant regional variations. By 1625 cases involving moral regulation far outnumbered those involving criminal activity or personal disputes in the business conducted by Essex JPs: in the more backward parts of Lancashire, on the other hand, in spite of sporadic earlier bursts of activity by the justices, the full imposition of moral reformation had to await Parliament's victory in the civil war.[19]

The western counties were not exempt from these developments. The Somerset JPs were especially alarmed about the disorders that accompanied public festivities: many unfortunate women, they lamented in 1632, had been indicted 'for murdering bastard children begotten at wakes and revels'.[20] Beginning in 1594 they issued a series of orders prohibiting church ales, whose frequent repetition indicates their ineffectiveness. The Wiltshire justices seem to have preferred to leave the matter to the ecclesiastical courts, but in Devon there were four sessions orders against church ales between 1595 and 1615, as well as assize orders in 1602 and 1627. A year later, a clerical petition led to a general order covering Somerset, Devon, and Dorset, which was repeated in 1632, fuelling the great controversy which culminated in the issue of Charles I's Book of Sports.[21] To that we shall return.

The campaign against the ancient feasts and popular recreations achieved mixed success. In some areas, as we shall see, it met with stubborn resistance, and everywhere it aroused a lingering nostalgia for the good old days on the part of people whose pleasures were being taken away. In the more firmly Protestant regions it made rapid headway. In 1576 William Harrison noted that the 'superfluous numbers of idle wakes' had already been 'well diminished'—a view confirmed by modern scholarship, as far as the eastern counties (Harrison's own area) are concerned.[22] Even in the arable midlands they were fast disappearing. At one time Leicestershire wills had often included bequests of malt for brewing at church ales, but after about 1570 these went the way of gifts of

[19] Wrightson, 'Puritan Reformation of Manners', ch. 7. James Tait, 'The Declaration of Sports for Lancashire (1617)', *Eng. H.R.* xxxii (1917), 565–7. Cf. Willcox, *Gloucestershire*, pp. 140–4.

[20] William Prynne, *Canterburies Doome*, 1646, p. 130. A recent study finds no statistical correlation between revels and illegitimate conceptions: G. R. Quaife, *Wanton Wenches and Wayward Wives: Peasants and Illicit Sex in Early Seventeenth Century England*, 1979, pp. 84–7. But see also Richard L. Greaves, *Society and Religion in Elizabethan England*, Minneapolis, 1981, pp. 214, 466–7.

[21] The relevant orders are listed in T. G. Barnes, 'County Politics and a Puritan Cause Célèbre: Somerset Churchales, 1633', *TRHS* 5th Ser., ix (1959), 109 and n., though the 1612 one is missed (see *SQSR* i. 75). See also S. K. Roberts, 'Alehouses, brewing, and government under the early Stuarts', *Southern History*, ii (1980), 58 and n. 46; and Keith Wrightson, 'Alehouses, Order and Reformation in Rural England, 1590–1660', in *Popular Culture and Class Conflict 1590–1914*, ed. Eileen and Stephen Yeo, Hassocks, Sussex, 1981, ch. 1. Information about Dorset is reduced by the absence of QS records before 1660, apart from an order book covering 1625–37. See F. J. Pope, 'Dorset Assizes in the Seventeenth Century', *DNHP* xxxiv (1913), 28.

[22] Harrison, *Description of England*, 1968 edn., p. 36.

bread for the poor. Where the feasts were held, there are significant signs of reluctance to participate.[23] Church plays, after a brief revival early in Elizabeth's reign, disappeared in Essex and Suffolk when the parish notables turned against them at about the same time. At Chelmsford they ended in 1576 and the costumes were sold, 'by the consent of divers of the parishioners'. By 1600, Dr Wrightson suggests, the communal sociability of the parish feasts had been replaced by the 'fragmented sociability' of the alehouse.[24]

The drive for order was conducted with particular urgency in towns beset by large numbers of the poor. The outlook of their rulers can be illustrated by a brief consideration of the fortunes of travelling theatrical companies. By the middle of James I's reign two generations of Puritan preachers had done their work: plays were widely seen as dangerous distractions for the poor, contributing to idleness and disorder. 'Those who spend their money on plays', declared the Puritan mayor of Exeter in 1618, 'are ordinarily very poor people'. Payments to companies to leave towns without performing became common after about 1616, sometimes on other pretexts—the plague was a favourite one—but usually out of concern for the work habits of the poor.[25] Norwich's policy was restriction rather than outright prohibition: no performances on Sundays or during musters and other public functions. Plays put on by local people at the time of the Florists' Feast survived in spite of Puritan disapproval. But the danger to the morals of the lower orders begins to feature in official arguments, especially after 1620. Permission is refused because of 'the poor, whose work cannot be wanted', or 'for fear of tumult of the people'. Some players with a patent from the Master of the Revels outstayed their permit in 1634, 'to the great hurt of the poor'. The corporation promptly petitioned against such patents, 'by reason that the maintenance of the inhabitants here doth consist of work and making of manufactures', but only in March 1641 did they get total control over visiting players. One applicant for permission to perform in Norwich sensibly offered to pay for an officer who would prevent 'poor people, servants and idle persons' from attending.[26]

Besides plays and processions, drinking, sabbath-breaking, and the

[23] Hoskins, *Midland Peasant*, pp. 182–3. Ware, 'Elizabethan Parish', pp. 73–4.

[24] Wrightson, 'Puritan Reformation of Manners', pp. 37–8. 'Extracts from an old Chelmsford Parish Account Book', ed. Archdeacon Mildmay, *Essex Archaeological Soc. Transactions*, ii (1863), 228. See also Cox, *Churchwardens Accounts*, pp. 275–6; and Hunt, *The Puritan Moment*, pp. 132–5.

[25] Murray, *Dramatic Companies*, ii. 6, 199–200, 272.

[26] *Minutes of the Norwich Court of Mayoralty 1632–1635*, ed. William L. Sachse, Norfolk RS xxxvi, 1967, pp. 81, 85, 129, 132–4, 175, 183. Murray, *Dramatic Companies*, ii. 340–60. Glynne Wickham, *Early English Stages 1300 to 1650*, 1959–81, ii, pt. i, 120. *The Knyvett Letters, 1620–1644*, ed. B. Schofield, Norfolk RS xx, 1949, p. 29. See also L. G. Bolingbroke, 'Players in Norwich, from the Accession of Queen Elizabeth until their Suppression in 1642', *Norfolk Archaeology*, xiii (1898), 12–19; and Ketton-Cremer, *Forty Norfolk Essays*, pp. 14–16.

playing of unlawful games all attracted the attention of urban moral reformers. Restrictions on unlawful games have a long history, antedating the Reformation by at least a century.[27] But even the 1541 statute did not trigger the sort of obsession with the problem that becomes visible in the records of many towns after 1570. Such games, a Southampton jury lamented in 1579, had greatly impoverished 'divers artificers of this town and other householders by lewd servants'. The complaint was familiar and so too was the ever-present religious justification. At Devizes the campaign began under a Puritan mayor, denounced by one of his enemies as 'a godly coxcomb'. God, as the divine Thomas Beard reminded his readers with a deluge of lurid examples, often punished drunkards and sabbath-breakers directly; but it was still the godly's duty to assist. If nothing was done and unlawful games were tolerated, another South-ampton jury declared in 1590, 'the great wrath of God hangeth over us'.[28]

Several English towns established notable reputations as bastions of moral reformation. Two of them—Gloucester and Salisbury—have recently received attention from historians. In both places religious and cultural reforms were combined with discipline and relief of the poor, with the objective of creating a godly 'city on a hill'. At Salisbury the old ways were going out even before the Puritan clique tightened their grip on the corporation in the 1620s. The Whitsun festivities in the city parishes had dwindled to 'children's dances', and these too disappeared by 1611, though declining receipts from 'Whitsun gatherings' were still recorded in one parish until 1619. It is unnecessary to recapitulate the aims and achievements of John Ivie and his friends, but one famous incident does deserve to be recalled because it so poignantly dramatizes the conflict between the old beliefs and the new. When Recorder Sherfield observed some women parishioners making 'low curtsies' in St. Edmund's church he asked one of them why they did it and was told 'that they made them to their Lord God, and to God the Father in the glass window'. Sherfield promptly smashed the offending stained glass.[29]

Sherfield's friends were never completely secure in their control of Salisbury. At Dorchester, on the other hand, the arrival of the formidable new rector, John White, in 1606 was quickly followed by an almost total Puritan ascendency. The town had a short way with visiting players, brusquely imprisoning the leader of one company in 1615 when he unwisely protested at a refusal to let his men perform. 'We have no waste

[27] There were prosecutions at Castle Combe, for example, between 1428 and 1452: Scrope, *Castle Combe*, pp. 244, 328.
[28] *Southampton Court Leet Records*, i. 55, 179, 283. *Annals of Devizes*, i, pt. i, 59–64. Beard, *Theatre of Gods Judgements*, pp. 150, 420–5.
[29] *Poverty in Salisbury*, pp. 46, 49, 58, 97. *Churchwardens Accounts of S. Edmund and S. Thomas, Sarum, 1443–1702*, ed. H. J. F. Swayne, Wilts. RS, 1896, pp. 161–9, 298–9, 303–9. Prynne, *Canterburies Doome*, p. 102. See also Slack, 'Poverty and Politics'; and Clark, 'Ramoth-Gilead'.

money for such idle things', the town fathers told a travelling puppeteer in 1661, and the statement adequately sums up their outlook through the century.[30] By the 1620s Dorchester was in the grip of an authoritarian Puritan regime which regulated the most minute details of its residents' lives with fanatical rigour. Swearing, tippling, sexual irregularities, 'night walking', absence from church, feasting and merry-making, and general idleness: these were the common targets of reformers everywhere. At Dorchester, under the stern eye of John White and his supporters they were pursued with an intensity bordering on a state of 'moral panic'. Of all the towns in the western counties, Dorchester was the one in which Puritan reformation was most systematically imposed.[31]

*

The whole campaign against popular disorder depended on the co-operation of the local élites, and in the last resort on their willingness to present offending neighbours to the courts. Not all the increasing number of prosecutions were made by Puritans in the name of moral order. Sometimes they were made against them: people accused of absence from church were often discontented Puritans who had gone 'gadding to sermons' elsewhere. But more often they do reflect middling-sort concern with the sins of the ungodly poor. The necessary Calvinist commitment was aided by increasing literacy. The 'educational revolution', reaching its climax in Elizabeth's reign, gave more people access to a culture of wider scope than that of their town or village.[32] Local legends and superstitions lost their appeal as printing (in John Aubrey's words) 'put all the old fables out of doors . . . frighted away Robin Goodfellow and the fairies'. Puritanism was the rational religion, and there were many who, like the courtier James Howell, deplored the growing involvement in religious controversy that literacy made possible: the result was 'that variety of dogmatists, which swarm among us'.[33]

Parishes might have practical as well as moral reasons for abandoning plays and ales. Besides their value as occasions for cultivating fellowship and good neighbourhood, the main function of the old feasts was to raise money for the church. But they were not the most efficient methods of fund-raising, as the example of Tewkesbury shows. Elaborate plays had been regularly presented there (and costumes often hired out to neigh-

[30] *The Case Book of Sir Francis Ashley J.P. Recorder of Dorchester 1614–1635*, ed. J. H. Bettey, Dorset RS vii, 1981, p. 10. 'The Diary of William Whiteway', ed. W. Barnes, *DNHP* xiii (1892), 72.
[31] The intensity of the campaign is clear in the Court Book, 1629–37, in DRO B2/8/1, and in the extracts printed by Mayo in *Dorchester Records*, pp. 650–69. See also H. J. Moule, 'Notes on a Minute Book belonging to the Corporation of Dorchester', *DNHP* x (1888), 73–9.
[32] The evidence on literacy is surveyed by Cressy, *Literacy and the Social Order*. See also Lawrence Stone, 'The Educational Revolution in England, 1560–1640', *P & P* no. 28 (July 1964), 41–80.
[33] Aubrey, 'Remaines', p. 290. *Epistolae Ho-Elianae*, ii. 526.

bouring parishes) until about 1585, but then they lapsed for fifteen years. In 1600 some expensive repairs to the abbey tower were needed, so after having been forbidden to hold a church ale the churchwardens again held plays in the abbey grounds during Whitsun week. Because the old costumes had long since been disposed of, new ones had to be rented; trumpeters and other musicians also had to be paid for. Tewkesbury's plays produced only a small profit, nothing like the sum required for the tower, and there were no more efforts to revive them.[34]

Other fund-raising methods besides plays and church ales existed, which also relied on the old voluntarist sense of obligation to the community. But these too were on the way out. In many parishes in 1600 money was raised by 'gatherings', collections made door-to-door, or sometimes, as at Sherborne, at an annual parish dinner. Another name for this practice was 'hoggling', and in some Somerset villages hoggling gifts were often paid in kind: eggs and bacon for Easter, for example.[35] But as new attitudes to charity and public duty replaced the old voluntarism, more systematic procedures, reflecting the businesslike outlook of the middling-sort parish notables, were adopted. Contributions to the church ought not to be left to the vague force of customary duty; they should be based on ability to pay, rationally assessed and legally enforceable. So church rates took the place of the older church ales, the hogglings and gatherings. Before 1609 the chapelries of Corston and Rodbourne had paid 'what they listed' for the repair of Malmesbury church, but in that year the inhabitants agreed to pay a quarter of the rate for the whole large parish.[36]

For Puritan reformers however, moral arguments against church ales were more important than pragmatic fiscal ones. The reform movement reflects the increasing determination of the respectable to control the turbulent recreations of their poorer neighbours. Whether initiated by county JPs or borough corporations, by village notables or reforming ministers, the campaign against popular festivals was almost invariably divisive. In that campaign Puritans naturally took a leading part. Puritan insistence on the distinction between the elect and the reprobate made the ideal of all-inclusive parish harmony unrealizable; as if, the unsym-

---

[34] GRO P 329, CW 2/1 (Tewkesbury Churchwardens accounts, 1563–1703), pp. 55–88, 130–1. Willcox, *Gloucestershire*, p. 242.

[35] DRO P 155, CW/72, 73 (Sherborne Churchwardens accounts, 1600–2). SRO D/D/Cd 28 (Depositions, 1599), *Badgworth churchwardens* v. *Hyde* (I am indebted to Patricia Croot for this reference). For a Gloucestershire example, see GRO P 124, CW/2/4 (Dursley Churchwardens accounts).

[36] WRO B/ABO 9 (Act Book, 1619–20), fo. 29ᵛ. The transition from 'hogglings' or 'gatherings' to rates can be observed in such parishes as Blagdon, South Brent, and Burrington: SRO D/D/Cd 71 (Depositions, 1631–5), *Derrick* v. *Allen*, 5 Mar. 1631/2; D/D/Cd 35 (Depositions, 1604), *S. Brent churchwardens* v. *Locke* (again I am indebted to Patricia Croot); D/P/bur, 4/1/1 (Burrington Churchwardens accounts, 1605–83). See also Ware, 'Elizabethan Parish', p. 77.

pathetic Robert Sanderson declared, 'none had interest in goodness . . . but themselves'—and Sanderson was as keen on proper observance of the sabbath as any moral reformer. Such people could be found in every region, including Sanderson's own county of Lincolnshire, where clergy like John Vicars at Stamford and John Cotton at Boston divided their parishes by the ferocity of their preaching against the ungodly, and sometimes organized the elect minorities in a Puritan covenant.[37] They had long existed, too, in the towns and villages of the Weald, where in Elizabethan times they had asserted their singularity by giving their children biblical names like Flee-Sin and Safe-on-High, urged on by ministers who made their parishes hotbeds of 'broil and contention'.[38] In the towns especially the resulting conflicts were so frequent in James I's reign as to cast much doubt on the view held by some modern historians that this was a tranquil interlude of peaceful co-existence within the English church.[39]

Examples of urban conflict can be culled from every part of England. William Fennor lamented how the genial sociability, the 'peace and neighbourhood' of his native town of Leeds had been destroyed by 'factious schisms and humours'. At Stratford-on-Avon in 1619 there were angry criticisms of a small reformist oligarchy (only seven people, it was said) for their divisive legalism and harshness towards the poor. The conclusion was becoming familiar: 'They have set all the town together by the ears, which is the true office of a Puritan'.[40] In the western counties a Puritan clique had emerged at Bridport by 1614, which included a former bailiff and other influential townsmen. Here too the main charge was divisiveness: they were attacked as schismatics who lured poor people to conventicles where a nonconforming minister and a young schoolmaster 'expounded parcels of scripture, counterfeiting preaching, and sang psalms, pretending to profess a more pure and zealous religion than others'. And there are the same charges of uncharitableness and vindictiveness as were levelled at the Stratford clique.[41]

In many of these urban conflicts it is often unclear which side was temporarily uppermost. What, for example, are we to make of the situation at Stafford in 1612? In that year the maypole was taken down and converted into fire-fighting ladders, yet morris dancing was still officially

---

[37] Holmes, *Lincolnshire*, pp. 42–3, 52, 62.

[38] Nicholas Tyacke, 'Popular Puritan Mentality in late Elizabethan England', in *English Commonwealth*, ed. Clark, Smith, and Tyacke, pp. 79–81.

[39] As argued, for example, by C. H. and Katherine George, *The Protestant Mind of the English Reformation, 1570–1640*, Princeton, 1961, chs. 1, 5, 6; and Nicholas Tyacke, 'Puritanism, Arminianism and Counter-Revolution', in *The Origins of the English Civil War*, ed. Conrad Russell, 1973, pp. 120–9.

[40] [William Fennor], *Pasquil's Palinodia, and His progresse to the Taverne*, 1619. C. J. Sisson, *Lost Plays of Shakespeare's Age*, Cambridge, 1936, pp. 188–96.

[41] PRO STAC 8/214/2 (*Miller v. Maries*, 1614).

permitted, the churchwardens laying out money for a new 'fool's coat' to be worn at 'the Hobby Horse'.[42] Usually, however, the circumstances are much clearer, and varying degrees of Puritan success can be detected. For the reformers did not have everything their own way, and many examples could be cited of towns in which some members of the élite vigorously, and with at least temporary success, protected the traditional culture. Events at Wells provide a striking illustration and deserve detailed examination.

In 1607 the churchwardens of St. Cuthbert's parish wanted to hold a church ale to raise money for a new bell and some repairs to the tower. After an unsuccessful application to a JP for exemption from the prohibitions, they were given permission by the Dean. The climax of the ensuing festivities was a magnificent procession in which all the traditional themes of popular legend were colourfully portrayed: the Lord of the May, the Pindar of Wakefield, Robin Hood, St. George and the Dragon, Noah's Ark, and the Sultan of Egypt, along with the usual morris dancers and giants. The joint blessing of civil and ecclesiastical authorities was symbolized by the presence of the mayor and corporation at a dinner at the church house, by the city plate displayed in the procession, and by the cathedral choristers singing hymns and anthems. So far it seems no more than a charming celebration of good neighbourhood in an unusually united community. However, the pageant also included a more controversial item: a representation of a spotted calf carried by a satyr. This was immediately recognized as a libel against a certain Mrs Yard, who had recently denounced the town maypole as a 'painted calf', and who had been linked by scandalous gossip with another Puritan, a wealthy clothier named John Hole. As constable in that very year Hole had made repeated attempts to stop the festivities. Here, surely, is a classic case-study of the Puritan individual at odds with the unreformed community. 'It was a hard matter', a citizen complained, 'when one man should stand against the mayor and masters of the whole town, and also refuse to go to the church ale with his neighbours.' Further cheerful libels against Hole were composed by inventive young wits (and much relished in cathedral circles), and there were more charivari in which the Puritans were remorselessly lampooned. In the end, alas, the mirth turned sour. The churchwardens were indicted at Assizes for holding an illegal church ale and the humiliated Hole took his tormentors into Star Chamber.[43]

In this case the Puritans were unusually ineffective. That Hole was a

[42] Frederick W. Hackwood, *Staffordshire Customs, Superstitions and Folklore*, Lichfield, 1924, pp. 16–17.

[43] Sisson, *Lost Plays*, pp. 162–85, provides a full account, but I have added some details from the main source, PRO STAC 8/161/1 (*Hole* v. *White*, 1608). The episode was followed by a new rating of the parish, with the usual results—a lot of arrears from 1612–14 were still outstanding in 1615: SRO D/D/Ca 191 (Comperta, 1615), Wells, St. Cuthbert's.

capitalist clothier, though, is surely significant: another reminder that this was in part a collision between different social worlds. Wells is a special case not so much because it was a cathedral city (so were Exeter, Gloucester, Norwich, and Salisbury, all places with strong Puritan factions) as because it was not yet afflicted with as acute a problem of poverty as existed in other towns. Even where poverty was more pervasive and the case for moral reformation correspondingly stronger, however, the Puritans encountered plenty of opposition.

Much of the resistance of the lower orders was of course inherent in the situation—a natural resentment at being pushed around. It can be sensed even at Dorchester in the frequent outbursts of arrested moral offenders—'I know you to be as good a whoremaster and drunkard as myself', one of them shouted at the constable in 1633—and in the traffic out of the town by people seeking pleasure in the less policed suburbs or the nearby parish of Fordington.[44] In other Dorset towns opposition was even more vocal. At Wimborne Minster a reform campaign began early in James I's reign. There was a petition 'to have down the organs' and the churchwardens were exceptionally energetic in prosecuting absentees from church. Yet sporadic resistance continued, with a maypole and morris dancing in 1608 which led to the usual disorders.[45] Weymouth experienced similar problems. The attack on unlawful games and sabbath-breaking was already well under way in 1618, a Puritan lectureship had been established, and the town had adopted the policy of paying theatrical companies to depart without playing. But in June 1618, at the height of the campaign, a crowd defied the mayor's order to disperse and marched off behind drums and trumpets to set up a maypole. The incident was followed by a rash of prosecutions for drunkenness, assault on the constables, and 'upbraiding and contemptuous speeches'.[46]

Opposition from below often had support within the élite, and it was then that it was most troublesome. At Winchester the mayor allowed a play to be performed in St. Peter's church on a Sunday; the constable arrested the performers. The disputes at Stratford-on-Avon got out of hand (there was a riot at the September fair in 1619 when officers tried to take down the maypole) because prominent townsmen, including several of Shakespeare's friends, were involved. Presumably it was their influence that enabled the May games to survive a little longer, for they

[44] DRO B2/8/1 (Dorchester Court Book), fo. 161ᵛ; see also *Dorchester Records*, pp. 661–2. The lure of the suburbs is apparent in *Ashley's Case Book*, pp. 31, 36, 45–7, 56.

[45] DRO P 204/CP 32 (Catalogue of Wimborne Presentments), ff. 5–7, 11, 15, 24, 31–3, 46–50, 58–61, 65–8. See also John Hutchins, *The History and Antiquities of the County of Dorset*, ed. W. Shipp and J. W. Hodson, 3rd edn., Westminster, 1861–73, iii. 263–6. Large numbers of presentments for absence from Easter communion were made at Wimborne in 1624, for example: DRO P 204, CP/13 (Peculiar Court Papers, 1619–40), no. 29.

[46] *Weymouth Documents*, pp. 59, 139; and see pp. 54–75 for the campaign in general.

were still being held in 1622, with morris dancing and a Robin Hood play.[47] Even places where the moral reformers gained complete control experienced periods of élite conflict. There was a brief one at Dorchester soon after White's arrival in 1606. One of his first moves was to get the magistrates to ban a touring theatrical company, Lord Berkeley's men. A conservative group led by the influential Matthew Chubb, a former MP for the town, obstructed the magistrates and circulated written libels attacking White, his allies in the corporation, and the whole 'counterfeit company and pack of Puritans'.[48]

At Dorchester the enemies of godly reformation were quickly routed. In other towns, however, conflict often simmered for years. At Salisbury the reformers had to contend with a formidable coalition of enemies— brewers entrenched in the corporation, cathedral clergy, and what Ivie called the 'great unjust rude rabble' of the town.[49] Lyme Regis provides another striking example of protracted cultural conflict. As at Dorchester, trouble began soon after the arrival of a committed Puritan, in this case John Geare, as vicar. In 1607, at his instigation, the churchwardens presented the mayor for allowing plays in the schoolhouse next to the church. A year later several burgesses were expelled from the corporation, among other things for supporting Geare, 'who hath been the cause of great factions and divisions amongst us'.[50] Geare's principal target was the 'Cobb Ale', the great annual feast to raise money for the Cobb, the quay on which Lyme's prosperity depended. From 1606 the churchwardens repeatedly complained about 'profane' ceremonies at the election of the Cobb-wardens, and about Whitsun processions headed by 'a drum, ancient, flag, and musical instruments . . . to fetch in boughs'. After breakfast at the Cobb house there was much carousing and skittle-playing in the churchyard. In 1610 the constables were prosecuted for permitting unlawful games and sabbath-breaking during the Ale, and by now people were becoming reluctant to serve as wardens. After a brief truce Geare was suspended (not for the first time) and retaliated by again charging the mayor and Cobb wardens with irreligious abuses.[51]

In the end the campaign was a failure. Geare had allies in the corporation who won some victories: around 1620, for example, Lyme began

[47] PRO STAC 8/94/7 (*Coleman* v. *Thorpe*, 1617). E. R. C. Brinkworth, *Shakespeare and the Bawdy Court of Stratford*, 1972, pp. 54–5.

[48] PRO STAC 8/94/17 (*Conduitt* v. *Chubb*, 1607). For White see Frances Rose-Troup, *John White The Patriarch of Dorchester*, New York, 1930.

[49] Slack, 'Poverty and Politics', pp. 183–92. *Poverty in Salisbury*, p. 122.

[50] DRO B7/D1/1 (Lyme Regis Corporation Orders, 1594–1671), p. 29. WRO, Dean's Peculiar, Presentments 1606–8, no. 59.

[51] DRO B7/D1/1 (Lyme Corp. Orders), pp. 36, 40, 42, 49, 51; B7/1/8 (Lyme Court Book, 1613–27), p. 174. WRO, Dean's Peculiar, Presentments 1606–8, no. 59; 1609, no. 24. There are brief but not very clear accounts of the conflict in Lyme Regis in A. R. Bayley, *The Great Civil War in Dorset 1642–1660*, Taunton, 1910, pp. 13–14; and G. Roberts, *Social History of the People of the Southern Counties of England in Past Centuries*, 1856, pp. 343–5.

making the familiar payments to theatrical companies to leave without performing. But the Cobb was another matter. In 1635 the churchwardens noted that the church porch was in a disgraceful mess, littered with 'vessels called tuns which serve for the use of the Cobb'.[52] Other old customs had also survived Geare's offensive. It was a local tradition, the churchwardens sadly reported in the same year, to make midsummer bonfires 'for the christening of apples as they call it'. During morning service on Ascension Day a great crowd gathered near the church, led by William Alford, their 'captain'. After much 'gunning and drumming and shooting' (which interrupted Geare's sermon) they marched noisily off into town. The constables tried vainly to disperse them, and eventually Geare asked Alford's father, who was in the church, to use his authority as a parent, a member of the corporation, and a JP. Reluctantly Alford did so, muttering audibly, 'what a prating . . . about nothing'.[53] Such incidents remind us that the transformation of even urban oligarchies was a slow and uncertain one.

*

In the countryside too the campaign against traditional culture reflected prevailing social divisions. It also intensified them, ranging the Puritan clergy and their converts among the parish élites against much of the rest of the population.[54] In one form or another the campaign can be observed in every part of the three-county area that is the core of this study: from Nettleton in the northern Cotswold fringe, where eleven men were fined in 1603 for gambling and another for 'playing out evening prayer at bowls with two strangers', to Charminster in the Dorset chalk country, where in 1609 fourteen men were presented for bowling in the churchyard.[55]

Some places were targets of especially sharp bouts of cultural repression, either because they were unusually disorderly or because the local élites thought they were. Ill-governed rural settlements adjacent to towns where reformers were taking over were particularly likely to provoke states of 'moral panic', as we have observed at Dorchester. The tithings of Leigh and Colehill, near Wimborne Minster, were subjected to similar attention, partly no doubt because they accounted for a high proportion of the numerous recusants in the parish.[56] Large sprawling parishes sometimes experienced similar outbursts of reforming frenzy. Westbury-on-

[52] WRO, Dean's Peculiar, Presentments 1635, no. 73. Murray, *Dramatic Companies*, ii. 327.

[53] WRO, Dean's Peculiar, Presentments 1635, no. 73. For midsummer bonfires and blessing the apples, see Aubrey, 'Remaines', p. 143.

[54] Wrightson points out that the withdrawal of wealthier villagers was a major factor in the decline of traditional festivals: 'Puritan Reformation of Manners', pp. 40–1; 'Aspects of Social Differentiation', p. 38.

[55] BL Add. MS 23151 (Nettleton Court Book), fo. 43ᵛ. WRO, Dean's Peculiar, Presentments 1609, no. 20.

[56] DRO P 204, CP/10 (Wimborne Peculiar, Act Book, 1601–3), pp. 63–6; P 204, CP/13 (Court Papers, 1619–40), no. 60.

Severn, on the edge of the Forest of Dean, was the scene of one such outbreak in 1610. It began when a group of young people on their way home from catechism 'fell to dancing, quaffing and rioting, and, as we heard', the churchwardens reported, 'scoffing and deriding at the doctrine of our minister'. A flood of prosecutions followed. Three of the women involved were also accused of incontinent living before marriage, two others of blasphemously teaching 'a counterfeit catechism upon the cards'. Altogether about fifty parishioners were presented on charges ranging from drunkenness and absence from church to fornication and harbouring pregnant women. The presentments provide a striking glimpse of the alternative culture that respectable parishioners were trying to eradicate. But contrary to the reformers' assumptions, adherents of that culture were not universally jovial drunkards and promiscuous fornicators. Several of the couples accused of sexual offences were in fact married by the time they were presented, and two of the women charged with harbouring were the mothers of the pregnant girls. Westbury-on-Severn in 1610 was being struck by a new force of moral reformation.[57]

As in the towns, it was around the parish feasts that some of the most bitter rural struggles were fought. The biographer of the Cheshire Puritan, John Bruen, sounds the usual note of reformist indignation:

Popery and profaneness, two sisters in evil, had consented and conspired in this parish [Tarvin], as in other places, to advance their idols against the ark of God, and to celebrate their solemn feasts of their popish saints . . . by their wakes and vigils, kept in commemoration and honour of them; in all riot and excess of eating and drinking, dalliance and dancing, sporting and gaming, and other abominable impieties and isolatries.[58]

Such attitudes were even more vehemently held by the Puritan clergy. Incensed by midsummer feasting in 1602, the curate of Winsley, Wiltshire, declared 'that all women and maids that were singers and dancers were whores, and as many as did look upon them no better than they'.[59]

Resistance to the reformers was easily inflamed among the young and disorderly. May games at Longdon, Worcestershire, were marred between 1614 and 1616 by violent affrays when men from neighbouring parishes invaded the proceedings. In 1615, some Longdon youths, reluctant to interrupt their morris dancing, ingeniously sent a poor excommunicated woman into the church, hoping to make the minister suspend the service.[60] Outsiders were often blamed for stirring up trouble. At

[57] GRO GDR 111 (Detections, 1610), Forest Deanery, Westbury-on-Severn presentments.
[58] William Hinde, *A Faithfull Remonstrance of the Holy Life and Happy Death of John Bruen of Bruen Stapleford*, 1641, p. 89.
[59] WRO, Bishop's Deposition Book 22a (1602–3), ff. 27[v], 31.
[60] *Worcester County Records: The Quarter Sessions Rolls*, i: *Kalendar . . . 1591–1621*, ed. J. W. Willis Bund, Worcester, 1899, pp. 254–5. For violence at village feasts see also Hunt, *The Puritan Moment*, pp. 132–3.

Easton Royal, Wiltshire, it was not a parishioner but a man from nearby
Burbage who in 1609 demanded of the parson: 'Why will you not let the
people dance? Better men than you will, for my lord [Hertford?] himself
will, and look upon them also'.[61]

It is another reminder that the old customs were often protected by
people in authority. In 1603 the censorious and corrupt Somerset JP,
Maurice Gilbert, unearthed 'a supposed misdemeanour for playing
Christmas sports in a bear's skin'. But it took place at a gentleman's house:
Gilbert did not proceed with the prosecution.[62] Denunciations of moral
crusaders came from obscure folk like the Wincanton man who called
them 'precisian, Puritan rogues' and hoped 'that the devils should have
them'. But they also came from people further up the scale, like the
Dorset gentleman Richard Christmas who in 1616 put a cat on a post in
the street, acclaimed it as the best preacher in the county, and said that
'there were none but rogues and whores that would hear sermons'.[63]
Traditionally-minded ministers could easily ignite the wrath of reformers
in their congregations. In 1610 the vicar of Bisley, Gloucestershire, made
his son lord of the Whitsun maypole; there was music and dancing for the
young people. 'Piping and dancing at a maypole and keeping of summer-
ale', the vicar preached, were as lawful as hearing the word of God. But
the maypole was erected 'against the goodwill of the honest and religious
disposed people': one of the churchwardens took the minister to court.[64]

Parishes could be divided in numerous ways by the cultural collision.
The transition from ales to church rates sometimes provoked acrimonious
disputes and even, as at Hannington, Wiltshire, in 1617, brawls in the
church.[65] At Ashton Keynes in 1602 the churchwardens presented their
predecessors for 'ill husbandring of their Ale'. There had been no profit
from the three-week-long festivity, so the retiring wardens ought to pay
for the minstrels out of their own pockets.[66] See-saw struggles between
the adherents of ales and rates often dragged on for years. There was an
annual church ale at Thatcham, Berkshire, until 1598, when the churchwardens got into trouble for it at the assizes. A few years later, after selling
the maypole for 2s., the parish went over to rating, but in 1617 the Whitsun
ale was revived. Only in 1621 was rating permanently established.[67]

[61] 'Extracts from Wiltshire QS Records', pp. 21–2. The Seymours acquired the manor of Easton at
the Dissolution, and built the church there: A. Audrey Locke, *The Seymour Family*, 1911, p. 30; H.
Saint Maur, *Annals of the Seymours*, 1902, p. 154.

[62] PRO STAC 8/43/3 (*Adams v. Gilbert*, 1603).

[63] SRO D/D/Ca 191 (Comperta, 1615), Wincanton, 6 Oct. PRO STAC 8/272/17 (*Sir R. Strode v. John Strode*, 1616). *Ashley's Case Book*, pp. 29–30, 32.

[64] GRO GDR 114 (Depositions, 1611–13), Christopher Windle, 21 May; John Clissold, 31 May
1611.

[65] WRO AW/ABO 5 (Act Book, 1616–22), fo. 27ᵛ. For similar disputes at Chilmark and Edington
see AS/ABO 13 (Act Book, 1620–4), ff. 22ᵛ, 169.

[66] WRO B/ABO 5 (Act Book, 1600–6), fo. 25ᵛ.

[67] Samuel Barfield, *Thatcham, Berks., and its Manors*, Oxford, 1901, ii. 93–112.

The erosion of rural traditions was also hastened by the adoption of more absolutist conceptions of property-rights, which could lead to the disappearance of commons formerly open to public use. At Bourton, Berkshire, a meadow had once been 'allotted to the youth of the parish there to make merry with their King-ale', but by 1611 the church ale had been abolished and the land yielded the parish only a monetary return.[68] Enclosure might also deprive villagers of their space for sports and festivals. Riots at Osmington, Dorset, between 1615 and 1622 chiefly concerned a field called the 'bowling green or butt close'. While the manor was held by the crown the residents retained rights of access, but after its purchase by a gentleman named John Warham it was enclosed and the inhabitants excluded. They offered to accept Warham's pasture rights if he would let them 'walk and bowl therein without interruption'. His refusal led to the destruction of his hedges and other violence.[69] A later case from Oxfordshire, though it occurred after the Restoration, vividly illustrates the growing acceptance of the sanctity of property. According to Robert Plot, the inhabitants of Eynsham had the right to cut down whatever trees the churchwardens marked, and on Whit Monday to haul the timber into the Abbey yard, 'whence if they could draw it out again, notwithstanding all the impediments . . . given the cart by the servants . . . it was then their own, and went in part at least to the reparation of the church'. The disorderly custom was ancient, but also highly 'inconvenient' to the landowner, so sometime before 1677 'the chiefest of the parish' agreed to end it.[70]

One further example of the cultural conflict that raged in so many English parishes during the first decade of James I's reign deserves attention, for in it the contrasting perceptions of the old festive customs are dramatically epitomized. The village of Rangeworthy, a few miles north of Bristol, was a detached part of the large parish of Thornbury, a chapelry whose curate was nominated by the vicar of Iron Acton. In 1611 the vicar decreed that the customary Whitsun revel should no longer begin on the sabbath. The villagers obediently curtailed their celebration to Whit Monday; it was preceded by a sermon of 'near three hours'. During the afternoon the constable of Thornbury Hundred, John Parker, was called to the scene. He found, he told Star Chamber, 'a most disorderly, riotous and unlawful assembly' engaged in 'unlawful games and most beastly and disorderly drinking'. The ringleaders, Parker decided, were four 'unknown persons who passed under the name of musicians, all of them being strangers having no habitations thereabouts nor appertaining to any nobleman or man of worth'—vagrants or master-less men, in other words. He tried to arrest the musicians and put them in

[68] WRO B/ABO 6 (Act Book, 1606–13), ff. 82, 105ᵛ.
[69] PRO STAC 8/293/12 (*Warham* v. *Symonds*, 1622).
[70] Plot, *Nat. Hist. Oxfordshire*, pp. 202–3.

the stocks, but was resisted by the villagers, who surrounded the stocks and rescued them. According to Parker, he and his handful of assistants were badly beaten up.

Viewed from this standpoint the Rangeworthy revel pitted a group of law-abiding reformers against a crowd of violent, drunken louts. To the villagers it seemed very different. Their defence was based on a familiar system of values. 'By all the time whereof the memory of man is not to the contrary', they declared, the revel feast had been held in Rangeworthy during Whitsun week. Its purpose was 'the refreshing of the minds and spirits of the country people, being inured and tired with husbandry and continual labour . . . for preservation of mutual amity, acquaintance and love . . . and allaying of strifes, discords and debates between neighbour and neighbour'. It had always included innocent diversions like 'wrestling, leaping, running, throwing the bar' as well as dancing and 'other honest sport'. On the day in question there was no excessive drinking—just a few young people dancing while the musicians played and some of the older inhabitants lingered to watch on their way home from the sermon. This idyllic scene was shattered only by the arrival of the arrogant constable, who provoked the crowd by his 'reviling speeches' against the dancers and musicians. Parker, they noted, was a known trouble-maker, a promoter of 'many suits and troubles . . . between neighbours and friends'. Worse, he was an adherent of nonconforming preachers, a precisian 'arrogating to himself a singularity of sanctity and religion'. They denied obstructing him, though they admitted that nobody had lifted a finger when Parker called for assistance. But the constable's subsequent complaints to the JPs had been dismissed as frivolous and malicious.[71]

What, if anything, lies behind this incident? The most significant fact is that Parker, like Hole at Wells, was a master clothier, the only one in Thornbury, where the industry had long been in decay. He employed a dozen weavers in the town and a few others in villages round about— though none, apparently, in Rangeworthy.[72] But Parker was not acting alone, for the Rangeworthy defendants admitted that the 'pretended sanctimony' he and his allies professed had won them 'a great name and estimation amongst the vulgar sort'. Reforming zeal had obviously been whipped up at Thornbury by the recent arrival of a Puritan minister, John Sprint, and may have spread among poor clothworkers (as it was certainly doing in the Wiltshire clothing district at this time), as well as inflaming men like Parker.[73] On the other side we have a village little touched by the

[71] PRO STAC 8/239/3 (*Parker* v. *Hooper*, 1611).

[72] R. Perry, 'The Gloucestershire Woollen Industry, 1100–1690', *Bristol and Glos. Archaeological Soc. Transactions*, lxvi (1945), 98.

[73] For Sprint see *DNB*; and Sir Robert Atkyns, *The Ancient and Present State of Glostershire*, 1712, p. 771.

stern individualism that helped to form the mental world of Parker and his allies; a village set in the rich farmland of the Severn Vale which even a century later still retained 'large commons'.[74] The Rangeworthy revel is thus a classic example of Jacobean cultural conflict. Rituals appropriate to a traditional society, enshrining ancient values of custom and good neighbourhood, were attacked by people in authority who put individual piety, sobriety, and hard work above the older co-operative virtues.

*

Thus far we have generally been considering a conflict between 'official' reformers and 'popular' defenders of traditional customs. Yet we have also encountered many people in authority who actively defended the old culture. They did so because it reflected their notion of what society ought to be—hierarchical, unified, and co-operative. Their actions were often isolated episodes, defensive moves triggered by particular local situations. But there were also more systematic attempts to preserve the festive customs, attempts that were part of a conservative ideological campaign to repair the vertical ties which bound the social structure together. In Charles I's reign, especially, upholders of monarchy and the Laudian church clearly recognized the utility of village feasts in making people more content with their lot and with the existing order.

Rural recreations had always been protected by a minority of the gentry; sometimes, their critics suspected, in order to court popularity among the common people. A Devonshire gentleman, Walter Wootton, defied sessions and assize orders and the opinions of the 'best affected sort' in his neighbourhood. 'Be of good comfort', he told the villagers of Harberton, '. . . he doubted not but to procure them their church ale, their Whitsun Lord and Lady, their fool and his horns and all again'.[75] Sir Edward Parham of Poyntington in south Somerset was alleged to have promoted a church ale with bull-baiting, and to have joined in the morris dancing, 'to get the love and affection of the common people'. Parham's defence was the conventional one that country festivals nourished 'love and familiarity amongst neighbours'. The reciprocal elements of paternalism and deference in all this are obvious, and indeed Parham's own household was a highly traditional one, retaining a style of clientage that was beginning to seem old-fashioned in the early seventeenth century.[76]

Formal clientage ties, however, were not essential to habits of good neighbourhood, and where such habits had declined they might still be

[74] Atkyns, *Glostershire*, pp. 616–17. For the county's agricultural regions see Willcox, *Gloucestershire*, pp. 3–11.

[75] PRO STAC 8/264/11 (*Somaster* v. *Wootton*, 1606).

[76] PRO STAC 8/291/12 (*Walton* v. *Parham*, 1606). The behaviour of Parham's dependents during brawls with townspeople at Sherborne was of a very old-fashioned, 'feudal' kind.

revived. So thought Robert Dover, the Norfolk-born lawyer who moved to Gloucestershire in 1611 and became the impresario of the Cotswold Games. Dover reorganized the defunct Whitsun revels which had traditionally been jointly held by the parishes of Chipping Camden and Weston-sub-Edge, on what was soon to be known as Dover's Hill. His purpose was to relate the old rural sports, in the words of his biographer, 'to classical mythology and Renaissance culture, whilst linking them with the throne and the King's Protestant Church'. It was a conscious attempt to bridge the gap between genteel and popular culture and reunify the whole community under its traditional leaders.[77]

The games were much frequented, Anthony Wood recalled, by the nobility and gentry, 'some of whom came sixty miles to see them'. For them there was hunting and horse-racing, for the common folk the typical Cotswold sports—wrestling, singlestick fighting, shin-kicking and the like—as well as plenty of drinking and dancing. In 1636 some of Dover's literary friends brought out a collection of poems to celebrate his achievements. Ben Jonson's contribution sums up the central message: the games 'advance true love and neighbourhood/And do both Church and Commonwealth the good'. Throughout the emphasis is on 'harmless merriment' as the expression of a political and social harmony threatened only by Puritans. You would find people of all factions on Dover's Hill, one contributor observed, 'save that I fear thou wilt not find a Zealous Brother there'.[78]

Such defences of rural festivals were not new. There had been a chorus of praise for them two decades earlier. 'He allows of honest pastime', wrote Sir Thomas Overbury of his ideal yeoman, 'and thinks not the bones of the dead any . . . the worse for it, though the country lasses dance in the churchyard after evensong'. Nicholas Breton's countryman also lauded the 'true mirth' engendered by dancing on the green or around the maypole, while William Fennor roundly condemned the 'envious nature' of the Puritan, and looked back to better days of 'honest neighbourhood, where all the parish did in one combine':

> Happy the age, and harmless were the days,
> (For then true love and amity were found)
> When every village did a May Pole raise
> And Whitsun-ales and May-games did abound.[79]

[77] *Robert Dover and the Cotswold Games: Annalia Dubrensia*, ed. Christopher Whitfield, 1962, p. 2; Whitfield's introduction provides a useful account of the Games. See also Dennis Brailsford, *Sport and Society: Elizabeth to Anne*, 1969, p. 103.

[78] *Dover and the Cotswold Games*, pp. 18–21, 134, 213. There is perhaps an irony in the fact that Dover revived the ancient rural customs only a few years after the manor of Campden had been bought by the London financier, Sir Baptist Hicks: Christopher Whitfield, *A History of Chipping Camden and Captain Robert Dover's Olympick Games*, Eton and Windsor, 1958, pp. 101–2.

[79] Overbury, in *Conceited Newes*, ed. Savage, p. 213. Breton, 'The Court and Country', p. 7. [Fennor], *Pasquil's Palinodia*. For an earlier defence of church ales, see Carew, *Cornwall*, pp. 141–2.

'Where all the parish did in one combine': to conservatives, parochial unity, not divisive reformism, was the best preservative of order. And that unity had to be cultivated and ritualized. Rogationtide processions, George Herbert thought, were vital for the strengthening of charitable and neighbourly feelings.[80] The Puritan habit of 'gadding to sermons' disrupted this unity, and there were those who saw its connection with other lapses from neighbourliness. Thomas Watts, a Norfolk rector, was later accused of having 'scandalized such as go about to hear sermons, and said they will not . . . lay a board cloth on Sunday, but will deceive their neighbours all the week day'.[81]

The first phase of the cultural counter-offensive produced James I's Declaration of Sports. Its original version (1617) was inspired by local conflict in Lancashire. Although the Lancashire JPs had sporadically suppressed popular festivals since the 1590s, this was still a heavily recusant and socially conservative county. Both of these facts had a bearing on the Declaration. If the JPs and clergy continued their repression, it was said, labourers and servants seeking recreation and relief from toil would be driven into the arms of the more tolerant Catholics. And popular revels were certainly encouraged by many of the county élite. On the day the problem had been brought to the King's notice by piping and dancing near the church he was attending, James went on to a 'rushbearing and piping', followed by country dances, at the house of his host, Sir Richard Houghton.[82] Lancashire's great magnate, the Earl of Derby, aided his paternalist sway by patronizing country customs. William Blundell mentions a sword-dance at the Earl's mansion, Latham House, in 1638, and also speaks of the 'lads of Latham' dancing a hornpipe named for the Earl's heir.[83]

The 1617 Declaration was reissued with minor revisions, and extended to the whole kingdom, in the following year.[84] There was some confusion about the precise scope of the 1618 Declaration—some people still professed to believe that it was limited to Lancashire—but it is striking how quickly the inhabitants of small towns and villages appealed to it against the reformers. Some of the attempts to set up the maypoles noted

[80] *Works of George Herbert*, p. 284.

[81] Bodleian MS J. Walker c. 6 (Eastern Association, Committee for Scandalous Ministers), fo. 46. For similar Laudian examples see John White, *The First Century of Scandalous Malignant Priests*, 1643, pp. 44, 49. Laudians could of course be as divisive as their enemies: see Anthony Fletcher, 'Factionalism in Town and Countryside: the Significance of Puritanism and Arminianism', *Studies in Church History*, xvi (1979), 293–4.

[82] Tait, 'Declaration of Sports', pp. 563–4.

[83] *A Cavalier's Notebook: Being Notes, Anecdotes and Observations of William Blundell of Crosby, Lancashire*, ed. T. E. Gibson, 1880, pp. 117, 234. Blundell makes frequent references to the survival of festivals in Lancashire. See also William S. Weeks, *Clitheroe in the Seventeenth Century*, Clitheroe, n.d., pp. 109, 115.

[84] Tait, 'Declaration of Sports', pp. 561–5.

earlier—at Weymouth and Stratford, for example—may have been provoked by it. The vicar of St. Mary's, Marlborough, reproved a parishioner for taking part in 'sport or merriment' on Midsummer Day in 1618 and was promptly told 'that the King did allow of it by his Book'. In the same county a minister intent on suppressing dancing at Wylye received a similar answer, while four Keevil men appealed to the Declaration when cited in ecclesiastical court.[85] At Fuston in Yorkshire there was a scuffle in the church when the minister preached against the Declaration and tried to suppress the old custom of rushbearing.[86]

James's Declaration did not end the campaign against local festivals. Attempts to overturn it by parliamentary action were unsuccessful, but town and county magistrates still retained much discretion. By the time Charles I's Declaration was issued in October 1633 fifteen years of growing national division had made the political dimensions of the issue even clearer.[87] The 1633 Declaration was a direct outgrowth of the great controversy in the western counties, in which Laud had compelled the reluctant Chief Justice Richardson to repeal the assize orders prohibiting ales and revels.

Looking for ammunition, Laud asked William Piers, Bishop of Bath and Wells, for information on the actual state of affairs in Somerset. The bishop's answer shows how well the Laudians understood the political implications of the conflict. Church ales, he confessed, had virtually disappeared, but revels or dedication feasts continued to flourish. Piers stressed their contribution to social harmony: 'for the civilizing of the people, for their lawful recreations, for composing differences by . . . meeting of friends' and for settling lawsuits which might otherwise have ended in Westminster Hall. But it was political harmony in which he was more interested. When the justices prohibited the feasts people had murmured that 'it was very hard if they could not entertain their kindred and friends once a year, to praise God for his blessings, and to pray for the King's Majesty, under whose happy government they enjoyed peace and quietness'. If people were denied their innocent pleasures they would be driven into alehouses and there talk of 'matters of church and state' or into conventicles.[88] Once again we find 'communal sociability' and loyalty

---

[85] WRO B/ABO 8 (Act Book, 1615–18), fo. 121; AS/ABO 13 (Act Book, 1620–4), ff. 270ᵛ–271ᵛ. Resistance to the Puritan campaign at Wylye and Keevil is well described by Ingram, 'Ecclesiastical Justice in Wiltshire', pp. 106–7.

[86] PRO STAC 8/180/11 (*Harryson* v. *Smithson*, 1620).

[87] The 1633 Declaration was in effect a reissue of James I's Declaration, with a postscript ordering that parochial dedication feasts be continued: *The Constitutional Documents of the Puritan Revolution 1625–1660*, ed. Samuel R. Gardiner, 3rd edn., Oxford, 1906, pp. 99–103. For the circumstances see Hill, *Society and Puritanism*, pp. 161, 194–5; and Barnes, 'County Politics', p. 119.

[88] *CSPD, 1633–4*, p. 275. *Church-Wardens' Accounts of Croscombe*, p. 246. See also Prynne, *Canterburies Doome*, pp. 141–2, 151.

associated with the traditional order; 'fragmented sociability' and political dissent with the new order of the Puritans.

The reformers' wrath at the 'Morris book' was hard to restrain.[89] Many who preached against it were silenced, but some found ways of limiting the time available for Sunday sports. A Leicestershire rector deliberately prolonged his sermons and composed long extempore prayers to keep his flock in church until it was too dark for their amusements.[90] But local defenders of traditional customs could usually rely on central authority to protect them.[91] Reformers could only watch and wait, taking comfort in the many edifying signs of the wrath of God, as when a churchyard wall collapsed on people assembled for a bear-baiting at Bunbury, Cheshire. The Book of Sports was morally objectionable. But it was also socially objectionable because, as the Puritan Henry Burton declared, the illicit pastimes encouraged the 'high contempt' of inferiors against superiors: 'the common vulgar against the magistrate and minister, servants against their masters, children against their parents, and wanton wives against their husbands'.[92]

From the Laudian side there was much clerical rejoicing. Even in East Anglia there were plenty of conservative ministers willing to give a lead to their parishioners, men such as John Lothwaite of Rockland St. Peter's, Norfolk, who read the Book with enthusiasm and turned up to shout 'well played!' at Sunday football matches.[93] For some of them there may have been an ingredient of cynicism. At Hougham, Kent, Henry Hannington curtailed his services to celebrate the Book of Sports and had 'beer laid into his house, and dancing and drinking there'. But he is also alleged to have said, 'let them pay me their offerings at Easter, and . . . go to the devil at Whitsuntide'.[94]

So the cultural counter-attack depended to some extent on élite sponsorship. We should not exaggerate this, however. Even in areas where Puritan reform had apparently been successful the old festive traditions had somehow survived among the lower orders, and in 1634 as in 1618 they quickly came out of hiding. Months before the issue of the 1633 Book news of the repeal of the local prohibitions spread through the Somerset villages. In May there was violence at a revel at Coleford, a

---

[89] The term was used by Sir Benjamin Rudyard: *Journal of Sir Simonds D'Ewes from the Beginning of the Long Parliament . . .*, ed. Wallace Notestein, New Haven, 1923, p. 6.

[90] Hoskins, *Provincial England*, pp. 179–80.

[91] For examples of intervention by central authority, see Burton, *Divine Tragedie*, pp. 9–10; Clark, *Provincial Society*, p. 365; A. R. Wright, *British Calendar Customs: England*, ed. T. E. Lones, 1936–40, i. 99. For the suspension of resisting clergy see Hill, *Society and Puritanism*, pp. 199–200.

[92] Burton, *Divine Tragedie*, p. 29 (many other instances are listed in pp. 3–25). For the Bunbury incident see Wright, *Calendar Customs*, iii. 4.

[93] Bodleian MS J. Walker c. 6 (Committee for Scandalous Ministers), fo. 44. For other East Anglian examples see White, *First Century*, p. 18; and *LJ* vi. 152.

[94] White, *First Century*, p. 48.

Mendip mining village. After order was restored a disgruntled alehouse-keeper complained that 'the constables had done more than they could justify . . . for he might go to the Cross at Wells and read a proclamation that all revels and all pastimes should be used'. This was a Puritan area, yet it witnessed other signs of cultural revival: the reappearance of a maypole at Dundry, for example.[95] Henry Burton's many instances of divine punishment inflicted on sabbath-breakers after 1633 are proof of the speed with which ales and revels had been resumed. Forty years of preaching by a godly minister at Woolston, Worcestershire, had done much to reform the inhabitants. But in 1634, encouraged by the Book of Sports, they had a Whitsun ale with maypole and morris dancing, 'continuing their rude revelling a week together'. In Kent the preacher Richard Culmer was threatened with violence when he tried to prevent the erection of a maypole, and even at Gloucester people tried to set one up.[96] In this aspect at least, Laudian policy was appealing to a large segment of the population, though not, of course, to the middling sort.

*

This discussion of the conservative cultural revival has dealt mainly with the countryside. In the towns the situation was somewhat more complicated. In many places, as we have seen, Puritans were well represented in the governing oligarchies. When this was the case, civic ritual was not abandoned completely, but it was modified and reformed to proclaim more clearly than ever the necessary messages of authority. Urban governors of all persuasions recognized the importance of the 'theatrical show' that accompanied public occasions, and in this they were supported by the central government. 'It is of great use', Lord Keeper Coventry noted in 1628, 'to maintain the ceremonies and insignia of these times', instancing the 'formalities and solemnities' at the welcoming of the assize judges by high sheriffs.[97] But the Puritans also had their own cultural forms, their own rituals, quite apart from the ones asserting civic authority. Certain festivals—like Gunpowder Treason—were especially dear to them, though in both town and countryside they were unfortunately likely to be marred by the unseemly behaviour of the unregenerate multitude. In towns where the Puritans had made less headway larger elements of the older pageantry survived, but even in them it was nearly always directed towards upholding and ritualizing the lines of power and obedience.

The urban experience was infinitely varied, and only a few examples can be given. Gloucester shows the impact of Puritanism on civic ritual in

<hr>

[95] SRO CQ 3/1/70 (Sessions Rolls, 1633), fo. 121. For the Dundry maypole see below, pp. 86–8.
[96] Burton, *Divine Tragedie*, pp. 13–14, 24–5. Clark, *Provincial Society*, p. 365.
[97] BL Lansdowne MS 620 (Notes on Star Chamber cases), fo. 71.

its extreme form. In the sixteenth century the city's identity had been regularly affirmed by occasions for popular feasting; now the populace stood by and admired the austere processions symbolizing the authority of their magistrates.[98] In less Puritan York the rich pageantry of the Corpus Christi plays was replaced in the 1580s by a more secular midsummer show. Colour and ritual did not disappear completely, but the central feature was the procession of civic dignitaries and armed citizens, and the messages of order and authority were even more clearly conveyed by the elaborate ceremonies which accompanied occasional royal visits.[99]

Chester deserves to be treated at greater length. The festive year there had included elaborate Whitsuntide plays and processions. The plays were abandoned in 1575 and although the Whitsun pageant continued, it too aroused Puritan opposition. In 1600 the mayor, Henry Hardware, put down the bull- and bear-baiting, had the giants used in the show smashed to pieces, and prohibited the traditional dragon, devil, and 'naked boys'. Some years later the traditionalists got the devils restored to the procession and in 1620 bull-baitings were revived, leading to the traditional rioting between the butchers' and bakers' companies.[100] The relative tolerance of some of the city's rulers did not, however, extend to encouraging idleness at times other than the great holidays. In 1615 the corporation complained of servants 'neglecting their masters' business' by going to plays, and imposed stringent restrictions.[101] Other kinds of popular recreation had long since been curtailed. The Shrove Tuesday football matches went out as early as 1539, when the competitive instincts of the companies were given less disorderly outlets in foot and horse-races. Eventually all these plebeian amusements were overshadowed by festivities dominated by the élite. In 1610 a horse-race for 'gentlemen of worship and quality' was inaugurated, its first running being preceded by a St. George's Day pageant. Some traditional elements were present: two giants 'with fireworks to scatter abroad', for example. But the main tableaux (depicting Fame, Mercury, the City, St. George, Peace, Plenty, and Love) presented less 'popular' themes than those in the one we have encountered at Wells. Plebeian inhabitants, in so far as they still participated in the festivities (and for most of them horse-racing was a spectator sport) did so simply as deferential actors in a celebration of 'the King's crown and dignity, and the homage to the King and Prince'.[102]

---

[98] Clark, 'Ramoth-Gilead', p. 178.

[99] *York Drama*, ed. Johnston and Rogerson, i. 392–421, 505, 600–7.

[100] *Records of Early English Drama: Chester*, ed. Lawrence Clopper, Toronto, 1979, pp. liv–lv, 97, 104–10, 197–8, 303–4, 331–2. George L. Fenwick, *A History of the Ancient City of Chester*, Chester, 1896, p. 370. Hardware's brother-in-law was the Puritan gentleman, John Bruen: Hinde, *Faithfull Remonstrance*, pp. 98–9.

[101] Murray, *Dramatic Companies*, ii. 235. *Chester Drama*, pp. 292–3.

[102] *Chester Drama*, pp. 41–2, 234–5, 258–61, 270. Fenwick, *Chester*, pp. 371–4.

Traditional popular culture had always upheld the social order. It was now being openly manipulated for this purpose by a section of the élite.

Everything said so far might suggest that militant Protestants and Puritans opposed virtually all kinds of public entertainment. This was not quite the case, for just as the early church had taken over many of the pagan feasts, so did Protestants acquire their own rituals, adapting older forms or providing substitutes for them. The most obvious English example is the replacement of the traditional Hallowe'en (31 October) by the fiercely anti-Catholic Gunpowder Treason day on 5 November. Hallowe'en, when goblins and spirits had to be propitiated, had come under the same official ban at the Reformation as other saints' days. But it was still occasionally celebrated: at Wellington, Somerset, for instance, as late as 1604, when the constable was beaten up by a disorderly crowd of revellers.[103]

There are some interesting parallels between Hallowe'en and Guy Fawkes Day rituals: the playing of goblin-like tricks on people who would not contribute to the festivities, for example. In 1606 Parliament ordered the annual observance of 5 November as a day of thanksgiving. It quickly became an occasion for affirming Protestant and national identity, its anti-Catholic meaning making it particularly attractive to Puritans. Failure to observe it automatically aroused suspicion: one of the charges against a Cambridgeshire minister denounced to the Long Parliament was that he 'never gave any thanks' on that day.[104] In the towns it provided one more opportunity for civic dignitaries to display their authority as they paraded formally to church. At Southampton in 1606 the corporation solemnized the day 'in scarlet gowns with prayer, evening and morning, and sermons'.[105] Everywhere the church bells were rung, and in larger towns there were public bonfires and fireworks.[106]

Gunpowder Treason might be dear to the hearts of Puritans, but it still provided tempting opportunities for mischief, and occasionally things got out of hand. Two Norwich men were so carried away in 1633 that they stole some doors to throw on the bonfire. There was often a good deal of drinking. At Everleigh, Wiltshire, the minister persuaded his parishioners to transfer the traditional Christmas drinking to 5 November, and the custom persisted for several years. On Guy Fawkes Day in 1613 a man got

---

[103] PRO STAC 8/124/2 (*Druston v. Calway*, 1604). The ringing of bells on Hallowe'en had been prohibited after the Reformation. The festival seems to have survived best in Scotland and Ireland: R. Chambers, *The Book of Days: A Miscellany of Popular Antiquities*, 1863–4, ii. 519–22; William Hone, *The Every-Day Book, or a guide to the year*, 1888–9, i. 704–8.

[104] *Journal of Sir Simonds D'Ewes*, pp. 38–9. For 5 November as a Protestant festival see Chambers, *Book of Days*, ii. 549–50; Wright, *Calendar Customs*, iii. 145–56.

[105] *Southampton Mayor's Book, 1606–8*, p. 48.

[106] At Bristol and Devizes, among other possible examples: Wright, *Calendar Customs*, iii. 147; *Annals of Devizes*, ii, pt. ii, 85–101.

into the pulpit in All Cannings church and edified his equally drunken companions with a mock sermon. Its connection with Gunpowder Treason is obscure, though as a fantasy expressing some typical male anxieties its meaning is clear enough: 'Man love thy wife and thy wife will love thee, and if she will not do as thou wilt have her, take a staff and break her arms and legs and she will forgive thee.'[107]

There were other dates with special meaning for Protestants. One was 17 November, the anniversary of Queen Elizabeth's accession, which later in the century produced celebrations very similar to those on the 5th. Before the civil war, however, there is no record of anything more elaborate than the ringing of church bells. This was most likely to happen in Puritan towns such as Dorchester and Stroud, which also ordered ringing for other Protestant occasions: Stroud for Prince Charles's return from Spain in 1623, and Dorchester in 1631 for the Swedish victory at Breitenfeld.[108] But such celebrations were not confined to outposts of Puritanism. More conservative Coventry rang the bells for 'the good proceedings of the Parliament' when Charles I accepted the Petition of Right in 1628. There were bells and bonfires for this in many places, but the Coventry celebrations were distinctly traditional, including a fencing display and a 'dancing horse' accompanied by plentiful supplies of beer and wine.[109]

Coventry people were also regularly entertained by itinerant puppet-shows, acrobats, and exhibitions of 'wonders'. Some of these had a Protestant or biblical flavour—portraits of the King and Queen of Bohemia and their children were exhibited in 1630, and a show representing the creation came twice later in the decade—but more often they were simply entertainments.[110] Puritan Norwich was more selective, but the corporation had no objection to shows with suitably improving messages like the waxworks featuring an effigy of King Gustavus, or William Gostlynge's 'portraiture of the city of Jerusalem'.[111] Advocates of moral reformation were quite willing to borrow cultural forms whose use in other hands they were trying to eliminate. The permitted entertainments, however, taught moral lessons—lessons of biblical and Protestant virtue—just as the reformers' austere civic processions taught lessons of duty and obedience.

*

[107] Ralph Whitlock, *The Folklore of Wiltshire*, 1976, pp. 75–6. WRO B/ABO 7 (Act Book, 1613–15), fo. 57.

[108] GRO P 328, CW/2/1 (Stroud Churchwardens accounts, 1623–1716), pp. 1, 4, 19, 22, 24, 33. DRO P 173, CW/1 (Dorchester, Holy Trinity accounts), ff. 48, 50, 52, 57, 61, 66ᵛ.

[109] Murray, *Dramatic Companies*, ii. 250–1 and n. See also *English History from Essex Sources 1550–1750*, ed. A. C. Edwards, Chelmsford, 1952, p. 71; and Conrad Russell, *Parliaments and English Politics 1621–1629*, Oxford, 1979, p. 389 and n.

[110] Murray, *Dramatic Companies*, ii. 247–53.

[111] *Minutes of Norwich Court of Mayoralty*, p. 100. Murray, *Dramatic Companies*, ii. 357.

Early seventeenth-century England thus displays many symptoms of cultural conflict. At the élite level the conflict ranged the Protestant country gentry and middling sort—the 'Country'—against what they perceived as the corrupt and popish extravagance of the Court and its hangers-on.[112] At the popular level it ranged many of the gentry, the Puritan clergy and their allies among the respectable parish notables against the bulk of their social inferiors and the poor. Elements of the élite such as the Laudian clergy and conservative laymen such as Robert Dover attempted to rescue and preserve the older festive customs because the values they expressed were closer to their own. The two cultural positions reflected the two conceptions of society that we have had frequent occasion to contrast: one stressing tradition, custom, and the co-operative, harmonious 'vertical' community; the other moral reformation, individualism, the ethic of work, and personal responsibility. It has already been suggested that these contrasts had a regional as well as a social base, but the question has not been examined in detail. In the chapter that follows we shall attempt to determine which areas of the three south-western counties remained more attached to the traditional culture, and which were more affected by the new.

[112] P. W. Thomas, 'Two Cultures? Court and Country under Charles I', in *The Origins of the English Civil War*, ed. Russell, ch. 6. See also Christopher Hill, *Milton and the English Revolution*, New York, 1977, chs. 2–5.

4

Regional Cultures

THE notion that cultural differences are in part the product of environmental ones is no modern invention. It was flatly stated in the later seventeenth century by John Aubrey: 'According to the several sorts of earth in England (and so all the world over), the Indigenae are respectively witty or dull, good or bad.'[1] Aubrey contrasts the cultures of the two principal regions of Wiltshire—the 'chalk' and the 'cheese' countries—beginning with the villagers of the chalk region:

On the downs, sc. the south part, where 'tis all upon tillage, and where the shepherds labour hard, their flesh is hard, their bodies strong: being weary after hard labour, they have not leisure to read or contemplate of religion.

In the 'dirty clayey country' to the north, on the other hand, the people

speak drawling; they are phlegmatic, skins pale and livid, slow and dull, heavy of spirit; hereabout is but little tillage or hard labour, they only milk the cows and make cheese; they feed chiefly on milk meats, which cools their brains too much, and hurts their inventions.

Dairy farming was only one reason for this region's cultural peculiarity. It was 'a woodsere country, abounding much with sour and austere plants, as sorrel', which made the inhabitants correspondingly taciturn. Cheese country folk were thus inclined to be 'melancholy, contemplative, and malicious', addicted to Puritanism, witchcraft beliefs, and compulsive litigiousness. The downlanders of south Wiltshire had none of these characteristics.[2] We may reject Aubrey's combination of traditional humouralism and botanical determinism, and still accept the possibility that he was right to identify major cultural differences between the two parts of his county.

Wiltshire was not unique in its variety. There were striking cultural contrasts over quite short distances in other parts of the country. The high

[1] Aubrey, *Nat. Hist. Wilts.*, p. 11. For connections between environment and culture see Julian H. Steward, *Theory of Culture Change*, Urbana, Illinois, 1963, ch. 2; and A. L. Kroeber, 'Cultural and Natural Areas of North America', in *Environment and Cultural Behavior*, ed. Vayda, p. 351 (I am indebted to Rhett Jones for this reference).

[2] Aubrey, *Nat. Hist. Wilts.*, pp. 11–12. *Top. Coll. John Aubrey*, p. 266. The prominence of milk products in the diet of people from dairying regions is (not surprisingly) confirmed by Jay Allan Anderson, '"A Solid Sufficiency": an Ethnography of Yeoman Foodways in Stuart England', Ph.D. thesis, University of Pennsylvania, 1973, pp. 248–50.

GLOUCESTERSHIRE ⊗1612
+1640
⊗1620
⊗1620
BERKSHIRE
COTSWOLDS
1620 +
1617
+
⊗1634
CHEESE COUNTRY
⊗1603
+1618
CLOTHING
DISTRICT
+1604
VALE OF PEWSEY
SOMERSET
+1617
+1624
1620
+
⊗1628
+1612
⊗1608
1616
+
1637
+
1628 +
+1608
HAMPSHIRE
+1627
CHALK COUNTRY
+1621
1618⊗
⊗1623
1621⊗
+1622
1623
+
1630
+
1610
+
1623+
1640+
1611
⊗1616
⊗
1612

⊗ Church ale
+ Other public revel
   (latest recorded date)
DORSET
0   5   10 miles

II Wiltshire regions and popular festivals, 1603–1640

incidence of biblical-text first names may be a sign of a very local Puritan
subculture in the Kent and Sussex Weald.[3] Geographical variations in the
popularity of certain sports also indicate the existence of regional cultures.
Some sports had an extremely local flavour, like the highly ritualized
Haxey Hood game played in the Isle of Axholme. Others were associated
with somewhat broader areas—hurling in Devon and Cornwall; cricket,

---

[3] Tyacke, 'Popular Puritan Mentality'.

in the early seventeenth century still confined to Kent and Sussex.[4] In Wiltshire itself the contrast between the sports of the two main regions in some ways bears out the truth of Aubrey's analysis.

Put simply, the typical team sport of the south Wiltshire downlands was football; the typical sports of the north Wiltshire cheese country were variants of bat-and-ball games, of which stoolball was in this period by far the most popular. Both sports, of course, had large followings in other parts of the country. Football, with its numerous local variants (camp ball in the eastern counties, bottle-kicking in Leicestershire) was played in all types of communities—town and country, open-field and wood-pasture alike.[5] A more or less ritualized combat between communities, often represented by virtually the entire young male population of whole parishes, it was an appropriate expression of parochial loyalty against outsiders, in which the identity of the individual was almost totally submerged in that of the group. Its disorderly violence made it an inevitable target of moral reformers; the Laudian clergy, by contrast, encouraged it as a harmless reinforcement of feelings of neighbourhood.[6] The submergence of the individual was not absolute: in an ecclesiastical court case at Berkhamsted in 1617 a young woman recalled sitting with her friends 'talking upon football players', presumably in tones of admiration.[7] But its collective character made it an appropriate game for communities with strong habits of co-operation, as in open-field arable villages, or fen villages with highly developed arrangements for common pasture.

Football was more firmly entrenched in the downlands than in north Wiltshire, though it was occasionally played there too. Bishops Cannings, on the edge of the downs north of Devizes, says Aubrey, 'would have challenged all England for music, ringing and football play'.[8] Prosecutions for playing football on Sundays were fairly common in the chalk country. In 1607 most of the parishioners of Alton Pancras, Dorset, including the vicar, travelled to Cheselbourne, another downland village, for a Sunday football match.[9] In Wiltshire matches are frequently

---

[4] Christina Hole, *English Sports and Pastimes*, 1949, pp. 55–6. E. O. James, *Seasonal Feasts and Festivals*, 1961, pp. 298–9. Carew, *Cornwall*, pp. 147–50. There is a huge literature on cricket; for a useful discussion of the early years, in which the south-eastern origins are clear, see Christopher Brookes, *English Cricket: The Game and its Players through the Ages*, 1978, pp. 10–24.

[5] Football was traditionally associated with Shrove Tuesday, but was also played at many other times of year. It was especially popular in the midland and northern counties and in East Anglia, and seems to have been particularly violent in the Fens: Enid Porter, *Cambridgeshire Customs and Folklore*, 1969, pp. 230–1. See also James, *Seasonal Feasts*, pp. 298–9, 300–4; Chambers, *Mediaeval Stage*, i. 150; and Robert W. Malcolmson, *Popular Recreations in English Society 1700–1850*, Cambridge, 1973, pp. 34–40.

[6] For some Essex examples see F. G. Emmison, *Elizabethan Life: Disorder*, Chelmsford, 1970, pp. 225–6; and White, *First Century*, pp. 19, 36–7.

[7] Bodleian MS Oxf. Archd. papers: Berks. c. 61 (Deposition Book, 1616–20), fo. 34.

[8] Quoted by Anne Whiteman, 'The Church of England 1542–1837', *VCH, Wilts.* iii. 40.

[9] WRO, Dean's Peculiar, Presentments 1606–8, no. 27.

recorded: on Collingbourne Down near Everleigh, at Charlton on the northern edge of Salisbury Plain, at Newton Toney and Kingston Deverill. Drinking at matches had familiar consequences. Richard Bowles of Tisbury was charged with 'unseemly fighting in the company at football'; he admitted it and also that he was drunk.[10] Evidence for football in early seventeenth-century Wiltshire comes largely from nucleated downland villages where local authorities often shared the community-oriented values of those who played it.

Football was less popular in the cheese country, but bat-and-ball games like stoolball and trap-ball were more widely played. Stoolball's popularity in north Wiltshire might be ascribed to the fact that its structure expressed, better than football, the more individualistic nature of the wood-pasture community. Stoolball was a team sport, to be sure, but wood-pasture villages were also communities. In stoolball, as in cricket, the confrontation between batsman and bowler is an individual one within a team context; there is an analogy here with the place of the individual in the wood-pasture village, which was still, however fragmented, a community. In both the game and the community the individual had a greater sense of his personal role.[11]

Stoolball was not confined to the cheese country: it was being played at Ombersley, Worcestershire in 1608, and was known in pasture and clothing districts of Lancashire between 1680 and 1715, as well as in Bedfordshire, Hertfordshire, and Norfolk a century earlier.[12] Games, like other cultural forms, are not constrained by the geographical boundaries convenient to modern historians, so it is not surprising that stoolball and trap-ball both spread into the northern part of the downland region. Stoolball was played at Broad Hinton, on the northern fringe of the Marlborough Downs, in 1631, trap-ball at Mildenhall near Marlborough in 1614, and Shrewton on Salisbury Plain, in 1620.[13] But as John Aubrey attests, stoolball's heartland was the region near the Wiltshire–Gloucestershire border. Colerne Down was 'the place so famous and frequented for it'.[14] People were presented for playing it on Sundays at Tetbury and

[10] WRO AS/ABO 11 (Act Book, 1612–16), ff. 195ᵛ, 197; 15 (1636–40), fo. 9ᵛ; B/ABO 7 (Act Book, 1613–15), fo. 72; 10 (1620–2), fo. 47; 11 (1622–33), fo. 29ᵛ.

[11] There were two variants of stoolball: a primitive form played with a paddle or the hand instead of a bat, and the more elaborate Wiltshire form played with a hard ball and a wooden staff resembling a modern baseball bat (Hole, *Sports and Pastimes*, pp. 59–60, and see also *Top. Coll. John Aubrey*, p. 77). I suspect that the simpler form was the one popular in other parts of the country, being played, for example, at village revels 'for a Tansy and a banquet of curds and cream': Breton, 'The Court and Country', p. 7. See also Brookes, *English Cricket*, pp. 11–12; Malcolmson, *Popular Recreations*, p. 42; and W. Carew Hazlitt, *Faiths and Folklore of the British Isles: A Descriptive and Historical Dictionary*, New York, 1965, ii. 569.

[12] Malcolmson, *Popular Recreations*, p. 42. PRO STAC 8/255/14 (*Sandys v. Jones*, 1608). HMC, *Fifth Report* (House of Lords MSS), p. 27. NRO C/S, 3/12 (Norfolk QS rolls, 1594–6), 38 Eliz.

[13] WRO B/ABO 7 (Act Book, 1613–15), ff. 73–74ᵛ; 11 (1622–33), fo. 115ᵛ.

[14] *Top. Coll. John Aubrey*, p. 77.

the nearby village of Rodmarton in 1609 and 1610, and at Castle Combe thirty years earlier. It surfaces at Slaughterford, Sherston Magna, and Broughton Gifford, all cheese country villages, in the same period. A Sherston man was late for church because the other players 'fell a-quarrelling with him', while one of those accused at Broughton Gifford claimed that he had been at church in a neighbouring village on the evening in question.[15] The 'fit' between football and the downlands, stoolball and the northern pasture regions, is not exact, but is sufficiently close to support Aubrey's point about their cultural dissimilarities.[16]

*

Aubrey was also right about the religious complexion of the clothing region, for Puritanism had struck strong roots there. It was promoted by many of the leading gentry, including the Haringtons, Horners, and Pophams in north Somerset, the Bayntons, Danvers, and Hungerfords in Wiltshire. With their encouragement, an array of Puritan preachers advanced the cause of reformation. Men like Humphrey Chambers of Claverton, Samuel Crooke of Wrington, Samuel Oliver of Cameley, and William Thomas of Ubley were exerting a powerful influence in north Somerset by the late 1620s.[17] When the Laudian hierarchy moved against lectureships, Bishop Piers found a number of north Somerset lectures deserving his attention at Bath, Bathford, Chew Stoke, Wrington, and elsewhere.[18] The clothing region was the scene of much resentful preaching against the Book of Sports: William Thomas of Ubley was among several prominent Somerset divines in trouble for it. At Batcombe, long a Puritan stronghold, the churchwardens were ordered to remove offensive monuments, including one describing their late rector as 'an enemy of heathenish revel'. Richard Allein's preaching at Ditcheat convinced one of his parishioners that 'a maypole was an idol' and another that 'it was a greater sin for a man to play at bowls on the sabbath day, than to lie with another man's wife on a week day'.[19]

[15] GRO GDR 108 (Office, 1609–10), ff. 5ᵛ, 19ᵛ, 33; 111 (Detections, 1610), Stonehouse Deanery presentments, Rodmarton, 10 Oct. Scrope, *Castle Combe*, p. 331. Whiteman, 'Church of England 1542–1837', p. 38. WRO AW/ABO 5 (Act Book, 1616–22), fo. 22ᵛ; AS/ABO 13 (1620–4), ff. 38, 42.

[16] Other bat-and-ball games were played in the Wiltshire pasture country, for instance the one traditionally played at Cley Hill near Warminster on Palm Sunday: Davies, *Life in an English Village*, p. 96. There is, to be sure, no positive evidence that this was being played in the early seventeenth century.

[17] A list of clergy serving the Chewton Mendip lectureship around 1630 includes all the four named, as well as other well-known Puritans from further afield: *SDNQ* xxiv (1943–6), 136. For Puritanism in Somerset see Margaret Stieg, *Laud's Laboratory: The Diocese of Bath and Wells in the Early Seventeenth Century*, Lewisburg, Pennsylvania, 1982, ch. 10.

[18] Stieg, *Laud's Laboratory*, p. 291. Underdown, *Somerset*, p. 22. For the whole subject see Hill, *Society and Puritanism*, ch. 3; and Paul S. Seaver, *The Puritan Lectureships: The Politics of Religious Dissent 1560–1662*, Stanford, 1970.

[19] Stieg, *Laud's Laboratory*, pp. 36, 292–3.

Throughout the western counties it was the towns and the rural clothing parishes that most obstinately resisted conformity to Laudian ritual. Central to the whole Laudian policy was the campaign to remove the 'Protestant' communion table from the nave and rail it off in the chancel as a 'popish' altar. In most parishes in the three-county area the churchwardens grumbled but complied. Opposition was most vocal, one of Laud's officials reported, 'in great clothing towns, because they see no such thing, as they say, in the churches of London'.[20] That inhabitants of the clothing districts were aware of what was happening in the capital because of their trading connections is likely, but it is not a sufficient explanation of their opposition. Parishioners of places such as Becking-ton, Mells, Stratton-on-the-Fosse, and Batcombe, all of which felt the strong hand of authority when they resisted, saw an altar as a popish innovation, a repudiation of the good old Protestant tradition of Queen Elizabeth's and King James's days. It set the minister on a different plane from his congregation, turning him into a priest who could perform, perhaps, the miracle of transubstantiation. It did not need the example of London to tell west-countrymen this.[21]

In Wiltshire and Dorset opposition to Laud was less vocal than in Somerset, partly because both counties were in dioceses with bishops less zealous than William Piers.[22] There had been, to be sure, some spec-tacular incidents, like Henry Sherfield's violence against the stained glass in St. Edmund's, Salisbury, which followed an attempt by the leading parishioners to remove the window and sell the church organ: they were forbidden to do either by the ecclesiastical court.[23] And in the Wiltshire clothing districts no less than in Somerset the divisive impact of Puritan-ism is clear. Consciousness of being part of an elect minority subject to the special demands of Puritan sainthood made many people in the cheese country dissatisfied with their beneficed clergy. Some went 'gadding to sermons' or formed conventicles, in both cases breaking the unity of the parish. Several Broughton Gifford men charged with forming a con-venticle in 1604 also admitted going to Melksham to hear sermons, because there were none in their own parish. Others at Farrington Gurney said that they went out of the parish 'to receive instruction by sermons for the salvation of their souls'.[24] North Somerset visitation returns in 1615 disclose widespread concern by the parish notables about the irregularity of preaching and catechizing. At Monkton Combe there

[20] Prynne, *Canterburies Doome*, p. 92.

[21] *Journal of Sir Simonds D'Ewes*, pp. 143–4. Stieg, *Laud's Laboratory*, pp. 296–301.

[22] Whiteman, 'Church of England 1542–1837', pp. 37–40. Majorie E. Reeves, 'Protestant Non-conformity', *VCH, Wilts.*, iii. 100–1. Bettey, *Dorset*, pp. 101–2, briefly surveys the extent of Puritanism in that county.

[23] BL Add. MS 22084 (Wilts. Sequestrations Register), fo. 55.

[24] WRO B/ABO 5 (Act Book, 1600–6), ff. 65–6. SRO D/D/Ca 191 (Comperta, 1615), Farrington, T. Cole, 13 Aug.

were only quarterly sermons; at Brislington the impropriator, Sir Francis Popham, had failed to provide for preachers; at Bathampton there had been a few sermons within the previous year but none recently; at Stanton Drew there were complaints about the parson being deaf, haunting alehouses, and not being licensed to preach.[25] The area's Puritanism cannot be entirely attributed to its clergy.

Conventicles like the one meeting at Chelwood 'in stables and out-houses' in 1635 were a natural consequence.[26] In these northern parishes, with their relatively broadly-based élites, dissatisfaction with the existing state of the church was shared by a fairly wide segment of the population. The 'middling sort' Puritans occupying responsible positions in their parishes tended to work for reform from within. People who were less economically secure were more likely to separate into their own congregations. There were separatists at Bradford-on-Avon in Elizabeth's reign, and in 1604 weavers from Castle Combe and other villages were attending conventicles at Slaughterford to hear preachers who included the Brownist Francis Johnson on a visit from Amsterdam. Among the Amsterdam exiles, indeed, there was a fair sprinkling of Wiltshire men and women, most of them textile workers.[27] We should not exaggerate the significance of incidents like the one at Box in 1603 in which a weaver and a 'roughmason' denounced the Prayer Book and denied the legitimacy of non-preaching ministers, but they at least indicate that Puritan opinions in this area were not confined to the village oligarchs. Gadding to sermons was not exclusively a cheese-country phenomenon. But where we find it we often also find conventicles and unauthorized visiting preachers, and such things were more common in the pasture country than in the downlands.[28] In 1620 a group of people from Burrington were presented for going to hear Samuel Crooke preach at Wrington; it may not be a coincidence that twenty years later Burrington welcomed a number of itinerant preachers who denounced episcopal authority, including the radical separatist William Erbury.[29] Payments to visiting preachers were common in the 1620s in Gloucestershire clothing villages like Dursley and North Nibley, and are further signs of the erosion of parish unity.[30]

[25] SRO D/D/Ca 191 and 194 (Comperta, 1615), *passim*. See also Stieg, *Laud's Laboratory*, pp. 188–9. It may be significant that the value of benefices was most seriously eroded by inflation in this, the Puritan part of the county (Stieg, pp. 126–7).

[26] Stieg, *Laud's Laboratory*, p. 293.

[27] Reeves, 'Protestant Nonconformity', p. 100. HMC, *Various Collections*, i (Wilts. QS MSS), p. 76.

[28] HMC, *Various Collections*, i. 71–2. For examples of gadding to sermons elsewhere in Wiltshire see Whiteman, 'Church of England 1542–1837', p. 37; and WRO B/ABO 8 (Act Book, 1615–18), fo. 3.

[29] SRO D/D/Ca 220 (Comperta, 1620), Burrington, 20 Sept. Erbury also preached to great crowds at Chew Stoke and other places in north Somerset in October 1640: Stieg, *Laud's Laboratory*, pp. 288–90 (on p. 289 'Barrington' should read 'Burrington').

[30] GRO P 124, CW/2/4 (Dursley Churchwardens accounts), fo. 38; P 230, CW/2/1 (N. Nibley Churchwardens accounts), 1625, 1628.

This erosion was most likely to occur in large, sprawling parishes than in smaller, compact ones—and large parishes were more common in wood-pasture than in field country. People who lived a long way from the church were likely to be detached from the communal life of that parish. The existence of several chapelries in a parish also tended to weaken parochial discipline by giving people a choice. Lawrence Bullock defended himself for attending the parish church at Sherston Magna, 'there being a sufficient minister and preacher', whereas the curate of the chapelry of Alderton, where he lived, was 'ignorant and such as from whom he can receive no spiritual counsel'.[31] People who did this were invariably told 'not to sever themselves from their own congregation'.[32] Even the less extreme form of gadding to sermons undermined parish order, and this was becoming particularly common in the pasture country in the early seventeenth century. Aubrey recognized that the contemplative spirit engendered by the vegetation was not the only explanation for the cheese country's Puritanism: 'That, and the Bible, and ease—for it is now all upon dairy-grassing and clothing—set their wits a-running and reforming.'[33]

There were many parishes in the wood-pasture area where after 1600 groups of the elect were detaching themselves from their neighbours. Sometimes the parish notables were themselves divided. At Stratton St. Margaret in 1613 one churchwarden, Lawrence Mellor, had to make his own presentment, complaining that 'none of my neighbours will . . . join with me'. He was clearly a Puritan, denouncing the minister for not preaching or catechizing, and other parishioners for sabbath-breaking; he admitted that he sometimes went to other parishes for sermons. His fellow churchwarden duly presented him for absence from church, while one of his victims labelled him the 'causer of this our troubles' and accused him of waging a vindictive campaign against the poor.[34]

Another sign of declining community identity in pasture parishes is their frequent failure to keep up Rogationtide perambulations. Even in the attenuated form permitted by earlier restrictions these seem to have been disappearing more rapidly in wood-pasture parishes than in fielden ones. The new hedges and enclosures of the market economy obliterated both the old physical landmarks and the traditions of sociability which

---

[31] WRO B/ABO 5 (Act Book, 1600–6), ff. 20ᵛ–21. The claim that churches in other parishes were closer than a resident's own parish church is made in WRO, AS/ABO 11 (Act Book, 1612–16), fo. 159ᵛ.

[32] WRO B/ABO 7 (Act Book, 1613–15), fo. 14. Cf. the later statement by Philip Henry that separatists 'pluck up the hedge of parish order', quoted in Christopher Hill, *Some Intellectual Consequences of the English Revolution*, Madison, 1980, p. 74.

[33] *Top. Coll. John Aubrey*, p. 266.

[34] WRO, Dean's Peculiar, Presentments 1616, nos. 43–7.

perambulation of the bounds had preserved. 'By reason of the new enclosures and multitude of hedges', the churchwardens of Netherbury, Dorset, declared in 1613, 'we have been for many years constrained to forbear going on procession or perambulation'. The inhabitants of Long Burton were willing to do it, they said ten years later, 'yet the grounds of the parish are so hedged in that we cannot go'.[35] Even when undivided ownership meant the survival of strong manorial control enclosures could prevent this annual affirmation of parish identity. At Rimpton, Somerset, there was no perambulation in 1615 'in regard their parish is enclosed and sufficiently known and belonging all to their lord'.[36] When common land at the parish boundary of Melcombe Regis was enclosed early in the century the perambulation appears to have been abandoned: by the time of the civil war one of the customary stopping places on the processional way, a common pound, had become a private dairy-house.[37]

With the exception of Melcombe Regis, all these are wood-pasture parishes, in areas that were culturally more conservative than the northern cheese country. Even where recent enclosures had not obstructed processional routes perambulations were disappearing. At Weston Bampfylde in 1615 the minister gave notice of the perambulation, 'but their parish came not'. At Ilchester the minister 'was ready, but none came'. At Lyme Regis the redoubtable John Geare had to give up the attempt in 1635 'because he could get none to go with him'.[38] In many places the key to the decline was the withdrawal of the middling sort. At Barkham, in the wood-pasture country south-east of Reading, the bounds were perambulated only once between 1603 and 1631: the minister blamed the substantial residents for refusing to 'provide drinkings for them at certain places where the gospels are usually read'.[39] The custom still held up in some west-country towns: Axbridge, for example, where in 1640 the churchwardens accounted for 14s. 6d. 'spent in the per-ambulation week', and even at Stroud, in the heart of the Gloucestershire cloth-making region.[40] Conclusions about the undermining of parochial solidarity have to be qualified by noting the bewilderingly varied nature of local circumstances. On the whole, though, it is clear that the wood-

[35] WRO, Dean's Peculiar, Presentments 1613, no. 83 (quoted by Bettey, 'Sheep, Enclosures and Watermeadows', p. 12); 1625, no. 82.

[36] SRO D/D/Ca 191 (Comperta, 1615), Rimpton, 12 Oct.

[37] *Weymouth Documents*, pp. 116–18. *CCC* i. 262–3.

[38] SRO D/D/Ca 191 (Comperta, 1615), Weston Bampfylde and Ilchester presentments. WRO, Dean's Peculiar, Presentments 1635, no. 73. Geare had been previously presented for neglecting the perambulation: Dean's Peculiar, Presentments 1613, no. 87; 1625, no. 72.

[39] WRO B/ABO 11 (Act Book, 1622–23), fo. 144ᵛ. See also cases at Beenham (B/ABO 6, fo. 56) and Bucklebury (B/ABO 11, fo. 58).

[40] SRO D/P/ax, 4/1/1 (Axbridge Churchwardens accounts), 1641. GRO P 328, CW 2/1 (Stroud Churchwardens accounts), p. 33 ff.

pasture parishes showed the least interest in maintaining the old
processional customs.[41]

*

The parishes of the clothing districts were more divided and less cohesive
than their counterparts in other regions—divided physically (because
they were so often larger in area), divided socially (because of the influx of
poor), and divided in religion (because of the frequent presence of knots
of Puritan reformers). Their parish élites had the same preoccupations
with order—with achieving a reformed, disciplined, industrious community—as their urban counterparts. They fought hard to suppress
drunkenness and disorder. Where they were united they could usually put
an end to the disorderly festivals at which drunkenness had been so often
legitimized. And in the clothing region the élites *were* more often united.
The attack on popular festivals therefore achieved greater success and
encountered less effective resistance in this than in other areas. This is a
difficult statement to prove because it relies heavily upon the argument
from silence.[42] Much remains obscure for lack of evidence. We simply do
not know whether festivities like the Palm Sunday gatherings on Cley
Hill, near Warminster, where, a later antiquary records, the country
people used to 'divert themselves with tumbling and rolling from top to
bottom', were interrupted in the early seventeenth century. Nor do we
know if the many north Wiltshire revels which Aubrey records survived
throughout the period or were revived after 1660.[43] As we shall see, some
revels undoubtedly did survive in the cheese and clothing districts
through unofficial action. But there is absolutely no positive evidence of
the holding of official church ales sponsored by parish officers between
about 1610 and the Laudian counter-attack in the 1630s. It is possible that
they were still held but that nobody bothered to present them in the courts
because there were no disturbances or because they were tolerated by the
local élites. Given the strength of Puritanism in the region this seems
unlikely.

The campaign against ales and revels had reached its climax, it will be
recalled, in the years around 1610. Where they had gone without resistance before that time, therefore, we have reasonably convincing evidence
of cultural change, and the evidence certainly suggests that this occurred
at an early date in the clothing districts. In the Gloucestershire textile
region, Minchinhampton abandoned its church ale around 1589, a few

---

[41] The decline of perambulation customs should not be exaggerated. The bounds were still being
perambulated in many places right down to the civil war: see Cox, *Churchwardens Accounts*, pp. 283–4.
Presentments often fail to indicate whether the lapse was an isolated one or part of a long sequence of
neglect which earlier churchwardens had not presented.

[42] An incident at Dundry in 1634 is a good example of the difficulties: see below, pp. 86–8.

[43] BL Add. MS 22836 (Maton collection), fo. 20. *Top. Coll. John Aubrey*, pp. 125, 139, 146, 185, 198.
Aubrey, 'Remaines', p. 212.

years after the arrival of a reformist minister, and regular sermons by visiting lecturers soon followed. At Dursley brewing utensils appear in the church inventories until 1592; then, after a gap in the accounts, they disappear and by 1603 a church rate has been adopted. Rates were introduced at Uley, another Cotswold clothing village, at least by 1570, and in many other Gloucestershire parishes they were already well established.[44] In none of these places is there any sign of serious trouble: it was in places like Rangeworthy, outside the clothing region, that resistance was likely to occur.

In the Wiltshire cheese country, too, church ales were becoming uncommon by the beginning of the century. At Biddestone, near Chippenham, a rate had been established before 1600; ales appear to have been on the way out by 1602 in Ashton Keynes; while at Calne the last church ale was held in 1603 and rating followed a year later. Steeple Ashton's church ale was still being held in 1583, but that may have been the last time before the parish went over to the collection of a Whitsun 'gift' and to a more formal rating in 1600.[45] It is not clear when ales were discontinued at Keevil, but it must have been before 1611, when the manor court ordered the demolition of the 'King house' at the request of the vicar, Francis Greatrakes, a moral crusader of long experience.[46] There was a 'clerk-ale' (an ale whose proceeds went to the payment of the parish clerk's wages) at North Bradley in 1628, but that is the only evidence of any kind of official church ale in this part of Wiltshire after 1610.[47]

North Somerset presents the same picture of Puritan success against church ales. The absence of presentments in so strongly Puritan an area must be significant. We know that ales were abolished at South Brent, a pasture village outside the clothing area, shortly before 1600, that there were signs of reluctance about holding ales at Glastonbury in 1589, and that many other parishes had church rates, or 'gifts' that were really rates under another name, by this time. At Blagdon the 'church gift' was collected from the 'holders of means' in the parish long before 1590, for example.[48] The impact of Richard Allein's preaching against maypoles at

[44] 'Minchinhampton Churchwardens Accounts', pp. 413, 418–19, 432–5. GRO P 124, CW/2/4 (Dursley Churchwardens accounts), ff. 11–27ᵛ, 30; GDR 114 (Depositions, 1611–13), *Downey* v. *Dauncey*, 10 Oct. 1612.

[45] WRO B/ABO 11 (Act Book, 1622–33), fo. 66; 5 (1600–6), fo. 25ᵛ. A. E. W. Marsh, *History of the Borough and Town of Calne*, 1903, pp. 372–3. 'Steeple Ashton Churchwardens' Accounts', ed. E. P. Knubley, *Wilts. N & Q* vi (1908–10), 425, 468, 472, 519–22.

[46] Ingram, 'Ecclesiastical Justice in Wiltshire', p. 102.

[47] *Records of Wilts.*, p. 91. There was a similar case at Thornford, Dorset, in 1628: DRO, QS Order Book, 1627–37, fo. 128ᵛ.

[48] SRO D/D/Cd 35 (Depositions, 1604), *S. Brent churchwardens* v. *Locke*; D/D/Cd 71 (Depositions, 1631–5), *Derrick* v. *Derrick and Allen*. Ware, 'Elizabethan Parish', p. 73 and n. Glastonbury had a church rate at least by 1613: SRO D/D/Cd 65 (Depositions, 1628–30), *Roode and King* v. *Gorge*, 1629.

Ditcheat, the inscriptions on the church wall at Batcombe, and all the other evidence of widespread Puritanism in the region, make it highly unlikely that villagers could have defied the sessions and assize orders that were in force until 1633 without there being somebody in the neighbourhood to denounce them and thus bring them to the attention of the historian.

Less formal merry-makings were another matter. Alehouses remained a universal problem. During the period of economic crisis around 1630 there was particularly strong concern about them in the northern clothing parishes. The usual arguments were deployed, as at Paulton in 1636, when the inhabitants complained about an alehouse which attracted servants and young people at unlawful hours, to the neglect of 'their parents' and masters' service'.[49] In Wiltshire too there were frequent complaints, including one from Bradford-on-Avon in 1628 which denounced alehouses for enticing 'poor workmen and day labourers' to drown their sorrows while their wives and children starved.[50] Petitions to the justices repeatedly stressed the impact of alehouses on the poor. Getting rid of alehouses was difficult; even harder was getting convictions for drunkenness. 'All men,' the constables of Calne complained '. . . love these cup companions so well that no man will take upon him to be a sworn witness.'[51]

Nor could communal sociability be suppressed entirely. The destruction of the 'King house' at Keevil provoked an obscene libel against the vicar, a not very surprising reminder that even in the Puritan areas cliques of respectable reformers were likely to be resisted by the more disorderly elements of their parishes. Church ales might no longer be sponsored by the substantial inhabitants, but this did not prevent young people gathering on Sunday evenings to enjoy themselves. At Whitsun 1624 a group of young men were charged with being 'at a dancing match upon a Sunday after evening prayer': one of them asserted that there was 'usually' dancing in Keevil on Sunday evenings, and cited James I's Book of Sports for its legality.[52] Revel feasts, which required less participation by parish notables than church ales, also continued in some villages in this area. The feast was held at Seend in 1613, and four years later there was dancing there in the evening of Ascension Day.[53] At Tockenham Wick on the eastern edge of the cloth-making region, the revel feast was held in September 1620, with the usual cudgel playing in the village street.

[49] *SQSR* i. xlv–xlvii, 121, 174–5, 235–6, 248; ii. 42–3, 120, 138, 140, 144, 160, 248–9, 269.
[50] *Records of Wilts.*, pp. 89–90, and see also pp. 25–6, 34, 86, 125, 140. HMC, *Various Collections*, i. 72, 79, 85, 97.
[51] *Records of Wilts.*, p. 35.
[52] WRO AS/ABO 13 (Act Book, 1620–4), ff. 270ᵛ–271ᵛ. Ingram, 'Ecclesiastical Justice in Wiltshire', pp. 102–3.
[53] WRO B/ABO 7 (1613–15), ff. 10ᵛ, 18, 25ᵛ; AS/ABO 12 (1616–20), ff. 125ᵛ, 135.

Violence erupted, however, when a gang of men from Wooton Bassett arrived, out for trouble and asking 'where were the middle sort of men in Tockenham?'[54] The invaders obviously knew from what level of society their enemies were likely to be drawn.

It would, of course, be absurd to expect the reform campaign to have succeeded completely. But in the clothing parishes feasts survived only with difficulty and without official tolerance. Similarly with presentments for playing unlawful games: there are occasional cases in this area, but they usually involve individuals rather than the larger groups often presented in other regions. An isolated case of Sunday skittles at Bradford-on-Avon, or the breaking of a church window during a snowball fight at Bromham, do not contradict the impression that these were distinctly Puritan places.[55] It was obviously impossible to suppress all occasions for popular merry-makings. Major fairs like Tann Hill Fair on the downs near Devizes, and Woodbury Hill Fair near Bere Regis in Dorset, attracted people from a huge area, and had recreational as well as economic importance. The multitude of lesser fairs everywhere provided various forms of popular amusement: there were ballad singers from London at Frome and Trowbridge fairs in July 1620. Fairs, as the reformers often complained, provided frequent opportunity for disorder and immorality.[56]

In North Somerset, too, the suppression of church ales did not end less official forms of merry-making. It would have been impossible to stop the sort of gathering that occurred at Bleadon on May Day, 1633, when a group of people (some from neighbouring villages) dined together, 'and were merry, as friends use to be when they meet'.[57] Organized revels were also held, in spite of parish officers' disapproval, in the very heart of the clothing region. An alehouse-keeper was presented by the church-wardens of Batheaston for allowing drinking during service time on a Sunday in June 1615: his house was 'full of strangers coming thither to be merry, it being the morrow after their revel feast'.[58] There was a revel at Cameley in the following year, with some minor disorders, 'upon a working day usually used for making merry', a phrase which suggests that this was not an isolated occasion.[59] But once again we should not expect

[54] WRO, QS Rolls, Michaelmas 1620, no. 197.

[55] The examples are from WRO AS/ABO 12 (Act Book, 1616–20), fo. 230ᵛ; AW/ABO 5 (Act Book, 1616–22), fo. 68ᵛ. For others see *Records of Wilts.*, pp. 29–30, 43, 57. The popularity of stoolball should again be noted.

[56] For Tann Hill Fair see *WAM* xxxiv (1905–6), 426; for Woodbury Fair, Hutchins, *Dorset*, i. 135. *Ashley's Case Book* contains many references to disorder and crime at the fair: see for example pp. 36–40, 63–5. The ballad-singers at Frome and Trowbridge are noted in WRO, QS Rolls, Michaelmas 1620, no. 186.

[57] SRO D/D/Cd 76 (Depositions, 1633–4), *Least* v. *Cabell alias Kinge*, 30 Apr. 1634.

[58] SRO D/D/Ca 194 (Comperta, 1615), Batheaston, 30 Sept.

[59] *SQSR* i, xlix. There was also a revel at Butcombe, or nearby, in 1616: SRO CQ 3/1/23 (Sessions Rolls, 1616), no. 77.

the old culture to disappear immediately and without trace. What is striking about such incidents in both north Somerset and Wiltshire is their relative infrequency. Presentments for playing unlawful games were similarly uncommon in this area; a case of bowls in the churchyard on the sabbath at Keynsham and another of card-playing at Saltford on St. James's Day, are almost the only ones for the whole of Bath Archdeaconry in 1615.[60]

We have already noted signs of a festive revival in north Somerset after the revocation of the judicial orders and the publication of the Book of Sports in 1633.[61] The Coleford revel was followed by other acts of defiance by enemies of the reformers, both in Somerset and in other western pasture or clothing parishes. There was a Whitsun ale at Corsham, Wiltshire, in 1634; one of the churchwardens encouraged the setting up of a maypole at Glastonbury; and a maypole also reappeared at Symondsbury, in the west Dorset pasture region.[62] The best documented case, however, is one in the north Somerset village of Dundry, perched on its hill overlooking Bristol. In 1634, much to the curate's disapproval, a maypole was erected in the 'church hay', the field next to the churchyard. The testimony in the case provides an unusual opportunity to see what lies behind the customary silence of the records in the wood-pasture region. Was the maypole erected as part of a festive revival made possible by the Book of Sports, or had there been a continuous tradition of festivity that would contradict the impression of previous Puritan ascendency?

Three things were not in dispute: the offending maypole was erected in May 1634; there had not been one immediately before that date; and villagers of 'the younger sort' were the principal instigators. The case before the ecclesiastical court arose out of a claim by the vicar of Chew Magna (Dundry was a chapelry within his parish) that the 'church hay' was in fact part of the churchyard. Those who asserted it was not included several men, their ages ranging between fifty-two and seventy, who deposed that there had been maypoles there, at least occasionally, in the past. The questions to which we need answers are, when? how often? with how long an interruption before 1634? Unfortunately the depositions are ambiguous, but they certainly imply that there had been a lengthy interruption, perhaps since the early years of the century. The speakers all had an interest in proving that the church hay had been continuously used as a site for maypoles, yet none of them specifically say this. Thus Joseph Smith, aged about seventy, says that 'in his youth and so upwards he hath

[60] SRO D/D/Ca 194 (Comperta, 1615), Keynsham and Saltford presentments.
[61] See above, pp. 67–8. In some places the revival may have begun somewhat earlier. In 1631–2 the Dursley churchwardens spent money on 'the arbour about the youth tree', the first time since 1572 that the arbour appears in their accounts: GRO P 124, CW/2/4, fo. 11.
[62] Burton, *Divine Tragedie*, pp. 12–13, 19–20. Suitable divine punishment was of course forthcoming in all these incidents.

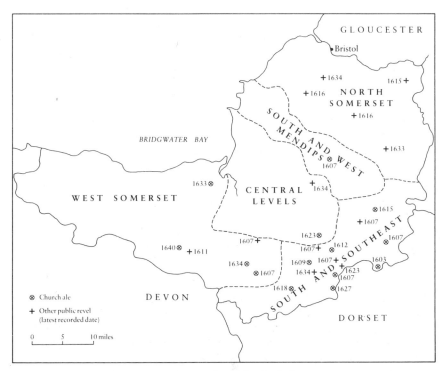

III Somerset regions and popular festivals, 1603–1640

seen and known maypoles and summer luggs' in the field. William Brock and William King, sixty-four and fifty-two respectively, say that there have been 'several' maypoles there. These are not very confident assertions of continuity, and given that the memory of even the youngest deponent would range back to before 1600, still leave open the possibility that maypoles had been absent from the festive scene at Dundry for some thirty or forty years.[63]

The depositions contain much information about the games that had been played in the Dundry church hay. Henry Lukins, a carpenter, provides an impressive list: 'dancing, sporting, kissing, bull-baiting, quoiting, bowling, shooting at butts, cudgel playing, tennis-playing', and others. Again, though, his language implies that there had been some interruptions. These pastimes, he says, had been pursued, 'In those days wherein recreations, sports and plays of several sorts were used'. He recalled them from 'his first time of memory and so for divers years

[63] This and the two following paragraphs are based on SRO D/D/Cd 71; 81 (Depositions, 1631–5; 1635), *Fabian* v. *Payton*. See also Stieg, *Laud's Laboratory*, pp. 144–6 for further ramifications of this case.

sithence', and had himself been 'divers and sundry times' either a participant or a spectator. Some of the sports, he deposed, had continued 'from
time to time . . . or some other like them'. Others give a similar story.
William Brock states that he 'in his youth and since hath several times'
played there. Brock adds that in 1620 he and King were churchwardens
and presented several Dundry youths for dancing in the church hay on the
sabbath, one of the offenders being Brock's own son. They had also
presented youths for playing fives against the church tower. Even the
curate, Simon Cotton, who was against the maypole and could not
remember any dancing, admitted that he had sometimes played bowls in
the church hay.

The depositions are ambiguous and it would be foolish to read too
much into them. Set in the context of everything else that we know about
north Somerset, however, they do not contradict the general thesis of this
chapter. Maypoles, revels, and rural sports had been part of the festive
culture of wood-pasture communities before 1600, had then come under
attack from reforming clergy and laymen, and until the revival of the 1630s
had survived only unofficially and in the margin, particularly as part of
(though not exclusively as) a youth culture. No group of reformers,
however dedicated and energetic, could possibly achieve total success,
and some of the recreations mentioned may have occurred at the time of
the St. Giles's Day fair, which everyone agreed had always been held at
Dundry.[64] The affair also illustrates the ambivalence typical of so many of
the parish notables, even in Puritan areas. The curate tried to stop the
maypole, but admitted that he had no objection to playing bowls. As
churchwardens Brock and King presented young people for dancing and
playing fives, but were quite willing to cite the games they had played in
their misspent youth to support the village's claim to the church hay.

*

The chalk downlands of Dorset and south Wiltshire, with their pre-
dominantly open-field arable farming, nucleated settlement patterns, and
more cohesive societies, present a striking contrast to the wood-pasture
area. The old festive customs were under attack in the chalk country too,
but in many places they held out longer, thanks to broader community
support, often including that of the parish notables. Aubrey, as we might
expect, stresses their survival in such areas as the Hampshire and Wiltshire downs, where fiddlers and drummers, 'good cheer and strong beer',
enlivened sheep-shearings and harvest homes. Robert Plot noted that in
open-field Oxfordshire in the 1670s there were 'many ancient customs

---

[64] There had been cudgel-playing in the churchyard at Chew Magna, the parent parish to Dundry,
in 1620: SRO D/D/Ca 220 (Comperta, 1620), Chew Magna, 20 Sept.

still retained here, abolished and quite lost in most other counties'. The records of secular and ecclesiastical courts confirm the general truth of these observations, and in this case we are less dependent on the argument from silence.[65]

The erosion of parochial identity that was occurring in the clothing districts proceeded more slowly in the downlands. There had always been a few Puritan ministers in downland pastures—Kethe at Childe Okeford in the 1560s, the elder Obadiah Sedgwick at Ogbourne St. Andrew four decades later, Gabriel Sanger at Sutton Mandeville in the 1630s, for example. Small towns like Shaftesbury on the fringe of the region contained their knots of reformers, not surprisingly given that they experienced the usual problems of over-population and poverty.[66] But the Puritans had made less headway in this area. Gadding to sermons was uncommon, if only because there were fewer sermons to gad to. Occasional outbursts of contempt for orthodox religion, like that of the Broad Sydling man who anticipated the Ranters by saying that 'the cup was his Christ', may reflect the irreligion of the disorderly as much as any tendency to separatism.[67]

Puritanism in fact encountered a good deal of hostility in this region, particularly in Dorset, where 'Puritan rogue' was becoming a stock term of abuse. Visitors to Dorchester from its more permissive rural environs were sometimes outraged by the treatment they received. 'It was a Puritan law which he spake', a Poxwell husbandman protested when his companion was warned for swearing by one of the town preachers. 'A plague of God on the slaves of Dorchester', a Cerne Abbas man shouted when arrested in the town for drunkenness.[68] Villagers with anti-Puritan squires or parsons were particularly inclined to such expressions. A lonely reformer at Broad Sydling, Richard Christmas's village, was assaulted in 1615 and denounced as 'Puritan knave'; Christmas stood surety for the culprits when they were brought before the magistrates.[69] Aristocratic influence may in part explain the resistance of some villages to cultural reformation: Donhead St. Mary, for example, a parish in an area with a large recusant population, thanks to the nearby presence of the Catholic Lord Arundell of Wardour.[70]

---

[65] Aubrey, 'Remaines', pp. 137–8, 143. Plot, *Nat. Hist. Oxfordshire*, pp. 200–2. See also Cox, *Churchwardens Accounts*, p. 263.

[66] Whiteman, 'Church of England 1542–1837', pp. 37–8. F. J. Pope, 'Puritans at Shaftesbury in the Early Stuart Period', *SDNQ* xiii (1912–13), 160–2.

[67] *Ashley's Case Book*, pp. 40, 42. The fact that Henry Devenish, a Puritan yeoman, stood surety for the accused man suggests that he may not have been totally irreligious.

[68] DRO B2/8/1 (Dorchester Court Book), ff. 139, 215ᵛ. For other examples see *Ashley's Case Book*, pp. 15, 21.

[69] *Ashley's Case Book*, p. 15.

[70] Church ales and plays were held in the parish at least until 1613, and between then and 1626 two residents of Donhead St. Mary were often employed as musicians at other chalk country parish feasts:

Conservative clerics, too, played their part. The parson at Milborne St. Andrew proclaimed that 'all that went to sermons were bawdy knaves, drunken knaves, lecherous knaves and thievish knaves'; given this sort of example it is not surprising to find the village tithingman among a group of men charged with drunkenness and playing skittles on Sunday.[71] Clergymen of this type fitted more comfortably into their parishes than did their more reformist brethren. Peter Waterman of Wootton Rivers on the edge of the Marlborough Downs was one of the dying breed of farmer-parsons. In 1646 he was charged with behaviour 'not befitting a minister of the gospel', by 'going to plough, filling the dung-pot, serving of hogs and the like'. Waterman was also a cultural traditionalist. His wife sold metheglin, there was card-playing at the parsonage, and Sunday skittle games outside.[72] Such homespun ministers were less acceptable to the literate, respectable laymen who now filled the parish offices in other areas. The churchwardens of Halstock, Dorset, presented their minister in 1613 because he 'goeth not decently in his apparel, and . . . hath used bodily labour not becoming his calling'.[73] In the downlands this was more likely to be tolerated: Waterman was not denounced for it until after the civil war. By the 1630s cultural traditionalism was naturally often accompanied by Laudianism. George Herbert's successor at Bemerton had a maypole set up at his front door, attended the bowls and skittle-playing on Sunday evenings, and entertained the fiddlers. He was also a 'great innovator' who had the communion table set altar-wise and referred to it as 'the blessed board'.[74]

But while paternalist squires and parsons encouraged the conservative mentality of these downland villages the survival of ancient rituals cannot be solely attributed to their influence. The outlook of the inhabitants was equally favourable to the old customs. Rogationtide processions, for example: they expressed both the villagers' sense of communal identity, and their interest in resisting encroachment on their lands by neighbouring parishes.[75] The withdrawal of the middling sort from the rituals

---

Records of Wilts., p. 35; WRO B/ABO 6 (Act Book, 1606–13), fo. 25ᵛ; AS/ABO 11 (Act Book, 1612–16), ff. 36ᵛ, 83; 12 (1616–20), fo. 200ᵛ; 14 (1624–30), fo. 74ᵛ. For recusancy in this area see J. Anthony Williams, *Catholic Recusancy in Wiltshire 1660–1791*, Catholic Record Soc., 1968, pp. 255, 257n.

[71] *Ashley's Case Book*, pp. 34–5.

[72] BL Add. MS 22084 (Wilts. Sequestrations Register), fo. 140. See also A. G. Matthews, *Walker Revised*, Oxford, 1948, p. 381.

[73] WRO, Dean's Peculiar, Presentments 1613, no. 78. See also Hoskins, *Essays in Leics. History*, p. 2; and Holmes, *Lincolnshire*, pp. 54, 56.

[74] BL Add. MS 22084 (Wilts. Sequestrations register), fo. 144; also Matthews, *Walker Revised*, p. 376.

[75] Conflicts between neighbouring villages following alleged alterations of processional routes are recorded in WRO, Treasurer's Peculiar, Presentments, Westbury, 1633; and Bettey, 'Agriculture and Rural Society in Dorset', p. 111.

of the 'roguing week', as William Kethe called it, was beginning: substantial parishioners were sometimes reluctant to provide the traditional cakes and ale. But the perambulation was still being kept up around 1630 at Tisbury and Dinton, Wiltshire, at Arne, Dorset, and other downland parishes. Perambulations were still the rule in the Berkshire downs, denial of hospitality still regarded as a violation of community norms. There were exceptions, but they do not undermine the conclusion that perambulations survived more widely in downland parishes in the early seventeenth century than they did elsewhere.[76]

Chalk country villagers were likely to combine to defend other festive traditions. By 1600, to be sure, church ales were beginning to disappear even in the downlands. At Winterslow, Wiltshire, the minstrels and morris dancers vanished from the 'King-Ale' before the first adoption of a rate in 1600. The ale was held again in 1602 and was succeeded by a 'Whit Monday's dinner', but there were disputes about it; in 1610 a parish meeting had to be held, with the agreement of those present 'set down in writing under their hands'.[77] Corfe Castle retained its church ale at least as late as 1611, but it may have been dropped soon afterwards.[78] At Bere Regis ales were held until 1614, when a rate was adopted. But there was fierce resistance to the change. The rate produced less than half the amount normally raised by the church ale, there were large unpaid arrears and apparitor's fees 'for following the suit against those that do refuse to pay the rate'. In 1616 Bere Regis returned to the old ways and held a successful church ale, making a new 'vizard for the players'. A gap in the churchwardens' accounts obscures the next few years, but by 1624 the struggle was over. The 1624 rate raised more than the earlier ales had done, and by now there were increasing revenues from the sale of church seats. Ales were as unnecessary to the repair of Bere Regis church as they had at last become unacceptable to its parish élite.[79]

James I's reign was a transitional period in many parishes. Disputes over church ales were fairly common, and probably lie behind some of the incidents, in the downlands as well as in the pasture country, in which churchwardens had difficulty in passing their accounts. At Edington in 1620 the village notables quarrelled so violently that a parish meeting

---

[76] Kethe, *Sermon at Blandford*, p. 19. WRO B/ABO 6 (Act Book, 1606–13), ff. 7, 14, 80ᵛ; 7 (1613–15), fo. 3; 11 (1622–33), ff. 27, 54, 94ᵛ, 96ᵛ, 115; AS/ABO 13 (1620–4), fo. 13ᵛ; 14 (1624–30), fo. 102ᵛ; Dean's Peculiar, Presentments 1606–8, no. 9. BL Add. MS 29776 (Pitt MSS), fo. 61.

[77] W. Symonds, 'Winterslow Church Reckonings 1542–1661', *WAM* xxxvi (1909–10), 29–33.

[78] DRO P 11, CW/1 (Corfe Churchwardens accounts, 1563–1633). After 1611 the accounts do not show whether or not church ales were held. I suspect that they were held in 1612 and 1620 when total receipts were over £10, but not in 1613–17 when they fell to around £3 or £4. In 1618 there was a special rate for some expensive repairs. Regular rating had been introduced by 1636: DRO P 11, CW/2 (Corfe accounts, 1633–1760).

[79] DRO P 213, CW/1–3 (Bere Regis Churchwardens accounts, 1607–24). WRO, Dean's Peculiar, Presentments 1620, no. 15.

IV Dorset regions and popular festivals, 1603–1640

broke up in chaos, while at Chilmark two years earlier a churchwarden
refused either to pass his accounts or to pay the new rate.[80] Local conflict
may explain other instances of apparently mystifying behaviour. At Cerne
Abbas the maypole survived the earlier Puritan attack, only to be cut down
to make a town ladder in 1635, just when maypoles were reappearing in
other places after the second Book of Sports.[81]

Other downland villages are less contradictory. In Wiltshire church
ales continued to receive the support of parish officials long after their
disappearance in the northern clothing region. Ales were held at Hatch,
near Tisbury, with the permission of the churchwardens, at least until
1616, and at Allington there was still a Whitsun ale in 1618, with much

---

[80] WRO AS/ABO 13 (Act Book, 1620–4), ff. 22[v], 169. Ingram, 'Ecclesiastical Justice in Wiltshire',
p. 217, notes the survival of traditional Hocktide binding customs at Chilmark (used by a local yeoman
as a pretext to seduce the wife of a poorer neighbour). Charlton Marshall, Dorset, is another parish
where the early adoption of a rate (1587) did not prevent continued Hocktide and May Day
celebrations receiving official parish support for years afterwards: DRO P 9, CW/1 (Charlton
Marshall Churchwardens accounts, 1583–1656), ff. 18, 20, 24[v].
[81] Wright, *Calendar Customs*, ii. 219. The parish already had a church rate by this time: DRO P 22,
CW/1 (Cerne Abbas Churchwardens accounts, 1628–85).

drinking and dancing.[82] At Mere, close to the western edge of the downs, elaborate Whitsun festivities presided over by a 'Cuckoo King', at which the 'Summer Lord' and his retinue from Gillingham were entertained with cakes and ale, were still continuing in 1621. Soon after that date, however, there was a general rating of the parish, and it may be no coincidence that payments to visiting preachers also start at about this time.[83] Dorset records are more fragmentary, but those that exist suggest a fairly late survival of church ales in downland parishes, along with the usual signs of growing conflict. In 1617 an ale at Puddletown was interrupted by shots fired into the church, and two years later the constables ejected a fiddler from the village over the opposition of some other residents. A Sunday ale with bull-baiting at Winterbourne Monkton in 1616 was denounced to the authorities by the minister, another at Litton Cheney in 1619 by the tithingman. But at Upwey, where the minister haunted alehouses, the parish élite was still behind the feasts; in 1618 both churchwardens were bound over to the assizes 'for keeping of a public ale'.[84]

The later survival of church ales is only one among many signs of the downlands' conservatism. Throughout the whole area a strong sense of neighbourliness and sociability linked the 'people of credit' with their inferiors. Revel feasts continued to flourish, with or without the sanction of parish officers, surfacing in the 1620s at Lavington, Longbridge Deverill, and Crockerton in Wiltshire and at Hanley in Dorset. From the same decade there is evidence of less organized dancing at Manningford Abbas, Barford St. Martin, Enford, and other downland villages.[85] Sunday games like bowls, throwing the hammer (popular at harvest time), and quoits were also widely enjoyed in the chalk region, as well as more brutal sports such as cock-shying, which continued at Winterslow right down to the civil war.[86]

Such incidents are sufficiently common to suggest that many of the middling sort of the chalk country shared with their poorer neighbours an older, more permissive concept of order. 'What had any justice to do with

[82] WRO AS/ABO 11 (Act Book, 1612–16), fo. 196; B/ABO 8 (1615–18), ff. 14ᵛ, 115ᵛ–116. Ingram, 'Ecclesiastical Justice in Wiltshire', p. 89.
[83] T. H. Baker, 'Notes on the History of Mere', *WAM* xxix (1896–7), 269–73. 'The Churchwardens' Accounts of Mere', ed. T. H. Baker, *WAM* xxxv (1907–8), 266–76. C. F. H. Johnston, 'Cuckowe-King', *Folk-Lore*, xviii (1907), 340–1. Whitlock, *Folklore of Wilts.*, p. 40. Mere had occasional ratings before 1621.
[84] *Ashley's Case Book*, pp. 23–4, 31, 51, 59, 61.
[85] WRO, QS Rolls, Michaelmas 1620, no. 212; B/ABO 6 (Act Book, 1606–13), fo. 54; AW/ABO 5 (Act Book, 1616–22), fo. 63ᵛ; AS/ABO 14 (1624–30), ff. 74ᵛ, 95ᵛ, 96ᵛ, 141; Bishop's Deposition Book 42 (1627–8), fo. 123ᵛ. See also Ingram, 'Ecclesiastical Justice in Wiltshire', pp. 174–6.
[86] For cock-shying see Symonds, 'Winterslow Church Reckonings', pp. 42–3. For examples of other sports: WRO AS/ABO 11 (Act Book, 1612–16), fo. 190ᵛ; 12 (1616–20), fo. 73; 13 (1620–4), ff. 118, 121ᵛ–122; 14 (1624–30), ff. 99ᵛ, 111; D/AB 28 (Act Book, 1622–7), fo. 179ᵛ.

his drinking?' a Milborne St. Andrew blacksmith demanded—a natural question in a village where, as we have seen, the parson and the tithing-man held similar attitudes.[87] Downland clergy and churchwardens often lent their support to Sunday football, or as at Kingston Deverill in 1632, refused to prosecute the players. Court records disclose many other instances of middling-sort tolerance for traditional amusements: a tithingman at Fisherton Anger who regularly plays bowls on the sabbath; a Shrewton churchwarden who allows his son to play trap-ball during service time; a Ludgershall churchwarden who is found among a group of midsummer revellers on a Sunday in 1616.[88] Perhaps the most striking case came to light at Newton Toney in 1621. The churchwardens had permitted cock-fighting in the chancel of the parish church, and urged a participant to get his bird away before it was discovered. They were also accused of allowing the bells to be rung at unseemly hours, and one of them had missed Sunday service to attend a football match.[89]

Other downland parishes were also strongholds of the older culture, Wylye and the adjoining parish of Steeple Langford among them. Dr Ingram has constructed a persuasive account of events in the former village. After a permissive period under a minister who did not object to games and dancing, in 1619 a new rector, John Lee, took over, put in his son as curate, and immediately began a programme of reform. The Lees were supported by some of the better-off villagers, including a rising yeoman named Thomas Potticary, but their opponents, led by a less successful yeoman, Thomas Kent, were more numerous. Kent was churchwarden in 1622, yet he was lax in church attendance, grumbled about the curate's long sermons, and disliked the new policy of regular communion services. His daughter, Susan Kent, found the preaching especially tiresome: 'such a deal of bibble-babble that I am weary to hear it'—and preferred to sleep through it.[90] Before the Lees' arrival the villagers' strong sense of neighbourly identity had been reinforced by frequent feastings and merry-makings. These were quickly resumed when Kent became churchwarden, with minstrels brought in to lead the dancing on Sunday afternoons at the 'common meeting place under the elm . . . near the church'.[91] When Kent's year of office was over, however, his daughter, like other youthful revellers, had to look for amusement elsewhere. The disapproving Thomas Potticary met her one Sunday evening on the road to Steeple Langford, 'there being dancing at an ale

[87] *Ashley's Case Book*, pp. 33–4.

[88] WRO B/ABO 8 (Act Book, 1615–18), ff. 23, 30ᵛ; AS/ABO 11 (Act Book, 1612–16), ff. 224ᵛ, 229ᵛ; 13 (1620–4), ff. 42, 44ᵛ; 14 (1624–30), ff. 74ᵛ, 76; 15 (1636–40), fo. 9ᵛ.

[89] WRO B/ABO 10 (Act Book, 1620–2), fo. 47.

[90] Except where otherwise stated, this paragraph relies on Dr Ingram's account: 'Ecclesiastical Justice in Wiltshire', pp. 104–8.

[91] *Records of Wilts.*, p. 58.

there'; on another occasion she organized a dancing match at Little Battington and paid for the minstrels herself.[92] By 1623 the parish officers of Steeple Langford were more tolerant than their counterparts at Wylye had now become. But in the following year things got out of hand there too, when some Steeple Langford men were presented for having 'unstripped themselves and danced . . . stark naked', one of them being also charged with fornication.[93] Even the most traditional concept of order did not extend to excesses of this kind.

The most conclusive evidence for cultural survival in the downlands dates from the 1620s; the change in national policy under Laud makes evidence from the following decades less useful. Unless disorder occurred or the law was violated in some other way there is no reason why festive episodes from those years should be recorded at all. The presentments of two Norton Bavant men for dancing and playing fives before evensong, or of a Bower Chalke man for entertaining company on Sundays with drinking and dancing, show only that the law was being enforced: such recreations were permitted only *after* evening prayer. We know that there was a Whitsun ale at Tolpuddle in 1634, after the Book of Sports, but only because Henry Burton records the appropriate divine punishment of one of its promoters.[94] Two cases, however, are more significant, and show the continuing vitality of ancient rituals in the region. At Westbury in 1637 a scandalized minister reported that young people had been lured away from church on Midsummer Day to a noisy revel presided over by 'Thomas Stafford, Lord of our Summerhouse, and Edward Sartaine, termed Lord Prince of that company'.[95] Even more shocking were the festivities at Broad Chalke at midsummer 1640, when young people attended a dancing match at the mill, featuring a mock-bishop and a good deal of nocturnal horseplay after the candles were put out: 'Catherine Sanger of Knoyle was set upon her head and was bishoped'.[96] Events like this confirm that the downlands were still bastions of traditional culture.

*

So far we have discussed only the contrasts between the clothing districts and the chalk country. But the downlands were not the only parts of the

---

[92] In spite of (or because of) her reputation among 'respectable' parishioners, Susan Kent was quick to take action to defend her good name when a neighbour made improper advances: WRO AS/ABO 12 (Act Book, 1616–20), fo. 155.

[93] WRO AS/ABO 14 (Act Book, 1624–30), ff. 30v–31.

[94] WRO AS/ABO 15 (1636–40), ff. 6v, 180. Burton, *Divine Tragedie*, p. 20.

[95] WRO, Precentor's Peculiar, Presentments 1614–40, Westbury, 27 June 1637. Ingram, 'Ecclesiastical Justice in Wiltshire', p. 89. Bull-baiting was also resumed at Warminster during this period: Whiteman, 'Church of England 1542–1837', p. 38.

[96] *Records of Wilts.*, pp. 131–2.

western counties where reformers encountered stubborn defence of old customs. There were pockets of resistance in other arable regions—the Cotswold fringe, for example—but also in pasture areas like south Somerset and Blackmore Vale where Puritanism had made fewer inroads than it had in the clothing parishes. Let us take these two regions in turn, beginning with the northern one.

In the arable regions of north-west Wiltshire along the slopes of the Cotswolds and in the flat pastureland of the north-east of the county, older festive customs certainly held on longer than in the clothing parishes. Even some of the smaller clothing towns held revel feasts well into the seventeenth century.[97] But the further the village from the clothing region the more likely it is that traditions survived. There was still a church ale at Kemble in 1612, and in the pasture country further east, between Cricklade and Highworth, conflicts over ales were still simmering in 1620. At both Castle Eaton and Hannington the churchwardens were unable to pass their accounts in that year because the profits of church ales were in the hands of third parties.[98] The most striking sign of cultural survival in this area comes from Long Newnton, near Malmesbury. The village had a picturesque custom of 'carrying the garland' on Trinity Sunday, to commemorate the royal grant of a common in Saxon times; the day ended with a parish feast. This continued almost to the eve of the civil war, but in June 1641 it ended in disaster, when a gang of Malmesbury men arrived, led by one 'with a hobby-horse, and bells on his legs'. Encountering the Long Newnton men with the garland, one of these apparently innocent morris dancers bellowed, 'Win it and wear it, come three score of you, you are but boys to we', and there was a bloody affray in which several defenders were seriously injured. Violence of this sort, like football a ritualized expression of communal rivalry, often occurred at revels: 'tis no festival unless there be some fightings' ran the popular saying. Like the garland ritual it was all very traditional, and reinforces the impression of cultural conservatism already suggested by this area.[99]

A similar conservatism is evident in the sparsely settled pasture country of west Somerset, and even more obviously in the wood-pasture region around Yeovil in the south of the county that extended into Blackmore Vale across the Dorset border. As in the downlands, there were still strong habits of co-operation and neighbourliness in these areas. They are

[97] The 'revel day' was still observed at Castle Combe in 1617, for example: WRO, QS Rolls, Michaelmas 1617, nos. 141–2.

[98] GRO GDR 114 (Depositions, 1611–13), *Creed* v. *Cowles*, 15 Jan. 1612/13. WRO AW/ABO 5 (Act Book, 1616–22), ff. 80ᵛ, 91ᵛ, 97.

[99] Aubrey, 'Remaines', pp. 192–4. *Records of Wilts.*, p. 141. BL TT, E. 1035 (7): Thomas Hall, *Funebria Florae, The Downfall of May-Games*, 1660, p. 10. Aubrey notes that around 1660 'one was killed, striving to take away the garland' at Long Newnton.

reflected in the words of an Exmoor husbandman recalling a summer Sunday evening 'after shear time' when he was 'in a green adjoining to the churchyard of Cutcombe . . . with others of his neighbours at bowls'.[100] The same spirit is even more apparent in Blackmore Vale, a region which had been less disrupted, it will be recalled, by agricultural change and social polarization than other pasture regions had been. Some Blackmore parishes had been affected by recent enclosure, but in others Rogation-tide processions continued to reflect the inhabitants' feeling of solidarity.[101] Both the Vale and the adjacent parts of Somerset were highly traditional in culture.

The region had not, of course, been exempt from the attentions of moral reformers. In 1596 the pious aristocrat, Francis Hastings, left bequests to North and South Cadbury, Halton, and Maperton, all south-east Somerset parishes, on condition that they held no more church ales. By the beginning of James I's reign ales had been replaced by rates in several Blackmore parishes, including Motcombe and Halstock.[102] A succession of Puritan preachers made Crewkerne a stronghold of godly order in the years after 1580, though the church retained its singing-men and organ, and the communion table was railed in without demur in 1635. Even at Sherborne, a more consistently conservative place, a Puritan minister exerted considerable influence during the same period.[103]

Yet in many places in the region both the local élites and their inferiors stoutly resisted many aspects of godly reformation. According to Sir Edward Parham, the Milborne Port church ale which he patronized in 1603 was supported by many 'substantial householders of honesty and good credit'. There were suspicions that Parham's enemies were en-couraged by the Puritan JP Maurice Gilbert, but those enemies were scarcely impressive moral reformers. Robert Smyth, a Sutton Montis yeoman subsequently alleged to have been murdered by clients of the Parhams, disturbed the patrons of a Sherborne inn when he arrived with fiddlers and started to dance, while his brother came to Sherborne to buy provisions for the 'feast Sunday' at Weston Bampfylde. In 1607 Robert Smyth was drunk 'three days together' at a church ale at Charlton Horethorne, an unfriendly witness declared; he was heard to 'whoop and hallooe', perhaps inspired by 'certain powder used there to provoke drunkenness'.[104]

---

[100] SRO D/D/Cd 76 (Depositions, 1633–4), *Hallett* v. *Edwards*, 26 Nov. 1633. For survival of ales and revels in west Somerset see Stieg, *Laud's Laboratory*, p. 225 (Old Cleeve, 1610), and below, n. 112.
[101] WRO, Dean's Peculiar, Presentments 1625, no. 73; 1635, no. 93.
[102] *The Letters of Sir Francis Hastings 1574–1609*, ed. Claire Cross, SRS lxix, 1969, pp. 117–18. DRO P 241, CW/3 (Motcombe Churchwardens accounts, 1604–1713). WRO, Dean's Peculiar, Presentments 1609, no. 37.
[103] *VCH, Somerset*, iv. 31.
[104] PRO STAC 8/266/6–7 (*Smyth* v. *Bishop*, 1608); STAC 8/291/12 (*Walton* v. *Parham*, 1606).

These villages are close to an area which received much attention from the justices in 1607, a year when the prohibitions against ales and revels were being widely ignored.[105] Investigation of an itinerant bull-keeper uncovered a revel at Adber near Yeovil, church ales at Ilton and Sherborne, and wakes at Sturminster Newton, Ilchester, and Stoke St. Gregory. But the most elaborate festivities were at Yeovil. The town had a rich festive heritage, its Robin Hood plays being performed as late as 1577; how complete the subsequent interruption had been is not clear. In 1607 the festivities were revived with the full support of the parish officers. There was dancing and drinking around the church house into the small hours, a boisterous procession headed by drummers and a lord of misrule went around gathering contributions, and the churchwardens allowed themselves to be carried on a cowlstaff amid great hilarity. Sober townsmen who protested were told that next year the pageant would be even more elborate, with 'a priest maid and a Maid Marion' and double the amount of ale.[106]

All this provoked yet another order by the Somerset JPs, repeating the prohibitions and ordering every parish to adopt a rating system. This may have had some temporary effect—ales were abandoned at Tintinhull in 1609—but the need for a further order in 1612 shows that compliance had not been universal.[107] There was a church ale at West Buckland in 1611, and three years later the parish clerk of Yeovilton was in trouble for holding an Easter ale.[108] Festivals continued in south-east Somerset in defiance of the authorities. At Pitcombe, near Bruton, in 1615 the churchwardens paid the minstrels to play for dancing in the churchyard; their successors presented them for it, but this was an issue that was already settled in less traditional areas. At Merriott, the 'play day' was celebrated in 1618; two years later there was a church ale with bull- and bear-baiting, and a churchwarden was accused of using the communion cup to serve alehouse beer. It is not clear exactly when church ales went out at Kingsdon, but it was probably in 1623, when the parish's brewing utensils were sold and the church house sublet.[109]

The evidence, as always, is fragmentary, but enough remains to show that south-east Somerset and Blackmore Vale was a distinctly conservative region. JPs and local reformers strove to impose moral discipline with only partial success. The respectable inhabitants of Trent, near the

[105] The most spectacular example is the elaborate pageant at Wells, already discussed.
[106] *SQSR* i. 5–6 (with some further details from SRO, QS Rolls 1607, no. 64). *SDNQ* xxviii (1961–7), 37. Barnes 'County Politics', p. 107n. Quaife, *Wanton Wenches*, p. 86.
[107] *SQSR* i. 7, 75. *VCH, Somerset*, iii. 264.
[108] PRO STAC 8/141/1 (*Fraunceis* v. *Ley*, 1612). *SQSR* i, intro., p. xlvii. There was a clerk-ale at Netherbury, Dorset, in 1609, with 'bull-baiting and other unlawful sports': WRO, Dean's Peculiar, Presentments 1609, no. 31.
[109] SRO D/D/Ca 191 (Comperta, 1615), Pitcombe, 6 Oct. *VCH Somerset*, iii. 119; iv. 60 and n.

Somerset–Dorset border, had to petition the justices against Abraham Brokes, 'a very dissolute and idle person', who in 1622 kept an unlicensed alehouse and promoted bull- and bear-baitings.[110] As in the downlands, parish officers were often ambivalent. An Oborne churchwarden could not resist an invitation to play bowls on the sabbath—but he presented himself to the ecclesiastical court for doing so. At East Coker the schoolmaster allowed his pupils to hold the traditional Easter cock-fighting; the village constable, a yeoman, was a spectator in 1615 and confessed that such sports had been permitted on other occasions. In the same parish a church ale was held as late as 1627.[111] Many of the ales and revels recorded in this area in the 1630s—at Montacute and Beer Crocombe, for instance—were probably revivals made possible by the lifting of the prohibitions in 1633. But at Cannington in west Somerset ales were held even before the orders were rescinded: the minister was rescued by a posse of villagers when he was summoned for permitting one. And at Langford Budville in the Vale of Taunton the revel feast was still officially sanctioned and the brewing vessels retained in the parish inventories, right down to the civil war.[112] Apart from Puritan towns such as Taunton and Wellington, both west and south-east Somerset resisted the campaign for moral reformation. Middling sort and lower orders alike still participated in the public rituals of a common culture.

*

Before we leave the subject of regional cultural contrasts, one other striking manifestation of them deserves our attention. We have already noted widespread fears of a breakdown of familial order in the early seventeenth century. These fears were particularly rife in wood-pasture areas. They may have been the product of a general sense of disorder caused by poverty and over-population. They may perhaps be related to the fact that in these places women often made greater contributions to household income (from spinning and the marketing of dairy products) than was normally possible for the wives of open-field arable farmers, and have been more assertive in consequence. They may also reflect anxieties about Puritan teaching on marriage. In the long run mainstream Puritanism did as much to reinforce as to weaken patriarchal authority. Still, the preachers always stressed the partnership aspect of marriage,

---

[110] *SQSR* i, intro., pp. l–li.

[111] WRO, Dean's Peculiar, Presentments 1620, no. 28. PRO STAC 8/49/6 (*Buckland* v. *Wood*, 1615). Barnes, 'County Politics', p. 108n.

[112] Barnes, 'County Politics', p. 120n. Prynne, *Canterburies Doome*, p. 378. *Western Circuit Assize Orders 1629–1648*, ed. J. S. Cockburn, Camden 4th Ser., xvii, 1976, p. 66. *Somerset Assize Orders 1629–1640*, ed. Thomas G. Barnes, SRS lxv, 1959, p. 22. M. B. McDermott, 'Church House at Langford Budville', *SDNQ* xxix (1968–73), 129–31. The later custom of 'clipping the tower' at Langford Budville suggests a strong sense of community identity: see Edward Jeboult, *Popular History of West Somerset*, 1893, p. 149.

and gave the wife a responsible role in the moral and spiritual ordering of the household. Among the more extreme separatists women often had considerable equality with men as church members.[113] Whether or not these are the reasons for it, an unmistakable feeling of unease about gender relations pervades the Puritan cheese and clothing region in the early seventeenth century. There were, however, many ritualized methods of dealing with unruly women. One form of these rituals, the 'skimmington', was a very distinctive part of the traditions of the Somerset and Wiltshire pasture country. It provides some further insights into the culture, as well as the social complexities, of that area.

All over Europe festive processions—charivari—had for centuries been employed to shame people who violated their communities' social or sexual standards. They were often an officially sanctioned component of legal punishments. A procession making discordant 'rough music' might accompany the 'carting' or 'riding' of a whore, the placarding or ducking of a scold. At Devizes in Elizabeth's reign couples convicted of fornication were 'led about the towns with basins', and this was a familiar practice in many places.[114] Such rituals were especially common in towns for punishing scolds. Scolding was originally primarily an urban problem: in medieval times there are few signs of rural anxiety about it. When concern began to intensify during Elizabeth's reign it was the towns which were most likely to invest in cucking-stools. By the early decades of the next century many west-country towns—Bridport, Dorchester, Lyme Regis, and Weymouth among them—were employing them.[115] They were also somewhat more common in wood-pasture than in arable villages, no doubt because the latter possessed better mechanisms for informal mediation. The difficulties the failure of such mechanisms could create in a place like Nettleton will be remembered. After 1614 the new cucking-stool there quickly fell into disuse, and when one of the scolds offended again in 1621 she had to be presented in the ecclesiastical court, since the manor court was unable to deal with her.[116]

Cucking-stools and charivari were also commonly employed against sexual offenders—and defiance of sexual norms was of course another form of female rebelliousness. If the magistrates failed, or were not required to act, neighbours were always ready to uphold morality and patriarchy. The public display of horns to ridicule the cuckolded husband and shame his wife was especially popular. Horns were of course the universal symbol of cuckoldry. 'Take that for the key to your bed-chamber door', a Norwich man shouted as he threw a pair of ox horns into a shop in

[113] See my essay, 'The Taming of the Scold', for this and the following pages.
[114] *Annals of Devizes*, i. pt. i, 35; pt. ii, 3.
[115] The evidence is summarized in Underdown, 'Taming of the Scold'.
[116] WRO AW/ABO 5 (Act Book, 1616–22), fo. 106ᵛ.

1609. The mere mention of them was enough to start a lawsuit. 'Fulbrooke hath longer horns than my cow', a countryman leered in Abingdon market-place—and William Fulbrooke promptly took him to court when he heard about it.[117] Great ingenuity was used in their display. We find them made out of branches used to decorate the church and attached to the targets' pew; in another case they are tied to the necks of geese. At Berkley in north Somerset in 1611, William Swarfe's mare was led around the village amid 'great laughter and derision, with great clamours, shouts and outcries'; the mare was wearing horns and a paper attached to her tail summoned Swarfe to appear at a 'court of cuckolds'. Whatever the method, the shaming was invariably effective. Rams' horns hung on the churchyard gate during the wedding of a Charminster couple caused much derisive laughter, 'to the great grief and scandalizing of them and their credits'.[118]

Incidents like this were distinctly more common in urban or wood-pasture communities than in arable villages. Out of sixteen recorded incidents involving horn rituals in the three western counties during the period 1600–60, only four occurred in places of the latter type. Wood-pasture villagers were especially concerned about female challenges to patriarchal authority, and to resort to public shaming rituals. And their rituals, including those against domineering wives (about whom, again, they seem to have been more worried than arable villagers were), were more elaborate and involved the playing of more clearly defined theatrical roles than did the undifferentiated rough-music processions of other regions.[119]

The charivari against unfaithful or violent wives, like other riding forms, was a ritual deeply rooted in folk memory—an 'antique show', to quote a well-known description in Samuel Butler's *Hudibras*.[120] The central ingredient was a rough-music procession to the offenders' house, headed by a drummer and a man wearing horns. If infidelity was the offence, poles or other implements, sometimes draped with a chemise, and surmounted by a horse's head or skull with horns attached, were shaken in front of the windows while the rough music was performed.[121] If

[117] NRO DEP/35 (Consistory Court Deposition Book, 1608), fo. 31ᵛ (I am indebted to Susan Amussen for this reference). Bodleian MS Oxf. Archd. papers, Berks. c. 155 (Deposition Book, 1594–1600), ff. 171ᵛ–2.
[118] PRO STAC 8/92/10 (*Graye and Swarfe* v. *Hoskins*, 1611). WRO, Dean's Peculiar, Presentments 1609, no. 18.
[119] As in France, where urban charivari tended to be more elaborate and theatrical than ones in rural villages: Natalie Z. Davis, *Society and Culture in Early Modern France*, Stanford, 1975, pp. 100, 109–10, 116–17.
[120] Samuel Butler, *Hudibras*, ed. John Wilders, Oxford, 1967, pp. 143–4. Cf. also Marvell's 'Last Instructions to a Painter', in *Poems and Letters of Andrew Marvell*, ed. H. M. Margoliouth, 3rd edn., Oxford, 1971, i. 156–7.
[121] Underdown, 'Taming of the Scold', pp. 129–31.

female dominance, represented by the wife's beating of the husband, was the offence, surrogates for the offenders (preferably the next-door neighbours) acted out the proscribed behaviour; the 'husband' in the position of humiliation, riding backwards on horse or donkey and holding a distaff, the symbol of female subjection, while the 'wife' (usually a man in women's clothes) beat him with a ladle. There were numerous regional variants—the more primitive 'riding the stang' in the northern counties, for example—but nowhere were they as elaborate or as clearly directed against the 'woman on top' as in the western cheese country.[122]

Although the term 'skimmington' (and its variants, 'skimmity', for example) was later to spread over much of southern England and into the American colonies, in the early seventeenth century this form of the ritual was a localized one centred in Somerset and north Wiltshire. Both the word and the ritual come straight out of the cheese country, for the implement used in the beating is a skimming ladle—used by women in the making of butter and cheese.[123] Skimmingtons against domestic offenders are recorded at various places in the pasture country between 1600 and 1660. The best documented ones are at Quemerford, near Calne, in 1618, and at Marden in the Vale of Pewsey in 1626, but they also surface at several places in north Somerset, including Cameley, Ditcheat, and Leigh-on-Mendip. And from not far away comes the rather earlier plasterwork panel in the great hall at Montacute.[124] In all these cases there are indications that the ritual was an extremely familiar one, so it is likely that a good many similar episodes went unrecorded. Skimmingtons were also sometimes aimed at violators of other community standards besides gender and sexual ones: as we shall see in the next chapter, there were some famous west-country ones against people who enclosed commons and otherwise threatened customary rights. Altogether the inhabitants of the cheese country seem to have had unusually well-developed mechanisms for enforcing community values.

There are, of course, some awkward problems here. First of all, skimmingtons contained obvious festive elements. The one at Ditcheat took place during Whitsun week, and people were induced to come 'to make merry with Skimmington' by the promise of plentiful supplies of beer. At Cameley, it happened during the revel feast; it was just a bit of innocent fun, the participants told the JPs, 'without any hurt done or misdemeanors otherwise at all'.[125] Yet this was the area in which the

---

[122] For the various 'riding' rituals see C. R. B. Barrett, 'Riding Skimmington and Riding the Stang', *Journal of the British Archaeological Assn.*, New Ser. i (1895), 58–68; and E. P. Thompson, ' "Rough Music": Le Charivari anglais', *Annales E.S.C.* xxvii (1972), 285–312.

[123] George E. Dartnell and Edward H. Goddard, *Glossary of Words used in the County of Wiltshire*, 1893, pp. 145–6. Joseph Wright, *English Dialect Dictionary*, 1898–1905, v. 475.

[124] Underdown 'Taming of the Scold'.

[125] SRO CQ 3/1/25 (Sessions Rolls, 1616), no. 23; CQ 3/1/86 (2) (1653), fo. 154.

suppression of the older festive culture had been most complete. The objection is not insuperable. As Dr Ingram's analysis shows, participants in skimmingtons tended to be drawn from the lower rungs of village society, with a fair sprinkling of people who had been in trouble with the law for other reasons. Although there is some occasional, not very convincing, evidence of encouragement by members of the élite, most people of higher rank—especially Puritans—disliked them for the same reasons that they disliked other disorderly features of the old culture. As we have already seen, there always remained a sort of under-class in these regions, hostile and resistant to Puritan reformation, and it was from this social level that skimmington performers were mainly drawn.[126] In these unstable wood-pasture villages, economic change and geographical mobility had weakened the ability of neighbours and kinsfolk to maintain order in the old informal ways. Different social groups had correspondingly different responses: Puritanism for the middling sort, skimmingtons for the lower orders. But though the responses were different, they were provoked by the same problem.

It might also be thought paradoxical that these highly developed collective rituals existed in the supposed individualistic cheese country rather than in the more co-operative, socially integrated arable parishes. But as the popularity of stoolball also shows, if the wood-pasture village was more dispersed and individualistic, it was still a community. Its inhabitants shared many elements of the common stock of culture, many assumptions about appropriate social and familial behaviour. The wood-pasture village enforced its social norms in its own way, by rituals which expressed the greater sense of individual identity which many even of the poorer residents were likely to possess. And lacking the resources of informal mediation available in arable villages through squire, parson, and more closely-bonded neighbours, they often had occasion to act in this way. Like stoolball, the skimmington is an appropriate expression of the culture of the cheese country.

*

John Aubrey was right: there were indeed important differences between the cultures of the wood-pasture regions and the arable downlands. In the former, popular festivals were outlawed and a new kind of moral discipline imposed with at least partial success. In the latter, traditional festivals and other plebeian amusements survived longer, and continued to reflect an older notion of community. We have, to be sure, qualified Aubrey's simple 'chalk and cheese' antithesis. Some other pasture

---

[126] Martin Ingram, 'Le charivari dans l'Angleterre du XVIe et du XVIIe siècle', in *Le Charivari*, ed. Jacques le Goff and Jean-Claud Schmitt, Paris, 1981, pp. 251–64.

regions—south and west Somerset, Blackmore Vale, parts of north Wiltshire outside the clothing districts—were as culturally conservative as the
downlands. These regions had less nucleated residential patterns than
chalk country villages, but resembled them in being less socially polarized, less affected by the pressures of a market economy or by the influx of
landless poor, than the clothing parishes and towns.

We have, of course, oversimplified the cultural history of the three
counties in the seventeenth century. The geographical boundaries
between regions were not as sharp as for analytical purposes, we have had
to depict them. Parishes like Mere, Warminster, and Westbury straddled
both downland and pasture zones; their urban cores (all were important
market towns) had much in common with the nucleated villages of the
sheep-corn region, while parts of their rural surrounds contained the
dispersed settlements found in the wood-pasture country. Many Blackmore Vale parishes, it will be recalled, also contained elements of both
settlement types: nucleated cores with the remains of common fields,
surrounded by outlying farms and hamlets carved out of the woodland
long after the original settlements were established.[127] If culture is related
to social structure, economic development and settlement pattern, we
should not be surprised to find corresponding complexities in the cultural
landscape. Some local contrasts were no doubt the result of élite
influence: hence the early disappearance of church ales at North and
South Cadbury, while in East Coker and Merriott, not many miles the
other side of Yeovil, they survived for decades longer. Batcombe and
Ditcheat, both reformed parishes thanks to a succession of preaching
ministers, were at the southern extremity of the Puritan region, within
walking distance of more conservative places like Bruton, Pitcombe, and
Castle Cary.

But if we look beyond these local variations, the overall patterns of
regional contrast are clear enough. The cultures of the major regions
were diverging, as their social structures were diverging, during the
half-century before the civil war. In the clothing parishes of the Wiltshire
cheese country and in Somerset north and east of the Mendips, the ethos
of Puritanism was coming to be shared not only by the substantial middling sort, but by many of the smaller property-owners and better-off
craftsmen as well. They never succeeded in eliminating completely the
disorderly recreations still popular among younger people and the poor,
but because of the breadth of Puritanism's appeal they were more
successful than their less numerous, more isolated counterparts in more
traditional areas. Even the undisciplined poorer folk of the cheese
country, their rituals suggest, shared some elements of the more individualistic outlook of their superiors, though they also retained highly

[127] Taylor, *The Making of the English Landscape: Dorset*, pp. 95–7, 120.

conservative notions of how society and the family ought to be ordered. In south Somerset, Blackmore Vale, the Wiltshire and Dorset downlands, a less polarized, more cohesive, somewhat more deferential form of society survived. So, inevitably, did older conceptions of good neighbourhood and community, and the festive customs in which they were articulated. These cultural contrasts are essential to an understanding of popular politics, a subject to which we now turn.

5

Popular Politics before the Civil War

ON a Sunday in April 1632, there was a riot outside the church at Newland in the Forest of Dean, when two forest officers were attacked by a hostile crowd. The officers were much hated figures in the neighbourhood, having recently arrested a certain John Williams, a miner who under the nickname 'Skimmington' had led a series of popular risings in the area. At least one of the assailants was armed with a stoolball staff.[1] By itself the incident is a trivial one. But the conjuncture of a riot, a forest community, 'Skimmington', and stoolball neatly encapsulates a whole complex of social and political forces, and provides a vividly symbolic illustration of how some of the cultural attitudes described in the preceding chapter were translated into politics.

Before we proceed further, though, we might pause to ask what 'politics' actually meant for the English common people in the early seventeenth century. Politics involves those matters pertaining to the *polis*, the community. There was a politics of the kingdom, a politics of the shire, a politics of the town or village, all in various ways related to each other. People were engaged with these several levels of politics in different ways according to their place in society. The marginal landholders, cottagers, and labourers were involved primarily in the third kind, and then only as subjects or victims of policies devised and implemented by others, except on the rare occasions when they combined in riotous protests serious enough to require the attention of the county governors, or even of King and Council. The better-off 'persons of credit', on the other hand, participated actively in village politics at parish meeting or at manor court, and were at least intermittently involved in the remoter politics of shire or kingdom as taxpayers, jurymen, and (occasionally) voters. They were also more likely to be literate and to have formed opinions on matters of national concern, especially during times of crisis.

Popular politics thus encompassed a wide range of attitudes and types of behaviour. Yet people of all social levels shared similar ideas about how their families and communities ought to be ordered: with due respect for legitimate authority, but also with the expectation of appropriate behaviour by their governors, which in turn meant due respect for law, natural justice, and customary rights. These ideas formed the basis for their

[1] *CSPD, 1631–3*, p. 312.

political attitudes, whether towards the matters that most immediately affected them—town governance, common rights, food supplies—or the more distant affairs of the kingdom. At the lowest level the most universal outlook was a conservative localism: a stubborn reliance on ancient custom, and a tendency to view national issues through the prism of town or village life. This did not mean blind submission to authority, for when authority fell short of the expected standard of good rule resistance was easily provoked. There were, then, some common values. They were expressed, however, in different ways in different regions. Political behaviour is an expression of culture, and like culture it often took distinctively regional forms.

*

The circumstances most likely to provoke popular political action, and in which the behaviour of different regions can best be compared, were ones involving an immediate threat to subsistence, such as the encroachment on common rights by enclosing landlords, or the failure of magistrates to enforce protective market regulations. In all kinds of community the first resort when customary rights were threatened was legal action: a petition to the justices, or a lawsuit with costs financed out of a common fund. If this failed there might be a gradual escalation of violence—verbal or written warnings, sporadic damage to property. We have encountered a case of this at Puddletown, where a landowning squire was the target, but village oligarchies might provoke similar threats. When a resentful inhabitant of Ramsbury, Wiltshire, was being escorted to the House of Correction he burst out 'that he hoped to see Ramsbury so in fire upon some of the best of the parish there'. If enough people were convinced that there was no justice in the courts, a chain of small-scale, isolated incidents might become sufficiently serious to merit the name of riot.[2]

Enclosure riots occurred occasionally in all types of regions. But there are some striking differences between those of the arable and those of the wood-pasture areas, which reflect some of the underlying cultural contrasts considered in the previous chapter. The political distinctiveness of the wood-pasture districts is clearly evident in the disorders which began in the western counties in 1626. The riots were provoked by the crown's sale of royal forests to courtiers and entrepreneurs who hoped to profit by enclosing and 'improving' hitherto under-utilized forest land. Although these were not, as sometimes pictured, totally arbitrary enclosures— agreement was reached with neighbouring manorial lords, and propertied farmers were compensated with leases from the new proprietors—the landless artisans and cottagers who swarmed in these woodland areas lost

---

[2] *Records of Wilts.*, pp. 115–16. For the escalation of protest see, for example, Fletcher, *Tudor Rebellions*, p. 69.

their rights of common almost completely.[3] The result was a serious breakdown of law and order. Gillingham Forest erupted in 1626, and sporadic rioting there reached a climax two years later when the sheriff of Dorset had to retreat after finding the rioters too numerous and well armed to be dispersed.[4] There were less violent disorders in Neroche Forest, in south-west Somerset, in 1629, and in the spring of 1631 more serious ones in the Forest of Dean, soon followed by others in the Wiltshire forests of Braydon, Chippenham, and Melksham and by at least one outbreak in Selwood. The arrest of John Williams did not end the troubles in Dean. Enclosures were still being thrown down in July 1633, and after an interlude of uneasy peace there was more violence by coal-miners in 1637.[5]

In all these riots villagers of middle and lower rank were combining to protest violations of their traditional rights by outsiders. The 'class' nature of the forest risings should not be exaggerated.[6] The targets were not local gentlemen and farmers, but the clique of courtiers and Londoners intent on disrupting the forest community in the name of improvement and private profit. They included the notorious monopolist Sir Giles Mompesson, Scots such as Sir James Fullerton and his stepson Lord Bruce, financiers such as Sir Sackville Crowe, and members of the unpopular Buckingham clan such as the Earl of Anglesey and Sir Edward Villiers. Most of the violence was directed against the property and agents of these outsiders. Apart from the labourers caught up in it, the only local people to suffer were collaborators like the servant of Sir John Hunger-ford who turned informer and had his house burned down in retaliation. The commoners' enemies were not the local gentry.[7]

Many of the rioters were, to be sure, people of little wealth or status. Gentlemen and yeomen had access to the courts if they were dissatisfied with their compensation, and were naturally reluctant to combine in riot with the disorderly poor, about whose 'lewd lives and conversations' they had been complaining for years. One respectable Dean householder kept his doors locked to prevent his servants joining the rioters. Yet even propertied farmers suffered from the enclosures. They received secure

---

[3] The most complete account of the western riots is by Buchanan Sharp, *In Contempt of All Authority: Rural Artisans and Riot in the West of England, 1586–1660*, Berkeley and Los Angeles, 1980. For the point discussed here see esp. pp. 134–55.

[4] The ringleaders were subsequently punished in Star Chamber and a precarious order restored: Sharp, *In Contempt*, pp. 86–9, 98.

[5] Sharp, *In Contempt*, pp. 87–96, 121, 208–18. See also E. Kerridge, 'The Revolts in Wiltshire against Charles I', *WAM* lvii (1958–60), 67–9; Barnes, *Somerset*, pp. 157–8; Bettey, 'Revolts', pp. 21–4; and Willcox, *Gloucestershire*, pp. 194–202. For earlier disorders in Dean see Sharp, pp. 191–2; and Willcox, pp. 193–4, 280.

[6] For reasons that will become clear, I do not accept Sharp's argument (*In Contempt*, esp. ch. 5) that only the poorest foresters were involved in the riots.

[7] Sharp, *In Contempt*, pp. 84–96, 101–2, 207. Barnes, *Somerset*, p. 157.

title to their now enclosed lands, but they also lost common grazing rights and were likely to be paying heavier poor rates to support their dispossessed neighbours.[8] They were unlikely to shed many tears over losses suffered by the outsiders who were the chief beneficiaries of disafforestation. Some felt strongly enough, or were under sufficient local pressure, to join the rioters. Of the seventy-four people convicted in the Gillingham outbreaks twenty-one were yeomen or husbandmen, an impressive number in proportion to the social composition of a forest community. In Braydon the proportion was even higher: eighteen out of thirty-four rioters whose occupations are known were propertied farmers, and one of the others was a gentleman.[9] Reports that the rioters had even more powerful support may have been exaggerated, but were not totally unfounded. Resistance in Neroche was openly encouraged by Lord Poulett, outraged by the impending loss of his hunting rights; a gathering of protesting countrymen at Ashill was organized by his ranger, and the men who passed the word around the villages included a constable, a bailiff, and other substantial men.[10]

The ambivalence of propertied opinion is clearly shown by the half-hearted measures taken by the local authorities to restore order. Repeated Council instructions to JPs and deputy-lieutenants to 'take better care for the peace of the country' produced only foot-dragging and excuses. The militia and the *posse comitatus*, composed of local men reluctant to fire on their poorer neighbours, were clearly unreliable. The sheriff of Dorset raised the *posse* against the Gillingham rebels but did not dare to attack, and efforts by the sheriffs of Wiltshire and Gloucestershire in Braydon and Dean were comically ineffective. Commands to mobilize the militia were generally ignored, and on the one occasion when the trained bands did turn out, their house-to-house search in a part of Dean Forest known to be swarming with rebels was a fiasco.[11] Attempts to use professional troops had similar results. Soldiers billeted at Shaftesbury mutinied and assisted the Gillingham men, while gunners brought from Bristol to bombard Cley Hill Farm in Selwood refused to open fire because they feared being indicted for murder—and tried by a local jury.[12] The long arm of Star Chamber was more effective, but the one resort to local judicial action—a commission of oyer and terminer in Dean—again revealed the state of public feeling. Numerous indictments were

[8] Willcox, *Gloucestershire*, pp. 156–7, 196. Kerridge, 'Agriculture c.1500–c.1793', p. 49.

[9] Sharp, *In Contempt*, pp. 128–9.

[10] PRO SP 16/131 (State Papers, Charles I), no. 16. See also Kerridge, 'Revolts', pp. 68–9; Barnes, *Somerset*, p. 158; Bettey, 'Revolts', p. 22; Sharp, *In Contempt*, pp. 110–11; and D. G. C. Allan, 'The Rising in the West, 1628–1631', *Ec. H.R.* 2nd Ser. v (1952–3), 80.

[11] Sharp, *In Contempt*, pp. 89–125, provides a rather different interpretation of all this.

[12] Sharp, *In Contempt*, pp. 88, 120–3. Allan, 'Rising in the West', p. 78. Bettey, 'Revolts', p. 23. Davies, *Life in an English Village*, p. 20. Kerridge, 'Revolts', p. 67.

obtained, but hardly any of the accused were rounded up to stand trial.[13] The attitude of the local justices emerges well from the Gloucestershire JPs' report on the affray at Newland. They agreed that popular resentment against Skimmington's captors was behind the riot, but excused it as unpremeditated and as a response to the two forest officers' provocations.[14] The western gentry regretted violence and riot, but they were distinctly unhappy about having to do the Council's dirty work.

Although the Skimmington rioters were for the most part cottagers and poor artisans, they were inspired more by localism than by class antagonism. 'Here were we born and here we will die', the Gillingham men declared when the sheriff came against them. There were long traditions behind the foresters' forcible defence of common rights: in Dean the name 'Robin Hoods' had been applied to participants in a 1612 outbreak. But the Dean men had a strong sense of legitimacy, and when they burned timber that the Earl of Pembroke had unjustly cut, they did so to shouts of 'God Save the King!'[15]

This combination of conservatism and rebelliousness is perhaps easier to understand if we consider the riots' 'skimmington' associations. The word served in north Wiltshire as a symbol for other kinds of threats to the well-being of a community besides those presented by assertive women. In 1625, when the men of Wilton invaded the neighbouring parish of Burbage 'with a jest to bring skimmington there', it was invoked as a pretext for a festive inter-village brawl, analogous to a football match.[16] A skimmington in this sense was something undesirable brought into the village by outsiders, and which, like an unruly woman, must be dealt with by communal action. The application of the term to the riots is logical enough. The disafforesting courtiers' antisocial behaviour is inspired by the spirit of 'skimmington', and is resisted by appropriately ritualized actions. At Mailescott in Dean in March 1631 the 'burying of Skimmington' was proclaimed. A procession of rioters broke down hedges and filled in ore pits sunk by the hated Mompesson, whose effigy was then ceremonially buried in one of the pits. The agent of another projector was warned that the rioters would return on May Day 'to do him the like service'.[17]

But 'skimmington' has other meanings. It also denoted a ritual action against the chosen target: to 'ride skimmington' was to take part in a demonstration against the skimmington in the pejorative sense. And the riots were headed by leaders who adopted the name: 'Skimmington' in the

---

[13] Sharp, *In Contempt*, pp. 114–15.

[14] *CSPD*, 1631–3, p. 312. A local jury refused to convict the assailants: Sharp, *In Contempt*, p. 102.

[15] Willcox, *Gloucestershire*, pp. 193–4, 279–80. Sharp, *In Contempt*, p. 191.

[16] WRO, Dean's Peculiar, Presentments 1625, no. 19; D/AB 28 (Act Book, 1622–7), ff. 180–1. See also Ingram, 'Le charivari', p. 255.

[17] Sharp, *In Contempt*, pp. 95–6, 129.

case of Williams, 'Lady Skimmington' in the case of the trio of leaders in Braydon. Skimmington briefly becomes a folk hero, similar to Robin Hood or to 'Captain Cobbler' and 'Captain Pouch' in earlier peasant uprisings, regarded as able to redress all sorts of popular grievances.[18] These then were skimmingtons (demonstrations) led by Skimmington (Williams and his counterparts) against Skimmington (Mompesson and company). We here encounter a rich complex of associations. A skimmington is something undesirable: the leaders defiantly assume the name, as if to restore the subverted moral order by inverting it yet again. In Braydon, where Skimmington was also a lady, we recognize the further element, of gender inversion. The three Braydon leaders dressed themselves in women's clothes, and were eventually punished by having to stand in the pillory so attired.[19]

Rituals of inversion were common in other parts of England. The customary world has been turned upside-down by enclosers; the protesters symbolically turn it upside-down again (dressing as women, parodying the titles and offices of their social superiors) in order to turn it right-side-up. The prominence of women in enclosure and grain riots is well known and is one more sign of rejection of the submissive ideal. Female rioters were often joined by men disguised in women's clothes. The practice had protective purposes, but it also involved elements of ritual inversion, and appropriately ritualized punishments were sometimes inflicted.[20] But although inversion rituals were known in other parts of England, nowhere were they as prominent a feature of the local culture as in these western wood-pasture regions. The greater sense of individual identity expressed in the 'domestic' skimmington ritual, the tension between individual and community reflected in stoolball: both helped to mould the character of the Skimmington riots. That one of the Newland rioters carried a stoolball staff is thus almost poetically appropriate. Many other features of the riots—the assaults on Council messengers, the burning of warrants, the rescue of prisoners, the reprisals against collaborators, the sheltering of suspects, the silent as well as the open resistance—further illuminate the culture of a region in which individuals could unite over wide areas when their rights were challenged. There was less collusion between the three main centres than has sometimes been

[18] As at Frampton-on-Severn: Sharp, *In Contempt*, pp. 105–6. For Capt. Cobbler see Fletcher, *Tudor Rebellions*, pp. 21–2; for Capt. Pouch, Edwin F. Gay, 'The Midland Revolt and the Inquisitions of Depopulation of 1607', *TRHS* New Ser. xviii (1904), 217n.

[19] Sharp, *In Contempt*, pp. 100, 104–5, 108, 129.

[20] After enclosure riots at Datchet, Bucks., in 1598 the women convicted were sentenced to the cucking-stool, the men to stand in the pillory in women's clothes: John Hawarde, *Les Reportes del Cases in Camera Stellata 1593 to 1609*, ed. W. P. Baildon, 1894, p. 104; and PRO STAC 5/K5/23, 5/K6/24 (*Kedermister v. Hales*, 1598). For women in riots see John Walter, 'Grain Riots and Popular Attitudes to the Law: Maldon and the Crisis of 1629', in *An Ungovernable People*, pp. 62–3.

supposed—the 'colonel' of the Gillingham group failed when he tried to get the Braydon rioters to join forces with him—but the foresters certainly knew what was happening in the other places, and had some sense of common purpose.[21]

The disorders had no explicit connection with other kinds of political or religious discontent. Still, in Braydon at least there were plenty of Puritans, and there is a possibly significant number of 'Puritan' first names in the list of rioters there. As for Dean, people at Newland were thought to have been stirred up by the curate, Peter Simon, who preached that 'setting the King's place and quality aside, we were all equal in respect of manhood unto him', though he denied any seditious intent. There is a hint of awareness of national politics in a Gillingham appeal to the Somerset JP Arthur Pyne, son of a man notorious for indiscreet speeches against the court, to intercede with the justices of assize on behalf of the victims of disafforestation. It seems unlikely that a JP from outside Dorset would have been approached for any other reason than his family's reputation of support for popular causes.[22]

The evidence for direct political associations is slender. Indirectly, however, the western riots had important political consequences. Disafforestation was one among several of Charles I's policies which upset the delicate balance between national and local institutions, between 'Court' and 'Country'. The west-country gentry and yeomen had no objection to improvement and enclosure, as long as they were the beneficiaries. When these things were done, however, for the profit of outsiders, and when in consequence they had to defend law and order against their aroused inferiors, it was a different matter. Disafforestation left the areas affected with a worse problem of poverty than ever, with a population less inclined to see the King as their benevolent protector or the court as anything but an oppressive, alien force, and with well-developed habits of collective action. When in 1642 the gentry and middling sort turned against the crown, they were to find willing support from the lower orders in these regions.

*

The forests were not the only sites of resistance to agricultural improvement. The eastern fens and their smaller Somerset counterparts offered similar opportunities for profit and provoked similar protests. Royal grants to entrepreneurial aristocrats and courtiers—the same sort of people as those behind the disafforestation projects—led to a series of

---

[21] Sharp disposes of earlier suggestions that Williams operated outside Dean: *In Contempt*, pp. 97–104.

[22] Kerridge, 'Revolts', p. 69. Sharp, *In Contempt*, pp. 110–11, 132–3. Barnes, *Somerset*, pp. 34, 70, 163, 262.

ambitious drainage schemes and aroused determined opposition by the poorer commoners. There were complicated lawsuits in which the inhabitants tried to protect their rights of common, but also intermittent rioting, which by 1637 had intensified and spread from Lincolnshire into other eastern counties. Events that year in Huntingdonshire show the familiar combination of popular action and connivance by members of the local élite. One of the fenlanders' gentry sympathizers was a hitherto obscure local squire named Oliver Cromwell.[23]

The Somerset drainage schemes were less successful and therefore provoked less violence. Like the foresters, the inhabitants of the Somerset levels could invoke long traditions of collective action to defend their rights.[24] As in the eastern fens, there had been earlier drainage projects, but it was only after Charles I's accession that serious efforts were made (under Exchequer commissions) to divide King's Sedgemoor between the King, the lords of adjoining manors, and tenants with rights of common. Some large landlords, such as the Earl of Pembroke and Sir John Stawell, would have received extensive tracts of drained and enclosed land. But the commissioners could not ignore the complaints of the lesser men of the affected parishes: the project would upset the intercommoning arrangements on which the villages around the moor depended. The King tried to drive a wedge between the propertied graziers and the poorer men with no written title: the former would be 'eased of such as pretend common there and have none'. But the farmers knew a swindle when they saw one, and the commissioners—influential men such as Sir John Horner and the formidable Sir Robert Phelips—dragged their feet and made the most of the legal problems they inevitably encountered.[25] Only the much smaller Aldermoor, near Glastonbury, was successfully drained. There was opposition there too—seditious mutterings by the commoners and a lawsuit by the Puritan William Strode. But the population affected in Aldermoor was too small to cause the county magnates serious alarm: they could do the King's business without much damage to their local reputations. In Sedgemoor they could not openly side with the commoners, but if they were to retain the trust of the freeholders and substantial men they would have to delay and obstruct, and they did so. The relations between gentry and middling sort were, as always, reciprocal.[26]

[23] H. C. Darby, *The Draining of the Fens*, 2nd edn., Cambridge, 1956, ch. 2. Thirsk, *Peasant Farming*, ch. 5. Holmes, *Lincolnshire*, pp. 124–30. Antonia Fraser, *Cromwell The Lord Protector*, 1973, pp. 52–5. Keith Lindley, *Fenland Riots and the English Revolution*, 1982, ch. 2.

[24] An earlier incident near Worle provides a good example: Harold Coward, 'The Wowwall: Some Aspects of Government and Land-Drainage early in the 15th Century', *Somerset Archaeology*, cxxiv (1980), 151–7.

[25] Barnes, *Somerset*, pp. 152–4. Williams, *Somerset Levels*, pp. 96–101.

[26] Williams, *Somerset Levels*, pp. 102–4. Barnes, *Somerset*, pp. 155–6. Underdown, *Somerset*, pp. 16–17.

Disafforestation and fen drainage are only the most spectacular examples of seventeenth-century agricultural improvement. Other kinds of enclosure also occasionally provoked disorder. Much enclosure in both arable and pasture regions was of course proceeding quietly and by agreement. There was some depopulating enclosure in both Dorset and Wiltshire—there are examples at Iwerne Courtney, in the Winterbourne valley, and at Hill Deverill, where the Ludlows enclosed the common fields and turned many of the tenants into day-labourers or paupers—but it was on a smaller scale than the forest schemes and produce far less upheaval.[27] Partial enclosure, for instance of demesne lands, leaving most of the common fields intact, was the more typical pattern. This might provoke litigation, as it did at Piddlehinton around 1618, for example, but it rarely led to riot.[28] Local society could accommodate itself to such changes, as long as they proceeded gradually. There were, to be sure, exceptional cases of downland villagers taking organized, quasi-political action. At Great Wishford in James I's reign a company of 'levellers' commanded by 'captains', wearing badges and red feathers, occupied a disputed meadow in a thoroughly ritualized way.[29] But most enclosure riots in the downlands were small-scale, confined to single villages, and lacked the political character of the 'Skimmington' outbreaks in the cheese country.

In other parts of arable England, however, enclosure sometimes provoked the same kind of class-conscious resistance that had been visible in 1549.[30] This is perhaps less paradoxical than it may appear. Much of the depopulating enclosure in the arable regions was undertaken by local squires, not by courtiers or outsiders. In the forest revolts the gentry sympathized with, or were at worst ambivalent towards the rioters; in the arable regions they were the enemy. Reports of violent language against the gentry in these outbreaks were certainly exaggerated by the authorities for propaganda purposes. But equally certainly, they were not invented. In Oxfordshire in 1596 there was talk of a plot 'to kill the gentlemen of that country and to take the spoil of them', buttressed by stories of earlier risings in Spain which had enabled the commons to 'live merrily there'. The folk memory was erratic, but it could also summon up better-based local traditions of a rising on Enslow Hill, where the peasants were 'hanged like dogs' after their surrender. Fifty years after it occurred, Kett's rebellion still lingered in the popular consciousness

[27] Bettey, 'Agriculture and Rural Society in Dorset', pp. 112–13. Kerridge, 'Agriculture c.1500–c.1793', p. 46.

[28] Bettey, 'Agriculture and Rural Society in Dorset', pp. 116–19.

[29] Kerridge, 'Revolts', pp. 65–6.

[30] Fletcher, *Tudor Rebellions*, pp. 61–3, 111. MacCulloch, 'Kett's Rebellion', pp. 41, 45–7, 55–7. Beer, *Rebellion and Riot*, pp. 68–73, 89–91, 108–12.

in Norfolk, awakening hopes of similar reprisals against the gentry.[31]

Complaints about depopulating landlords were common in the midland counties in the sixteenth century, and they continued after Elizabeth's death. When James I passed through Northamptonshire on his way to London in 1603 he was beset by great crowds complaining of recent enclosures by Sir John Spencer and other 'wolfish lords, that have eaten up poor husbandmen like sheep'. Four years later there was a full-scale revolt in the area, in which the rioters were described as 'levellers' and 'diggers'—not yet with the revolutionary connotations that the terms acquired forty years later, but it was not an unthinkably long step from levelling fences to levelling social distinctions. The title of a paper thrown into a Northamptonshire village church during the rising, 'The Poor Man's Friend and the Gentleman's Plague', shows what was on the minds of at least some of the rioters. This was a rising of the peasantry against their own gentry.[32]

We should not exaggerate, of course. On both sides embryonic class feeling was muted by traditional notions about a properly ordered society. The Council deplored the relative moderation displayed by the midland magistrates and their reluctance to use force; the JPs in turn blamed the 'great backwardness' of the militia, composed of men from the same communities as the rioters. Not all the midland gentry were ruthless enclosers, and it was those that were who armed their servants and forcibly dispersed the rebels. For their part, the rebels made the customary noises about their loyalty to the King and announced that they would go home peacefully if the magistrates would promise to redress their grievances. Even in the most extreme circumstances the reciprocal ties between rulers and ruled did not vanish completely.[33]

So the inhabitants of arable regions had no difficulty about combining to protest when their rights were threatened. The rituals they often used in doing so clearly reflect the solidarity of their communities; processions with flags, rough music, and the ringing of church bells were familiar features. After harvesting corn from disputed ground in 1611, rioters at Oundle, Northamptonshire, marched into the village 'with bagpipes playing, ringing of bells by the space of one whole day and a night, with hallooeing and throwing up of hats from the top of the steeple'. At Coleby,

[31] Gay, 'Midland Revolt', pp. 238–9. NRO C/S 3/12A (Norfolk QS Rolls, 1597), Gallow hundred presentment; C/S 3/15 (1605–6), Information of R. Braye, 4 Apr. 1606 (I am indebted to Susan Amussen for these references). See also Sharp, *In Contempt*, pp. 20–1.

[32] 'The True Narration of the Entertainment of his Royal Majesty' (1603), in *Stuart Tracts*, ed. C. H. Firth, Westminster, 1903, pp. 40, 42. Gay, 'Midland Revolt', esp. pp. 214 and n., 215–17, 240–1. Holmes, Lincolnshire, pp. 96–7.

[33] Gay, 'Midland Revolt', pp. 215, 217n., 240.

Lincolnshire, in 1616, the parishioners took advantage of the Rogationtide perambulation to level some recent enclosures.[34] But after 1607
anti-enclosure riots in the fielden areas were highly localized, involving
only the inhabitants of isolated villages acting against an immediate threat.
They show few of the more organized, 'political' characteristics of the fen
and forest riots, in which people from much wider areas co-operated for
longer periods of time and in ways which required the performance of
more clearly defined individual roles.

*

Riots provoked by food shortages or high prices reveal similarly conservative popular attitudes. They tended, naturally, to occur in clusters
after especially bad harvests, as in the 1590s, and in times of depression
and unemployment like the 1620s. As the cloth industry was largely
situated in regions that were not self-sufficient in food production it
naturally followed that the clothing districts were usually the worst
affected. North-east Somerset, the JPs of the neighbourhood reported in
1623, 'a great part of it being forest and woodlands, and the rest very
barren for corn', was particularly vulnerable.[35] So were the adjoining
parts of Wiltshire. The aims and methods of food rioters and the reaction
of the authorities to them exemplify many of the same characteristics of
popular protest that we have observed in the enclosure outbreaks.

The typical grain riot was directed against people, usually outsiders,
transporting grain to markets outside the area affected.[36] The ports of the
Thames estuary, the Norfolk and Essex coast, and Southampton were all
places through which grain was funnelled to London or other English
markets or exported to the continent, and all were the scenes of occasional
riots during this period.[37] In the western counties river traffic was often
interrupted. Starving clothworkers seized barges on the Severn between
Gloucester and Bristol in 1586, and there were similar incidents in
Somerset in 1629, on the Parrett near Langport and the Tone at North
Curry.[38] Corn 'badgers' carrying supplies to Bristol from the Wiltshire
market towns were natural targets of hard-pressed clothworkers. War-

[34] PRO STAC 8/121/20 (*Deane* v. *Clement*, 1611). Holmes, *Lincolnshire*, p. 12.

[35] Quoted in Underdown, *Somerset*, p. 18. For harvests see W. G. Hoskins, 'Harvest Fluctuations
and English Economic History 1480–1619', in *Essays in Agrarian History*, ed. Minchinton, i. 93–116;
and 'Harvest Fluctuations . . . 1620–1759', *Agricultural Hist. Rev.* xvi (1968), 15–31. Walter and
Wrightson, 'Dearth and the Social Order', p. 27, argue that most grain riots occurred *in* grain-
producing areas when supplies were being exported. It will be seen that in the western counties,
however, they tended to occur in wood-pasture regions on the fringes of the producing areas.

[36] Walter's 'Grain Riots and Popular Attitudes to the Law' is an excellent case-study.

[37] Peter Clark, 'Popular Protest and Disturbance in Kent, 1558–1640', *Ec. H.R.* 2nd Ser., xxix
(1976), 368. Sharp, *In Contempt*, pp. 19–22, 29–31.

[38] Willcox, *Gloucestershire*, pp. 135–9. Clark, 'Ramoth-Gilead', p. 175. Sharp, *In Contempt*, pp. 15,
27–8.

minster was one of the biggest markets in the country, and it is not surprising to find grain from there being seized by rioters during the 1595 dearth. There were further outbreaks in the nearby clothing districts in 1614 and 1622; in the latter year east Somerset was again affected and in Gloucestershire there were renewed plans to interrupt barges on the Severn. Finally, in November 1630 carts carrying grain from Warminster to Bristol were stopped on Midford Hill near Bath and their contents seized by about a hundred rioters.[39]

But riot, as always, was the ultimate weapon, to be resorted to only when other means of persuasion had been exhausted. Mere rumours of impending violence might be sufficient. There was talk of a rising at Weymouth in 1622, of cutting the mayor's throat and making a 'black day' for merchants who were shipping away victuals—enough to bring the plight of the poor to the corporation's attention.[40] But formal petitions to the JPs or even to Whitehall were at least as common, and probably more effective. Some unemployed Wiltshire clothworkers petitioned the Council in 1620, with a covert threat of violence: 'to starve is woeful, to steal ungodly and to beg unlawful', but '. . . to endure our present estate anywhile is almost impossible'. Riot was only the final stage, to be avoided if possible, of a lengthy process designed to force government to perform its expected ameliorative role.[41]

When riots did occur, the participants were naturally the poorest members of society with least to lose. The prominent role played by female rioters has often been noted.[42] At Southampton in 1608 a group of women refused to wait while the corporation debated what to do about a ship being loaded with grain for London: they boarded it and seized the cargo. Women were thought to be the likely rioters in the incident at Weymouth in 1622, while at Dorchester in 1631 a group (some of them inmates of the workhouse) stopped a cart in the mistaken belief that it contained wheat; one of them complained of a local merchant who 'did send away the best fruits of the land, as butter, cheese, wheat etc, over the seas'.[43]

The language used by food rioters occasionally expresses a generalized hostility to the rich and privileged, as in the alleged words of some Somerset rioters in 1596, 'that the rich men had gotten all into their hands,

[39] Sharp, *In Contempt*, pp. 18, 23–4, 28–9.
[40] *Weymouth Documents*, p. 67.
[41] Sharp, *In Contempt*, p. 71. See also Willcox, *Gloucestershire*, pp. 174–6; and Walter, 'Grain Riots and Popular Attitudes to the Law', p. 67.
[42] See above, n. 20. For further examples see Clark, 'Popular Protest', pp. 368–9, 376–7; and Sharp, *In Contempt*, pp. 22, 29, 35–6.
[43] *Assembly Books of Southampton*, i. 61–3 (the Corporation could not believe that the women had acted spontaneously and accused the Town Crier and other men of having 'animated' them). *Weymouth Documents*, p. 67. DRO B2/8/1 (Dorchester Court Book), ff. 100ᵛ–101ᵛ.

and will starve the poor'.[44] Outbursts of this kind were more common in
the 1590s than they were later. From that decade comes the menacing
query of an Essex labourer, 'What can rich men do against poor men if
poor men rise and hold together?' and the statement of a Norfolk man that
if the poor had to use violence to get food 'they would knock down the best
first'.[45] But such language was more often directed against selected
targets—forestallers, dealers, exporters—and then only as a means of
forcing the élite to perform their properly paternalistic functions. 'If a
hundred were of his mind', a Somerset stonemason declared in 1630,
'they would kill some of those rich men that the rest might sell corn
cheaper'.[46] Violence was apt to be counter-productive, and many would
have agreed with the Hampshire man who protested in 1586 'that he never
heard any like attempt to come to good', and advised his neighbours to
take the more acceptable way of petitioning.[47]

Petitioning implies a belief in a natural order of society protecting the
interests of rich and poor alike, which the authorities can be expected to
enforce once the misdeeds of individuals are brought to their notice. Even
riot can be seen in this light, for the intention was usually to compel
authority to maintain a traditional order, rather than to overturn it.
Religious teachings and government pronouncements alike contributed
to the prevailing belief that shortages were the result of individual greed
and sin rather than of a system of market relations or the pursuit of class
interests.[48] Food rioters and petitioners were inspired by the values of a
vaguely sensed 'moral economy', in contrast to the values of the market
economy now being adopted by increasing numbers of the middling sort.
It is true that there are few known cases of *taxation populaire*, in which corn
was sold off at the 'just' rather than the market price. But there are some.[49]
Just as intimidation rather than actual physical violence was the hallmark
of most of the riots, so too was the careful respect for legitimate
procedures and even for property rights. The carts should not pass, a
Kent rioter declared in 1596, but he added that he and his fellows could
not 'touch the corn'; all they could do was halt its shipment 'in her
Majesty's name'. In the same county in 1631 the cry 'One half . . . for the

[44] Sharp, *In Contempt*, p. 36.
[45] Samaha, 'Gleanings from Criminal-Court Records', p. 73. Clark, *Provincial Society*, p. 249;
'Popular Protest', pp. 380–1. Sharp, *In Contempt*, pp. 37, 41–2. Charges of sedition often arose from
loose talk in alehouses: Peter Clark 'The Alehouse and the Alternative Socity', in *Puritans and
Revolutionaries: Essays in Seventeenth-Century History presented to Christopher Hill*, ed. Donald
Pennington and Keith Thomas, Oxford, 1978, p. 66.
[46] Sharp, *In Contempt*, pp. 36–8.
[47] Ibid., p. 40. Cf. the statement by an Essex man quoted by Walter and Wrightson, 'Dearth and
the Social Order', p. 28.
[48] Clark, 'Popular Protest', pp. 370, 378–9. Walter and Wrightson, 'Dearth and the Social Order',
pp. 28–9, 31, 34.
[49] There are instances in Kent and at Southwark in 1595: Clark, 'Popular Protest', p. 368. But cf.
Walter and Wrightson, 'Dearth and the Social Order', p. 33; and Sharp, *In Contempt*, pp. 33–4.

King, the other for them' was heard, in effect a claim to the reward promised in royal proclamations to those who uncovered violations of export regulations. The same concern for legality was evident in Wiltshire in 1614 and Somerset in 1629, when rioters asked local officials to take charge of allegedly illegal shipments they had intercepted.[50] The incident at Dorchester two years later is a striking illustration of popular attitudes. When the women stopped the cart, wrongly thought to contain wheat, one of them declared that 'she would have corn for her money', and the carter replied that 'if it had been wheat and fit for them they should have it'. The intention was to pay for the wheat, not to steal it, and the carter clearly thought that people in want had the right to buy it at a fair price rather than see it shipped away.[51] Grain riots, like protests against enclosure, demonstrate the intense legalism of popular politics, as well as the readiness of the inhabitants of towns and villages, particularly in the wood-pasture and clothing districts, to take direct action to defend their rights.

*

In their resistance to disafforestation and fen drainage, in their demands for the enforcement of traditional market regulations, the common people of England were expressing a set of values deeply rooted in their culture, which also had important political implications. Behind the regional differences we have been discussing, there was a political culture shared by people in all areas, a culture whose elements included assumptions about the permanent validity of ancient laws and customary rights, and about the existence of appropriate modes of government in church and state. Popular political horizons were necessarily largely bounded by the limits of town and village, shire and region. To what extent, though, it is natural to ask, could commoners look beyond the parish pump to the wider politics of the kingdom? And to the degree that they did so, what was the nature of their involvement in that broader national politics?

The conflicts among the élite of early Stuart England are sufficiently familiar to require only the most cursory recapitulation. Recent historians have uttered some wise cautions about viewing these years as an inevitable 'high road to civil war' marked by an ever-increasing polarization of 'Court' and 'Country'.[52] It may be that the sharpness of the division in Parliament has been exaggerated, yet this was nevertheless a period in which large numbers of Englishmen became suspicious of a Court that appeared contemptuous of ancient legal rights, a hotbed of extravagance,

---

[50] Clark, 'Popular Protest', pp. 374–5. Walter and Wrightson, 'Dearth and the Social Order', p. 33.

[51] DRO B2/8/1 (Dorchester Court Book), fo. 100ᵛ.

[52] The most persuasive exposition of this view is by Conrad Russell, *Parliaments and English Politics*. For critical responses see the articles by Theodore K. Rabb, Derek Hirst, and Christopher Hill, *P & P* no. 92 (Aug. 1981), 55–124.

corruption, immorality, foreign culture, and, worst of all, perhaps even popery. James I's attempt to play the role of mediator in the divisions of Christendom baffled gentlemen brought up in the simpler days of Elizabethan Protestant fervour; his son's incoherent foreign policy—leading to inglorious failures at Cadiz and the Isle de Rhé—did little more than expose the weaknesses of a ramshackle administrative system, and provoke dispute over the crown's attempted remedies. Wartime fiscal burdens, the impressment and billeting of soldiers, reform of the militia: all aroused fears of arbitrary government and centralization. Members of Parliament found themselves, to their increasing discomfort, at the point of intersection between national and local priorities.[53] Both in the parliaments of the 1620s, and less openly in the decade of 'personal rule' that followed, the gentry articulated the grievances of a wide spectrum of 'Country' opinion. They articulated those grievances: they did not create them.

There is in fact plentiful evidence that in the early seventeenth century ordinary Englishmen had opinions on national issues that reflected their underlying concern for law, custom, and 'good rule'. They tended, naturally enough, to view these issues primarily in terms of their impact on their local communities. A man at Lyneham, Wiltshire, got so carried away during a Sunday morning argument in the churchyard in 1618 that he disturbed the congregation by talking 'somewhat loud . . . about the composition money for the King'.[54] As the national political temperature rose, more and more of the clergy and gentry were moved to remind their inferiors of the relevance of the kingdom's grievances to their own affairs. Edmond Peacham, rector of Hinton St. George, was tortured and died in prison in 1616 when his draft of a sermon on court misgovernment was construed as treasonable. 'Write on, Minterne, write on', a Dorset parson shouted ten years later when he observed a parishioner taking notes of his denunciations of injustice and corruption: 'I . . . would speak so much though the King were in presence'.[55] And in the same year Hugh Pyne, *Custos Rotulorum* of Somerset, was imprisoned for advising the grand jury to present the recent militia reorganization as an 'extortion' on the county, and for declaring that the King was 'stript and governed by a company of upstarts'. Statements like this, and incidents like the removal of the mighty Sir Robert Phelips from the commission of the peace and from his militia command because of his resistance to royal policies, were bound to affect the opinions of lesser men.[56]

[53] Russell, *Parliaments*, esp. ch. 5, and pp. 323–6, 331–40.

[54] WRO AW/ABO 5 (Act Book, 1616–22), fo. 30.

[55] Samuel R. Gardiner, *History of England . . . 1603–1642*, 1883–6, ii. 272–6. *Ashley's Case Book*, p. 91; the quotation is from the original, BL Harleian MS 6715, fo. 74.

[56] *Diary of Walter Yonge . . . 1604 to 1628*, ed. George Roberts, Camden 1st Ser., xli, 1848, pp. 110, 114. Barnes, *Somerset*, pp. 34, 163, 249, 262–3.

The early years of Charles I's reign were thus the crucial period of politicization. By 1627 the circulation of subversive writings had become ominously common: libels, Attorney-General Heath declared, were 'the epidemical disease of these days'. They were found hanging on a bush near Dunmow, Essex, in a shop in Norwich, speaking mysteriously of preparations for some violent action. Some, like those sung by three home counties fiddlers, were openly aimed against the King's chief counsellor, the Duke of Buckingham.[57] Disaffection was spreading even among the military: when Londoners, conscripted as punishment for resisting the 1626 Forced Loan, arrived at Portsmouth, troops from the garrison demonstrated in their favour.[58] By January 1628 the scholarly Sir Robert Cotton was worrying over the strength of feeling 'amongst the better sort of the multitude'. In the ensuing Parliament there was a chorus of reports of popular resentment against the soldiers who swarmed in the southern counties. 'Our poor men say, shall I work for this soldier?' a Kent MP declared, 'The farmer says, shall I be a slave to them?'[59] The bells and bonfires which greeted Charles I's reluctant acceptance of the Petition of Right, and the ballads and seditious verses which celebrated the subsequent assassination of Buckingham, all confirm the impression that political matters had by now assumed a large place in the popular consciousness.[60]

But if the common people were becoming more politically aware it might still be argued that they were not autonomous, that they were in fact the pawns and agents of their superiors. Certainly the hierarchical structure of this society, with its patriarchal ideology, ensured that the gentry could expect, and draw on, a deep fund of deference.[61] Such expectations persisted even in the less closely governed wood-pasture parishes. Sir Barnaby Samborne of Paulton in north Somerset was enraged when his servant was arrested on a charge of bestiality. He was not a JP, Samborne conceded, but he was 'sufficient enough to deal with his own man'.[62] Even some of the larger clothing towns were subject to aristocratic influence: by the Hungerfords and Pophams at Chippenham, the Earl and Countess of

---

[57] *The Court and Times of Charles the First*, ed. Thomas Birch and [R. F. Williams], 1849, i. 203–4, 207. BL Lansdowne MS 620 (Notes on Star Chamber cases), fo. 50.

[58] *Court and Times of Charles I*, i. 172, 178.

[59] Kevin Sharpe, *Sir Robert Cotton 1586–1631*, Oxford, 1979, p. 182. *Commons Debates 1628*, ed. Robert C. Johnson, Mary F. Keeler, Maija J. Cole, and William B. Bidwell, New Haven, 1977, ii. 253 (and see also pp. 127–8, 168–70, 304, 365, 399, for similar complaints). See also Willcox, *Gloucestershire*, pp. 100–2.

[60] See above, chapter 3, n. 109. Bonfires were reported in some places, following false rumours that Buckingham was to be sent to the Tower: *Court and Times of Charles I*, i. 362.

[61] Which explains why historians have usually confined their investigations of early Stuart politics to the aristocracy and gentry.

[62] PRO STAC 8/106/15 (*Carew* v. *Samborne*, 1605).

Marlborough at Westbury, for example.[63] In more socially conservative regions clientage relationships were even more likely to be taken for granted. Words uttered during a quarrel between some Dorset gentlemen at Blandford in 1619 catch some of the spirit of such places; Thomas Pomfret was asked 'whom he . . . did serve and whose man he was?'[64] Consciousness of the ties which bound them to superiors made the gentry all the more likely to insist on respect from those below them.

Still, deference was not automatic; it had to be earned. Beyond their immediate dependents it was not likely to be available to even respectable Catholics like the Stourtons and Arundells of Wardour, much less to the abominable Earl of Castlehaven at Fonthill Gifford (executed for a variety of sensational sexual offences in 1631).[66] For a gentleman to aspire to effective leadership in his county he had to win the respect of his inferiors, to cultivate them and attend to their, as well as his own, grievances. The process can be clearly recognized in the rise to pre-eminence of Sir Robert Phelips in Somerset, the only one of the three western counties in which connections between local and national politics can be clearly traced.[66] Phelips and his great rival, Lord Poulett, pursued fundamentally different tactics. Poulett assumed that the road to local power lay through Court favour; except in Neroche (where his personal interests were involved) he treated the lesser people of the shire with contempt. Phelips, on the other hand, played the role of 'the country's only friend', the defender of local interests in such matters as the militia and Ship Money, the man to

[63] BL Add. MS 34566 (Jackson collection), fo. 58. Derek Hirst, *The Representative of the People? Voters and Voting in England under the Early Stuarts*, Cambridge, 1975, p. 199. PRO E 179/199/408 (1642 Assessments), Hundred of Westbury. See also *VCH, Wilts.* viii. 149–64.

[64] PRO STAC 8/240/12 (*Pomfret v. Morton*, 1614).

[65] The Earl's family were bad neighbours for other reasons besides the sexual orgies—suspected recusants who were accused of having a Stalbridge man murdered during a dispute over the rectory. Arms were seized at Fonthill in 1625; the Earl denied recusancy, but the Attorney-General was probably right in saying that 'in the morning he would be a Papist and go to mass, and in the afternoon a Protestant and go to a sermon'. *Complete Collection of State Trials*, ed. T. B. Howell, 1816, iii. 401–26. PRO STAC 8/277/7 (*Castlehaven v. Bishop*, 1617). *Ashley's Case Book*, intro., p. vii. *CSPD, 1619–23*, pp. 97, 143, 323; 1625–6, pp. 170, 182, 184; 1629–31, pp. 371, 415. See also G. E. C[ockayne], *Complete Peerage*, rev. edn., 1910–59, iii. 86–7.

[66] Wiltshire politics have often been viewed as a power-struggle between the Herbert and Seymour families: G. A. Harrison, 'Royalist Organisation in Wiltshire, 1642–1646', Ph.D. thesis, University of London, 1963, pp. 14–15, 37–42; Morrill, *Revolt*, pp. 43–4. This seems to me an exaggeration: there is no sign that faction leaders like Sir Henry Knevet and Sir John Thynne were in any real sense Herbert clients. See Alison Wall, 'Faction in Local Politics 1580–1620: Struggles for Supremacy in Wiltshire', *WAM* lxxii–lxxiii (1977–8), 119–33; and S. T. Bindoff, 'Parliamentary History 1529–1688', *VCH, Wilts.* v. 114–17, 135, 139–40. Dorset was run by a closely related group of gentry families headed by the Strangways of Abbotsbury and Melbury Sampford. The arrival of the Digbys at Sherborne in 1616 does not seem to have affected the relative harmony of the gentry élite. See D. Brunton and D. H. Pennington, *Members of the Long Parliament*, 1954, pp. 153–67; Mary F. Keeler, *The Long Parliament, 1640–1641: A Biographical Study of its Members*, Philadelphia, 1954, pp. 44–5, 353–4; and J. P. Ferris, 'The Gentry of Dorset on the Eve of the Civil War', *Genealogists' Magazine*, xv (1965), 104–16.

whom petitions for relief on a host of minor problems were naturally addressed. His victory over Poulett depended on his gaining 'the good opinion of the country'. The common people, Poulett recognized too late, would 'applaud any man . . . unwilling to lay burdens upon them'.[67] The espousal of popular policies, far more than expectations of deference, was the key.

The limits of deference are apparent in electoral as well as in county politics. The assumption that tenant votes could routinely be delivered by their landlords was common enough—it was made, for example, in the 1614 Somerset election. But the early seventeenth-century electorate was both more numerous and less easily controlled by the élite than historians used to suppose, and middling-sort voters had to be wooed, not commanded. As one of the Somerset candidates in 1614 lamented, 'we have to do with a wavering multitude which are apt to alter in the instant that I have done'. The aristocracy had not yet mastered the skills of electoral manipulation that were to serve them so well in the eighteenth century. Indeed, the growth of a wider, more independent electorate, free from aristocratic and Court control, was being encouraged by influential MPs: men such as Sir Richard Grosvenor firmly believed that the freeholders shared their own priorities. The canvassing of voters and the 'theatrical show' of processions were becoming more common, especially in the counties and in large urban constituencies. At Gloucester in 1604 the victorious John Jones paraded his supporters through the streets 'in riotous and triumphant manner like a conqueror', a popular celebration, it was noted, hitherto unknown in the town.[68]

So Englishmen of the middling sort were becoming more involved in national policies in the early seventeenth century than ever before. Then as in later periods they were often preoccupied with matters that may seem unrelated to the broader themes of national debate. Yet disputes over the appointment of a parish clerk at Blandford, over the authority of a bailiff at Thornbury, over the extent of ecclesiastical jurisdiction in cathedral cities, continually sharpened already deep-rooted habits of participation and self-government. Even so powerful a nobleman as the Earl of Pembroke had to submit to years of litigation with the recently incorporated town of Shaftesbury.[69] Internal conflicts provided further training in processes of law and politics, as in the protracted disputes over the control of borough lands at Malmesbury and Chippenham between town oligarchies and residents deprived of rights of common. The

[67] Barnes, *Somerset*, pp. 37, 89–90, 269–70, 282, 284–7, 290–5.

[68] Hirst, *Representative of the People?*, chs. 4–5, esp. pp. 67, 104–5; also pp. 113–15, 121. Edith Farnham, 'The Somerset Election of 1614', *Eng. H.R.* xlvi (1931), 588, 590. Cust and Lake, 'Sir Richard Grosvenor', pp. 43–4. Willcox, *Gloucestershire*, p. 33.

[69] PRO REQ 2, *Pope v. Prince*, 1604; STAC 8/280/9 (*Taylor v. Hilpe*, 1608). *Municipal Records of the Borough of Shaftesbury*, ed. C. H. Mayo, Sherborne, 1889, pp. 7–8, 16–17, 47–56.

crown's manifest preferences for oligarchic government drove the poorer townsmen of many such places into an 'oppositionist' stance.[70]

But there were, after all, wider issues. It has become a familiar commonplace that in the early seventeenth century provincial Englishmen generally viewed national politics through the prism of localism. This does not mean, however, that they were totally detached from the broad questions of constitutional debate, for what was national politics but the resultant of countless forces arising from the interaction between Westminster and the localities? The Ship Money controversy is an obvious example of these interactions. At one level it appears to involve the principled opposition of men like John Hampden, at another to be simply a confusion of local disputes over ratings and assessments. But the two levels are inextricably connected. It was natural for yeomen and husbandmen to limit their protests to technical matters such as ratings rather than to stick their necks out and challenge the legality of the tax—that sort of thing was for the gentry. When by 1636 it became clear that Ship Money was not to be an occasional emergency levy, but a permanent annual tax, rating disputes proliferated in a way that reveals increasing popular discontent. In Somerset, the source of more appeals to the Council over ratings than any other county, resistance received covert encouragement by county magnates such as Phelips, as it did in Dorset by men such as Sir Walter Erle. The Puritan William Strode was the first to refuse to pay, in 1636, but already the money was only being extracted from the country people, as the sheriff of Dorset reported, 'like drops of blood'. Strode's example was followed first by a 'general underhand resistance', and then by outright defiance, by threats and violence against unhappy tithingmen, and by the forcible recovery of distrained goods.[71]

The point is that Ship Money, like so many other aspects of Charles I's policy of centralization, was *new,* and thus an affront to popular as well as élite notions of law and good rule. In 1638 the Somerset grand jury complained of 'the great and heavy taxations by new invented ways upon the county', of which Ship Money was of course the most burdensome.[72] The defence of local rights and interests was only one aspect of a general defence of ancient custom. Complaints about assessments in Somerset

[70] PRO STAC 8/130/2 (*Elkington* v. *Palmer*, 1608); STAC 8/290/22 (*Webb* v. *Cowper*, 1613). Sir Richard Luce, *History of the Abbey and Town of Malmesbury*, Malmesbury, 1979, pp. 96–8. Kerridge, 'Revolts', p. 65. Hirst, *Representative of the People?*, p. 198 (and see pp. 45–6, 56–7, 142, for other examples of local issues). See also Manning, *English People*, pp. 146–7.

[71] Barnes, *Somerset*, pp. 209–33. Bayley, *Dorset*, pp. 4–5. Cf. also Willcox, *Gloucestershire*, pp. 122–32; Clark, *Provincial Society*, pp. 358–60; Fletcher, *A County Community*, pp. 205–9; Holmes, *Lincolnshire*, pp. 130–7; J. S. Morrill, *Cheshire 1630–1660: County Government and Society during the English Revolution*, Oxford, 1974, pp. 28–9; and Kent, 'English Village Constable', pp. 40–4. For the general subject of localism, see Morrill, *Revolt*, pp. 24–9; and Holmes, 'County Community', pp. 65–6.

[72] *Somerset Assize Orders, 1629–40*, p. 60.

often focused on alleged departures from the 'Hinton rate', the system adopted in 1569, which had by now acquired an almost mystical authority.[73] That Ship Money was in many ways a more rational, equitable tax was irrelevant, for as Sir Henry Slingsby reflected, 'The common people judges not with things as they are with reason or against; but long usage with them is instead of all'.[74] Long usage; custom; traditional rights: the common people had their own version of that 'ancient constitution' to which their superiors in Parliament were so constantly appealing. The connection between local and national liberties was becoming all too clear. The clique of courtiers who had ridden roughshod over the rights of the western foresters, was the same clique that was advising Charles I to violate the country's liberties in such matters as the Forced Loan, arbitrary imprisonment, and Ship Money. Whether it was local or national liberties that were in question, the instinctive reaction was the same: the appeal to ancient law. When the King was trying to revive the forest laws in his favour in 1634, a member of an Essex grand jury empanelled for that purpose promptly demanded to see a copy of King John's charter.[75]

The rhetoric of MPs about the ancient rights and liberties of Englishmen were thus directly echoed by their inferiors. Sometimes, indeed, MPs betrayed an uncomfortable feeling that taken out of context their arguments might lead to dangerous conclusions. In a debate on the issue of whether Englishmen could legally be compelled to fight outside the kingdom, Sir Dudley Digges suggested that they 'rather cover the power the subjects have than let it be openly spoken abroad, that mean men may not know it, which perhaps if they should would be inconvenient'.[76] Rights and liberties were all very well for respectable men of substance, but it would be highly 'inconvenient' if the rude multitude should claim them. Yet even Digges took patriotic price in the virtues of free Englishmen: 'In Muscovy one English mariner with a sword will beat five Muscovites that are likely to eat him.' Sir John Eliot agreed: the King's greatness resided in 'the freedom of his people, to be a king of free men, not of slaves'.[77] In opposing the Forced Loan and other illegalities, the aristocracy and gentry did more than set an example of resistance—they actively encouraged the freeholders to join them. Tracts against the Loan were aimed at a wider spectrum of opinion than the gentry. They were circulated at county meetings and the Earl of Lincoln had one entitled, *To*

---

[73] Barnes, *Somerset*, pp. 213–14, 217.

[74] *Diary of Sir Henry Slingsby*, ed. Daniel Parsons, 1836, p. 68.

[75] *Journal of Sir Simonds D'Ewes*, p. 150. See also *English History from Essex Sources*, pp. 72–3. Ancient documents guaranteeing local rights, like the 'Mowbray deed' at Haxey in the Isle of Axholme, were venerated in much the same way as *Magna Carta*: see Holmes, *Lincolnshire*, pp. 11, 124.

[76] *Common Debates 1628*, ii. 287.

[77] Ibid. ii, 66; iii. 8.

all true-hearted Englishmen, dispersed among the freeholders. So resistance to the Loan was more broadly-based, more than the 'luxury for the gentry' that it has been called, encompassing many men of lesser rank who refused to pay and suffered imprisonment or punitive impressment in consequence.[78]

We have observed that gentlemen like Sir Richard Grosvenor assumed that the middling sort shared the same attachment as the gentry to the laws, the Protestant religion, and the rightful place of Parliament in the constitution. There is plentiful evidence to suggest that they were not mistaken. The gentry who in county after county returned the same answer to the request for the 'Free Gift' of 1626—that they would assist the King only in 'a parliamentary way'—were not speaking only for themselves. The commoners might plead more mundane excuses, as did those of Yorkshire who fell back on 'the late dearth of corn, the present dearth of cattle, and the want of trade'; but they were not in the habit of making such collective responses to demands for parliamentary subsidies.[79] The popular assumption that there was only one legal mode of authorizing emergency taxation was even clearer later in the year. When the subsidy-men of Westminster were asked to subscribe to the Loan, they responded with shouts of 'A Parliament! A Parliament!'.[80] The instinctive appeal to Parliament was not confined to fiscal matters, and it survived even in the years of the 'personal rule'. When in 1636 the Beckington churchwardens were told to rail in their communion table as an altar, they remonstrated with Bishop Piers: 'they thought they could not answer it to a Parliament'.[81]

There was, then, a right and proper way of doing things, and there was a wrong, and hence tyrannical way. On this gentry and middling-sort voters agreed, for they shared important elements of a common political culture, and their resistance to perceived illegalities thus reinforced each other's. How far down the social scale this rough consensus went is less clear. But the behaviour of the poor and oppressed in grain and enclosure riots suggests that such people did indeed have their own notions of political

[78] The phrase, 'luxury for the gentry', is Russell's: *Parliaments,* pp. 333–4. But see *Court and Times of Charles I,* i. 190–1, 202, 206–7, 222, 231; *Diary of Walter Yonge,* pp. 100–10; Willcox, *Gloucestershire,* pp. 117–21; Holmes, *Lincolnshire,* pp. 105–7; and Holmes, 'County Community', pp. 68–9. I am grateful to Richard Cust for allowing me to read chapters of his 'The Forced Loan and English Politics 1626–1628', Ph.D. thesis, University of London, 1984, which provides impressive evidence that resistance to the Loan and other policies of Charles I was not simply orchestrated by the aristocracy and gentry.

[79] Willcox, *Gloucestershire,* pp. 116–17. Holmes, 'County Community', pp. 67–8. *Memoirs of the Reign of Charles the First: The Fairfax Correspondence,* ed. G. W. Johnson, 1848, i. 73–4. It also seems reasonable to suppose that earlier élite protests against unparliamentary taxation, as in 1614 and 1622, also had some popular support: see Gardiner, *History of England,* ii. 266–70; iv. 295; and *Diary of Walter Yonge,* p. 61.

[80] *Court and Times of Charles I,* i. 130–1.

[81] *Journal of Sir Simonds D'Ewes,* p. 143.

right and wrong. These notions were often expressed in nostalgic yearnings for a vanished past, as in the opinion of the Essex labourer in
Elizabeth's reign that 'it was a merry England when there was better
government': that was how the popular mind worked.[82] The rhetoric of
MPs about legal rights and liberties was bound to have most impact on the
literate, tax-paying middling sort, but even at the lowest level of society
there were standards by which government could be judged.

And by those standards many aspects of early Stuart government were
found wanting. The cultural stereotypes of 'Court' (corrupt, effeminate,
Popish, tyrannical) and 'Country' (virtuous, patriotic, Protestant, liberty-
loving) were steadily gaining ground during James I's reign.[83] The very
word 'courtier' was becoming a term of abuse, enough to provoke a libel
suit, as Hugh David, parson of Chelvey, Somerset, found when he called a
neighbouring gentlemen one. How courtiers were viewed at Bath, already
a fashionable resort with plenty of experience of them, is suggested by a
libel of which a certain Mall Perman complained in 1614:[84]

> Of all the whores that I have known
> From Court that came unto our town,
> There's none compares with muddy Mall,
> That plays the whore from spring to fall.

Court corruption and extravagance became increasingly conspicuous.
The scandalous events (including the murder of Sir Thomas Overbury)
preceding the marriage of James's favourite, Somerset, to the divorced
Countess of Essex provoked much hostile gossip; so did the expensive
masques that accompanied the wedding. 'Pompous vanities', the Devon
diarist Walter Yonge lamented of similar festivities put on by Buckingham
ten years later, '. . . the country being in poverty'.[85] By the mid-1620s,
antipathy to courtiers was often surfacing in contested elections. Even
Lord Poulett was not above using it for electoral advantage, alleging that
Phelips had 'forsaken the country and was turned courtier' when he
temporarily allied with Buckingham in 1625. In the long run it was of
course Poulett who suffered through being identified with the Court, a
perception strengthened by such actions as his henchman Stawell's
billeting of soldiers on Taunton voters who had supported Phelips in the
1628 election.[86]

---

[82] Samaha, 'Gleanings from Criminal-Court Records', pp. 68–73, esp. p. 69. Cf. the comment of
the Essex preacher, George Gifford, quoted in Hunt, *The Puritan Moment*, p. 148.

[83] For the stereotypes see Perez Zagorin, *The Court and the Country: The Beginning of the English
Revolution*, 1969, pp. 33–9; and Stone, *Causes of the English Revolution*, pp. 105–7.

[84] PRO STAC 8/160/17 (*Gorges v. David*, 1605); STAC 8/237/26 (*Perman v. Bromley*, 1614).

[85] *Diary of Walter Yonge*, p. 98. For the impact of court scandals see Lawrence Stone, *The Crisis of
the Aristocracy 1558–1641*, Oxford, 1965, pp. 393–4, 664–8.

[86] Hirst, *Representative of the People?*, p. 180 (and see pp. 140–4 for other examples of hostility to
courtiers). Russell, *Parliaments*, pp. 20, 213, 218. *Diary of Walter Yonge*, p. 115. *Commons Debates 1628*,
ii. 254–5, 564–73; iii. 419–26.

A general dislike of the Court and its policies, from the Forced Loan to Ship Money, was present in all parts of England, and we do not need to involve regional cultural differences to explain it. Political feeling ran highest, to be sure, in the towns. Resistance to the 1626–7 Loan was most vocal in London, and the rejoicings that followed the King's acceptance of the Petition of Right and the death of Buckingham were noisier there than elsewhere. Not long before Buckingham was assassinated, his confidant and astrologer, Dr Lambe, had been lynched by a London mob, amid shouts that 'if his master was there, they would give him as much'.[87] Provincial towns witnessed nothing like this violence, but by the 1620s it was often becoming clear where their sympathies lay. As early as 1618 the Lyme Regis corporation made difficulties about the distribution of Richard Mocket's *God and the King,* a monarchist tract which the Council had ordered to be bought by every householder and taught in every school.[88] Obstruction of the billeting of troops in 1628 was most likely to occur in the towns—at Dorchester, for instance, where the corporation was soon to make its position clear by presenting a silver cup to the borough's MP, Denzil Holles, when he was imprisoned after the 1629 dissolution. At Gloucester in the same year Parliament's Remonstrance against tunnage and poundage was formally entered in the town's records.[89]

All these, of course, were Puritan towns, and it is indeed significant that political as well as religious grievances were often most clearly articulated by Puritans. A preaching tailor, 'the prophet Ball', was prominent in the agitation against the Loan in London in 1626; when arrested by Council messengers he 'quoted scripture to them mightily'.[90] A letter audaciously addressed to Charles I in January 1629 by Robert Triplet, an Islington brewer, further illustrates the connection. Triplet urged the King to govern in harmony, not conflict, with Parliament, and to appoint to his Council sound Protestants and 'commonwealth's men' like Sir Edward Coke. But the central thrust of Triplet's letter was protest against the excessive favour being extended to Catholics, especially the toleration of Jesuits and seminary priests, who now 'much more abound in England than they did in Queen Elizabeth's days'.[91] The yardstick of good government, as always in popular politics, was the imagined harmony and Protestant integrity of the good old days.

[87] *Court and Times of Charles I,* i. 364–5.
[88] DRO B 7/1/8 (Lyme Regis Court Book, 1613–27), p. 179. For Mocket's book see Schochet, *Patriarchalism,* pp. 88–90.
[89] *CSPD, 1628–9,* p. 131 (and see also p. 578 for an example of attitudes to Dorchester held by Court servants). Derek Hirst, 'Revisionism Revised: The Place of Principle', *P & P* no. 92 (Aug. 1981), 92. Clark, 'Ramoth-Gilead', p. 181.
[90] *Court and Times of Charles I,* i. 154, 159.
[91] *CSPD, 1628–9,* p. 452, with some further details from PRO SP 16/132, no. 35.

Triplet's laments about Court favour to Catholics express one of the most enduring elements in popular politics: anti-Catholicism. Years of exposure to Foxe's *Acts and Monuments*, of incessant hammering at the theme by Protestant preachers, had created a national mythology of a beleagured nation, saved from the forces of evil only by repeated providential interventions as in 1588 and 1605, which might yet be overcome by the enemies of God and the kingdom if vigilance was relaxed. Fortified by the great annual ritual of Gunpowder Treason Day, fear of popery provided a crucial bonding element for Protestants of all social ranks. At the local level, to be sure, there could be a good deal of tolerance. Catholic gentry and peers such as the Stourtons and Arundells could live in harmony with their neighbours, and might indeed be protected against outsiders. When in 1626 a party of drunken soldiers plotted to extort money from two inoffensive recusant ladies at Corscombe, Dorset, local people warned the household of impending trouble and the constable even succeeded in arresting some of the culprits. Still, there were occasional alarms about the danger of Catholic rebellion—in Dorset and Wiltshire during the invasion scare of 1625, for instance, and at Bristol in 1636.[92]

The full extent of 'Country' suspicions that Charles I's Court was deeply infected with popery and that a connection existed between this fact and the prevailing threat to English liberties, was to become strikingly apparent in 1640. The speed with which these suspicions then erupted suggests how far they had been spreading subterraneously during the previous decade. Suspicions were further encouraged by the Arminian campaign within the Church of England, for Laudian ritual and tolerance of ungodly sports could all too easily be interpreted as signs of Catholic sympathies. The popular religious mood of the 1630s was conservative, and there is little sign of any widespread demand for a radical reconstruction of the church. A growing minority might go gadding to sermons, vote with their feet by joining the exodus to New England, or even form separatist conventicles.[93] But all that most people seem to have wanted was the reversal of Arminian innovations which had been so divisive (paradoxically, given that Laud's intention was to restore the kingdom's natural harmony) and a return to the moderate Protestantism of the days of Queen Elizabeth and King James.[94]

[92] *Ashley's Case Book*, pp. 94–5. F. J. Pope, 'Roman Catholics at Benvill, Dorset', *SDNQ* xiii (1912–13), 348–9. The 1625 invasion scare is evident in *CSPD, 1625–6*, pp. 170–82. For the subject in general see Robin Clifton, 'Fear of Popery', in *Origins of the English Civil War*, ed. Russell, ch. 5.

[93] This is not to deny that a submerged form of Presbyterianism survived within the church, as for example among Lancashire Puritans. See R. C. Richardson, *Puritanism in North-West England: A Regional Study of the Diocese of Chester to 1642*, Manchester, 1972, pp. 66–9.

[94] For Laudians rather than Puritans as divisive innovators see Tyacke, 'Puritanism, Arminianism and Counter-Revolution'. The moderate gentry's view of Laudian divisiveness is well illustrated in Everitt, *Community of Kent*, pp. 52–4.

Until about 1637 the Laudian campaign appeared to be succeeding, on the surface at least. In Somerset Bishop Piers stamped out overt opposition to the Book of Sports, put down Puritan lectureships and their 'factious and disorderly sermons', and got a good many communion tables moved altar-wise. Laud was impressed: the diocese was 'in marvellous good order for all things'. It was, of course, a delusion. Many church-wardens simply omitted to present violations of Laudian injunctions, and the return *'omnia bene'* could conceal a multitude of Puritan sins.[95] Suspicion of the entire programme simmered through the country, ready to be precipitated into action by some catalytic event. Proliferating tithe disputes; increasing signs of disrespect for the ecclesiastical courts; middling-sort rumblings of discontent over the 'morris book'; these were symptoms that in religion as in politics the 'personal rule' offended deeply rooted notions of public order held by many thousands of English folk.[96]

*

All this was common to the whole kingdom, and makes it easier to understand the virtually unanimous demand for reformation of both church and state—articulated by the gentry in Parliament but shared by their inferiors in the provinces—of 1640. The unanimity, however, while conspicuous in political matters, was less profound in matters of religion. As we have observed in earlier chapters, there were marked regional variations in the intensity of Puritan feeling, variations which help to explain the subsequent division of the nation into two sides capable of fighting a civil war. Opposition to Laudianism was fiercest in the wood-pasture areas, and especially in the clothing districts. In these parishes it was strongest among the middling sort, the parish oligarchies of yeomen and clothiers who had for so long been struggling to impose their notions of godly discipline upon the disorderly poor, and who now took the lead, as at Mells and Beckington, in resisting Laud's altar policy. But it was not confined to the middling sort, for there were many lesser folk in the clothing parishes who went gadding to sermons, attended conventicles and flocked to hear itinerant preachers.[97] The Beckington church-wardens' answer to Bishop Piers shows an awareness of the connection between religious and constitutional issues and, again, there is no reason to suppose that lesser men were unconscious of it. Even where there was no overt resistance to the altar policy, resentment at the overturning of

---

[95] 'Documents of the Laudian Period', ed. J. Armitage Robinson, in *Collectanea*, ii, ed. T. F. Palmer, SRS xliii, 1928, pp. 208–11. For the connivance of churchwardens see Spufford, *Contrasting Communities*, pp. 266–70.

[96] Hill, *Society and Puritanism*, esp. pp. 322–3, 338–41, 373–4. Clark, *Provincial Society*, pp. 361–73. Spufford, *Contrasting Communities*, pp. 232–8. Fletcher, 'Factionalism'. Stieg, *Laud's Laboratory*, ch. 10.

[97] Stieg, *Laud's Laboratory*, pp. 287–90, 297–301.

hallowed parish custom must have been fanned by the expense of making the change, which often included costs for attendance at the ecclesiastical court.[98]

We should not exaggerate the regional contrasts. Feelings could run high even outside the wood-pasture area. When the Amesbury church-wardens were presented for not railing in the communion table, they declared in court 'that their consciences were as good as any man's in the company' and were duly held in contempt for it.[99] In all areas many parishes were apathetic, many were divided. It was a common practice in west-country villages, it was observed in 1634, to choose one Puritan and one non-Puritan churchwarden. This could lead to contention and liti-gation, as at Beaminster, where two churchwardens were suing each other energetically at this time.[100] But among moderate men, arrangements like this could prevent disputes from getting out of hand and splitting the community, and this was more likely to be the case in the more cohesive downland parishes. In such places there might be hostility to the Laudian programme among a minority, but among the majority there was likely to be an equally deep dislike of the Puritan reformation which had attempted to extinguish their seasonal feasts and Sunday pleasures.

So when the political atmosphere was transformed by the meeting of Parliament in 1640 there was a surface unity among all sorts and con-ditions of Englishmen, but the seeds of division had long since been sown. The unity was on political matters like Ship Money, centralization, and the threat to ancient liberties: on these the Long Parliament spoke for a nation in which high and low, town and country, arable and pasture regions were, in so far as they understood the issues, of one mind. But religious and cultural differences of long standing ensured that the potential for future strife still existed. Richard Baxter recalled that before 1640 anyone who took religion seriously enough to go gadding to sermons 'was made the derision of the vulgar rabble, under the odious name of a Puritan'; his own father was so labelled 'only for reading Scripture when the rest were dancing on the Lord's day, and for praying . . . in his house, and for reproving drunkards and swearers, and for talking sometimes a few words of Scripture and the life to come'.[101] The conflict, it must again be stressed, was partly rooted in social divisions. But it was also rooted in regional and cultural ones.

*

[98] Charges arising from moving the communion table are recorded, for example, in Gloucester-shire churchwardens' accounts: GRO P 34, CW/2/1 (Barnsley, 1609–55), 1636; P 107, CW/2/1 (Daglingworth, 1624–1803), 1637; P 328, CW/2/1 (Stroud, 1623–1716), p. 29.

[99] WRO AS/ABO 15 (Act Book, 1636–40), fo. 22.

[100] HMC, *Fourth Report* (House of Lords MSS), p. 131.

[101] *Reliquiae Baxterianae*, pp. 2–3.

The unity of 1640 was fleeting, but for a time it was real enough. The meeting of the Long Parliament in November awakened universal expectation that church and state could be reformed, good governance restored, through the co-operation of King, Parliament, and 'Country'. 'We dream now of nothing more than of a golden age', wrote the Devon squire John Bampfield, in a typical expression of the prevailing optimism.[102] Eventually the menacing outbursts of popular violence which erupted as the political temperature became more feverish and the hand of authority weaker—by London mobs shouting against Strafford and the bishops, rural mobs destroying fences and drainage works—divided the propertied nation into a 'party of change' and a 'party of order'.[103] But in 1640 the underlying social, religious, and cultural divisions were hidden behind the façade of outward political unity.

The divisions which led to civil war were sharpened by the intrusion of the popular element into national politics. The process was already under way, as we have seen, in the 1620s, and it received further impetus in 1640. In many constituencies, to be sure, the elections to both the Short and Long Parliaments followed familiar patterns: contests for local pre-eminence with no ideological basis, expressions of the territorial power of aristocrats or gentry magnates. The influence of the Earl of Warwick in Essex may have been aided by the coincidence between his views and those of so many of the Puritan gentry and freeholders, but his control over the county was in other respects of a very traditional kind. So too were the methods by which gentry candidates in such counties as Kent obtained votes from their neighbours and tenants.[104] But if it is a mistake to ignore the older form of electoral politics, it would be equally wrong to neglect the new. A broader, more independent electorate had been a striking feature of the 1620s, and it became an even more critical one in 1640. As in the earlier decade, many moderate country gentlemen welcomed and encouraged this development, assuming (with good reason) that their views on the church and the constitution were shared by their inferiors. When the Commons considered the Great Marlow election dispute in November 1640, the staunchly conservative Sir Simonds D'Ewes declared 'that the poorest man ought to have a voice, that it was the birthright of the subjects of England'.[105]

---

[102] HMC, *Fifteenth Report*, vii (Seymour MSS), p. 64. For other examples of the mood of expectancy see Stone, *Causes of the English Revolution*, pp. 51–3; and David Underdown, *Pride's Purge: Politics in the Puritan Revolution*, Oxford, 1971, p. 14.

[103] See Manning, *English People*, ch. 3.

[104] Holmes, *Eastern Association*, pp. 22–4. Everitt, *Community of Kent*, pp. 69–83, esp. pp. 71, 79. For the 1640 elections see also Hirst, *Representative of the People?*, esp. pp. 147–51.

[105] *Journal of Sir Simonds D'Ewes*, p. 43.

It is scarcely surprising that the 1640 elections provoked an unprecedented degree of popular involvement and excitement. Issues like Ship Money, the military burdens imposed by the Bishops' Wars, and concerns about the church, frequently surfaced in the campaigns. Often, of course, they did so in local terms, with hostility to Ship Money expressed in denunciations of corrupt collectors rather than arguments about constitutional legality.[106] In some counties local and national issues neatly coincided, as in Lincolnshire, where voters were advised in the spring to 'Choose no Ship sheriff, nor Court atheist, No fen drainer, nor Church papist'. In the same election in Kent an observer remarked how 'the common people had been so bitten with Ship Money they were very averse from a courtier'. The Northamptonshire poll was enlivened by shouts of 'No Deputy Lieutenants', and both there and in other counties the zeal of the Puritan clergy in animating voters against Court candidates was widely noted. This gave rise to the myth of a co-ordinated campaign, carried on by the 'cunning underhand canvass . . . the greater part of the kingdom over', of which a Gloucestershire Laudian complained. But such tactics are not a sufficient explanation of the success of 'Country' candidates in the 1640 elections. The necessary ingredients for that success were ready to hand in the popular political mind.[107]

Nowhere was this more evident than in the three western counties. By the time the Short Parliament met, efforts to collect Ship Money were collapsing. Scarcely half the Somerset hundreds even rated their inhabitants, and the ones that did were paralysed by the usual assessment disputes. Most constables simply gave up, fearing abuse and violence by the 'resolute men' of their neighbourhoods more than the now feeble hand of Whitehall. By August 1640 Somerset had produced only £300 of its £8,000 assessment. Resistance was less unanimous in Wiltshire and Dorset, but they too exhibited signs of the taxpayers' strike that was spreading throughout the kingdom.[108] Attempts to raise forces against the Scots aroused equally widespread resistance. Asked for the means of refusers of coat-and-conduct money, constables threw up their hands: they would have to 'bring in the names of every man'. All three counties eventually collected some troops, but there were massive desertions and repeated mutinies in one of which a Catholic officer was murdered, during the march to Yorkshire. Wiltshire soldiers broke open the county gaol and released people imprisoned for refusing to pay their militia taxes. At Wellington townspeople watched approvingly when another Catholic

[106] In Sussex, for example: Fletcher, *A County Community*, p. 246.

[107] Holmes, *Lincolnshire*, p. 138. Everitt, *Community of Kent*, p. 71. Clark, *Provincial Society*, pp. 385–6. Hirst, *Representative of the People?*, p. 151. Holmes, *Eastern Association*, pp. 22–3. Willcox, *Gloucestershire*, pp. 33–6, and 36n.

[108] Barnes, *Somerset*, pp. 232–3. *CSPD*, *1640–1*, p. 81. Bindoff, 'Parliamentary History 1529–1688', pp. 133–4.

officer was killed by forces from Devon who then disbanded and went home.[109]

Though muted by the survival of older traditions of electioneering, there are echoes of this popular ferment in both 1640 elections. Borough patrons such as Attorney-General Bankes at Corfe Castle and the Earl of Pembroke in a string of Wiltshire towns could still get their nominees elected.[110] But clients could no longer be taken for granted. Minehead's patron Alexander Luttrell thought it wise before the October election to discharge his tenants of 'all quay duties which are now demanded of them in my name'. Even closed corporations like Chippenham felt the winds of change. The locally powerful Sir Edward Baynton was elected, to be sure, but he had been a Ship Money sheriff and his supporters were angrily denounced as 'rogues or knaves'.[111] Local issues, were often decisive. But they sometimes interacted with national ones, as at Salisbury. In both 1640 elections there the Recorder, Robert Hyde, and Pembroke's secretary, Michael Oldisworth, were returned by a Court-inclined corporation in which the old reforming oligarchy was by now a minority; their defeated opponents, two Puritan aldermen, were generally supported by the godly middling sort. Hyde stood for the cathedral interest, the gentry of the close, and the alliance of brewers and clergy who had sabotaged the Puritans' poor relief scheme. He had outspokenly defended Ship Money, and he also opposed Puritan lectureships, and declared that the children of 'mechanic men' ought not to be educated. The elections reflect a longstanding urban cultural conflict, but ideological as well as local issues were at stake in the Salisbury contest.[112]

Their varied franchises make the boroughs fickle guides to public opinion. The larger county electorates provide a more reliable index, though generalized conclusions are difficult because contests were so often avoided by gentlemen seeking to preserve harmony in their shires, and because of the frequent paucity of the evidence.[113] Dorset and Wiltshire both avoided contests in 1640. In the former the oligarchy of governing families retained its cohesion, and in the latter (in the spring election at least) the authority of the Herberts and Seymours remained intact. These were still united communities: at the Long Parliament

---

[109] *CSPD, 1640*, pp. 220–1, 313–14, 318, 436–7, 476. Barnes, *Somerset*, pp. 275–6. Bayley, *Dorset*, p. 13. Eugene A. Andriette, *Devon and Exeter in the Civil War*, Newton Abbot, 1971, p. 41.

[110] Keeler, *Long Parliament*, pp. 44, 70–2. Violet A. Rowe, 'The Influence of the Earls of Pembroke on Parliamentary Elections, 1625–41', *Eng. H.R.* l (1935), 251–2.

[111] SRO DD/L/48 (Luttrell MSS), no. 1. Keeler, *Long Parliament*, p. 70. *Records of Chippenham*, p. 59.

[112] Paul Slack, 'An Election to the Short Parliament', *BIHR* xlvi (1973), 108–14; and see also Slack, 'Poverty and Politics', and *Journal of Sir Simonds D'Ewes*, pp. 98–9, 430–2.

[113] The Somerset JPs' attempt to make a 'peaceable election' in 1624 had foundered on the rocks of faction: Farnham, 'Somerset Election of 1614', p. 584n. Herefordshire provides an example of an election agreement by the gentry: BL Add. MS 11044 (Scudamore MSS), ff. 253–4.

election in Dorset a statement of the county's grievances—Ship Money and the like—was read to the assembled freeholders and enthusiastically acclaimed.[114] In more politically divided Somerset, on the other hand, a county where echoes of the great Phelips–Poulett conflict still rumbled, the 1640 elections provoked greater animosity, and were marked by a striking degree of popular participation.

Charles I's decision to call a parliament early in 1640 at once 'begot much joy amongst all country people', Edward Phelips, Sir Robert's son, observed.[115] Edward proved incapable of holding his now deceased father's faction together, but a new political grouping quickly emerged to complicate matters for the Pouletts. The new group was known as the 'Robins', their candidate in the election as 'Robin Hood'. These terms clearly suggest an appeal to the people, and this is confirmed by the names of several aspirants to the role of Robin Hood: William Strode, famous for resisting Ship Money; John Ashe, who had egged on the Beckington churchwardens and had been in trouble for distributing Puritan pamphlets; and the man eventually selected, the Puritan gentleman Alexander Popham, a highly appropriate Robin Hood, some thought, because he was under sentence of outlawry for debt.[116] All were the sort of people likely to appeal to middling-sort voters upset about Ship Money and Laudian innovations. The fact that Strode and Ashe were upstart clothiers only recently established on the fringes of county society might have made them all the more attractive to 'Robin' voters. A list of 'Little Robins'—minor gentry and yeomen who supported Popham—confirms that this was indeed a popular, Puritan, faction.[117]

In the end Popham was defeated, though his running-mate Thomas Smyth, Poulett's son-in-law, was elected. Smyth had not openly identified himself with the Robins, but he must have received their second votes. He won because he had both the Poulett interest and the popular Puritan Robins behind him: Popham's defeat shows that one without the other was still not enough. The fact that the Pouletts were again successful (though with different candidates) in the Long Parliament election suggests that their territorial strength in south-east Somerset remained

---

[114] Brunton and Pennington, *Members*, pp. 153–9. Keeler, *Long Parliament*, pp. 44, 70, 157, 211–12, 260, 325–7, 353–4. Hirst, *Representative of the People?*, p. 183. Anthony Fletcher, *The Outbreak of the English Civil War*, 1981, pp. xxvi–xxvii. Bindoff, 'Parliamentary History 1529–1688', pp. 136–7.

[115] *Calendar of the Correspondence of the Smyth Family of Ashton Court 1548–1642*, ed. J. H. Bettey, Bristol RS xxxv, 1982, p. 150. The expectations of the Beckington churchwardens will be recalled: above, p. 126.

[116] Christie, *Shaftesbury*, i. 33–4. *Calendar of Smyth Correspondence*, pp. 150, 154–6, 195–7. For the civil war careers of Strode, Ashe, and Popham, see Underdown, *Somerset*.

[117] The lists of 'Little Johns' and 'Little Robins' are printed in *Calendar of Smyth Correspondence*, p. 196; almost all the latter are identifiable as future supporters of Parliament in the civil war. Clarendon's comment about status-rivalry, in *History of the Rebellion*, ii. 296, is clearly relevant to people like Ashe and Strode.

unimpaired, and that they had at last learned how to cultivate the freeholders. Both victors in the autumn went up to the Long Parliament as
typical 'Country' spokesmen, and by 1640 this was not a totally implausible
position for the Pouletts. They had, after all, obstructed disafforestation
in Neroche, and had been on the Puritan side in the church ales dispute.
The Robins were symptoms of a new political order; the Pouletts' success
in containing them shows the older one was far from dead.[118]

*

Comfortable assumptions that the lower orders shared the gentry's preference for moderate reform were soon put to the test. Some had been
sceptical from the start. Mob violence after the dissolution of the Short
Parliament caused the scholar James Howell to worry about the threat of
popular insurrection: 'strange principles' had been infused into the
common people.[119] There soon appeared many impressive indications of
the intensity of popular feeling—the joyful crowds which greeted the
released Star Chamber victims, the uglier ones which demonstrated
against the hated Strafford and gave vent to 'universal rejoicing' at his
execution. The revolutionary street politics of 1641 in London are sufficiently well known not to need recapitulation.[120] They provide, however,
the essential background to the process of division which led to civil war.
Few Parliament men had any desire to enlist the common people as
anything but law-abiding voters or petitioners. Yet in executing Strafford,
destroying Star Chamber and other prerogative institutions, and discussing far-reaching reforms of the church, they were themselves striking
at the whole frame of authority. The common people, Sir Henry Slingsby
lamented, were bound to think themselves 'loose and absolved from all
government, when they should see that which they so much venerated so
easily subverted'.[121]

   'Loose and absolved from all government': the spectre of popular
upheaval loomed in much else besides the violence against Strafford and
the bishops. The fens and forests again erupted at this time, and by 1642
parts of the eastern counties were in a state of virtual rebellion. Like those
in the western forests ten years earlier, the fen riots were directed mainly
against courtiers, peers, and projectors—outsiders destroying the
customary economy in the name of profit and 'improvement'. They
naturally took on an anti-Court colouring, and the fenmen again received
a good deal of sympathy and support from Commons' leaders like Oliver
Cromwell. Lincolnshire rioters who defied the authority of the Lords

[118] For the Long Parliament election see Keeler, *Long Parliament*, p. 62; Hirst, *Representative of the People?*, p. 115; and *Calendar of Smyth Correspondence*, pp. 160–1.
[119] *Epistolae Ho-Elianae*, i. 352.
[120] Manning, *English People*, pp. 2–3, 10–18. Fletcher, *Outbreak*, pp. 6, 15–16.
[121] *Diary of Sir Henry Slingsby*, p. 68.

conceded that 'if it had been an order of the House of Commons' they would have desisted.[122]

In the more placid Somerset levels there were few echoes of these dramatic disturbances. However, recent enclosures by the Earl of Hertford in Godney Moor were invaded by rioters who broke down fences and gave out 'threatening speeches'.[123] The western forests, too, were quieter than those in other parts of England, but there were riots in Neroche in October 1641, and more serious ones in the Forest of Dean, which effectively destroyed Sir John Wintour's ambitious enclosures. That Wintour was a Catholic and the Queen's secretary provides one more link with the wider politics of the kingdom.[124] The outlook of enclosure rioters was, as usual, fundamentally conservative (though there were some expressions of class feeling in arable Oxfordshire), their rituals highly traditional. In Yorkshire, it was reported, rioters 'had their pipe to go before them, and their ale and cakes to make themselves merry'.[125] But in the 'distracted times' of 1642, with depression again enveloping the clothing districts and political uncertainty disrupting trade of all kinds, even such normally harmless outbreaks seemed threatening to the gentry. 'There is no trust to be put in the common people; they have neither constancy nor gratitude', Lord Conway complained as early as May 1640.[126]

Disorders fuelled by religion reveal even more strikingly the growing split between the moderate gentry and clergy and an aroused minority of the lower orders. Before 1640 was out petitions were flooding into Parliament against the isolated Laudian remnant—against Bishop Piers, against the parsons of Beckington, Mells, and other villages which squirmed under Arminian innovations. There were no Root-and-Branch petitions from the western counties, but the proceedings against the bishops aroused much popular interest there: the Cheddar church-wardens bought a collection of parliamentary proceedings to keep the parish informed.[127] Gentlemen who had stoutly expressed their counties' grievances during the elections were soon, like the Dorset MP Lord

---

[122] Manning, *English People*, pp. 124–37. Thirsk, *Peasant Farming*, pp. 125–6. Holmes, *Lincolnshire*, pp. 139–40, 153–7. Fletcher, *Outbreak*, pp. 312, 377. Lindley, *Fenland Riots*, ch. 3.

[123] *LJ* iv. 262. The Lords subsequently noted that the destruction of enclosures had been 'more frequently done since this Parliament began than formerly': ibid., p. 312.

[124] Sharp, *In Contempt*, pp. 216–18, 222. Fletcher, *Outbreak*, p. 81. For enclosure riots elsewhere in England see *LJ* v. 199; HMC, *Fifth Report* (House of Lords MSS), p. 37; D. H. Pennington, 'County and Country: Staffordshire in Civil War Politics', *N. Staffs. Journal of Field Studies*, vi (1966), 15; and Sharp, *In Contempt*, pp. 222–4.

[125] *Memoirs of the Verney Family during the Civil War*, ed. Frances P. Verney, rev. edn., 1970, ii. 86. For class feeling in Oxfordshire see Fletcher, *Outbreak*, p. 378.

[126] HMC, *Portland*, iii. 64. For the 'decay of trade' and the fear of disorder see Manning, *English People*, pp. 99–110; and Fletcher, *Outbreak*, pp. 375–9.

[127] *CJ* ii. 36, 50, 73. *Historical Collections*, ed. John Rushworth, 2nd edn., 1721–2, iv. 61. *Journal of Sir Simonds D'Ewes*, pp. 143–4, 542. Hirst, *Representative of the People?*, p. 182.

Digby, to denounce the 'irregular and tumultous assemblies of people' accompanying mass petitioning. The Wiltshire magnate Sir John Danvers thought that allowing 'lewd persons' to petition exposed Parliament to an inundation of beggars'.[128]

Such people might deplore the excesses of popular politics, yet their own actions were helping to stimulate them. Digby himself appealed to the people by having his speech in defence of Strafford printed. As the political fissure widened, both sides engaged in systematic propaganda campaigns to influence public opinion, calling on sheriffs, mayors, and preachers to distribute official declarations like the Grand Remonstrance and the King's Answer to the Nineteen Propositions. Leading politicians made sure their country friends were kept well informed: Sir Robert Harley used the official post to send 'advertisements of the proceedings in the Parliament' to the bailiff of Ludlow, for the benefit of 'the Puritan party' of the neighbourhood.[129] Public demonstrations like the carefully orchestrated civic receptions for Charles I during his return from Scotland in November 1641, or the noisy London outbursts in support of the Five Members two months later, were equally significant propaganda exercises. By the summer of 1642 even the King was making speeches to the Yorkshire freeholders.[130] There were still those who claimed, as Nathaniel Tovey did in Leicestershire in January 1642, to 'live in darkness and ignorance and know not which end of the world stands upwards', but such isolation was becoming, at least for the literate middling sort, unusual. The widespread rumour-mongering of which Tovey complained itself shows that political discussion was no longer the exclusive preserve of the gentry.[131]

At the local level, the most effective propaganda weapon was the county petition, designed to demonstrate the maximum degree of public support for the aims of its promoters. County petitions of course expressed the aspirations of their clerical and gentry authors, and sceptics such as those who thought Bedfordshire countrymen incapable of understanding their 'subtleties and dangerous insinuations' may have been partly right.[132] Still, as Mr Fletcher has shown in his comprehensive survey of the 1641–2 petitions, they can less easily be dismissed as artificially contrived 'parrot' petitions than some historians have supposed. Self-interested claims about their numerical support can be discounted, yet it is clear that many

---

[128] Manning, *English People*, p. 6. BL Stowe MS 184 (Dering correspondence), fo. 31.

[129] Fletcher, *Outbreak*, pp. 16, 77, 291–2, 296–7. Penry Williams, 'Government and Politics at Ludlow, 1590–1642', *Shropshire Archaeol. and Nat. Hist. Soc. Transactions*, lvi (1957–60), 290. One way of dealing with unwelcome parliamentarian propaganda is shown in the case of the Canterbury minister reported in *LJ* v. 244; and HMC, *Fifth Report* (House of Lords MSS), pp. 33, 40.

[130] Fletcher, *Outbreak*, pp. 160–2, 182–5, 233.

[131] PRO SP 46/83 (Warner MSS, 1636–44), fo. 51.

[132] Quoted in Fletcher, *Outbreak*, p. 289.

of them did express the consensus of a wide spectrum of local society.[133] Petitions from the three western counties were at first relatively uncontroversial, like the one from Somerset in February 1641 complaining about Ship Money and militia abuses. Efforts to get Dorset ministers to subscribe a clerical Remonstrance calling for religious reformation had only limited success, though John White was one of the delegation presenting it to Parliament.[134] By the end of 1641, however, the intensity of political and religious division is reflected in elaborately organized petitions of a far more partisan nature. The Somerset petition in defence of episcopacy, presented in December, claimed over 14,000 signatures, and there were similar documents from Dorset and Wiltshire. This campaign against Puritan reformation was answered in the early months of 1642 by another series of petitions in support of Parliament's measures, to which all three counties again contributed.[135]

The arousal of public feeling was most dramatic in matters of religion. Middling-sort Puritans might content themselves with implementing orders to remove altar rails and superstitious monuments, with reviving lectureships and with religious exercises preparing them for further reformation. 'All our business', it was reported from Devonshire in October 1641, 'is to pray and pay, and our chiefest farmers . . . begin to bristle up for a lay eldership'.[136] But in many places popular hostility to Laudian ritual was too intense for people to be content with quiet methods of reform. Incidents involving the violent destruction of altar rails, 'popish' monuments and stained glass occurred in all parts of the country, and were particularly common in London and the home counties. Sometimes they provoked a good deal of festive rejoicing, which may have attracted people who were far from Puritan. At Latton, Essex, a bonfire of altar rails was combined with a beer party in the church porch; at Chelmsford the smashing of stained glass occurred in the aftermath of Gunpowder Treason celebrations.[137]

Some of these outbreaks were, to be sure, encouraged by members of the élite. After the Commons ordered the removal of altar rails and superstitious monuments in September 1641 Sir Robert Harley went down to Herefordshire for a hectic orgy of image-smashing. Wigmore cross was 'beaten to pieces, even to dust, with a sledge'; the cross and

---

[133] Fletcher, *Outbreak*, chs. 3, 6, and pp. 289–90. For another view of petitions see Morrill, *Cheshire*, pp. 46, 53; and Everitt, *Community of Kent*, pp. 86–7, 95.

[134] *CJ* ii. 77, 81. Fletcher, *Outbreak*, pp. 92–3. *Journal of Sir Simonds D'Ewes*, pp. 277, 313.

[135] Underdown, *Somerset*, pp. 26–7. Fletcher, *Outbreak*, pp. 191–200, 284–8.

[136] *CSPD*, 1641–3, p. 144. Among lectureships founded or revived in 1642 were ones at Martock, Shepton Mallet, and Bridport: *CJ* ii. 610, 692; HMC, *Fifth Report* (House of Lords MSS), pp. 28, 37.

[137] *English History from Essex Sources*, pp. 76–7. Hunt, *The Puritan Moment*, pp. 292–3. For similar events in other Essex parishes see Sharpe, 'Crime and Delinquency in an Essex Parish', p. 105; and Philip L. Ralph, *Sir Humphrey Mildmay: Royalist Gentleman*, New Brunswick, NJ, 1947, p. 167. See also Fletcher, *Outbreak*, pp. 109–10; and Manning, *English People*, pp. 33–6.

stained glass at Leintwardine received similar treatment.[138] Few incidents of this type are recorded in the western counties: in the Puritan parishes of north Somerset and the Wiltshire cheese country the work was evidently done quietly by the parish élites, while in the more conservative down-lands and Blackmore Vale covert toleration of Laudian rituals may have continued. When a 'fair crucifix' was smashed in Wells Cathedral in April 1642 it was blamed on an outsider, a visiting Londoner. Still, there were enough symptoms of religious radicalism—reports of separatist conventicles in north Somerset, of women preachers in Wiltshire—for moderate opinion to take alarm. Dorchester Puritans denounced the disorderly sects, demanding 'pious reformation not confusion', and the godly Somerset magistrate John Harington spoke out against them at the January 1642 Quarter Sessions. 'Ungodly and pernicious attempts' to 'innovate or alter anything in the service of God or the decent order lawfully used . . . in the Church' ought, he declared, to be severely punished.[139]

*

The religious extremism which men such as Harington feared was con-fined to a noisy minority. Its adherents would have made little headway if they had not been able to tap a large fund of anti-Catholic prejudice. Suspicion of Catholics was, as we have seen, one of the most basic common denominators of popular politics, easily ignited in times of crisis. A steady drumbeat of accusation and innuendo, assiduously encouraged by John Pym and other leaders in Parliament, aroused widespread fears of a vaguely defined yet profoundly threatening popish conspiracy by courtiers, army officers, and Laudian bishops against the liberties of Protestant England. The riots that erupted in London after the dis-solution of the Short Parliament were directed against the Queen's household, the Catholic peers, the Papal agent—and Archbishop Laud. The 'great fear' of Catholic conspiracy, fed by rumours of Army plots fomented by the Queen to put an end to Parliament altogether, steadily intensified during the following year. Earlier local panics were dwarfed by the ones that followed the Irish Rebellion in the autumn of 1641. Papists everywhere were believed to be collecting arms, plotting to burn towns. Sir Robert Harley's warnings to his family caused panic in Herefordshire and the adjoining counties; in every village people were 'up in arms, with watch all night in very great fear'. Rumours that Irish rebels were coming,

[138] HMC, *Eleventh Report*, vii (Bridgewater MSS), p. 147. Manning, *English People*, pp. 34–5.
[139] HMC, *Wells Dean and Chapter*, ii. 426. Fletcher, *Outbreak*, p. 112 (and see also pp. 118–19). *The Diary of John Harington, M.P. 1646–53*, ed. Margaret F. Stieg, SRS lxxiv, 1977, p. 102.

inspired by nothing worse than the arrival of a few Protestant refugees, swept through the West Riding clothing districts.[140]

In the western counties too anti-Catholic feeling helped to rally the populace behind the cause of Parliament. Commissioners had already disarmed most of the local recusants, but the news from Ireland reignited the always smouldering anxieties. Minehead and other western ports swarmed with refugees retailing lurid stories of Catholic atrocities, there were rumours that Irish papists had landed, and that local Catholics were holding suspicious meetings and collecting arms. It is no coincidence that Somerset people subscribed enthusiastically to the 'Irish Adventurers' scheme.[141]

However slender their foundation, such fears were easily turned to political account. In early 1642 petitions from the localities had one recurrent theme: all the troubles of the kingdom—religious, political, economic—were the fault of the 'popish Lords and bishops'. The depression of the cloth trade, the inhabitants of Tavistock complained, was caused by 'dread of the Turks at sea, and of popish plots at home'. The fishing industry, a Plymouth petition declared, had been disrupted by Irish rebels encouraged 'by certain popish and ill-affected lords and bishops'. County petitions from Dorset, Somerset, and Wiltshire, and from many other places, had the same refrain: the papists were on the march and could only be frustrated by the exclusion of the bishops from the House of Lords.[142]

These anxieties could also be turned against local targets. Allegations of sympathy for popery were easily directed at anyone unsympathetic to Parliament's programme of reformation. By the beginning of 1642 this was happening in Dorset, where the Digbys had long since abandoned their earlier 'Country' position. There were complaints of their 'large revenues and multiplicity of tenants who are for the most part recusants, and impetuous resisters of the Protestant religion'; a potential nucleus of armed resistance to Parliament. In fact only some seventy recusant households could be found in the whole of Blackmore Vale, the centre of the Digbys' territorial power, and many of these were probably tenants of the Catholic Lords Stourton and Arundell of Wardour.[143] Catholicism was thus being used (consciously or unconsciously) as a code word to

[140] Robin Clifton, 'The Popular Fear of Catholics during the English Revolution', *P & P* no. 52 (Aug. 1971), 23–55. Manning, *English People*, pp. 22–30, esp. pp. 27–8. Fletcher, *Outbreak*, pp. 59–61, 136–40, 200–7.

[141] Underdown, *Somerset*, p. 28. Andriette, *Devon and Exeter*, pp. 47–8. Fletcher, *Outbreak*, pp. 201, 203, 250.

[142] Andriette, *Devon and Exeter*, pp. 44–6. Underdown, *Somerset*, pp. 28–9. Fletcher, *Outbreak*, pp. 200–14.

[143] Clifton, 'Popular Fear of Catholics', p. 47. For Arundell and Stourton influences see Williams, *Recusancy in Wiltshire*, pp. 255–7; and Ferris, 'Gentry of Dorset', p. 109. Their strength is confirmed by an undated list of Dorset recusants in PRO SP 30/24/7 (Shaftesbury papers), no. 530.

describe the undoubted religious and cultural conservatism of the region. Sympathy for the traditional order, for the Laudian church and for the ancient festive culture it had protected were equated in the mind of the Puritan middling sort with the machinations of Catholic agents.

Beliefs of this kind blended with more explicitly political elements to form the popular stereotype of the 'Cavalier' whose emergence, along with the corresponding stereotype of the 'Roundhead' on the other side, both reflected and heightened the division of the kingdom. Stereotypes—cultural constructions that express in a form of public shorthand the negative characteristics of opponents—are the inevitable product of deep-seated political divisions. When they acquire an aura of total moral exclusiveness, providing symbolic expression of fundamentally opposed ideologies and moral codes, they intensify pre-existing divisions and solidify group identities. They are of course of particular value when complicated political issues have to be articulated in forms readily accessible to large, imperfectly informed populations. Such was the case in England in 1642.

The 'Cavalier' stereotype combined other components with the Catholic one. A crucial element was the 'swordsman' figure, derived from the impression that Charles I was surrounded by irresponsible, swaggering soldiers, intent on destroying English liberties and taking bloody aristocratic revenge for the plebeian slights heaped upon the King, Queen, and Court. Popular fear and dislike of soldiers had a long history stretching back far beyond the 1620s, and was reawakened by the Army plot and other scares of 1641. The violence of Lunsford's soldiers in London at the end of the year confirmed these old prejudices. By the following spring fear of Cavalier swordsmen had spread far throughout the countryside, stimulated by exaggerated rumours of the London violence, and by the sight of the King's aristocratic guards at York.[144]

Political, religious, cultural, and social prejudices all converged in the formation of the rival stereotypes. Puritan perceptions of the Herefordshire JP Wallop Brabazon, a leading enemy of the Harleys, provide a good example. He had been 'very forward' in urging payment of Ship Money, had violated common rights, entertained papists in his house, licensed a tenant to keep an alehouse where bowling on the sabbath was permitted, and as churchwarden had introduced Laudian innovations and forced the parish to employ an organist who also taught music to Brabazon's children. Only the military element is missing, and that was added when Brabazon became a Commissioner of Array and brought soldiers into the neighbourhood. Brabazon was not himself a papist, but his connections and his Laudian views made it easy for him to be loosely identified as one.

[144] Fletcher, *Outbreak*, pp. 172, 231. See also the excellent discussion of the stereotypes in Malcolm, *Caesar's Due*, ch. 6.

By 1642 'papist', 'Malignant', and 'Cavalier' were virtually interchange-able synonyms, all three conjuring up the figure of a menacing, armed enemy of Protestantism and English liberties.[145]

The corresponding 'Roundhead' stereotype, like its Cavalier equiv-alent, contained a kernel of truth, sharpened, exaggerated, and cari-catured to create a composite symbol. The notion that opposition to Charles I was confined to a handful of ill-disposed Puritans, shattering the old harmony of English society by their divisive individualism and sanctimonious rejection of popular amusements, was a convenient fiction for Royalists. Not all Puritans were kill-joys, and not all Parliamentarians were Puritans, but the ones that were offered an easy target for abuse and ridicule. Like 'Cavalier', the label 'Roundhead' evoked a combination of responses. It was a term charged with social meaning, expressing the contempt felt by officers and gentlemen for people of inferior rank; Pym and his allies were self-interested upstarts turning the world upside-down, 'to make subjects princes and princes slaves', as an East Anglian jingle put it.[146] At another level it encoded a set of religious and cultural assumptions: Roundheads were Puritans who wore their hair short and were against maypoles and honest recreations. No matter that many Parliamentarians were not Puritan in anything but the loosest sense of that term. The cavalier mob who assaulted a group of inoffensive Lincolnshire gentlemen as Roundheads after a coronation-day celebration at York in March 1642 showed how deeply the notion had taken root. Throughout the spring and summer the stereotypes regularly surfaced in outbreaks of mutual invective as communities divided throughout the length and breadth of England.[147]

We are again reminded that the divisions of 1642 were as much cultural as religious or political. The war, Baxter reflected, 'was begun in our streets before king or parliament had any armies'.[148] Its origins lay, in other words, in that same cultural conflict that had for so long ranged Puritan minorities against their neighbours. Baxter knew this from his own experience. When he went to Kidderminster as lecturer in 1641 he encountered a typically divided wood-pasture parish: 'an ignorant, rude and revelling people for the greater part', but also 'a small company of converts, who were humble, godly, and of good conversations'. The former—mostly poor journeymen and servants—still had their revel

[145] HMC, *Portland*, iii. 76. BL Loan 29/50 (Misc. Harley papers), Leominster petition [1642?]. See also Fletcher, 'Factionalism', p. 296; and *Outbreak*, pp. 302–6, 410–11.

[146] Fletcher, *Outbreak*, p. 294.

[147] Fletcher provides many examples: for example, *Outbreak*, pp. 280–1, 370. There were cries of 'Roundhead' during the disputes at Leominster: BL Loan 29/121 (Harley papers), J. Tombes to Sir R. Harley, 31 July 1642. The term was already in common use in Herefordshire: *Letters of the Lady Brilliana Harley*, ed. T. T. Lewis, Camden 1st Ser., lviii, 1854, pp. 170–2.

[148] Quoted in Fletcher, *Outbreak*, p. 409. It will be seen that my reading of Baxter's meaning differs from Fletcher's.

feast, where they 'brought forth the painted forms of giants and suchlike foolery', and they rioted when the godly churchwardens tried to remove the churchyard cross and the 'popish' images. The familiar socio-cultural polarization was soon solidified in the popular stereotypes. 'If a stranger passed, in many places, that had short hair and a civil habit', Baxter tells us, 'the rabble presently cried, "Down with the Roundheads"; and some they knocked down in the open streets'. Baxter was driven from Kidderminster and took refuge at Puritan Gloucester.[149] The stage was set for civil war.

*

The political unity of 1640 foundered in the renewal of religious and cultural conflict. The immediate precipitant of civil war—the constitutional dispute over the militia power—concealed more fundamental antagonisms that went beyond matters of government to differences about the very nature of society. These divisions existed in every community, every region. Yet, as the next chapter will show, some regional patterns are unmistakable. In some areas the dominant outlook was shaped by those of the gentry and middling sort who pressed unwaveringly for 'godly reformation' and regarded Cavaliers as agents of 'popery and profaneness'.[150] In others the public mood was set by those who saw in the traditional order and its communal rituals the only guarantee of social harmony, and feared the disruptive consequences of Puritanism more than the mythical popish conspiracy.

Most people, understandably, were appalled at the prospect of civil war and tried to stay out of it as far as possible. As we shall see, though, a preference for neutrality did not necessarily mean indifference to the outcome. And even the more partisan shared elements of a large common stock of ideas about society and government, shaped by long collective experience in the ordering of their communities. The handful of zealots, particularly on the side of Parliament, who rejected these traditional values have an historical importance out of all proportion to their numbers. But their failure to establish the New Jerusalem they yearned for was in the end the result of the tenacious attachment of most of their countrymen to ancient laws and customs.

In 1641 the common system of values was skillfully translated into political language. A national oath of loyalty, the Protestation, was enacted by the Commons during the great fear of a counter-stroke against Parliament by Charles I. Initially the oath was taken only by MPs and by

[149] *Reliquiae Baxterianae*, pp. 20, 24, 40–1. Many similar comments could be cited: for example, those of John Tombes on the 'ignorant and superstitious' common people at Leominster: HMC, *Portland*, iii. 76. Fletcher notes the presence of sabbatarian, anti-festive elements in some of the 1642 petitions: *Outbreak*, p. 219.

[150] Hinde, *Faithfull Remonstrance*, p. 6.

voluntary subscription in a few parishes, but in January 1642 it was sent down into the countryside and the clergy ordered to administer it to all adult males.[151] Its subscribers swore to maintain 'His Majesty's royal person and estate': the patriarchal, monarchical core of the social and political order. They swore to defend 'the power and privilege of Parliaments, the lawful rights and liberties of the subjects': the ancient constitution and laws from which stemmed the rights of individuals and of the kingdom's component communities. And they swore to preserve 'the true reformed Protestant religion expressed in the doctrine of the Church of England, against all Popery and popish innovation': the religion which united, rather than divided them. Patriarchy; law; liberty; the Protestantism of Queen Elizabeth's days: the Protestation expressed a set of simple, unifying ideas which were to surface again repeatedly in popular politics during and after the civil war.

The Protestation was originally designed to cement public opinion behind Parliament, and to isolate Catholics and other 'malignants'. In the hectic early months of 1642 it became a powerful parliamentarian symbol, carried on pikes and swords by Londoners demonstrating their support of the Five Members, worn in the hats of Buckinghamshire gentlemen accompanying their county petition to Westminster.[152] It could be used, in other words, for highly partisan purposes. But it was also available as a statement of basic principles that transcended the disputes now dividing the kingdom. The reading of the Protestation after morning service, and the solemn ceremony of subscription, must have been unforgettable experiences for many humble villagers as they publicly affirmed the unity of the nation. The fracturing of that unity by civil war did not eradicate the appeal of the Protestation's simple, obvious statement of consensus ideas. Like their predecessors in the forest and fen riots with whom this chapter opened, the subscribers to the Protestation had their own ill-defined, yet deeply felt version of the ancient constitution.

[151] Text in *Documents of the Puritan Revolution*, ed. Gardiner, pp. 155–6. The returns are calendared in HMC, *Fifth Report* (House of Lords MSS), pp. 120–34. For the circumstances surrounding the Protestation see Fletcher, *Outbreak*, pp. 15–16, 77–9, 209–10.

[152] Fletcher, *Outbreak*, pp. 185, 196, 209.

6

The Civil War and the People

THE English people shared a large fund of common values, yet in 1642 they were sufficiently divided to fight a civil war. Before the patterns of wartime allegiance in the three western counties can be analysed, however, a brief review of military events in the region is required. The war in the west had four phases: a year of parliamentarian ascendency ended by the royalist victories of the summer of 1643; a year of royalist domination ended by the arrival of the Earl of Essex's army in June 1644; a third year of turmoil in which the three counties were subjected to repeated devastation by the forces of both sides; and a final phase from the arrival of the New Model army in June 1645 to the ultimate victory of Parliament. This bald summary grossly over-simplifies the complex realities of war—the petty skirmishes, the survival of besieged garrisons in the midst of hostile territory, above all the constant misery, bloodshed, and terror inflicted upon the population. But these matters must be given a chronological setting.

The war began in August 1642 with the Marquis of Hertford's attempt to execute the King's Commission of Array. Hertford briefly established himself at Wells, but was driven out by a great popular uprising in which men from north Somerset and the adjacent parts of Wiltshire and Gloucestershire converged on the Mendips.[1] Hertford quickly retreated to the Digbys' castle at Sherborne. This stronghold was defended with better success, but before September was out he again had to evacuate his dwindling forces, some to South Wales, some to Cornwall. Parliament's local levies had shown little enthusiasm at the siege of Sherborne, but a Dorset MP was probably not wrong in reporting universal relief at Hertford's departure. Royalists were rounded up, and the local forces were 'something violent upon the Papists'.[2] In the course of the ensuing winter the fall of Marlborough, Malmesbury, and Devizes brought much of north Wiltshire under royalist control (its proximity to Oxford made this virtually a frontier area), and until the spring of 1643 garrisons held Abbotsbury, Corfe, Portland, and Wardour Castle for the King. There was some occasional skirmishing in other places—a pitched battle

---

[1] The summary of military events in the west that follows is based on Bayley, *Dorset*; Underdown, *Somerset*; and *Memoirs of Edmund Ludlow*, ed. C. H. Firth, Oxford, 1894, i, App., pp. 439–81.
[2] HMC, *Portland*, i. 64.

between the Puritan villagers of Batcombe and their royalist neighbours of Bruton, some renewed resistance by the townsmen at Sherborne when Parliamentarian troops from Somerset went there to secure the castle in April 1643. But throughout the first year of the war the Roundheads were, for the most part, in control.

The situation was transformed in the summer of 1643 by powerful royalist forces from outside the region. Sir Ralph Hopton's Cornish army was joined by cavalry from Oxford under Hertford and Prince Maurice, and by the beginning of August the three counties had been recovered for the King. Of the two great battles of this campaign, Lansdown was inconclusive, but at Roundway eight days later the Parliamentarians were routed.[3] Rupert's capture of Bristol completed the cavalier triumph. Only the Dorset ports of Poole and Lyme, and some scattered garrisons along the western borders of Wiltshire (of which Wardour was regained by the Royalists in March 1644) held out for Parliament. There were occasional forays from these places—the Lyme Roundheads raided as far afield as Chard, while forces from Poole seized Wareham in December 1643 and held it for several months—but these were only minor dents in the royalist façade. On the surface life seemed to have returned to something like normality. Government by the JPs in Quarter Sessions replaced Parliament's innovative rule by emergency committees, and the royalist clergy returned to their pulpits. All three counties were still subject to the inevitable burdens of taxation and recruiting, but there was no open challenge to the royalist ascendancy.

The prelude to the third phase was the recovery of Malmesbury by forces from Gloucester in May 1644, which enabled the Roundheads to regain control of north-west Wiltshire. More important was the arrival, early in June, of the Earl of Essex with his whole army, on the first stage of the expedition that was to end in disaster at Lostwithiel; a month later the King himself came in pursuit. For the next year the region was repeatedly traversed by marauding armies, ruined by the multiplying garrisons of both sides. During their marches through Dorset and Somerset both Essex and the King energetically wooed public opinion, with a deluge of proclamations, sermons, speeches by the generals, even by the King himself. During his return march in the autumn, after the victory at Lostwithiel, Charles launched a second propaganda campaign, posing as the pacific monarch whose overtures had been repeatedly rebuffed by a bloody-minded Parliament. The resulting petitions for peace on the King's terms were unproductive, but the scheme was taken up by Sir John Stawell a few months later when he tried to steer 'Country' opinion into royalist channels through another series of such petitions, using the same

[3] For an argument that Lansdown was a parliamentarian victory see John Wroughton, *The Civil War in Bath and North Somerset (1642–1650)*, Bath, 1973, pp. 81–2.

slogan, 'One and All'. In the mean time garrisons on both sides proliferated, Puritan Taunton was twice besieged and twice relieved (in
December 1644 and May 1645), and there was much confused fighting in
both Wiltshire and Dorset. Apart from Malmesbury, all Parliament's
major strongholds in Wiltshire were lost by February 1645, but in Dorset
the tide ran in the other direction, as local forces under Sir Anthony
Ashley Cooper mopped up several royalist outposts. The plight of the
ravaged counties was made even worse by the arrival of George Goring's
predatory army early in 1645. When the spring came the countrymen
showed that they could stand no more, and 'Peace-keeping associations'
of Clubmen bent on protecting their homes and communities from
destruction emerged spontaneously in all three counties.

The final phase began at the end of June 1645, when the full force of the
New Model under Fairfax and Cromwell, fresh from their victory at
Naseby, marched into the west. They smashed Goring at Langport on 10
July, and twelve days later, after conciliating the Clubmen of central
Somerset (those in Wiltshire and Dorset had been less friendly) they
stormed Bridgwater. Early in August Cromwell bloodily dispersed the
Wiltshire and Dorset Clubmen at Hambledon Hill, near Blandford;
Fairfax then took Sherborne, marched north and forced Rupert to surrender Bristol on 10 September. He was assisted by a popular uprising
similar to that of August 1642, for the Clubmen of north Somerset
thronged to the Parliament's cause. While the New Model advanced
westwards in the autumn to end the war in Devon and Cornwall,
mopping-up operations began in the three counties behind them. Royalist
garrisons at Devizes, Lacock, and Longford surrendered in September
and October, and although north Wiltshire still suffered from sporadic
raids by forces from Oxford (Marlborough was briefly in cavalier hands
in January 1646), only a few doomed castles hung on through the winter.
Corfe surrendered to Parliament in February, Portland and Dunster not
until April.

*

So much for the military campaigns; what of the war's actual impact on the
population of these counties? The most obvious impression the evidence
leaves is one of misery and havoc, confirming the not very original
conclusion that war, and particularly civil war, is hell. Much of the distress
cannot be quantified—the emotional scars of bereaved widows and
parents, the psychological scars of families divided by the war, the physical
scars of the maimed, the financial scars of the ruined. England may not
have 'turned Ireland', as a London news-writer thought was the case after
Rupert sacked Marlborough in December 1642, but some places came
uncomfortably close to a state of social breakdown. No part of England

suffered more than the western counties and the adjacent Severn Valley and Welsh border regions, in which the most protracted and ruinous campaigns of the war occurred.[4] War taxation; the quartering of soldiers; plundering; the physical devastation of town and countryside: these were universal realities for the population of all regions, royalist and parliamentarian alike.

The financial burdens were bad enough in parliamentarian south-east England, where circumstances permitted tolerably regular, systematic procedures of government. Even in that more fortunate region the war made Charles I's earlier exactions pale into insignificance. By 1645 Parliament's assessments were raising more money in Kent in a month than Ship Money had produced in a year. Taxation on this scale could be collected only by an emergency administrative system which bypassed traditional local institutions. The Royalists showed greater respect for the old ways of government—county assessments were endorsed by grand juries or county meetings, appeals heard by the JPs. But if less innovative than Parliament's, royalist taxation was in the end even more oppressive, since the military were often directly involved in its collection.[5] One form of wartime taxation, the excise, aroused special hostility. Both sides adopted this new and unpopular fiscal expedient, but Parliament's excise was never enforced in the western counties until after the war. The Royalists, however, were driven to it by 1644. Vague promises that it would lead to relief from the hated weekly contributions were soon dismissed as the 'mere tricks of courtiers'. The Somerset JPs and gentry were obstructive; at Wells the mayor went into hiding rather than publish the proclamation, and when the excise commissioners arrived one of the aldermen told a crowd in the market place that they came 'to rob and devour the people'. Excise officers were assaulted on market day at Bridgwater; the Governor refused to provide troops to protect them, and his soldiers (local men) joined in the attack. The officials were warned, they reported, that if they continued their work, 'the Country would certainly drive us out with stones'.[6]

For much of the war, chronic military instability prevented either side in the west from establishing anything resembling normal tax-collecting procedures. Instead, the inhabitants were subjected directly to the demands of rival armies and garrisons. Such demands, backed by threats

[4] Ian Roy, 'England Turned Germany? The Aftermath of the Civil War in its European Context', *TRHS* 5th Ser. xxviii (1978), esp. pp. 128, 141. Alan Everitt thinks that impressions of the war's destructiveness have been exaggerated: *The Local Community and the Great Rebellion*, Hist. Assn. Pamphlet G.70, 1969, pp. 24–6.
[5] Morrill, *Revolt*, pp. 80–5.
[6] BL Harleian MSS 6802 (Sir E. Walker MSS), fo. 279; 6804, ff. 143, 284–7. See also Edward Hughes, *Studies in Administration and Finance 1558–1825*, Manchester, 1934, pp. 119–26; Maurice Ashley, *Financial and Commercial Policy under the Cromwellian Protectorate*, Oxford, 1934, ch. 7; Morrill, *Revolt*, p. 85; and Morrill, *Cheshire*, p. 99.

of plunder and destruction, often led to enforced payment to both sides. In May 1643 Sir William Waller ordered the hundreds near Cirencester to pay contributions to his army, but the royalist Earl of Crawford arrived soon afterwards, 'threatening fire and sword if they paid him a penny' and ordering them to pay it to him instead.[7] The double burdens on the Wiltshire clothing towns during the first winter of the war are apparent in the records of Chippenham: three contributions to Sir Edward Hungerford's Parliamentarians, two to the Royalists at Malmesbury, as well as a fine of £200 for their earlier assistance to Hungerford. As the war ground on, so did dual contributions: to Hungerford, Waller, and Massey, but also to Hertford, Prince Maurice, and other royalist commanders. Other west-country towns and villages had similar experiences.[8] It was the spiralling burden of contributions, as much as any other grievance, that precipitated the neutralist revolts of 1645, and their regulation through deals with local garrisons was one of the Clubmen's first priorities.[9]

Taxation was a universal burden; so was the quartering of soldiers. In some counties the costs it inflicted on the inhabitants far exceeded the sums raised by taxation—in Buckinghamshire they were almost three times as much. After the war the subcommittees of accounts collected some striking information. In the hundred of Wellow, near Bath, claims for quartering parliamentarian soldiers down to 1646 amounted to £1,202.10s.8d, not much less than the total subscribed to Parliament under other headings, such as the 'Propositions' of 1642.[10] This accounts only for the hundred's outlays for Parliament: the Royalist's demands must have been of comparable size. Some compensation for parliamentarian quartering was eventually forthcoming, but only after years of delay.[11]

Quartering became especially severe during the terrible winter of 1644–5. At Winterbourne Earls in Wiltshire, old John Nicholas, father of Charles I's Secretary, was 'never free from billetting of soldiers of both sides, sometimes thirty, forty or fifty men and as many horses three or four days and nights together'. Quartering, Buckinghamshire country people complained, let soldiers 'eat the meat out of their children's mouths', and

---

[7] BL Add. MS 18980 (Rupert MSS), fo. 72. For an example of double contributions in Oxfordshire see David Underdown, 'The Problem of Popular Allegiance in the English Civil War', *TRHS* 5th Ser. xxxi (1981), 70.

[8] *Records of Chippenham*, pp. 209–13. For the problems of the clothing districts see Roy, 'England Turned Germany?', pp. 138–40. For other west-country places, HMC, *Salisbury*, xxii. 375–9; *Annals of Devizes*, i, pt. ii. 115; Underdown, *Somerset*, pp. 69, 77–8; *The Minute Books of the Dorset Standing Committee*, ed. Charles H. Mayo, Exeter, 1902, p. 398.

[9] *LJ* vii. 485.

[10] Morrill, *Revolt*, p. 86 (but cf. John Broad, 'Gentry Finances and the Civil War: The Case of the Buckinghamshire Verneys', *Ec. H.R.* 2nd Ser. xxxii (1979), 185–6). PRO SP 28/242 (Committee of Accounts papers), fo. 104.

[11] Villages near Shepton Mallet, for instance, were paid only in 1650 for quartering that had occurred five and six years earlier: PRO SP 28/242, ff. 112–34.

if the fare was not good enough loud were their complaints.[12] Efforts to persuade commanders to remove their forces were rarely successful. In the later stages of the war Chippenham sent repeated messages to Skippon and Fairfax at Bristol, 'for removing the soldiers from hence', but to no avail. Only if the troops were completely out of hand was action likely to be taken.[13]

Ill-paid and poorly disciplined troops inevitably resorted to plundering. Soldiers on both sides appropriated money, food, livestock and goods, with or without their officers' consent. At Winchester in December 1642 parliamentarian troops fired on their own officers when they tried to restrain them from pillage. It made little difference which side people were on: friend was as likely to be looted as neutral or enemy.[14] How far plundering had entered into the fabric of wartime life is evident from the plea of Mary Wilde of Market Lavington, accused in 1644 of stealing clothes from various houses in the Devizes area: she had bought them, she declared, 'from several troopers'. True or false, it was a plausible story.[15] The western counties produced a familiar litany of complaints: of tenants unable to pay rents, vacating their holdings. In Wiltshire late in 1644, Sir Edward Nicholas's steward found that 'no money could be had from any body, only complaints of plundering and losses'.[16] North Somerset, two roundhead commanders declared, still contained 'as fruitful parts as are in England to quarter in'. If this was true, it was not saying much, and elsewhere in the region the ravaged landscape proclaimed the contrary. The plight of the western counties were made even worse early in 1645 by the arrival of Goring's infamous rabble. Royalists and Parliamentarians alike condemned their 'horrid outrages and barbarities', and even in the next century John Oldmixon noted that in Somerset 'Goring's crew' were 'remembered with abhorrence'.[17]

There were many other ways in which the war weighed heavily upon the population: the impressment of soldiers (to be discussed in the next chapter), and the demands for forced labour to carry supplies or work on fortifications, for example. The two were sometimes related. When the Gloucestershire Royalists sent out warrants for labourers to come to

[12] Donald Nicholas, *Mr. Secretary Nicholas (1593–1669) His Life and Letters*, 1955, p. 199. *Letter Books of Sir Samuel Luke*, p. 514. Underdown, *Somerset*, p. 78.
[13] *Records of Chippenham*, pp. 213–14. Parliament was constantly having to deal with complaints about the misbehaviour of troops in the south-eastern counties: see *CSPD*, 1644–5, pp. 298–9, 463; *CJ* iv. 5, 28, 38, 58; Bulstrode Whitelocke, *Memorials of the English Affairs*, Oxford, 1853, i. 372, 389.
[14] HMC, *Fifth Report* (House of Lords MSS), p. 60. See also Broad, 'Gentry Finances', pp. 184–5; Morrill, *Revolt*, p. 86; Roy, 'England Turned Germany?' pp. 136–7. For plundering of Birmingham Royalists by their own troops see BL TT, E. 258 (21): *Perfect Occurrences* 31 Jan.–7 Feb. 1644/5.
[15] *Records of Wilts.*, p. 145. For plundering in Dorset see F. J. Pope, 'Sidelights on the Civil War in Dorset', *SDNQ* xii (1910–11), 52–5.
[16] BL Egerton MS 2533 (Nicholas papers), fo. 390.
[17] Underdown, *Somerset*, pp. 81, 87. *Ludlow's Memoirs*, i. 465–6. Bayley, *Dorset*, p. 240.

Bristol rumours spread that the men were to be pressed as soldiers; the authorities had to issue a denial and promise that they would be paid for their work.[18] The wonder is not that the Clubmen rose in revolt in the spring of 1645, but that they did not do it sooner. There had been sporadic violence against soldiers earlier in the war in many parts of England—in the Severn Valley north of Bristol in 1643, for example, in Sussex in the following year—but it was only after Goring's arrival in the west that it became organized and systematic.[19]

The war's oppressions were universal in their impact, affecting regions of all types and of all political character. They might cause adverse popular reactions for one side or the other in areas that were generally sympathetic. When Rupert threatened Bristol in February 1643 the Parliamentarians were able to raise 1,000 men in north Somerset at short notice; against Hopton five months later they were unable to raise even a hundred, two local Roundheads complained, 'so much was the Country distasted with taking free quarter, horses, disorderly plundering even from the best affected'.[20] On the other side, by the autumn of 1644 the Royalists' plundering, their 'cruel and inhuman acts to the country people', had alienated many in Devonshire who had been 'strong for the King, and cry for Bishops and the Book of Common-Prayer'. Rival propagandists naturally made the most of such situations, and in this respect Goring was a particular windfall for Parliament.[21]

Both sides also recognized the adverse effects that plundering and free quarter had on their own popularity. But the contrast in their behaviour is significant. The Royalists showed some solicitude for the gentry-controlled institutions of local government, for the authority of JPs and Quarter Sessions, but were less interested in reforming abuses which fell most heavily on the middling and small property-owners. Among the generals the 'hard men' (as John Morrill has labelled them) were all too often out of control. It cost them dearly in Wiltshire, where half the King's commissioners resigned in the autumn of 1644 and others deliberately

---

[18] *CSPD, 1644*, p. 235. For other instances of forced labour see PRO SP 28/249 (County Committee papers: Worcs.), Frogmorton returns; GRO P 63, CW/2/1 (Bromsberrow Church-wardens accounts, 1631–1700).

[19] For the Severn Valley violence see Ian Roy, 'The English Civil War and English Society', in *War and Society: A Yearbook of Military History*, ed. B. Bond and I. Roy, 1975, pp. 37–41. For Sussex, Fletcher, *A County Community*, p. 274; and Charles Thomas-Stanford, *Sussex in the Great Civil War and the Interregnum 1642–1660*, 1910, p. 166.

[20] BL TT, E. 70 (1): *Colonell Fiennes His Reply to a Pamphlet*, 1643. *Bellum Civile. Hopton's Narrative of the Campaign in the West*, ed. C. E. H. Chadwyck Healey, SRS xviii, 1902, p. 88. Parliamentarian leaders in Wiltshire and Dorset were already alarmed at their loss of popular support even before the royalist invasion of 1643: *Ludlow's Memoirs*, i. 452; Bayley, *Dorset*, p. 88.

[21] BL TT, E. 256 (19): *Perfect Occurrences*, no. 9 (4–11 Oct. 1644). Even the ruthless Sir Richard Grenville protested at the Royalists' excessive requisitioning of horses and oxen in 1644: BL Add. MS 15750, fo. 20. For reports of Goring's outrages see BL TT, E. 26 (9): *Perfect Passages*, no. 14 (22–8 Jan. 1644/5); and E. 258 (14): *Perfect Occurrences*, 10–17 Jan. 1644/5.

obstructed recruiting, as well as in the counties of the Welsh border.[22] Parliament, on the other hand, showed less respect for established institutions, replacing them with *ad hoc* committees responsible to Westminster and often staffed by men from outside the old governing circles, but was distinctly more responsive to popular complaints about the behaviour of its troops. In October 1642 plundering by roundhead forces in Somerset and Dorset 'much incensed the country against them': Parliament ordered them to join Essex's army and subsequently sent down the MP John Ashe to hear complaints.[23] Two years later the Parliamentarians at Lyme gained a good reputation for defending neighbouring villages from plundering, a policy which paid dividends in popular support: Dorset countrymen enraged by the atrocities of royalist troops helped the Weymouth garrison to round them up. We should not exaggerate the contrast. Parliament's commanders sometimes encouraged their troops to plunder, as at Blandford in July 1644 in retaliation for the town's hostile attitude.[24] But for the most part their forces were less oppressive than the King's.

*

The natural, inevitable response to these calamities was a universal yearning for peace. The pacific, neutralist sentiments widespread at all levels of English society during the civil war have been well described by recent historians and need little recapitulation.[25] The wealthy could, if they were lucky, escape from war-torn regions by going to London or even the continent. The Gloucestershire gentleman Christopher Guise fled to London, he tells us, to avoid having to 'engage myself in some party which I did not like'. John Aubrey's royalist tutor advised his pupil to move from Wiltshire to the capital and live 'safe and unengaged from a bad and prosperous or a good but declining cause'.[26] The less affluent had no such choices. They could, however, support or even initiate moves to end the war or limit its destructiveness.

Various avenues to peace were repeatedly explored: the negotiation of local truces; the organization of mass petitioning campaigns addressed to King or Parliament; and the formation of a neutralist 'third force'.

[22] Morrill, *Revolt*, pp. 83–4, 93, 101, 103–4. Harrison, 'Royalist Organisation in Wilts.', pp. 221–6, 370–1.

[23] *CSPD, 1641–3*, p. 402.

[24] Bayley, *Dorset*, pp. 221–2. Whitelocke, *Memorials*, i. 279, 324.

[25] See Morrill, *Revolt*, ch. 3; Everitt, *Local Community*; Everitt, *Community of Kent*, pp. 116–24, 219–28; Morrill, *Cheshire*, pp. 65–74; Fletcher, *A County Community*, pp. 284–8; and B. S. Manning, 'Neutrals and Neutralism in the English Civil War 1642–1646', D.Phil. thesis, University of Oxford, 1957.

[26] *Autobiography of Thomas Raymond and Memoirs of the Family of Guise of Elmore, Gloucestershire*, ed. G. Davies, Camden 3rd Ser., xxviii, 1917, pp. 87, 124. Bodleian MS Aubrey 12, fo. 35.

Neutrality agreements or negotiated truces were essentially matters for the gentry and military men and are of interest to us mainly because they set examples of peacemaking which lesser men could follow. Agreements by local magnates to keep the peace were common in the early months of the war: Dr Morrill has discovered them in twenty-two English counties. Cheshire, for example, declared against both the Militia Ordinance and the Commission of Array and resolved to prevent outside forces from entering the county, while Staffordshire tried to raise a local force of 1,000 men for this purpose. Such expressions of community-centred localism were shattered by the great national division, and after the fighting started, attempts to end it by truces—in Yorkshire and again in Cheshire, for example—suffered similar fates.[27] In Dorset early in 1643 the leading gentry of each side agreed to disband their troops and to oppose 'all forces whatsoever that shall enter that county'. A temporary cessation was worked out between the Cornish Royalists and the Devon Roundheads; the Dorset leaders attended a meeting at Exeter to discuss making it permanent and extending it to the other western counties. But none of the expected participants from Somerset turned up, and pressure from Westminster soon put an end to the project.[28]

Peace petitions were no more fruitful. The leading Wiltshire gentry petitioned the King for peace in October 1642, and there were similar moves at Bristol and Salisbury, at a time when a massive peace campaign was under way in London and the south-eastern counties. Its promoters, gentry of mildly royalist outlook, upset by the recent Stour Valley riots and other outbreaks of popular violence, made much of the war's disastrous effect on trade and the prospect of 'a German devastation', as a Norfolk petition put it. The London Common Council was besieged by a mob shouting 'Peace! Peace!' and an apprentices' petition was accompanied to Westminster by a crowd of some 3,000 people.[29] Events in London were watched closely in the provinces, and may have encouraged the Dorset gentry in their efforts to achieve a neutrality agreement. In the following August, when Parliament itself was beset by rival mobs demonstrating for and against the war—the peace demonstration involved a striking intrusion of women into the political scene—the neutralist MP for Poole,

---

[27] Morrill, *Revolt*, pp. 36–7, 113; *Cheshire*, pp. 66–9. Manning, *English People*, p. 211.

[28] *CJ* ii. 991, 1002–4. HMC, *Portland*, i. 100–3. Andriette, *Devon and Exeter*, pp. 82–3. Bayley, *Dorset*, pp. 63–4. The peace moves appear to have been initiated by the Dean of Exeter, William Peterson: Bodleian MS J. Walker c. 4, fo. 217.

[29] Samuel R. Gardiner, *History of the Great Civil War 1642–1649*, 1886–91, i. 86–7, 95. Anthony Fletcher, 'The Coming of War', in *Reactions to the English Civil War 1642–1649*, ed. John Morrill, 1982, pp. 40–2. Holmes, *Eastern Association*, pp. 42–6, 53, 61. Harrison, 'Royalist Organisation in Wilts.', pp. 125–6. See also *LJ* v. 500–1, 507–8, 511–12, 524–5, 545–6; and HMC, *Fifth Report* (House of Lords MSS), p. 61.

William Constantine, reported to his friends in Dorset on the growing split between the peace and war parties.[30]

There were no further peace moves in the western counties until the autumn of 1644. During Charles I's return march from Cornwall a proclamation called on his subjects to accompany him in arms towards London (under the command of 'gentlemen of quality of their own countries'), to force his enemies to end the fighting. This produced Somerset petitions to both King and Parliament for peace on royalist terms, and a county meeting at Wells to mobilize popular support.[31] The campaign had less success in war-torn Dorset, and in Wiltshire the King's commissioners were in too much disarray to undertake it. The sheriff and a few of the gentry announced, however, that they would 'join in the same course' as their counterparts in Somerset, and in mid-October large numbers of countrymen assembled at Salisbury to answer the King's summons.[32] In fact this was merely an attempt to raise the country for the King masquerading as a peace movement, and the deception was obvious to many people. At West Camel the royalist rector bullied a reluctant parishioner, saying 'it should be the worse for him' if he did not sign. At Wrington one of the churchwardens gave information against refractory neighbours, 'and what rebels they were that did refuse', while his parliamentarian colleague was imprisoned for refusing to co-operate.[33]

The royalist petitioning campaign failed. But it left behind a sense of the legitimacy of peace efforts which was further encouraged by some of the royalist gentry during the winter. On 17 November, after the second battle of Newbury, Sir John Stawell and other leading Somerset Royalists went to the Court, then at Hungerford, with a petition for the removal of burdensome cavalier troops from the county. Instead of relying on plundering soldiers, Charles should reawaken the popular longing for peace. Once more the western counties would send petitions to Parliament, accompanied to London by 'many thousands of the most substantial freeholders' under the slogan 'One and All'. In the end the united community would succeed where the military failed.[34] Stawell's version of the 'One and All' scheme foundered on harsh military realities: even the local commissioners recognized that a war had to be fought, troops recruited, taxes levied. But popular pressure for peace continued during

[30] Bodleian MS Tanner 62, fo. 262. For the women's peace demonstration see Patricia Higgins, 'The Reactions of Women, with special reference to women petitioners', in *Politics, Religion and The English Civil War*, ed. Brian Manning, 1973, pp. 190–8.

[31] Underdown, *Somerset*, pp. 79–80.

[32] William Sanderson, *A Compleat History of the Life and Raigne of King Charles*, 1658, pp. 728–9. *Letter Books of Sir Samuel Luke*, pp. 672–3. Harrison, 'Royalist Organisation in Wilts.', p. 306.

[33] J. Batten, 'Somersetshire Sequestrations during the Civil War', *Somerset Archaeol. and Nat. Hist. Soc. Proceedings*, iv, pt. ii (1853), 69–70. 'Wrington Churchwardens Accounts 1633–75', *SDNQ* xxii (1936–8), 95.

[34] Clarendon, *History of the Rebellion*, iii. 504–5. Underdown, *Somerset*, pp. 91–2.

the winter, encouraged by unrealistic hopes from the negotiations between King and Parliament at Uxbridge. 'Multitudes of people', perhaps as many as 5,000, supported a Buckinghamshire peace petition, and when the Uxbridge treaty collapsed each side showed its concern for public opinion by blaming the other for the breakdown. The Cavaliers, a London newsbook concluded, were 'like to prove losers in the affections of the common people'.[35]

The last of the three avenues to peace—the notion of a 'third force' to impose a settlement—was foreshadowed by the early experiments in counties such as Staffordshire and Cheshire. Throughout the war Parliament's more zealous supporters constantly suspected neutrals and more moderate men of their own side of plotting such schemes. The Earl of Denbigh was accused of intrigues with Royalists to promote a third force in the midlands in 1643.[36] In the autumn of 1644 rumours of covert royalist attempts to create or take over a third party were especially widespread; supporters of the 'One and All' petitions were labelled the 'third party, or new Covenanters'. It is possible that at Hungerford Stawell may have met people who wanted to use 'One and All' as the basis for a third force, and that such talks continued during the winter while the Uxbridge negotiations were in progress.[37] The third force did not materialize in the form envisaged by the politicians, but word of these discussions may have filtered down into the villages and contributed to the climate of opinion in which the Clubmen emerged in the following spring.

The risings of the Clubmen—the most massive popular movement of the entire civil war period—thus have a long pre-history. They enlisted a population with strong traditions of collective action and with deep-rooted notions about public order and governance, affronted beyond endurance by the destructiveness of civil war, the vicious misbehaviour of soldiers on both sides, and the collapse of the familiar institutions of

[35] BL TT, E. 273 (2): *Kingdomes Weekly Intelligencer*, no. 90 (4–11 Mar. 1644/5). For the Buckinghamshire petition see *LJ* vii. 187, 193; *CJ* iv. 46, 50; Whitelocke, *Memorials*, i. 386–7; HMC, *Bath*, iv. 239; BL Add. MS 18982 (Rupert MSS), fo. 37; BL TT, E. 258 (24): *Perfect Occurrences*, 7–14 Feb. 1644/5; and E. 273 (13): *Mercurius Aulicus*, 23 Feb.–2 Mar. 1644/5.

[36] *CSPD, 1649–50*, pp. 444–7. *The Committee at Stafford 1643–1645*, ed. D. H. Pennington and I. A. Roots, Manchester, 1957, intro., p. lxxvi. For an example of the equation of moderate Parliamentarians with the 'Third Party' see BL TT, E. 21 (3): *Parliament Scout*, no. 76 (28 Nov.–5 Dec. 1644).

[37] BL TT, E. 21 (30): *Parliament Scout*, no. 78 (12–19 Dec. 1644). There are some mysterious features of the Hungerford discussions and the possibility of contact with Sir Anthony Ashley Cooper on the parliamentarian side cannot be completely ruled out. See Clarendon, *History of the Rebellion*, iii. 505; iv, 13; and John Locke, 'Memoirs relating to the Life of Anthony First Earl of Shaftesbury', in *The Works of John Locke*, 11th edn., 1812, ix. 266–70. Christie, *Shaftesbury*, i. 40n., points out Locke's inaccuracies; but cf. K. H. D. Haley, *The First Earl of Shaftesbury*, Oxford, 1968, pp. 46, 69n. There is a curious gap in the record of Ashley Cooper's activities between December 1644 and May 1645, and it is worth noting that the first great meeting of the Wiltshire and Dorset Clubmen in May took place within a few miles of his house at Wimborne St. Giles.

church and state. The protests of the gentry against the military, culminating in the resignation of the Wiltshire commissioners, and their promotion of peace petitions, encouraged people of lesser rank to explore other ways of ending the fighting. These were not the deferential reflexes of people who could do nothing without gentry leadership. There were indeed those who feared the democratic implications of the Club movement: 'They will have an army without a king, a lord, or a gentleman almost', a parliamentarian newsbook complained.[38] In fact the risings were revolts of whole communities, not merely 'the rabble'. In the sporadic violence against soldiers that preceded the major outbreaks the hand of local gentlemen can often be seen—for example at South Brent in April 1645, where the squire, John Somerset, played a notable part in resisting the Cavaliers.[39] But the villagers erupted because they were enraged by the soldiers' conduct, not because Somerset ordered them to do so; Somerset joined in because he was a member of the community.

The risings in the south-western counties were triggered by the march of Goring's turbulent army through Dorset at the end of February 1645. Some of his soldiers were killed in a clash with villagers at Godmanstone, and soon there were reports that nearly 1,000 countrymen were in arms to resist the Cavaliers. Waller and Cromwell, who were shadowing Goring, tried to win over this 'Country party' (as a newsbook described them), but without success, and by the end of March the Dorset Committee had disbanded the few who were still in arms.[40] They surfaced again on 12 May, when some 3,000 assembled between Shaftesbury and Blandford. On the 25th there was a great meeting at Gussage Corner, attended by men from both Dorset and Wiltshire, at which articles of association were adopted. Within the next few weeks there were gatherings all over the downlands, from Badbury in the south to Upavon on the northern edge of Salisbury Plain, from Whiteparish near the Hampshire border westward to Mere. The first major assembly in Somerset occurred near Castle Cary on 2 June, and by the time Langport was fought Clubmen were on foot all along the Poldens and across the levels. Fairfax encountered a great crowd of them on Sedgemoor soon after the battle, receiving a friendlier reception than he apparently expected. Later in that war-torn summer other organized bands appeared in the Quantocks and throughout the clothing districts.[41]

*

[38] BL TT, E. 296 (27): *Moderate Intelligencer*, no. 24 (7–15 Aug. 1645). See also Sanderson, *King Charles*, p. 817.
[39] Underdown, *Somerset*, pp. 90–1. Sir Moreton Briggs played a similar role in an incident in Shropshire in which royalist troops were disarmed: BL Add. MS 18981 (Rupert MSS), fo. 225.
[40] See David Underdown, 'The Chalk and the Cheese: Contrasts among the English Clubmen', *P & P* no. 85 (Nov. 1979), 30, and references there cited.
[41] Underdown, 'Chalk and Cheese', pp. 32–3, 37, 45–6; *Somerset*, pp. 98–9, 105–8, 111–13, 116.

The Club risings harnessed all the earlier yearnings for peace in a single popular movement. In the short run the Clubmen wanted to protect their communities from plunder and to reduce the burden of contributions. In the longer run they wanted to end the war altogether. Some groups of Clubmen were more inclined to favour the King, some the Parliament, and they blundered into several violent clashes with the forces of both: with Goring's crew, with the Cavaliers garrisoning Devizes; with Roundheads at Sturminster Newton in June, near Bridport in July, and at Hambledon Hill in August.[42] But the risings have a significance that goes beyond these immediate circumstances. Whichever side they favoured, all showed by their words and actions how tenaciously the older popular system of values had survived the war years.

The Clubmen had their own version of those principles of 'Liberty and Property' for which, Parliament never tired of asserting, the war was being fought. It is clear in the methods of the election of two or three of 'the abler sort' from each parish to run their associations (with a dash of participatory democracy in the occasional mass meetings).[43] It is clear in their repeated appeals to ancient law, their invocation of Magna Carta, their denunciations (as by the Sussex Clubmen) of 'insufferable, insolent, arbitrary power . . . contrary to all our ancient known laws, or ordinances of Parliament'.[44] The central place of 'property' in the Clubmen's programme is clear in all their statements, from the simple banners proclaiming 'If you offer to plunder or take our cattle,/Be assured we will bid you battle', to the more elaborate manifestos denouncing 'plunder and all other unlawful violence'.

One striking feature of the Clubmen's declarations is the constant repetition of the four points of the Protestation of 1641. The Protestation's original purpose was to cement loyalty to Parliament, yet its effectiveness depended on the very breadth of its appeal. Throughout the war the Protestation provided an automatic refuge for people unable, or unwilling, to take sides. In August 1642 the Dorset grand jury expressed bafflement at the 'contrary commands' of the Militia Ordinance and the Commission of Array, but they were entirely willing to defend the King's prerogative, the privilege of Parliament and 'the laws of this realm, according to the tenour of our late Protestation'.[45] Appeals to the document surface in the 1643 truce negotiations in the western counties, and in the peace petitions of 1644. A version of it, with the addition of some

[42] Underdown, 'Chalk and Cheese', p. 33, and references there cited.
[43] Morrill, *Revolt*, p. 199. Underdown, *Somerset*, pp. 98–9, 107.
[44] Morrill, *Revolt*, pp. 105, 198.
[45] PRO SP 16/491, no. 117. The Dorset petition is wrongly ascribed to Somerset in *CSPD*, 1641–3, p. 371.

words against 'sectaries and schismatics', appears in an oath of association which the Royalists imposed on the western counties earlier in that year.[46] The Protestation provided the peace-seeking majority with a programme and a vocabulary. Its four points are present in embryo in the declaration of the Wiltshire and Dorset Clubmen of 25 May 1645, and appear more explicitly in many later statements. The maintenance of 'the true reformed Protestant religion', the King's prerogatives, the privileges of Parliament, and 'the liberties and properties of the subject' were, the Wiltshire Clubmen pointed out in their July petition, 'the main four articles of that general Protestation, to which the body of this kingdom hath formerly sworn'.[47] A desire for peace on this conventional, conservative basis was the strongest element in popular politics, except for a small minority of militants, in 1645, and indeed throughout the war.

Even in a kingdom shattered by civil strife there thus remained important continuities in popular politics. Similar continuities existed in the concurrent struggles over customary rights. If the war brought burdens, it also brought opportunities for the recovery of lost advantages. Much of the wartime disorder, to be sure, was the product of immediate circumstances. 'Now men are lawless, trees and hedges are carried away without controlment'; tenants 'use their landlord how they list for their rents, taking this to be a time of liberty': such are the typical complaints of landowners during the war.[48] The massive increase in arrears of rents requires no ideological explanation. The crisis arose from sheer necessity: people defaulted because they had nothing left with which to pay. Deserters and other masterless men who took to a life of crime were not engaging in a form of social protest, but simply trying to survive, at the expense of the honest poor as well as the rich. It was the country people, not the gentry, who complained in 1645 about a gang of robbers 'in the woods about Buckingham . . . who are neither for the King nor Parliament, but lurk there up and down on purpose to rob the passengers'.[49]

Some kinds of wartime lawlessness, however, were clearly related to pre-war social discontents. Rioting against forest enclosers and fen drainers had again erupted in 1641 and 1642. In the Forest of Dean the lines of division merged neatly with national political ones: the Dean foresters naturally took the side of Parliament against their oppressor, the royalists (and Catholic) Sir John Wintour. On the other side of England, in the Isle of Axholme, there is a clear connection between the

---

[46] *The Association, Agreement, and Protestation of the Counties of Somerset, Dorset, Cornwall and Devon*, Oxford, 1644. See also Underdown, *Somerset*, pp. 72–3.

[47] BL TT, E. 292 (24): *The Desires, and Resolutions of the Club-Men of the Counties of Dorset and Wilts.*, 1645. Morrill, *Revolt*, pp. 105, 197.

[48] Oxfordshire VCH Office, Glympton papers, J. W[heate] to Wm. Wheate, [1643–4?]. Hants RO, Catalogue of Kingsmill MSS (typescript), no. 1362. See also Stone, *Family and Fortune*, p. 149.

[49] BL TT, E. 266 (37): *Perfect Occurrences*, 2 Jan. 1645/6, under 23 Dec. 1645.

inhabitants' resistance to the drainage works and their allegiance to Parliament. Elsewhere, although rioters might appear to adopt a royalist or a parliamentarian stance, they often had other, more immediate, priorities. The drainage projectors included some powerful parliamentarian magnates, and it is not surprising that the fen population sometimes swung over to royalism in retaliation. Crowland became a notable cavalier stronghold, while disorders in the Isle of Ely in 1643 had to be suppressed by parliamentarian troops from Wisbech and Cambridge; a JP was told by rioters that 'he was no justice, for he was against the King and all for the Parliament'.[50] The mass invasions of deer parks in south-east England at about this time produced some similar statements, like that of the mob at Farnham, who told a keeper that 'they cared not what Parliament did or said'. The real issue was not the authority of Parliament, however, but the right of the community to resources unjustly appropriated by individuals. 'They came for venison and venison they would have', rioters in Waltham Forest announced, 'for there was no law settled at this time'.[51]

There were attacks on deer parks in the west country: one on the Earl of Middlesex's park at Forthampton, Gloucestershire, for example. Often the culprits were soldiers, as in April 1643, when Hungerford's men killed deer in Longleat Park and seized livestock on Horningsham Common belonging to the Catholic Arundells.[52] At this time the Earl of Salisbury's steward was 'in continual fear as well of rogues as soldiers who range up and down the country taking men's goods by force', and countrymen near Pewsey had to implement 'club law' to recover cattle, sheep, and cloth taken from them by marauding Welshmen.[53] Soldiers, especially outsiders, were obvious targets to be resisted, but some people were quite ready to take action against their landlords, if opportunity arose. Pembroke's enclosures at Aldbourne were attacked early in 1643, and in May, when Maurice's troops sacked Salisbury's mansion at Cranborne, the local tenantry gleefully joined in the destruction of the rolls in which their copyholds were recorded. The Earl also suffered at the hands of his Somerset tenants when his tithes at Martock were appropriated by the poorer inhabitants.[54]

The war enabled victims of pre-war disafforestation to embark on another round of resistance. Hatred of the recent enclosures still smouldered in the western forests. Enclosures in Braydon and Selwood

[50] HMC, *Fifth Report* (House of Lords MSS), p. 93. See also Manning, *English People*, pp. 187–8; and Holmes, *Lincolnshire*, pp. 152–7, 163–6.

[51] HMC, *Fifth Report*, pp. 51–2. Manning, *English People*, pp. 190–2. See also Sharp, *In Contempt*, p. 223.

[52] Manning, *English People*, p. 192. *Ludlow's Memoirs*, i. 447.

[53] HMC, *Salisbury*, xxii. 374. Morrill, *Revolt*, pp. 102–3. Harrison, 'Royalist Organisation in Wilts.', p. 385.

[54] Stone, *Family and Fortune*, pp. 148–9.

THE
VVorld turn'd upside down:

OR,

A briefe description of the ridiculous Fashions of these distracted Times.

By **T. J.** a well-willer to King, Parliament and Kingdom.

London : Printed for *John Smith*. 1647.

1. *The World Turned Upside Down:* Title page of a 1647 pamphlet. *BL, TT E. 372 (19)*

A. Rioters outside Lambeth Palace, 1 May 1640. *BL, TT E. 116 (49), fo. 2*

B. Riot in Westminster Hall, 27 Dec. 1641. *BL, TT E. 116 (49), fo. 9*

2. DISORDERS IN LONDON, 1640–1

The Ministers and people solemnly take the Protestation in all Churches over the Kingdome.

A. A minister and his parishioners take the oath. *BL, TT E. 116 (49), fo. 4*

The Countie of Buckingham cometh to London the very same day of the Lords & Comons so quarded, with their Petition to the Parl: Carrying the Protestation on their staves on horseback, and the Counties of Essex, Hertford, Barkshire, Surrey, & others, followed them, in like maner, shortly after.

B. Procession of the Buckinghamshire petitioners, 11 Jan. 1642. *BL, TT E. 116 (49), fo. 7*

3. THE PROTESTATION

A. Soldiers on the march. *BL, TT E. 86 (23), frontis.*

23. May. 1643. Voted that if Queene Pawning the Iewells of y Crowne in Holland & there with buying Aemes to affist the Warr against y Parlam! & her owne actuall performances with her popish army in the North was high Treafon & tranfmited to the Lords; images, Cruci-fixes papiftecall bookes in Somerfet and Iameses ware burnt and y Capuchin friers fent away

B. Roundhead soldiers burn 'popish' images, 1643. *BL, TT E. 365 (6), p. 23*

4. CIVIL WAR

The 2 of May. 1643. y^e Crosse in Cheapeside was pulled downe, a Troope of Horse & 2 Companies of foote wayted to garde it & at y^e fall of y^e tope Crosse dromes beat tru-pets blew & multitudes of Capes warre throwne in ye Ayre. & a greate Shoute of People with ioy, ye 2 of May the Alma na-ke fareth, was ye invention of the Crosse. & 6 day at night was the Leaden Popes burnt, in the pla-ce where it ftood with ringinge of Bells, & a greate Acclamation & no hurt done in all these actions.

A. Demolition of Cheapside Cross, 2 May 1643. *BL, TT E. 365 (6), p. 21*

10 of May the Boocke of Sportes vpon the Lords day was bu-rnt by the Hangman in the place where the Crosse ftoode, & at Exhange

B. Burning of the Book of Sports, 10 May 1643. *BL, TT E. 365 (6), p. 21*

5. CULTURAL CONFLICT

A. Roundhead and Cavalier. *BL, TT E. 238 (21), title*

B. The Exciseman, from a broadsheet entitled *A Dialogue betwixt an EXCISE-MAN and DEATH.*
BL, TT 669 f. 21 (58)

6. POPULAR STEREOTYPES

A. The war as an opportunity for cuckoldry. *BL, TT E. 114 (14), title*

B. Skimmington beats her husband.
Bodleian, Douce L. 4, frontis.

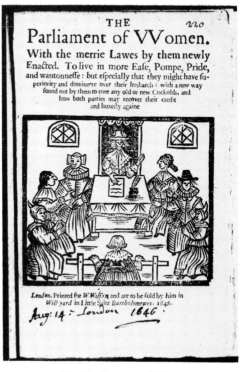

C. The Parliament of Women.
BL, TT E. 1150 (5), title

7. THE THREAT TO PATRIARCHAL ORDER

A. The 'riding' of a monopolist, 1641. The sentence above
this woodcut in the original reads: 'The manner and forme how
Projectors and Patentors have rode a Tylting in a Parliament time.'
BL, TT E. 156 (16), p. 8

B. The charivari theme used in political caricature, 1647.
BL, TT 669 f. 10 (114)

8. CHARIVARI

were destroyed early in the war by 'the poor of the neighbouring parishes', and others thrown down in Neroche had still not been restored ten years later.[55] Disorders in Gillingham Forest were encouraged by roundhead soldiers quartered near Shaftesbury who joined villagers in destroying hedges and fences. They were soon marched away, but in April 1643 there were further outbreaks in which men armed with clubs and muskets marched behind drummers to their work. The protests died away during the more stable royalist rule after Roundway, but in 1644 authority collapsed and the inhabitants once more took the law into their own hand. The men of Gillingham and Motcombe joined in the Club outbreaks in the spring of 1645, but still with their own priorities: on their way to a rendezvous they found time to dismantle the forest enclosures yet again.[56]

The wartime riots in Gillingham closely resemble those of fifteen years earlier. There is the same careful selection of targets, violence being used primarily against the representatives of the enclosing aristocrats: Thomas Brunker, the Earl of Elgin's agent, went in fear of his life and his servants were repeatedly beaten up. Some of Elgin's tenants were also attacked, but the purpose was less to inflict physical harm than to terrorize them into abandoning their holdings or stopping payment of rent. The rioters showed the same respect for their version of law and custom as their predecessors. New enclosures could be broken down, but property of longer standing was not damaged. Sir Edward Nicholas, who had a lease of Gillingham Park, was told about the June 1643 riots by his steward, who noted: 'They have not touched the Park nor . . . the lawn, because they were anciently enclosed'.[57] In return, the rioters met the same ambivalent response from the local forces of law and order as had been the case in the 1620s. When the Dorset *posse comitatus* was mustered against the rioters in 1643, only a score of unarmed men turned up. One of the JPs, Matthew Davis, repeatedly bailed people to answer at assizes which were unlikely to be held, and although his colleague William Whitaker was more severe it was only because he was a client of Elgin's—and the rioters cut down his orchard in revenge. Military commanders like Strode and Hungerford tried to round up suspects, but prisoners were invariably allowed to escape by sympathetic soldiers.[58]

The rioters showed their old qualities of determination and resourcefulness. The fortunes of war often short-circuited official action—on 3 July 1643, for example, Ludlow was ordered to round up suspects at Mere, Gillingham, and Motcombe, but ten days later Parliament's

[55] Sharp, *In Contempt*, pp. 242–6. *LJ* vi. 30.

[56] Sharp, *In Contempt*, pp. 224–32, 239–42, 248.

[57] Nicholas, *Secretary Nicholas*, p. 182.

[58] Besides the JPs' actions noted by Sharp, *In Contempt*, pp. 230–2, they committed three other men to the Assizes for riot and two for throwing down hedges: WRO QS Order Book 1641–54, Michaelmas 1643.

authority in the area was conclusively destroyed at Roundway. It would probably have made little difference if the battle had gone the other way.[59] War conditions made resistance easier, but the old skills were there to draw on. Collective action needed leaders, and it found them in men like John Phillips, a tanner who had been prominent in the pre-war riots, and who in January 1644 again led the men of Mere against the restored enclosures, riding his horse through the broken hedges in symbolic assertion of their rights. On other occasions, Elgin later complained, the foresters 'set two at a time to work, pretending thereby to avoid a riot', showing not only that they knew the law, but also that their movement was as disciplined and co-ordinated as ever.[60]

The Clubmen's appeals to the Protestation and the Gillingham foresters' attacks on enclosures may seem very different in nature. Both, however, reflect the survival of notions of law and custom that we have repeatedly seen reflected in popular politics in the years before the war. Most people wanted a return to the world they had known—a world in which heads of households regulated their families and ran their communities in parish and manor court, within a framework of law protected by monarch, Parliament, and benignly paternalistic JPs, and of religion provided by a moderately Protestant church. The war dislocated that order far more violently than Stuart centralization had done, even if it provided occasional opportunities to recover lost common rights. The English people wanted peace, on whatever terms would best guarantee a restoration of that vanished order. Unfortunately many of them disagreed on what those terms might be.

*

We confront at last the division of the English people into two contending parties, into Roundheads and Cavaliers. In all areas they experienced burdensome taxation and quartering, plunder and devastation, the dislocation of economic life, of community order and government. Everywhere a majority tried, as far as they could, to stay out of the fighting, to minimize its disruptive impact, and even, if possible, to end it. Yet they also divided in a civil war. People fought and died in the England of the 1640s, and unless we are to dismiss the whole question of popular allegiance as an illusion and attribute the varying loyalties of different regions solely to the influence of their élite leaders, the regional contrasts demand explanation. And regional contrasts there very clearly were. Some parts of the western counties were distinctly more royalist, some more parliamentarian, than others.

---

[59] *LJ* vi. 15, 30, 48, 118.
[60] HMC, *Sixth Report* (House of Lords MSS), p. 40. Sharp, *In Contempt*, pp. 241–2.

But, we may ask, how do we know that they were 'really' more royalist or more parliamentarian? How can we penetrate behind often ambiguous actions to uncover the real preferences and intentions of individuals, much less of whole communities? Even the more politically aware gentry often changed sides, placidly conformed to each in turn, or were manoeuvred into supporting one or the other through force of circumstance. 'Both sides', Dr Morrill points out, 'were riven by feuds and a majority had no deep-seated convictions behind their choice of sides'.[61] Take for example, the wartime mayors of Wells, Robert Morgan and William West. Until 1642 there is nothing in the record to distinguish them: they performed the same civic duties, signed the same petitions. But the war made Morgan a Parliamentarian, West a Royalist, in each case because their mayoralty coincided with the temporary local predominance of the party in question. They may have had ideological motives when they took sides, but if so, we have no evidence of them.[62]

The problems raised by neutralism and circumstance, hard enough to disentangle when we are dealing with the élite, are obviously infinitely compounded when we turn to the hazily documented multitudes. War service under compulsion—by impressment or at the command of landlords or employers—is a sufficiently complicated subject to require separate discussion in a later chapter. Even without this problem we have difficulties enough. Villagers, we have observed, often had their own priorities, and many unrelated matters, such as the settling of old scores, might temporarily align them with one of the contending armies. A Stalbridge family named Ridout enlisted soldiers in their quarrel with relatives at Henstridge over a debt. The troopers threatened one of the Henstridge Ridouts that they would 'cut him as small as herbs to the pot', beat him up, and seized the disputed bond. The war also created new sources of antagonism. The constable of Burbage did his duty by requisitioning two of Francis Barber's carts for Waller's army. But Barber had two sons on the other side and when the tide turned in favour of the Royalists they had the constable's horses seized in retaliation, threatening not to 'leave him while he was worth a groat'.[63] It would be a rash historian who assigned the Ridouts or the Burbage constable to one side or the other on this sort of evidence.

[61] Morrill, *Cheshire*, p. 74. See also Morrill, *Revolt*, esp. pp. 45–6; and Pennington, 'County and Country', pp. 12–25.
[62] David Underdown, 'A Case Concerning Bishops' Lands: Cornelius Burges and the Corporation of Wells', *Eng. H.R.* lxxviii (1963), 22–3. On the general subject of urban localism see Roger Howell, 'The Structure of Urban Politics in the English Civil War', *Albion*, xi (1979), 111–27; and 'Neutralism, Conservatism and Political Alignment in the English Revolution: The Case of the Towns, 1642–9', in *Reactions*, ed. Morrill, pp. 67–87.
[63] Pope, 'Sidelights on the Civil War in Dorset', p. 53. Underdown, 'Problem of Popular Allegiance', p. 91.

The problems are not, fortunately, as intractable as they may appear. Neutralism, for example, was not always absolute. People might sensibly want to avoid risking life and limb, might wish to escape the war and till their fields in peace, and still prefer one side to the other. The preferences might not be strong enough to provoke them into hopeless resistance to a dominant power, but in times of conflict it could be clearly visible in a reluctance or willingness to provide armies with supplies or intelligence. Neutralism could coexist with real differences of regional outlook. The vagaries of individual behaviour, too, can be allowed for. At the beginning of the war John Mowdy of Upton Lovell, Wiltshire, maintained his son in the King's service; later, 'when Parliament began to prevail', the son changed sides and was threatened with disinheritance.[64] On which side, we might perhaps ask, do the Mowdys belong? In fact, though, we are concerned less with the Mowdys than with the village of Upton Lovell and the whole downland area in which it was situated, in other words with group rather than individual behaviour.

Group behaviour: the war involved a far wider segment of society than the gentry. If any further proof of this is required, it can be found in the emphasis placed by both sides on propaganda. The inhabitants of the western counties, like those of all other parts of England, were constantly bombarded with sermons, declarations, and pamphlets, all aimed at influencing a broad spectrum of opinion. Hertford's arrival in August 1642 was followed by a hectic competition for popular support, in which the Parliamentarians had the better of it. The Commission of Array was in Latin and, as Clarendon ruefully observed, its enemies translated it 'into what English they pleased', trying to persuade the middling sort that it would impose a ruinous level of arbitrary taxation, and the poor that it would return them to a state of feudal bondage. Intemperate expressions of class feeling by Lord Poulett were sedulously magnified, and an impression successfully created that Hertford's party consisted only of outsiders and papists who had come to 'enthral the people', through their power to 'take what they please of any man's estate'. Hertford's disclaimers were no more effective than his attempt to counter the popish charge by labelling the Roundheads as men 'known to despise the Common Prayer Book, and to favour Brownists, Anabaptists, and other disturbers of all order and government'.[65]

The rival stereotypes—the swaggering, tyrannical, popish, plundering Cavalier and the canting, divisive, and socially subversive Roundhead— remained the staple fare of propaganda throughout the war.[66] The

---

[64] BL Add. MS 22084 (Wilts. Sequestrations Register), fo. 140.

[65] Clarendon, *History of the Rebellion*, ii. 296. HMC, *Fifth Report* (House of Lords MSS), p. 44. See also Underdown, *Somerset*, pp. 31–2, 38–9; and Manning. *English People*, pp. 157, 181–2.

[66] The sermons of Thomas Holt, royalist vicar of Westonzoyland, noted in *LJ* v. 669–70, are a good example. For some others see *Politics, Religion and Literature in the Seventeenth Century*, ed. William . Lamont and Sybil Oldfield, 1975, ch. 3.

anti-Catholic line was particularly effective for Parliament when Charles I began employing troops from Ireland in the latter part of 1643. Even in the royalist regions this led to widespread disaffection among both the gentry and the lower orders. Royalist soldiers at Bridgwater mutinied when they heard of the landing of Irish troops at Minehead and Bristol and there were similar signs of hostility in other places.[67] The issue was heavily stressed in June 1644. Essex and the Cornish peer, Lord Robartes, made inspiring speeches to the countrymen who came flocking into Weymouth and Chard to list themselves as volunteers; Hugh Peter, the greatest of the army preachers, thundered against the 'barbarous intruders'—the Cavaliers and their Irish mercenaries—at open-air meetings in Dorset. The deluge of propaganda helped to reignite enthusiasm for Parliament, for example at Dorchester, where the townspeople, women as well as men, fiercely resisted royalist assaults on two occasions later in the summer. The Royalists countered as best they could, depicting the Roundheads as the oppressive invaders who had used foreign forces (in this case the Scots); the argument appears in the King's speech appealing for his subjects' 'hearts, and hands, and purses' at the great meeting near Ilchester in July.[68] The propaganda competition shows how both parties recognized that the common people were not just obedient ciphers. They could, and often did, take sides.

*

The patterns of civil war allegiance in the western counties have an unmistakably regional character. This will be demonstrated statistically in the next chapter, but even an impressionistic survey using familiar sources reveals that some areas were strongly parliamentarian, others distinctly royalist. The most solidly parliamentarian region was the dairying and cloth-making country of north Wiltshire and north Somerset; the pasturelands of west Dorset and the Somerset levels were on the same side, though less enthusiastically. Support for the Royalists was strongest in the downlands, in Blackmore Vale and the adjoining parts of south Somerset, and in the hill country to the west. The towns generally followed the same paths as the rural areas that surrounded them, though there were some notable exceptions—Wells was royalist, Dorchester and Taunton strongly parliamentarian. Before we consider the reasons for these contrasts, it may be useful to examine the evidence in more detail.[69]

[67] Joyce L. Malcolm, 'All the King's Men: the impact of the crown's Irish soldiers on the English civil war', *Irish Historical Studies*, xxi (1979), 247–8.

[68] *CSPD, 1644*, p. 271. Bayley, *Dorset*, pp. 188, 194–208. John Vicars, *Gods Ark Overtopping the Worlds Waves* (pt. iii of *England's Parliamentary Chronicle*), 1646, pp. 264–5. Whitelocke, *Memorials*, i. 274, 280. Underdown, *Somerset*, pp. 75–6.

[69] The geographical division is briefly summarized in Underdown, 'Problem of Popular Allegiance', pp. 75–7.

First the northern clothing districts: the region which produced the great uprising of August 1642, in which the husbandsmen and cloth-workers assembled to drive away Hertford's Cavaliers. Many armed only with 'pitchforks, dungpicks, and suchlike weapons', they showed their Puritan sentiments in the praying and psalm-singing that echoed through their encampment on the open hills. Hertford could assemble only the mutinous fragments of a trained-band regiment (most of whom deserted) to supplement the gentry's levies from their households and estates in other parts of the county.[70] After Hertford's departure the political temperature quickly abated, but in the following year the region's loyalties were again apparent. After Lansdown, says Clarendon, Waller was easily able to reinforce his army, thanks to 'the inclinations of the three counties of Wilts, Gloucester, and Somerset, which joined about Bath in the most absolute disaffected parts of all three'. The royalist commander Hopton admitted that the 'general inclinations of the Country' were against him: he could get neither recruits, supplies, nor intelligence of Waller's movements.[71]

The Royalists' victories enabled them to rule the region, but not to elicit the kind of popular support that had been available to their enemies. The inhabitants' acquiescence should not surprise us: the history of the civil war is full of examples of towns and regions whose sensible reluctance to court martyrdom seems to bely their earlier enthusiasm. The local forces who pursued Hertford to Sherborne ran 'as if the devil had been in them', the Earl of Bedford complained, under bombardment from the castle.[72] But though the inhabitants of the clothing parishes might wish to avoid service far from home, might complain of the burdens imposed by Parliament as well as King, might obey and even serve the Royalists under duress, their respective attitudes to the two sides are clear. When Fairfax arrived in the summer of 1645 the true sympathies of the population were revealed. In a second great general rising, the Clubmen of the region once more turned out massively for Parliament.[73]

The parliamentarian allegiance of west Dorset and the Somerset levels was more ambiguous, and in the latter case is mainly demonstrated by the behaviour of the local Clubmen. The parliamentarian towns, too, exhibit some striking alternations between zeal and acquiescence. Poole, Dorchester, Bridport, and Taunton were quick to raise and drill volunteers in August 1642, and in these places the middling sort were strongly for the Parliament. At Dorchester roundhead zeal was extended to the lower orders by the dissemination of rumours that Cavaliers were coming to

[70] Underdown, *Somerset*, pp. 32–8.
[71] Clarendon, *History of the Rebellion*, iii. 89, 94–5. Underdown, *Somerset*, p. 61.
[72] Underdown, *Somerset*, p. 41.
[73] Ibid. p. 113.

burn the town. In 1643, confronted with menacing royalist power many such places, to be sure, quickly caved in. But Dorchester showed greater resolution in 1644, Lyme and Taunton dramatically more so in sieges that made them famous in Puritan annals.[74]

The arable regions were clearly on the other side. Throughout the war both downland Dorset and the Wiltshire chalk country displayed mildly royalist inclinations. There was at least as much neutralism as in other areas, but whenever popular sympathies for one side or the other surface they usually do so in royalist form. The downlands provided, in the force led by Richard Rogers of Bryanston, the one segment of the Dorset trained bands to assist Hertford at Sherborne. Corfe Castle served as a rallying-place for the royalism of the Isle of Purbeck, a region appropriately described by the roundhead Sir Walter Erle as 'very malignant'. The inhabitants of neighbouring downland villages took part in a royalist attempt on Weymouth in February 1645, an incident that has no parliamentarian parallel in the region.[75] Downland Wiltshire provides a similar picture—few dramatic incidents, but a general impression of solid, if unenthusiastic, support for the King. This was, for example, the only part of Wiltshire in which the Royalists succeeded in getting significant numbers of subscriptions to their Oath of Association during the winter of 1643–4. Most of the towns in and on the edge of the downlands in both counties had similar sympathies.[76]

The royalism of the downlands is revealed even more clearly by the behaviour of the Clubmen of this area. If the Clubmen had been totally neutralist, with no preference for either side their natural course in July 1645 would have been to support the New Model as the best hope for a quick ending to the war. They did not do this. They had resisted Goring's troops, and there were occasional skirmishes between Clubmen from the northern part of Salisbury Plain and royalist forces from Devizes. But their antagonism towards the Parliamentarians is much more consistent. London propagandists routinely exaggerated the extent to which the Clubmen were pawns of the Cavaliers, collaborators in 'Jesuitical plot of the enemy'.[77] They were wrong about the conspiracy, but right about the downland Clubmen's ultimate allegiance.

Blackmore Vale and south-east Somerset displayed a similar attachment to the King's side, though again with frequent symptoms of

---

[74] *CJ* ii. 733. *LJ* v. 229, 262, 310–11. HMC, *Fifth Report* (House of Lords MSS), pp. 42–3. *CSPD, 1641–3*, pp. 364–5, 375–6. HMC, *Portland*, i. 47. Clarendon, *History of the Rebellion*, iii. 127–8, 157. See also Bayley, *Dorset*, pp. 45–9, 99–100; and Underdown, *Somerset*, pp. 50–1.

[75] Bayley, *Dorset*, pp. 55, 57, 82–7, 91. Underdown, 'Problem of Popular Allegiance', p. 76.

[76] Harrison, 'Royalist Organisation in Wilts.', pp. 243–7. *Ludlow's Memoirs*, i. 93, 95. Whitelocke, *Memorials*, i. 279.

[77] BL TT, E. 296 (12): *The Kings Answer to the Propositions for Peace*, 1645. For the conduct of the downland Clubmen see Underdown, 'Chalk and Cheese', pp. 33–4.

neutralism and occasional backsliding. Bruton and Wincanton, a news-book lamented in 1642, were at 'the centre and heart of all the malignants' of Somerset, and this was born out on many occasions later in the war. There was a minor royalist uprising in the area in February 1643, and in 1645 the local Clubmen aligned themselves with the royalist groups from Dorset and Wiltshire rather than with their more parliamentarian counterparts in the Somerset levels.[78] Beyond their immediate domain at Sherborne, the Digbys at first seem to have had little success in raising men from Blackmore Vale. Sherborne, however, was firmly royalist: when roundhead troops went to secure the place in April 1643 they were violently resisted by the inhabitants, who shouted 'Kill the Parliament dogs!'[79] The Royalists had more success in the Vale in 1644, and a London sneer that many of Sir Lewis Dyve's soldiers were armed only with 'hedge-stakes, prongs, sheep-hooks, tar-boxes, and such like rural implements' is itself a confession that they were local men. And the Clubmen of Blackmore Vale stood firmly with the downlanders in the weeks leading up to the scuffle at Hambledon Hill and the subsequent fall of Sherborne to Fairfax.[80]

*

The geographical patterns are already clear enough. How are we to explain them? Of the four principle interpretations of popular behaviour outlined in the first chapter the 'class' explanation obviously has most relevance to the northern clothing districts. Class is a concept that can be applied to seventeenth-century English society only with the greatest possible caution. We can identify 'horizontal' social divisions existing across the boundaries of village, town, and region—between landowners, tenant farmers, artisans, and labourers. We can identify certain interests shared by members of each group. But it is not so easy to detect the element of consciousness necessary to transform a status or occupational group into a class. Most people still thought of themselves in 'vertical', local terms: as members of communities. Within those communities they were very conscious of their status and their roles as masters or servants, but were much less conscious of possessing an identity of interests with other masters or servants throughout the land. Still, as we have seen, a process of social differentiation was under way, more noticeably in some places than in others, and where this was happening wartime allegiances sometimes reflected a rudimentary sense of class identity.

---

[78] Underdown, 'Problem of Popular Allegiance', pp. 76, 83; *Somerset*, pp. 44, 99, 116.

[79] Bayley, *Dorset*, p. 66.

[80] BL, TT, E. 23 (16): *Mercurius Britannicus*, no. 64 (30 Dec. 1644–6 Jan. 1644/5). See also Underdown, 'Chalk and Cheese', pp. 44–5.

Throughout the war utterances by leaders of both sides repeatedly betray their fears of the consequences of appealing to, and arming, the common people.[81] It was a common assumption that the King's side was that of the gentry: 'the King would have the better', the Earl of Danby told his steward, 'for the gentry would stick by him, but the Parliament had only the common people'. This idea was widely accepted by Parliamentarians as well as Royalists. Thomas Stephens, sheriff of Gloucestershire in 1645, conceded that 'almost all the gentry were ever for the King', while in Wiltshire Edmund Ludlow lamented how many of them 'were contented to serve his arbitrary designs, if they might have leave to insult over such as were of a lower order'. Many were the royalist sneers at the lowly social origins of the Roundheads, typified by Sir Edward Walker's comment on the Warminster watchmaker who commanded the garrison at Woodhouse, Wiltshire: 'a person of equal quality with many of the rebels' officers'.[82] Fears that the poorer sort were motivated by class hatred of the gentry were further inflamed by incidents like the Stour Valley riots along the Essex–Suffolk border in 1642, which seriously alarmed local Parliamentarians as well as Royalists.[83] Elsewhere, however, embryonic class feeling was kept under élite control and channelled into support for Parliament. Dr Manning has argued persuasively that it provided a significant motivation for the clothworker–smallholders of the West Riding of Yorkshire and of south Lancashire, and for the metalworkers of the Birmingham area.[84] Even in these areas, though, its extent should not be exaggerated. The goal of Puritan reformation certainly inspired many of the middling sort. But outside the Stour Valley there are few signs of hostility to gentry as a class, or of anything beyond a desire to resist the imagined Catholic–Cavalier conspiracy.

The partially realized class feeling is evident in the clothing districts of the western counties. John Corbet's account of the civil war in Gloucestershire presents a version of the alignment familiar in Baxter and other commentators. At Bristol, says Corbet, 'the King's cause and party were favoured by two extremes in that city; the one the wealthy and powerful men, the other of the basest and lowest sort, but disgusted by the middle rank, the true and best citizens'. Corbet distinguishes between 'the true commons of the realm and the dregs of the people; the one the most vehement assertors of public liberty, but the other the first rise of tyrannical government'. The Royalists, in both city and county, were the

[81] Among many other possible examples: 'Memoirs of Denzil, Lord Holles', in *Select Tracts Relating to the Civil War in England*, ed. Francis Baron Maseres, 1815, i. 191; HMC, *Fourth Report* (De La Warr MSS), p. 309; BL TT, E. 21 (25): *Kingdomes Weekly Intelligencer*, no. 85 (10–17 Dec. 1644).

[82] HMC, *Sixth Report* (House of Lords MSS), p. 113. *Ludlow's Memoirs*, i. 96, 469. Sir Edward Walker, *Historical Discourses upon Several Occasions . . .*, 1705, pp. 39–40.

[83] Manning, *English People*, pp. 171–8. Holmes, *Eastern Association*, pp. 43–4, 51.

[84] Manning, *English People*, pp. 199–219, 246–7.

party of the rich and their dependents, 'the needy multitude'. For Parliament, on the other hand, 'the yeomen, farmers, clothiers, and the whole middle rank of the people were the only active men'.[85]

Parliament's strength in the cheese and clothing country was clearly related to the social structure of the region. The MP John Ashe was at pains to stress that the Somerset rising of August 1642 cut across class lines, comprising 'all the gentry, and yeomanry, and lusty youths that inhabited in the north-east part of the county'. But his own evidence belies that claim. Not only were many of the local gentry with Hertford at Wells, but the presence of Horners, Pophams, and a few other magnates could not disguise the acute shortage of suitable officers. Then and later the constant refrain was, 'we are lost and spoiled if we have not commanders': it was the Royalists who had the natural leaders, the gentlemen and their sons.[86] Throughout the war Parliament had most success in recruiting its forces from the middling sort of the clothing districts, a fact that was obvious to their enemies. When Wardour was plundered by forces from north Wiltshire and Somerset in May 1643 the Roundheads sold lead piping from the castle at 6*d*. a yard, a Royalist noted, 'as these men's wives in North Wiltshire do bone-lace'.[87] The limits of the middling sort's enthusiasm for Parliament were soon apparent. In their own countryside the men of the clothing parishes would join, or at least co-operate, with Parliament's forces, as they again showed in 1643 and 1645. But outside it their zeal tended to evaporate very quickly. They depended heavily, too, on gentry leadership, and even the independent Clubmen seem to have raised no objection to being recruited as auxiliaries to the New Model under Alexander Popham's command.[88]

Class feeling may help to explain the solidarity of the clothing districts for Parliament. But for it to be a sufficient explanation would require a much more consistent parliamentarian activism that in fact existed, and a perception of the war in terms wider than the localism which made the inhabitants so reluctant to serve outside their own area. It would also require a greater tendency to independent action even against the interests of the parliamentarian gentry, and (presumably) some indications that the poor, who did not share the ideological commitment of the middling sort, looked to the Royalists for protection against their oppressive parish élites. In some of the larger towns—Bristol, Gloucester, and Salisbury, for example—signs of Corbet's alliance of the wealthy and poor against the middling sort can be detected. But most places reveal no such division. Taunton, Dorchester, and the Dorset port towns went solidly for the

[85] Corbet, 'Military Government of Gloucester', pp. 306–7.
[86] [John Ashe], *A Perfect Relation of All the Passages and Proceedings of the Marquesse Hartford* (1642). Underdown, *Somerset*, pp. 37, 41.
[87] *Ludlow's Memoirs*, i. 450.
[88] Underdown, *Somerset*, p. 115.

Parliament; Shaftesbury, Blandford, Wareham, and Wells equally so for the King. Towns as well as rural villages still behaved as communities.[89]

The second available explanation of allegiance—deference—is, like the 'class' hypothesis, more satisfactory for some areas than for others. Assumptions that servants would follow their masters, tenants their landlords, were almost as commonly made in the seventeenth century as they have been by later historians. All over England forces were raised, especially for the King, by men who could expect their tenants to follow them. It was a commonplace that leadership depended on wealth and rank. 'I have not chosen beggars or unskilful men to places of command', the parliamentarian Sir Samuel Luke declared, 'but such as can with their credits sustain their companies three months from mutinies'. In turn, tenants with an influential overlord depended on him for protection. 'Unless Sir Edward Nicholas stand for the hundred', a Wiltshire man complaining about royalist taxation declared, 'we are all undone.'[90] In some parts of the country expectations that peers and gentlemen could command automatic loyalty were not ill-founded. The Marquis of Newcastle in the north-east, the Earls of Derby and Worcester in Lancashire and Wales respectively, all made huge contributions of manpower to the King's armies. In Lancashire, an observer noted, the Stanleys' bountiful hospitality earned them 'much love and more applause': with the help of their client gentry they raised much of Lancashire for the King, though not the clothing region around Manchester. On the other side, the Earl of Warwick's influence was one (though not the only) source of the solid parliamentarianism of the county of Essex in the early stages of the war.[91]

There were no peers in the western counties with anything like this authority. Pembroke, the biggest man in Wiltshire, already detached from the county by his career at Court, soon became Parliament's governor of the Isle of Wight and had little directly to do with Wiltshire. His estates lay principally in the downlands, at places like Broad Chalke, Dinton, and Wylye which were certainly not parliamentarian strongholds.[92] Hertford too was absent from Wiltshire for most of the war, and was unable to carry even Marlborough, in the heart of his family's territory, into the King's camp in July 1642. Assertions that the Herbert–Seymour rivalry was still the 'unchangeable basis of local politics' in wartime Wiltshire are not altogether convincing.[93] The Digbys had more control over Sherborne, and their 'multiplicity of tenants' in north Dorset had been noted not long

[89] For fuller discussion of the towns see the two articles by Howell cited in n. 62 above.

[90] *Letter Books of Sir Samuel Luke*, p. 274. BL Egerton MS 2533 (Nicholas papers), fo. 388.

[91] Manning, *English People*, pp. 230–2. Holmes, *Eastern Association*, pp. 37–40.

[92] *Surveys of the Manors of Philip, First Earl of Pembroke and Montgomery 1631–2*, ed. E. Kerridge, Wilts. Archaeol. and Nat. Hist. Soc. Records Branch, ix, Devizes, 1953.

[93] Morrill, *Revolt*, p. 44. For the Seymours' estates see CCC ii. 1329, 1507; *VCH, Wilts.* ix. 57, 80, 82, 122; x. 23, 111, 177; xi. 109, 113–14; xii. 169, 172–3.

before the war. Still, they were relative newcomers, and under the manorial customs of Blackmore Vale even their copyholders had strong security of tenure. So although Sherborne was consistently loyal to the Digbys, the surrounding area was, as we have seen, more ambivalent.

In all three counties the gentry counted for more than the peers. The gentry's leadership was most effective in the royalist areas, where paternalist social relations had survived better than they had in the clothing districts. The authority of Dorset landowners such as Richard Rogers and Sir John Strangways must have been aided by their apparently comfortable relations with their tenants, and while at Corfe Castle the Bankes family were newcomers and not especially paternalistic, their presence was important throughout the Purbeck region.[94] The royalism of the downland Clubmen cannot be dismissed as simply the product of deference; still, it is striking how many of the minor gentry who were involved (and inevitably took leading roles) had been in arms for the King. John Fussell, formerly deputy-governor of Weymouth, is a good example. He had been deputy-steward of the Earl of Salisbury's Cranborne estates since 1624, succeeding the Puritan Richard Sherfield after his dismissal for oppressing the tenantry. During the war he was openly disloyal to his employer, boasting that he had been asked to handle local lawsuits against him, and refusing to give up records in his custody. The tenants had no love for the absentee Earl, as they showed when Cranborne was plundered in 1643, but a local man like Fussell was another matter. It is not surprising that they preferred Fussell's benign supervision to Sherfield's harshness.[95]

Tenant support was not always so easily obtained. Sir John Stawell's recruits in west Somerset early in the war were alleged to be mainly his tenants-at-will, 'so that if they would not obey his command, he might out with them'. Parliamentarian writers excused the desertions before Sherborne in September 1642 as the actions of countrymen who held leases for lives from the very people they were fighting: 'when they saw their landlords express their fury out of the mouth of a cannon, they began to think that if they stood to it, they should not renew their lives.[96] It is in fact unlikely that west Somerset landlords were any more oppressive than those of other regions. Tenant deference always contained elements of fear and self-interest, but if the Royalists had relied on fear alone it is unlikely that they would have found many to follow them for long. Stawell may or may not have been a harsh landlord, but he was also noted for his

[94] Ferris, 'Gentry of Dorset', pp. 112–13.

[95] Underdown, 'Chalk and Cheese', pp. 35–6.

[96] Quoted in Manning, *English People*, p. 233; and in Ashton, *Civil War*, p. 175. There are lists of Stawell manors in BL Add. Charters, 28283; and G. D. Stawell, *A Quantock Family: The Stawells of Cothelstone and their descendents*, Taunton, 1910, p. 81.

'great hospitality', and even Lord Poulett had good credentials with the foresters of Neroche.[97]

The strength of royalism in the downlands, Blackmore Vale, and west Somerset was obviously partly the product of the authority of the peers and gentry over their tenants. The deference hypothesis is, however, a less convincing explanation for the behaviour of regions such as north Somerset and north-west Wiltshire. Such local magnates as the Horners and Pophams, Bayntons and Hungerfords played their part in harnessing the enthusiasm of the clothing districts for Parliament, and the rising of August 1642 was preceded by gatherings of neighbours and tenants at Mells, Hunstrete, and other gentlemen's houses. Yet there were also plenty of influential royalist gentry in the region. The inhabitants could have followed Hopton, Sir Francis Dodington, and Thomas Smyth into the royalist camp; instead large numbers of tenants of all three—at least forty of Smyth's, John Ashe tells us, and many of Hopton's 'unto his very gate'—took part in the great gathering on the Mendips.[98] Even in areas with stronger paternalist ties between landlord and tenant there are plenty of examples of defiant behaviour by dependents. Henry Coresey, constable of Salkley hundred in 1642, was a tenant of the Seymours, but this did not deter him from helping to secure the magazine at Marlborough for the Parliament.[99] Individuals were usually less courageous, but collectively even husbandmen and craftsmen could make choices that did not necessarily coincide with those of their superiors, particularly if there were forces from the other side in their neighbourhood to protect them. Excessive insistence on tenurial authority might in these circumstances, as the Earl of Derby discovered in Lancashire, be counter-productive.[100]

Where the sympathies of the gentry coincided with those of the population—as in parliamentarian Suffolk and Wealden Sussex, or in royalist west Somerset and downland Dorset—élite leadership was little impaired by the civil war.[101] But where a landlord was seriously out of step with the general opinion of the neighbourhood war conditions might make it impossible to impose his authority. Dodington, Hopton, and Smyth found this out in north Somerset in 1642, as did Salisbury at Cranborne in the following year. Deference was still a functioning element in the political culture of areas like the downlands. Even there,

[97] *Commons Debates 1628*, iii. 422.
[98] [Ashe], *Perfect Relation*. See also *LJ* v. 278–9; and Underdown, *Somerset*, pp. 35–9.
[99] BL Add. MS 32324 (Seymour MSS), fo. 47. For other examples of tenant defiance see *LJ* v. 681; HMC, *Fifth Report* (House of Lords MSS), p. 86; *Twelfth Report*, ix (Southwell MSS), pp. 550–1. Constables of course often did as they were told and obeyed each side in turn: for a woeful complaint by one of them in Wiltshire see Roy, 'Civil War and English Society', p. 29.
[100] Manning, *English People*, pp. 217–18. B. G. Blackwood, *The Lancashire Gentry and the Great Rebellion 1640–1660*, Chetham Soc. 3rd Ser. xxv, 1978, p. 52.
[101] *Suffolk and the Great Rebellion*, ed. Alan Everitt, Suffolk RS iii, 1960, pp. 25–6. Fletcher, *A County Community*, pp. 281–2, 296, 326–8.

however, it was a reciprocal relationship between rulers and ruled, not a one-way street in which authority was imposed on a population of obedient ciphers. The parish gentry of Wiltshire and Dorset, often of mildly royalist persuasion, who joined the Clubmen, made it easier for their dependents to do so too, but they did not command them. Just as the 'class' explanation offers a partial explanation of the wartime behaviour of the clothing districts, so the deference hypothesis provides a partial explanation of the allegiance of the royalist regions. In neither case, however, is it a complete one.

*

We are thrown back, then, on some version of localism. The first priority of all but two tiny politicized minorities of Englishmen, we have been assured, was the defence of the local community against outside threats of every description—the state, the warring armies, the adherents of alien ideologies. There was that familiar common fund of assumptions about society, about church and state—the primacy of custom and ancient law, the reciprocal rights of King and Parliament—the assumptions underpinning the Protestation. The civil war affronted these assumptions, so most people took sides in it, if at all, only under compulsion or out of an opportunist desire to get it over quickly by supporting the strongest side.[102]

About much of this there can be no dispute. Localism surfaces repeatedly in the peace movements, but it is also frequently reflected in the behaviour of many people who appear to have taken sides. Even at times of greatest popular excitement, national events were often viewed from a localist perspective. The 1642 Mendip rising was, among other things, a rising of the 'Country' against outsiders. Many of Hertford's Cavaliers were established local gentry, but to the countrymen they were 'incendiaries' who had abandoned their communities to bring in an alien instrument, the Commission of Array, to oppress them. Always the enemy is the outsider: the Irish, the Welsh, the malignant Cavalier coming to burn the town, the foreigner from the next village, the 'Batcombite'.[103] Royalists and Parliamentarians alike confronted the stubborn narrowness of provincial horizons. In 1644 Sir Ralph Hopton was more successful than he had been two years earlier in recruiting his tenants and neighbours in east Somerset, apparently because he told them they were needed to resist an expected French invasion. Finding that this was not

[102] Among numerous statements of the localist position see Everitt, *Local Community*, esp. pp. 8, 23; and Morrill, *Revolt*, esp. p. 89.

[103] Underdown, *Somerset*, pp. 39, 44. For similar perceptions of the Cavaliers elsewhere see Manning, *English People*, pp. 179, 206–7.

true most of them deserted.[104] In a sermon to the Hampshire Clubmen in 1645, the New Model chaplain William Beach denounced the reluctance of the countrymen to turn against the Royalists—people who asked 'are they not (some of them) of our kindred? of our Country? nay, of our religion?' Beach turned localism on its head, demanding how they could endure 'two garrisons of Country-destroyers' (at Basing and Winchester) 'and not contribute your clubs to the rooting of them out?'[105]

Beach might deplore the neutrals' localism, but even those who fought, from the officers to the obscurest of the rank-and-file, constantly showed the same parochial outlook. Only with the greatest difficulty could troops be induced to serve outside their homelands. Commanders regularly complained about the problem. 'Multitudes of men' had been raised, Essex reported from the western counties in 1644, but they wanted 'to serve under their own countrymen, and not be listed in my army', in which they might be marched into distant parts.[106] The Committee of Both Kingdoms had long and sad experience with citizen-soldiers, 'men of trade and employment', frequently allowing them to be sent home after representations from county committees.[107] The example, if one were needed, was set by the gentry. It was 'the usual mistake of particular associations', says John Corbet, 'to confine every enterprise to their own counties, and divide the commonwealth into so many petty kingdoms'. The Eastern Association, by far the most successful of Parliament's regional groupings, encountered much foot-dragging by its member counties; when its army was in turn absorbed by the New Model there were renewed protests.[108] Even nationally-politicized leaders betrayed their localism: Ludlow, for example, was distinctly unhappy about orders to take his regiment into Hampshire to besiege Basing House, 'it not being properly my work', he complained, 'who was raised by and for the county of Wilts'.[109]

If this sort of outlook animated so partisan a figure as Ludlow, we should naturally expect to find it among those who were less ideologically committed. People of all social levels saw the protection of their families and of the social and material fabric of their communities as their first duty. The frequent changes of side—easiest to observe among the gentry but probably even more common among their inferiors—were often the

---

[104] E. Green, 'The King's March through Somerset, 1644', *Somerset Archaeol. and Nat. Hist. Soc. Proceedings*, xxiv, pt. ii (1878), 44.

[105] BL TT, E. 304 (3): William Beach, *More Sulphure for Basing . . . A Sermon at the Siege of Basing*, 1645, p. 20.

[106] *CSPD*, 1644, p. 335. *LJ* vi. 616. Walker, *Historical Discourses*, p. 41. See also Underdown, *Somerset*, p. 74.

[107] Underdown, 'Problem of Popular Allegiance', pp. 72–3.

[108] Corbet, 'Military Government of Gloucester', p. 357. *Suffolk and the Great Rebellion*, pp. 33–4. Holmes, *Eastern Association*, chs. 4–5, 9–10.

[109] *Ludlow's Memoirs*, i. 105.

result not of cynical opportunism, but of a rational defence of local priorities. For a neighbourhood to flaunt its preference in the face of an enemy was to invite disastrous retribution, and fear of this was evident in the spring of 1643 even in parliamentarian north Wiltshire. The country people, a local commander complained, 'seemed very forward whilst Sir William Waller was present, but altered their minds so soon as they did see him with his army to be departed from them'.[110] An exchange between the ousted mayor of Wells, Robert Morgan, and his deputy, Robert Rowley, captures the true essence of localism. When the Royalists ordered Morgan's expulsion from the corporation Rowley asked, 'that if it should be his hap to put the said command in execution that he would not be offended with him'. Morgan replied that he understood perfectly and 'was contented to be put forth of his place of Mastership with all his heart'. He was thereupon expelled 'until it be further considered of'.[111]

There can be no argument about the importance of localism in the civil war. But it did not always lead to neutrality. We have identified marked contrasts in the distribution of allegiance in the three counties, marked variations of outlook that were regional rather than narrowly parochial in character. Those contrasts, it has been suggested, are connected with the relatively advanced stage of social polarization reached in the clothing districts, and with the survival of a more homogeneous, paternalist society in the arable regions. To be fully understood they need to be placed in the context of the regional cultural contrasts observed in earlier chapters. The 'fit' between pre-war culture and civil war allegiance is not exact, but it is close enough. The downlands and Blackmore Vale were very different in social structure, economic life, and settlement patterns. But they were both strongholds of cultural conservatism, and they were both royalist in the civil war. In all areas we find an attachment to localism: the cultural differences explain why the localism of some regions produced a preference for Parliament, of others for the King.

The eighteenth-century historian John Oldmixon, who grew up in a Puritan household at Bridgwater, regarded cultural conflict as absolutely central to the civil war. In 1642, he asserts, Somerset was 'Protestant and sober' and thus hostile to the Cavaliers, 'excepting those gentry and peasantry who had opposed the putting down revels and riots'.[112] The point could be restated as an assertion of the primacy of the religious issue. Provided we remember that the disputes between Puritans and their enemies were not confined to doctrine and church polity, but were

[110] Ibid. 446. In Dorset in 1644 the Earl of Warwick feared that the popular support he was enjoying would quickly disappear if a royalist army arrived: *Documents Relating to the Civil War*, ed. J. R. Powell and E. K. Timings, Navy RS cv, 1963, pp. 156–7.
[111] Underdown, 'Case Concerning Bishops' Lands', p. 22.
[112] John Oldmixon, *History of England During the Reigns of the Royal House of Stuart*, 1730–5, i. 208.

related to conflicting conceptions of personal morality and social discipline, this is perfectly acceptable. Baxter made essentially the same point:[113]

Not that the matter of bishops or no bishops was the main thing (for thousands that wished for good bishops were on the Parliament's side) . . . But the generality of the people . . . who were then called Puritans, precisians, religious persons, that used to talk of God, and heaven, and Scripture, and holiness . . . adhered to the Parliament. And on the other side, the gentry that were not so precise and strict against an oath, or gaming, or plays, or drinking, nor troubled themselves so much about the matters of God and the world to come, and the ministers and people that were for the King's Book [of Sports], for dancing and recreations on the Lord's days . . .

People on both sides in the civil war often engaged in symbolic behaviour, used recognizable cultural codes to assert their identities, to provoke or ridicule their enemies. For Royalists the maypole was a natural symbol. At Oxford shortly before the war the 'loose and licentious' people decorated one with a picture of a man in a tub, 'to describe a Roundhead', and used it for musketry practice, amid loud hilarity; there were similar scenes at Ludlow and other places.[114] On the other side, the symbolic targets were usually vestiges of Laudian ritual. In attacking them, Puritan militants did not always display the stern sobriety we might perhaps expect. The letters of Nehemiah Wharton, a London apprentice who served as a volunteer for Parliament early in the war, repeatedly reveal the troopers' high spirits as they left a trail of burnt altar rails and broken stained glass across the home counties and the midlands. In Northamptonshire, Wharton reports, one returned to camp 'clothed with a surplice, hood, and cap, representing the Bishop of Canterbury'. At Hereford during morning service in the cathedral, 'the pipes played and the puppets sang so sweetly, that some of our soldiers could not forbear dancing in the holy choir'. At Coventry they took 'an old base priest . . . and led him ridiculously about the city', and held a ceremonial riding and ducking of a whore who had followed the army from London.[115] Playful elements relieved the iconoclasm of many other units. Soldiers at Oxford fired at the statues on St. Mary's church, and at Canterbury, after vandalizing the cathedral, they used a statue of Christ on the Southgate for musketry practice, 'and there was much joy when they hit it either in the head or face'. When Cromwell's troops entered Winchester in 1645 they

---

[113] *Reliquiae Baxterianae*, p. 31.
[114] *Life and Times of Anthony Wood*, i: 1632–1653, ed. Andrew Clark, Oxford Hist. Soc. xix, 1891, p. 49. Hill, *Society and Puritanism*, pp. 185–6. *Letters of Brilliana Harley*, p. 167.
[115] 'Letters from a Subaltern Officer', ed. Sir Henry Ellis, *Archaeologia*, xxxv (1853), 311–14, 318, 320, 332.

plundered the cathedral muniments, using some of them to make 'kites . . . to fly in the air'.[116]

The western counties had their share of such episodes, some of them having a distinctly regional flavour. When the north Somerset country-men entered Wells in August 1642 they smashed the cathedral stained glass, plundered the Bishop's Palace, and paraded a painting of the Virgin Mary stuck on a pike at the head of a derisive procession. They came, of course, from an area in which Laudian ritual had been particularly unpopular, and in which the charivari was a deeply-rooted cultural form. In the following spring Wells was twice the scene of similar violence by troops recruited largely from the clothing districts. They pulled down whatever images and crucifixes were left in the cathedral and the Palace, wrecking 'all such monuments or pictures they espied, either of religion, antiquity, or the kings of England', a significant combination of symbols.[117] An incident in the pasture country of north Devon is a striking example of popular symbolic action. When the Earl of Bath came to read the Commission of Array at South Molton, his Cavaliers were resisted by the country people, among them a butcher's wife who 'came running with her lap full of ram's horns to throw at them'. Cavaliers were courtiers, and thus by definition cuckolds and otherwise morally despicable.[118]

The civil war repeatedly reveals the kind of cultural division that Baxter describes in Worcestershire. At Hereford, says Wharton, the royalist inhabitants were inveterate sabbath-breakers, 'totally ignorant in the ways of God, and much addicted to drunkenness and other vices, but princi-pally unto swearing'. At Oxford the 'sober and religious gospellers' were driven away by the 'dissolute crew' of royalist citizens and students.[119] Parliament's propagandists naturally exploited this theme: localist rebels in Kent in 1645, for instance, were dismissed as people whose 'custom was always to drink and roar as long as their money lasted'. It was well known, a newsbook sneered, what the downland Clubmen meant when they demanded the ancient laws: 'the old vanities and superstitions of their forefathers, the old necromantic order of prelacy, and the wondrous old heathen customs of Sunday-pipings and dancings, with the meritorious maypoles, garlands, galliards, and jolly Whitsun-ales'.[120]

---

[116] *Wood's Life and Times*, i. 63. HMC, *Fifth Report* (House of Lords MSS), pp. 48–9. Underdown, 'Problem of Popular Allegiance', p. 92.

[117] John Vicars, *Jehovah-Jireh. God in the Mount*, 1644, p. 134. HMC, *Wells Dean and Chapter*, ii. 427. E. Green, 'On the Civil War in Somerset', *Somerset Archaeol. and Nat. Hist. Soc. Proceedings*, xiv, pt. ii (1867), 70.

[118] Quoted in Andriette, *Devon and Exeter*, p. 63.

[119] 'Letters from a Subaltern Officer', pp. 331–2. HMC, *Portland*, i. 56–8. Cf. also *Reliquiae Baxterianae*, pp. 40–1.

[120] Everitt, *Community of Kent*, pp. 215–16. BL TT, E. 298 (24): *Mercurius Britannicus*, no. 95 (25 Aug.–1 Sept. 1645).

Popular royalism was commonly attributed to the slavish subservience to monarchy that such a culture engendered. This was why, John Corbet thought, 'the common people addicted to the King's service have come out of blind Wales, and other dark corners of the land' where the gentry and clergy had 'endeavoured the undermining of true religion, to promote a blind and irrational worship, that might bring forth an ignorant and slavish generation of men'. Even in solidly roundhead areas the influence of the royalist clergy was much feared. Henry Downhall, the non-resident rector of Toft, Cambridgeshire, refused to permit the establishment of a lectureship, 'fearing lest the parishioners should grow too heavenly wise, desiring to keep them in slavery'. The connection between ignorance and royalism was clear, at least to Puritans such as Sir Samuel Luke, who complained that people in the neighbourhood around Newport Pagnall were 'mostly Papists and atheists and extremely averse to Parliament'.[121]

In the western counties royalism was thus most widespread in regions where both traditional social relations and the old festive culture had survived, and where victory for Parliament would have cultural as well as political consequences: in the downlands, in south Somerset, and Blackmore Vale. Towns in and on the edge of these regions, like Blandford, were notable strongholds of royalism. Salisbury, where the lower orders had also experienced the full rigour of Puritan reformation, was conspicuously so. When Ludlow's broken cavalry fled there in July 1644, the inhabitants 'made a great shout at our coming into the town, rejoicing at our defeat'.[122] The contrast with Dorchester, where Puritan discipline had been even more ferocious, is striking. At Salisbury the leadership of the cathedral clergy and their allies in the victualling trades gave the anti-Puritan feelings of the poor a legitimacy which they lacked at Dorchester, with its more united élite.

Legitimacy and leadership: this does not mean that popular royalism was simply imposed from above. Certainly the downland clergy did their duty in exhorting their parishioners to take the royalist Oath of Association and in other ways to obey the King's commands, but only a handful of villagers seem to have objected to this. In every parish there were people of opposite opinions, yet even during periods of parliamentarian ascendency they rarely tried to get rid of royalist ministers; only after Parliament had won the war did the unity of the downland parishes break down.[123] Some parsons felt, no doubt, that their parishioners had no business thinking for themselves. Christopher Ryly, rector of Newton Toney, argued that 'laymen ought not to meddle with the scripture and

---

[121] Corbet, 'Military Government of Gloucester', p. 304. Bodleian MS J. Walker c. 6, fo. 14. Matthews, *Walker Revised*, p. 79. *Letter Books of Sir Samuel Luke*, p. 42.

[122] *Ludlow's Memoirs*, i. 93. See also Underdown, 'Chalk and Cheese', pp. 36–7.

[123] Morrill, *Revolt*, pp. 91–3.

that women ought not to read the scripture'. Many people swallowed this line and said, a New Model chaplain complained, 'we are not book-learned; and by whom should we be taught, if not by these?'[124] Still, these were men who expressed as well as moulded the opinions of their flocks, and their rhetoric, their depictions of Parliamentarians as socially and politically disruptive, effectively played on their listeners' prejudices. Their choice of epithets is often revealing. Peter Waterman of Wootton Rivers denounced the Earl of Essex as 'a cuckold and a rebel' and Parliament as 'a company of tinkers and pedlars'. The threat to parish unity posed by radical Puritanism was evoked in allegations that leaders such as Pym and Lords Brooke and Saye were separatists. The laity were constantly edified by a familiar stock of allusions, including comparisons of Parliament's rebellion to that of the 'powder traitors' or the revolt of Absolom against King David.[125]

Several of these royalists preachers were enthusiastic defenders of the old festive culture, and as we have seen, there were many such parsons in the downland villages. All over England there were places where older notions of community lingered throughout the war; Mr Fletcher cites villagers in Cheshire who denounced Puritan divisiveness and lamented the loss of Rogationtide processions and other 'customs which we have had in former times'.[126] But nowhere was the resistance to Puritan reformation as stubborn as in the downlands. Civilian as well as clerical Royalists saw their opportunity. A speech to the Clubmen of Alderbury Hundred by Sir Bartholemew Pell in 1645 shows the kind of argument to which the Wiltshire countrymen were thought susceptible. 'If the Parliament prevail', Pell reminded them, 'your religion is lost, your marriages, your christenings, your burials be all lost, as appeared by the Directory which they have set forth'.[127] The royalism of the downland villages was an appropriate expression of the local culture.

The same forces were at work in the pasture regions of south-east Somerset and Blackmore Vale, where traditional culture had survived before the war just as tenaciously as in the downlands. Some of the royalism of these areas can no doubt be attributed to the influence of great magnate families like the Berkeleys of Bruton and Yarlington. The Bruton–Batcombe skirmish in February 1643 followed recruiting for the King in the neighbourhood by the younger Berkeleys. The clergy they installed, men such as Bernard Banger at Yarlington and Guy Clinton at Alford, were strongly royalist, and Clinton's son took an active part in the affray at Bruton. Other south Somerset ministers such as William Haskett

[124] BL Add. MS 22084 (Wilts. Sequestrations Register), fo. 148. Matthews, *Walker Revised*, pp. 379–80. Beach, *More Sulphure for Basing*, p. 22.
[125] BL Add. MS 22084, ff. 130–1, 133, 140, 142, 144. Matthews, *Walker Revised*, pp. 369–70, 377.
[126] Fletcher, 'Factionalism', p. 291.
[127] BL TT, E. 297 (4): *Heads of Some Notes of the Citie Scout*, no. 4 (19 Aug. 1645).

at Maperton and Anthony Richardson at West Camel had similar views, and some may have shared the outlook of their more disorderly parishioners.[128] There had been a few royalist clergy in the northern parishes—Alexander Huish at Beckington, Henry Ancketyll at Mells, Andrew Bowerman at Frome—but there they were at odds with their more influential parishioners. In south Somerset this was less likely to be the case.

The parishes of the Bruton–Yeovil area had clung to their festive rituals long after they had been suppressed in the clothing districts. These preferences survived in the 1640s. After Castle Cary church was damaged early in the war, the churchwardens spent money for 'setting up the pieces of the organs and ... the stone-work that did stand before the communion table', though they soon had to stop paying the organist's salary, so it may be that the organ was wrecked beyond repair. When Parliament's soldiers confiscated the vestments in 1643 the parish promptly borrowed replacements from North Cadbury.[129] Other places were less fortunate. At Tintinhull soldiers took the surplices, 'cut them in pieces', and gave them to the poor. Images and vestments were disappearing from many villages, yet in some they survived for much of the war. There was still stained glass to be smashed and an organ to be pulled down at South Petherton by Essex's defeated cavalry in August 1644. Both ritual and the royalism that protected it were part of the cultural matrix of the region. When we find the Bruton congregation singing 'malignant psalms', we do not have to conclude that they sang because Sir Charles Berkeley ordered them to.[130]

To conclude: both parliamentarian and royalist areas exhibit many symptoms of localism, but localism did not necessarily lead to neutrality. South Somerset, Blackmore Vale, and the Dorset and Wiltshire downlands tended towards royalism partly because of the influence of their gentry and clergy, but also because these relatively cohesive communities shared a common culture which the increasing extremism of parliamentary Puritanism seemed to threaten. North Somerset and north-west Wiltshire were parliamentarian not only because of the authority of gentlemen such as Popham and Hungerford over their tenants, of great clothiers like the Ashes over their workpeople, not only because of the influence of the godly middling sort in the cloth-making and dairying parishes, but also because this region too had its own distinctive culture. It was, to be sure, one that was in part imposed by the Puritan élite and towards which the poor were often hostile, but embedded in it were notions of popular independence of the sort reflected in the skimmington ritual. And the preaching clergy like the Alleins at Batcombe reached

---

[128] Matthews, *Walker Revised*, pp. 309–10, 314, 318.
[129] SRO D/P/cas, 4/1/1 (Castle Cary Churchwardens accounts, 1628–1706).
[130] Underdown, *Somerset*, pp. 44, 78. Matthews, *Walker Revised*, p. 310.

many people below the middle rank of society. It was a royalist writer who noted Samuel Crooke's success in persuading 'thousands of poor people' in the Wrington area to support Parliament.[131]

The clergy, royalist or parliamentarian, led by persuasion and example, not compulsion. So too did the gentry in regions where their leadership remained effective, which was not everywhere. Both had weapons of influence, authority, and habits of command, but those weapons were effective only when a majority of their subordinates supported their use. The greater deference of the downlands, the embryonic class feeling of the middling sort in the clothing districts, were both related to the contrasting cultures of these regions.

[131] BL TT, E. 70 (8): *Mercurius Aulicus*, no. 39 (25 Sept.–2 Oct. 1643).

7

The Geographical Distribution of Allegiance

THE argument of this book so far rests on an impressionistic use of descriptive evidence. That evidence seems to support the hypothesis that regional contrasts in popular allegiance in the civil war were related to regional cultural differences. Is there any way of testing this hypothesis more precisely, by statistical analysis? In any attempt to do so we enter the usual minefield that awaits the quantifying historian using imperfect data. The sources make it possible to calculate the numbers of gentry who outwardly supported the two sides, but there are no contemporary lists that might provide a basis for similar calculations about the rest of the population. What quantifiable evidence exists tells us more about the distribution of Royalists than of Parliamentarians. And, of course, it is totally silent on the extent to which outward allegiance reflects real preferences—on what proportion of apparent supporters of each side were really neutrals driven into their respective camps by compulsion or force of circumstance.

The most obvious approach to statistical analysis is through an examination of military recruiting. But this is fraught with formidable difficulties. Only a minority of the male population actually bore arms in the war, and many of those who did had very low levels of commitment. Even among those with enough property to surface in the records of Parliament's Committee for Compounding we find people who served both sides, enlisted to escape their debts, or did so under compulsion as tenants or servants of greater men.[1] We do not have to believe all these stories, but there must have been a grain of truth in some of them. Below the level of the élite this sort of situation was obviously even more common. The armies of both sides were heavily recruited from the poor and the marginal, composed to some unquantifiable extent of men who served under compulsion—either the direct compulsion of impressment or the command of landlord or employer, or the indirect compulsion of poverty, the lure of 'pay and plunder'. Richard Gough could recollect a

---

[1] The following are some of the excuses that occur in Somerset cases in *CCC*: served both sides (iii. 1778); debts (ii. 1412); tenants of Earl of Hertford (ii. 1289–90); servants to royalist magnates (ii. 1320, and iii. 1678).

score of men from his Shropshire village who fought in the wars, almost
all for the King. They included a small farmer heavily in debt, the bastard
son of a cooper, the son of a man hanged for horse-stealing, a ruined
weaver, a vagrant tailor, and a man and his three sons who were so
marginal that they lived in a cave.[2] Such people were plentiful in most
communities and regions, and their appearance in civil war armies tells us
nothing conclusive about the loyalties of the more stable inhabitants.

There are other difficulties. Armies were recruited in very miscel-
laneous ways, and the resulting units on both sides were of correspondingly varied character. There were units raised by noblemen and
gentlemen, especially on the King's side, from their tenants and dependents. There were the trained bands. At the beginning of the war
Parliament relied heavily on them. In many counties—Wiltshire is one of
them—the King's commanders, on the other hand, quickly disarmed and
disbanded them. Both sides, in other words, recognized the generally
parliamentarian outlook of the small property-owners who, in theory,
made up the rank-and-file of the militia. In fact many of these people were
sending substitutes now that real fighting was in prospect, so service in
even a trained band regiment may indicate only that the person concerned
needed the money—though mercenary motives and some degree of
preference for one side over the other are not necessarily incompatible.
Finally, there were forces made up wholly or partly of conscripts.
Impressment, increasingly resorted to by both sides as the war dragged
on, obviously makes it impossible to penetrate to the real allegiance, if
any, of the people involved. Soldiers were sometimes conscripted by both
sides at different times, or enlisted in the enemy army when taken
prisoner. Any conclusions based on the places of origin of such unwilling
recruits must therefore be viewed with the greatest caution.[3]

Even if we had adequate information about the social and geographical
origins of civil war soldiers we should have difficulties enough. But we do
not have that information. One promising source, regimental muster-
rolls, rarely provides any indication of the common soldiers' places of
origin, and there are in any case hardly any muster-rolls from the western
counties. Far more useful for the region we are studying are the lists of
former soldiers to whom pensions were subsequently paid; they are, as
we shall see, much more voluminous for royalist soldiers than for
Parliamentarians, but even for the latter some tentative conclusions can

---

[2] Gough, *Myddle*, pp. 71–2, 133–4, 149–50, 226–7, 232–4.
[3] On disarming the trained bands see Harrison, 'Royalist Organisation in Wilts.', pp. 188–91;
Malcolm, *Caesar's Due*, pp. 45–6, 48–9. On the hiring of substitutes see Lindsay A. Boynton, *The
Elizabethan Militia*, 1967, pp. 110, 175, 220–1; Willcox, *Gloucestershire*, pp. 80–98. Examples of
prisoners enlisting with their captors are noted in Malcolm, *Caesar's Due*, pp. 110–11; Peter Young
and Wilfred Emberton, *The Cavalier Army: Its Organization and Everyday Life*, 1974, p. 30; C. H. Firth,
Cromwell's Army, 1902, p. 37; and *Wood's Life and Times*, i. 88.

be drawn from them. The distribution of Royalists indicated by the pensions lists can also be compared with a third source, the long lists of suspected Royalists collected by Cromwell's Major-Generals in the winter of 1655–6. These provide us not with soldiers, but with people who were believed to have royalist sympathies, which may be quite a different matter. Nevertheless, if marked local variations in the strength of royalist support existed, we might expect there to be some correlation between the distribution of pensioners and of 1655–6 suspects. Most of this chapter will be devoted to an analysis of these three types of evidence—muster-rolls, pensioners, and Protectorate suspects. Before that analysis can be undertaken, however, somewhat more detailed consideration of civil war recruiting is necessary, so that the statistics can be properly evaluated.

*

Our problems would of course all be solved if we could assume that we were dealing with committed partisans of the two sides, who went off to war in the spirit that legend attributes to Cromwell's pious Ironsides. It is undoubtedly true that the proportions of volunteers in the two armies affected their relative morale and fighting spirit. 'Plentiful experience teacheth', a newsbook announced in 1644, 'that none but volunteers do the work on both sides.'[4] The regiment in which the Londoner Nehemiah Wharton enlisted in 1642 contained many men who were motivated, as he was, by strong religious feelings, and who had the further advantage of retaining close ties with their home communities. The religious enthusiasm is evident in the soldiers' pious fits of psalm-singing, and their cheerful iconoclasm against images and altar rails, while the community ties are apparent in Wharton's own continuing identification with the household to which he had belonged as an apprentice.[5] The initial enthusiasm, to be sure, quickly began to wane when expectations of a quick end to the conflict were not fulfilled. The London regiments fought bravely at Edgehill and on many other occasions during the first year of the war, but by the time of Waller's campaign in Hampshire in late 1643 they were becoming mutinous and unreliable. Even then they could be persuaded to stay in the field long enough to help Waller win at Alton on 13 December, and were still sustained by the knowledge that they had a community behind them. A few weeks earlier, their regimental narrator records, 'we had much provision . . . from our neighbours where our regiment was raised, which was very thankfully received'.[6]

The deterioration of the London forces was clearly in part the result of the increasing proportion of soldiers who had enlisted for pay. Not that

[4] BL TT, E. 44 (14): *A True and Perfect Journall*, no. 2 (30 Apr. 1644).
[5] 'Letters from a Subaltern Officer', pp. 316–18, 320, 323, 330.
[6] Elias Archer, *A True Relation of The Marchings of The Red Trained Bands of Westminster . . . under the command of Sir William Waller*, 1643, pp. 2, 9–10.

they had been perfect even in 1642. They had habitually plundered other units in their own army, and even the officers were not safe. By the time his regiment reached Northampton on 7 September Wharton was already becoming disillusioned. When the men came on parade that morning, he reports, 'many of them discovered their base ends in undertaking this design, and demanded five shillings a man, which, they say, was promised them monthly by the committee, or they would surrender their arms'.[7] The predominance of mercenary motives was even clearer by the time of Waller's expedition a year later. While the 'Red' regiment was at Brentford awaiting some laggard companies, its narrator reports, 'divers of our men . . . went back to London, some hiring others in their room, others wholly deserted us'. There were further desertions during the march, and after the failure of an assault on Basing House some of the officers asked Waller to be realistic and retreat: 'many of the soldiers were hirelings, and their money being spent, they began to think of their return'. The officers were right: after a second failure there were serious mutinies. Waller himself blamed 'the hirelings which were promiscuously taken up', suggesting that they might have been deliberately infiltrated by the Royalists.[8]

Waller's difficulties during the Hampshire campaign well illustrate the complexities of any attempt to deduce political allegiance from military service. Some of the volunteer citizen-soldiers responded to their general's pleading and gave good service at Alton. But to men with no political stake in the war appeals to honour and duty were meaningless; if unpaid, they vented their frustrations by resorting to plunder, or simply deserted and went home. Forces raised in the counties were similarly varied in composition, and likely to be equally unreliable, though sometimes for different reasons. Parliament's reliance on volunteers of middling-sort status, like the 'yeomenry and husbandmen' serving under Sir Thomas Myddleton on the Welsh border early in 1645, had both strengths and weaknesses. On the one hand it gave them soldiers who knew what they were fighting for; on the other, it gave them men of localist outlook who expected to be consulted and were not obedient slaves to military discipline. As a London newsbook observed, men of this kind 'will not without much difficulty be obtained to endure such hardship, having estates of their own, which must needs sometimes be looked unto'. Repeatedly they had to be sent home when it was clear that they would serve no more.[9] Royalist commanders experienced similar problems— localism on the part of volunteers, desertion on the part of unpaid mercenaries. Both converge in a protest by one of Rupert's officers when ordered to march from Bristol, where he had been raising men in

---

[7] 'Letters from a Subaltern Officer', pp. 321–2.
[8] HMC, *Portland*, i. 154–5. See also Gardiner, *Civil War*, i. 293–5.
[9] BL TT, E. 269 (14): *A Diary, or an Exact Journall*, no. 39 (6–13 Feb. 1644/5).

February 1644: 'I doubt we shall lose some of our recruits, for want of new clothes, which hath been their chiefest allurement.'[10]

Forces raised in provincial towns were even more localist. The contrast between the more ideologically committed middling sort and their poorer neighbours who served only in the town is clear at Dorchester. Joseph Cuffe of that town served in the county forces as a trooper, having been 'set forth with a horse and arms and maintained in that service' by his mother and stepfather. Cuffe, like any other volunteer, still had to be paid, and he died with £25 arrears owing him, part of which was later paid to his mother by the Dorset County Committee.[11] Cuffe served in the wider county arena; for the defence of the town Dorchester had to raise part-time soldiers from among the poorer inhabitants. At first the town followed the old practice of requiring householders to maintain soldiers and pay them directly themselves, but finding this inefficient, on 2 December 1642 they ordered 'that the pay for the soldiers raised and maintained by several persons' should in future be provided from a general rate, collected weekly in each parish. The men so raised were normally part-timers: on 24 February 1643 'the three captains of the town' received £6 'to pay poor soldiers that served the two days this week'. Such men were not likely to make impressive soldiers, and it is not surprising that Dorchester surrendered so promptly to the Cavaliers in the summer. But the enlistment of poor men was common in royalist as well as parliamentarian towns: Shaftesbury, for example, decided in 1644 'to raise a stock for powder and to pay poor men that go on the alarms'.[12]

The line between volunteers and conscripts, then, is not always a clear-cut one, and does not necessarily entitle us to say that volunteers were ideologically committed and conscripts were not. The royalist Sir William Vavasour certainly made no such distinction when he reflected on the weakness of his position at Hereford, where he had only 'townsmen and a 100 pressed men to defend this place'.[13] Presence in, or proximity to, a garrison town must have turned many people into *de facto* conscripts. George Burrowes claimed to have been 'enforced by his master' to serve the Parliament in the defence of Taunton, George Loope to have served the King at Corfe Castle 'against his will', as he later protested, 'his house and his living being very near thereunto'.[14] Many were the complaints by officers on both sides about the quality of troops raised by compulsion: 'broken reeds, not to be confided in', a parliamentarian newsbook

---

[10] BL Add. MS 18981 (Rupert MSS), fo. 45.

[11] *Dorset Minute Books*, p. 32. On the maintenance of soldiers see also Firth, *Cromwell's Army*, p. 243.

[12] *Dorchester Records*, pp. 681–2, 684. *Shaftesbury Records*, p. 30.

[13] BL Add. MS 18981 (Rupert MSS), fo. 150.

[14] SRO CQ 3/1/99 (Sessions Rolls, 1660–1), no. 15. *Dorset Minute Books*, p. 93. Cf. the statement of George Hemynge of Worcester: Underdown, 'Problem of Popular Allegiance', p. 74.

characterized them.[15] But as the war continued both sides increasingly had to resort to impressment. At first it was done without formal authorization. Countrymen were simply rounded up and forced to serve by force or fraud. According to the Earl of Stamford, who was no doubt trying to counter royalist propaganda about the loyalty of the Cornishmen, during the siege of Plymouth the Cavaliers lured country people from Cornwall by inviting them to share in the forthcoming plunder, and then forced them to serve in the King's army. But the Roundheads were no more scrupulous. After his defeat at Roundway, Waller was alleged to have engaged in forcible recruiting in Gloucestershire; royalist scouts 'met divers running from their houses, lest Waller should compel them to serve him'.[16]

More formal and systematic methods of conscription, under which both sides required constables to produce quotas of men from their hundreds and parishes, eventually became the rule. In the western counties the Royalists began it during the winter of 1643–4, and it soon became a regular feature of their recruiting methods. Instructions issued by the King's commissioners at Devizes in April 1644 show the persistence of old assumptions. The Wiltshire constables were to impress only those 'for their quality fit to be common soldiers': single men who were not covenanted servants, 'mechanics' rather than husbandmen. They were to exempt married householders and as far as possible all others who were under household discipline.[17] Troops of this quality were of course likely to desert, as hundreds of Dorset men pressed in the summer of 1644 were said to have done, or even to join the enemy. Sometimes this brought retribution. When Sir Francis Dodington recaptured Wardour Castle for the King in March 1644 he promptly shot as deserters two of the garrison who had previously been impressed into the royalist army.[18]

The pace of royalist conscription accelerated as the fighting in the west approached its climax. Competition for recruits by the numerous small garrisons in Wiltshire added to the pressures on the population. The commander at Longford House was one who tried to expand his catchment area, complaining that the hundreds in which he had been allowed to impress were so few 'that I am not able to get near the number of men which is assigned me'.[19] In January 1645 Hopton was given authority to

---

[15] BL TT, E. 44 (14): *A True and Perfect Journall*, no. 2 (30 Apr. 1644).

[16] HMC, *Fifth Report* (House of Lords MSS), p. 71. BL Add. MS 18980 (Rupert MSS), fo. 86.

[17] Firth, *Cromwell's Army*, pp. 21–3 and n. *Docquets of Letters Patent . . . under the Great Seal of King Charles I at Oxford*, ed. William H. Black, 1838, pp. 130, 163, 198, 202, 214. For impressment in other areas see also Holmes, *Eastern Association*, pp. 164–5; Ronald Hutton, *The Royalist war effort 1642–1646*, 1982, pp. 92–3; and Malcolm, *Caesar's Due*, pp. 109–10.

[18] *CSPD*, 1644, p. 239. *Ludlow's Memoirs*, i. 80.

[19] BL Add. MS 15750, fo. 27.

impress 4,000 men in Somerset, and there were additional demands for men in April when the Western Association agreed to raise yet another large force. As the Royalists' plight became more desperate their concern for observing traditional social distinctions inevitably began to waver, and after Goring's arrival there were repeated reports, suitably magnified by London propagandists, of the conscription of householders and similar cavalier atrocities. Hostility to impressment merged with other sources of resentment against the military to produce the early Clubmen risings, in the course of which there were frequent reports of people rescuing conscripted neighbours by force.[20]

Systematic impressment on the parliamentarian side had begun much earlier in other parts of England, but in the west it seems to have been introduced only when the war in the region had been virtually won. After the fall of Bristol in September 1645 the region was subjected to heavy demands for recruits for Fairfax's army—2,000 men from Somerset alone—and even if it is unlikely that the counties came anywhere near meeting their quotas, the bitterness impressment was causing shows that it was not simply a paper burden. In both Somerset and Dorset impressment was a major factor in provoking renewed disorders by Clubmen in 1646.[21]

For the parish officers charged with filling their quotas, impressment, whether for King or Parliament, was one way of getting rid of local undesirables. Neither side could afford to be selective. When the Cavaliers occupied parliamentarian north Wiltshire in 1643 they raised troops where they could find them, whatever the sympathies of the population. At Calne, for example, the constables' accounts include numerous outlays of 'press money' for men conscripted by the royalist Col. Chester. No doubt Calne temporarily exported some of its disorderly and idle poor, though in individual cases impressment could also be used to punish political dissenters. The Broad Chalke tithingman tried to fill up his quota for the Royalists in March 1644 by conscripting one of the few Roundheads in the village even though he was both lame and elderly, offering to let him off only if he would recall his son from the Parliament's service and make him fight for the King instead.[22]

*

[20] For example, BL TT, E. 260 (6): *The generall Account of the Proceedings in Parliament*, 1645, p. 3. See also Underdown, *Somerset*, p. 96.

[21] *Memorials of the Civil War: Comprising the Correspondence of the Fairfax Family*, ed. Robert Bell, 1849, i. 250. *Dorset Minute Books*, pp. 7, 27. The difficulty of meeting impressment targets is clear from the situation in the south-eastern counties in October 1645: *CJ* iv. 299; and 'Documents illustrating the First Civil War', ed. Godfrey Davies, *Journal of Modern History*, iii (1931), 70–1.

[22] *Guild Stewards' Book of the Borough of Calne 1561–1688*, ed. A. W. Mabbs, Wilts. Archaeol. and Nat. Hist. Soc. Records Branch, vii, 1953, p. 61. BL Add. MS 22085 (Wilts. Sequestrations Register), fo. 20. Holmes, *Eastern Association*, p. 166, discusses the impressment of local undesirables.

Volunteers, mercenaries, conscripts: civil war armies were of such varied composition that it is obviously unsafe to deduce local differences in popular allegiance solely from variations in the proportions of troops supplied to the two sides by different regions. Still, even people recruited for pay must in many cases have had some vague preference for the side they were serving—they could, after all, equally well have sought similar rewards from the other side—and even conscripts were products of communities whose general outlook they would naturally have tended to share. So it is not altogether useless to investigate the common soldiers' places of origin. We shall find, indeed, that the investigation discloses regional patterns, some of which are significantly confirmed by other evidence.

Let us begin with the Parliamentarians: where did their soldiers come from? To answer the question with absolute confidence we should need to analyse the muster-rolls of every unit that fought in the war. A few isolated rolls are not of much use to us: we are not much the wiser for knowing that a dozen men from a particular village served in a given regiment. To evaluate this information we should need to know how many served in other units, and how many served on the other side. It is true that the handful of muster-rolls and regimental accounts surviving from other parts of England that include the soldiers' places of origin, suggest that regiments were often distinctly local in character. The accounts of Christopher Copley's troop in the army of Parliament's Northern Association, for instance, show this very clearly. Copley's seat was at Wadsworth in the West Riding, and a high proportion of his men also came from that highly Puritan region. The frequent repetition of surnames suggests also that there was a good deal of kin solidarity. One of Copley's corporals, later promoted to quartermaster, was James Nayler, soon to achieve radical notoriety; he and four other Naylers in the troop all came from the Wakefield area or not far away.[23]

Very little such evidence, unfortunately, survives for west-country regiments. Some imperfect information about the places of origin of a handful of parliamentarian soldiers in Dorset early in the war can be extracted from the accounts of a troop of horse raised by Sir Walter Erle. When it was formed in September 1642 it mustered fifty-two men, and another fifty-one served in it in the course of the next year. What little can be discovered about the geographical distribution of these 103 troopers suggests only that Erle's troop was not recruited from its commander's tenants and neighbours in the way that Copley's was in Yorkshire. Sir

[23] Worcester College, Clarke MS 4/2, Accounts of Copley's troop. Out of 64 men in the troop from identifiable places, 44 were from the West Riding. One solitary trooper (a man from Mere, Wilts.) came from the western counties.

Walter's territorial base was in east Dorset, where he owned manors and other lands at Charborough, East Morden, Lytchett Matravers, and Wareham. Only one trooper—a Wareham man—can be certainly traced to any of these places, and it is virtually certain that none of the 103 came from any of the three rural parishes. The troop drew recruits from almost every part of Dorset (though few from Blackmore Vale), and some of its members may have come from outside the county. At least six were from Dorchester, of whom two were subsequently promoted to commissioned rank.[24]

In the absence of adequate muster rolls, we are thrown back on the sources which record payments of pensions or gratuities to former parliamentarian soldiers. Numerous such payments were made by the JPs of many English counties between 1646 and 1660. The orders authorizing them do not always indicate the soldier's place of residence, but this information is given in thirty cases in Somerset and forty-four in Wiltshire. Dorset has no extant Quarter Sessions records for this period, but the minute-book of the County Committee serves as a usable substitute. Between 1646 and 1650 the Dorset Committee regularly made orders for the payment of arrears to former soldiers, and for small gratuities to men in extreme poverty or to their widows. This yields us another twenty-eight parliamentarian soldiers whose places of residence are known.[25]

We thus have a total of 102 parliamentarian soldiers in the three counties derived from these sources. The only pattern they disclose suggests a preponderance of soldiers from urban centres: twenty out of twenty-eight in Dorset, twenty-two out of thirty in Somerset, twenty-six out of forty-four in Wiltshire. Places with strong Puritan reputations are not surprisingly well represented: there are awards to thirteen Dorchester men, eleven Taunton men, and seven men from Wellington. This is to be expected; more surprising is the apparently infrequent grant of pensions to men from rural areas otherwise identifiable as generally parliamentarian in sympathy. Among the Somerset awards there are only two men known to be from the northern clothing parishes—one each to Freshford and Mells—and although there are a few more in the Wiltshire cheese country there is no really significant concentration of them even there. It may be that roundhead soldiers from the clothing districts were drawn

[24] PRO SP 28/128 (Military Accounts, Dorset). The troopers' places of residence have been extracted from *The Dorset Protestation Returns preserved in the House of Lords, 1641–2*, ed. Edward A. Fry, Dorset Records, xii, 1912; *Dorset Minute Books*; and *Dorchester Records*. Where the Protestation is the only source for a trooper's place of residence, only those with relatively uncommon names which occur only once in the returns have been included in this analysis. For Erle's estates see Hutchins, *Dorset*, iii. 498.

[25] *SQSR* iii, *passim*. (The Somerset QS Minute Book is missing from 1656, but some later petitions survive in SRO QS 164). WRO QS Order Books, 1641–54; 1654–68. *Dorset Minute Books, passim.*

from the more prosperous middling elements, or that variations in the availability of poor relief account for the disparity: that indigent soldiers from the villages could find other sources of assistance.[26] But the numbers are far too small to provide a solid base for generalization, as they are for conclusions about the impact of the gentry's territorial influence. The only place where it can be detected is Maiden Bradley—three of the four pensioners from that place served under Edmund Ludlow, who owned the manor.

*

With royalist pensions we are on much firmer ground. As usual the sources present some thorny technical problems, but they are not insoluble, and they enable us to chart the geographical distribution of popular royalism with greater confidence. Under an act passed by the Cavalier Parliament in 1662, the JPs of each county were required to pay small pensions to maimed or indigent former soldiers who served the King faithfully, or to their widows.[27] The territorial distribution of Somerset's pensioners cannot be determined because of the incompleteness of the record: there is no surviving Quarter Sessions minute-book for the three years during which most of the pensions were granted. For the other two counties, however, we have satisfactory records, from which the names and parishes of large numbers of people to whom pensions were granted between 1662 and 1667 have been recovered: 327 individuals from identifiable places in Wiltshire and 815 from Dorset.[28]

One thing is immediately striking: the much larger number of pensioners in Dorset, which was the smaller of the two counties. Suspicions that this might arouse about the completeness of the Wiltshire records are, however, allayed by the discovery that the two county benches obviously followed quite different policies. The Dorset justices were distinctly the more generous, less inclined to make total indigence the test of allegiance, and they chose to make many small awards (usually of £1 per annum) rather than to pay larger sums (usually a shilling a week) to fewer people, as was the policy in Wiltshire. As we shall see, many of the Dorset pensioners were husbandmen and small craftsmen—impoverished by the war, no doubt, as the language of the statute required them to be, but not the totally indigent paupers or labourers that we might perhaps

[26] I am indebted to John Morrill for this suggestion.
[27] 14 Car. II, c.9: *Statutes of the Realm*, v (1819), 389–90.
[28] WRO QS Order Book, 1654–68. DRO QS Order Book, 1663–74. Many of the Dorset pensions are tabulated in R.G.B[artelot], 'Dorset Royalist Roll of Honour, 1662', *SDNQ* xviii (1924–6), 89–93, 165–7, 200–3; xix (1927–9), 43–6, 139–42. See also Underdown, 'Problem of Popular Allegiance', p. 77, n. 32.

expect.[29] Armed with a Grand Inquest presentment insisting that only the 'truly indigent' be relieved, the Wiltshire magistrates, on the other hand scrutinized applications more carefully, with a stricter definition of indigence.[30] But even if the Wiltshire JPs were rigorous, there is no evidence that they were more so for one part of the county than for another. The procedures followed in both counties, different though they were, and the existence of pensioners in all the main regions of each, suggest that the listings are reasonably complete. It might be argued, though, especially in more restrictive Wiltshire, that the pensions are as much a guide to the location of poverty as to the location of Royalists, and this problem will have to be considered. One other possible element of distortion should be noted: the efforts of a conscientious squire or parson, concerned to see that his dependents got what was due to them, may have inflated the statistics in some places.[31]

The geographical distribution of pensioners has been compared with estimates of population of the principal regions of the two counties.[32] For this analysis, Wiltshire has been divided into three: the wood-pasture cheese and clothing parishes of the north-west with the addition of a handful of parishes in the 'butter' country of the south-west and in the south-eastern woodlands; the sheep-corn country of the chalk downlands; and a third, less geographically defined intermediate category which includes the north-western Cotswold fringe, where a mixture of sheep-corn and pastoral agriculture prevailed, along with a number of large, scattered parishes containing nucleated cores (sometimes towns such as Warminster and Westbury) and a few rural parishes such as Edington which also shared both types of rural economy.[33]

The pensioners amount to 2.88 per thousand of the population of Wiltshire. Taking the three regional categories as wholes, with no distinction between rural and urban parishes, the differences between them are not particularly striking, apart from a possibly significantly higher figure for the intermediate parishes.[34] Only when distinctions are made between urban or large parishes (of over 1,000 population) and smaller towns and villages do clear differences emerge. The rural areas

[29] The Dorset JPs began by making these £1 awards as a temporary measure while they considered 'how to settle pensions on them': B[artelot], 'Dorset Roll of Honour', p. 90. But the awards were often repeated, in effect becoming annual pensions: at the July 1665 sessions, for example, many awards went to men who had been granted the same sums a year earlier.

[30] WRO QS Rolls, Michaelmas 1662, Grand Inquest presentment.

[31] For example, at Sherborne.

[32] For the sources and methods used in arriving at population estimates for Wiltshire and Dorset, see Underdown, 'Problem of Popular Allegiance', pp. 93–4: Appendix.

[33] I have adapted the classification of Wiltshire agricultural regions in Kerridge, 'Agriculture c.1500–c.1793', to my own purposes, also making use of information on individual parishes from other volumes of *VCH, Wilts*. 'Towns' are places listed as such in John Adams, *Index Villaris. An Alphabetical Table of all the cities, market-towns . . . in England and Wales*, 1680.

[34] See below, Appendix II, Table 1.

show a rough uniformity across the three zones. But in the towns, large
and small, and in the more populous villages, there are some obvious
variations. The small market-towns of the cheese country, most of them
outside the main clothworking area, show surprising royalist strength,
though this is largely accounted for by two places: Highworth (for some
time a royalist garrison) and Wootton Bassett. Pensioners seem to have
been somewhat less common in the small towns of the chalk country,
though the figures again conceal wide variations: Hindon and Ludgershall produced about fifteen pensioners per thousand, Market Lavington
close to the average number, Aldbourne, Amesbury, and Heytesbury
hardly any.[35]

The population of these places is so small that generalization is
hazardous. With the larger towns and heavily populated villages, however,
greater confidence is possible. The statistics clearly contradict the objection that we are dealing solely with an indicator of poverty. The worst
poverty was concentrated in the clothing towns, yet places such as
Bradford-on-Avon, Calne, Chippenham, and Trowbridge contained
only a trivial scattering of pensioners. Indeed, the overall figure of 1.18 per
thousand for the clothing towns is almost entirely accounted for by
Devizes, where there had been a royalist garrison. Even the fragmentary
records from the 1650s disclose more roundhead pensioners than this in
places like Chippenham and Melksham. The conclusion is clear, though
scarcely surprising: few royalist soldiers were recruited from the larger
clothing towns, apart from those raised by impressment.[36]

Indigent Royalists were somewhat more common in the larger towns of
the chalk country, though even there the figure is only fractionally higher
than the average for the whole county. Much more impressive are the
concentrations of pensioners in towns in the intermediate category,
straddling both chalk and cheese countries: Downton, Mere, Warminster, and Westbury.[37] What do these places have in common? They
were all market towns set in large rural parishes that stretched into both
downland and wood-pasture zones. They thus contained nucleated cores
surrounded by rural hinterlands of scattered settlement, with areas of
both pasture and sheep-corn husbandry. Mere, Warminster, and Westbury were all important corn markets—Warminster's was one of the

[35] Highworth: 12.73 per thousand. Wootton Bassett: 7.82. Hindon: 15.44. Ludgershall: 14.19.
Market Lavington: 4.80. Aldbourne: 0. Amesbury: 1.18. Heytesbury: 1.43.
[36] Bradford: 0.61 royalist pensions per thousand. Calne: 0.59. Chippenham: 1.37. Trowbridge:
1.17. Devizes: 3.27. Melksham: 0. Parliamentarian pensions: Chippenham: 2.05 per thousand.
Melksham: 1.50. For poverty in the clothing towns see Ramsay, *Wiltshire Woollen Industry*, pp. 72–84;
Slack, 'Poverty and Politics' pp. 168–73; Ingram, 'Communities and courts', pp. 133–4. Calne, as we
have seen, was subjected to royalist impressment, as no doubt were the other clothing towns. But it
appears that only volunteers were eligible for pensions: Young and Emberton, *Cavalier Army*, p. 167.
[37] Downton: 8.67 per thousand. Mere: 11.90. Warminster: 2.80. Westbury: 4.39.

biggest in the western counties. Downton, on the edge of the south-eastern woodlands, was a borough in decay, while both Warminster and Westbury had significant cloth industries, Westbury's being in a state of particularly acute depression.[38] Here, then, poverty may indeed affect the statistics, indicating either a higher ratio of indigent to other royalist soldiers, or a possibly heavier recruitment in places where economic life—in both the corn markets and the clothing industry—was disrupted by the war. Warminster was in an area troubled by more frequent fighting than was the case in most of Wiltshire, and it had also received a larger number of the recorded parliamentarian pensions than any other place in the county.[39]

The Wiltshire evidence suggests that the political sympathies of the population limited royalist recruitment only in the region where Puritanism was most deeply entrenched—the larger clothing parishes. Neither the forms of agriculture (arable or pasture), nor the settlement patterns (nucleated or scattered) seem to have had much to do with it. But we are dealing with rather small numbers and, given the restrictive attitude of the Wiltshire JPs, with soldiers who must have been drawn from the poorest levels of society. When we turn to Dorset, however, we have the advantage of much larger numbers, the generosity of that county's magistrates having rewarded more than three times as many people, relative to total population, than was the case in Wiltshire. The discrepancy obviously precludes direct statistical comparison between the two counties, but at the same time it makes the Dorset returns a more useful guide to the actual distribution of royalist soldiers, and a much less automatic indicator of the distribution of poverty. This is an important point, and fortunately there is positive evidence as well as mathematical logic to support it.

A complete analysis of the social status of the Dorset pensioners is impossible because the Quarter Sessions records do not include occupational descriptions. However, the occupations of over a quarter of the pensioners can be retrieved from the lists of suspected Royalists compiled in 1656.[40] It is of course always hazardous to assume that identical names from the same village in two different documents refer to identical people: John Smith the 1662 pensioner may or may not be John Smith, husbandmen, the 1656 suspect. Still, the fact that in many villages a large

[38] *VCH, Wilts.* viii, 110–11, 115–16, 168–9, 175. In none of these cases is it possible to determine how many pensioners came from the town and how many from the out-parish. In a very few cases occupational descriptions are given: the 13 pensioners from Westbury, for example, include two weavers, a fuller, a tiler, and a husbandman, as well as a man from the hamlet of Chapmanslade.
[39] Eight. Several of them went to the widows of men hanged by Sir Francis Dodington at Woodhouse in 1644: see Underdown, *Somerset*, p. 75.
[40] BL Add. MS 34012: 'A Booke containing the names of all such persons as are specified in severall Lists received from the Deputies of Generall Disbrow Major Generall for the Counties of Wilts: Dorset: Devon: Cornewall: Somerset: Gloucester', 1655[–6].

proportion of the names correspond surely entitles us to suppose that in many cases they refer to the same people. At Cerne Abbas four of the five names in one list of pensioners are repeated, with occupational descriptions, in the 1656 returns; at Okeford Fitzpaine three out of four; at Wimborne ten out of fifteen—and these include relatively uncommon names like Will. Hurlock, John Peley, Roger Perham, and John Thedam. Analysis of this group of pensioners is therefore a worthwhile exercise.

The most striking result of such an analysis is the impression it provides that many pensioners were people of some economic independence, rather than day-labourers or paupers. Of the 212 pensioners whose names are repeated in the 1656 lists, no less than 117 were tradesmen, skilled or semi-skilled craftsmen (tailors, victuallers, weavers, and the like); 71 were husbandmen; and only 15 are described as being from unskilled labouring trades. Even these are described by other terms—masons, loaders, shepherds, and so on—and not a single one is described simply as a labourer.[41] Even conceding the frequent ambiguity in the use of occupational terms ('husbandmen', for instance, could mean anything from a substantial copyholder to someone little better than a cottager), and conceding that the craftsmen and husbandmen concerned must have been impoverished ones, the figures do something to correct the impression that the royalist armies were recruited only from the sort of marginal flotsam that Richard Gough describes. If this is true of the pensioners, it is likely to be even more true of the much larger number of royalist soldiers who did not receive pensions because they were not impoverished.

Let us now return to the geographical distribution of the entire group of Dorset pensioners—all 815 of them. What does their geographical distribution suggest? As in Wiltshire, it suggests only minor differences between the levels of royalist recruiting in some of the rural areas— notably the chalk downlands and the pasturelands of south and west Dorset—with the downlands, indeed, producing fewer Royalists than the pasturelands.[42] Once again it is in the towns that we find the most striking contrasts. With the exception of Puritan Dorchester, the larger towns of the chalk country, or those on its borders, contained significantly more royalist pensioners than the towns of the pasture region, with especially high concentrations at Shaftesbury and Blandford. Shaftesbury resembled Warminster in being an important market through which the corn of the downlands was sold to the pasture regions further west. It had long been afflicted with a serious poverty problem—containing 300 'begging people' in 1621, it was said—and its trade had been 'much impaired' by the dislocation caused by the nearby Gillingham Forest enclosures. After the war it was if anything more impoverished than

[41] See below, Appendix II, Table 2.
[42] See below, Appendix II, Table 3.

ever.[43] Many of the smaller chalk towns had similar problems—Cerne Abbas, it will be remembered, was afflicted with large numbers of poor cottagers. It is not surprising to find relatively high percentages of pensioners there or in similar places like Bere Regis and Milton Abbas, or in a small garrison like Corfe Castle. Tenurial influence no doubt played its part at Corfe, as it may have done at Cranborne, the only Dorset chalk town with virtually no pensioners.[44] The inhabitants who had looted the Earl of Salisbury's court rolls must still have been sufficiently in awe of him not to enlist in the army of the other side.

As in the chalk country, the proportion of royalist pensioners in the towns of the pasture regions of west and south Dorset also varied widely, but at a level generally below that of the chalk towns. Lyme, in keeping with its Puritan reputation and long months of siege, harboured only one pensioner, while Weymouth and Melcombe Regis are also below the average for towns in this region. Bridport, with a much higher figure (though no higher than for the county as a whole), is the only exception to the generally parliamentarian character of the Dorset ports. The inland towns of west Dorset—Beaminster and Netherbury, perhaps better described as large villages—follow the pattern of Wiltshire towns like Wootton Bassett in having moderately high concentrations of Royalists.[45] In Dorset as in Wiltshire parliamentarianism thus appears to depend more on economic activity (in Dorset maritime rather than industrial) than on settlement patterns. And once again the royalist soldiers are concentrated in market towns which contained large numbers of the recruitable poor in a time of wartime economic disruption.

Of the remaining Dorset regions, little need be said about the sparsely-populated heathlands, which seem to be suspiciously under-represented in the returns. The sharpest departures from the country-wide average occur in Blackmore Vale, the region of mixed farming and stock-rearing to the south and south-east of Sherborne. Some, though not all, of the Vale's distinctiveness is accounted for by the huge concentration of pensioners at Sherborne: 141 in a population of just under 2,500, or 57.72 per thousand. There is nothing like this in any other place in either Dorset or Wiltshire, and it is easy to see why. Sherborne was garrisoned for the King for long periods, while the authority of the Digbys at the castle was sufficient to ensure that virtually every able-bodied male was in arms at one time or another, and that those eligible were both encouraged to apply

[43] Shaftesbury: 30.86 per thousand. Blandford: 29.10. Dorchester (including Fordington): 2.94. For poverty at Shaftesbury see *Shaftesbury Records*, p. 52; Bettey, 'Revolts', p. 23; and *Dorset Minute Books*, p. 250.
[44] Cerne Abbas: 12.86 per thousand. Bere Regis: 23.17. Milton Abbas: 22.08. Corfe Castle: 21.07. Cranborne: 0.87.
[45] Weymouth and Melcombe Regis: 4.74 per thousand. Bridport: 16.00. Beaminster: 14.29. Netherbury: 13.42.

for, and likely to receive, their pensions. But even without Sherborne, Blackmore Vale was impressively royalist, with more than twice the percentage of pensioners to be found in the chalk villages. At Gillingham and Motcombe, the sites of the recurrent protests against disafforestation, the large number of pensioners may reflect poverty among people displaced by enclosure.[46]

This, however, does not dispose of the smaller villages of the Vale, for which we can only resort to the cultural explanation. Blackmore Vale it will be recalled, was a region in which mixed farming, with cattle-grazing rather than dairying predominating, had not led to the breakdown of traditional community ties. Many Blackmore Vale villages contained nucleated centres, though they were less nucleated than the downland villages, with outlying hamlets and isolated farms carved out of the woodland long after the original open-field settlements had been established.[47] Throughout the area, big royalist landlords like the Digbys and the Berkeleys across the Somerset border had extensive manorial holdings. It was also, as we have seen, a region of marked cultural conservatism, in which traditional festive rituals had survived, often with the encouragement of the parish élites, right down to 1640. The heavy concentration of royalist pensioners thus seems to confirm the impression, already suggested by other kinds of evidence, that popular royalism was a product of local cultural forces.[48]

We should again remember, however, that we have at best been measuring only military recruitment, which may not necessarily accurately reflect the political sympathies of the regions involved. The ability to recruit depended as much on local military predominance as on popular sympathies. The distribution of pensioners may seem to contradict the previous impression of parliamentarian loyalty in the rural parishes of north Wiltshire and the west Dorset pasturelands, but does not necessarily invalidate it. The poor and the marginal from those regions may have been drawn into the King's armies in much the same proportion as those from the downland villages, but it does not automatically follow that the more established residents who stayed behind were royalist in their sympathies. An inclination to withhold supplies and intelligence, as Hopton discovered in north Wiltshire in 1643, may be more revealing of the general outlook of a region than the Royalists' success in recruiting some of the poorer inhabitants.

*

[46] Gillingham: 22.00 per thousand. Motcombe: 27.29. Sturminster Newton, with 25.00, also has a high figure.

[47] Taylor, *Making of the English Landscape: Dorset*, pp. 95–7, 120.

[48] Underdown, 'Problem of Popular Allegiance', p. 83.

How far levels of recruiting corresponded with the loyalties of a broader segment of the population can perhaps be determined by examining the other principal statistical source available to us. In the latter part of 1655 Cromwell's Major-Generals were instructed to take security for good behaviour from all suspected Royalists—people of small property as well as the wealthier delinquents who were assessed for the new Decimation Tax. The names of those required to give security were recorded in a central office in London.[49] Unfortunately for the inhabitants, but fortunately for the historian, the western counties were within the domain of one of the most energetic and conscientious of the Major-Generals, Cromwell's brother-in-law John Disbrowe. Compared with those of most other counties, the west-country returns are consequently unusually numerous, providing 384 named suspects from Wiltshire, 1,507 from Dorset, and 1,713 from Somerset.[50] Places of residence and occupational or status descriptions are given for nearly all of them.

Before we can analyse either the social or geographical distribution of the suspects we need first to know whether the lists are reliable and complete. There is no evidence to show exactly how they were compiled—presumably it was done in each county by the Major-Generals' assistants, the 'commissioners for securing the peace of the Commonwealth', on the basis of returns from the parishes. There may well have been marked variations in the efficiency and enthusiasm of town or village authorities (as there manifestly were between those of different counties), and as with the pension lists, it would be rash to read too much into the returns.[51] Wiltshire's much smaller number of suspects may imply that its commissioners were less zealous than those of Dorset and Somerset, though the discrepancy is in part explained by the fact that entries are recorded from only thirteen of the county's twenty-eight hundreds, all of them in the downlands and the small dairying enclave in the south-west. There are some less serious gaps in the Dorset and Somerset returns, including a noticeable absence of names from west Somerset and from many Blackmore Vale parishes. But with these exceptions the main regions of both counties are well represented.

When the returns are broken down by status and occupational description, it is immediately obvious that they tell us little about the outlook of the very poor; the Protectorate officials made the conventional assumption that independent heads of households were the only people

---

[49] Paul H. Hardacre, *The Royalists during the Puritan Revolution*, The Hague, 1956, pp. 129–30. Morrill, *Cheshire*, pp. 281–2.
[50] See above, n. 40.
[51] Morrill comments on these local differences: *Cheshire*, p. 282.

who mattered politically. And only male heads of household, at that—just one solitary widow is named among the 3,600 suspects in the three counties. The Royalists listed represent a cross-section of the political nation, but one that is heavily skewed towards the upper and middle ranks.[52] The sympathies of people at the top of the hierarchy were naturally more visible—and of more concern to the government—than those of lesser people. Peers, gentry, and professional men comprise almost one tenth of the suspects, whereas they were only half that proportion of the population as a whole. At the other end of the scale, only four suspects are described as labourers (three in Somerset, one in Dorset), and not one by the term 'servant'. Yet servants and labourers made up over half the population of seventeenth-century England. There are to be sure, those other occupational terms—mason, shepherd, and other designations of unskilled trades—which might be translated as 'labourer' in other contexts. But people from such unskilled trades account for only 7.5 per cent of the west-country Royalists from whom it was thought necessary to extract security in 1656.

This bias in the returns does not mean, however, that they are of no value as a guide to the social contours of popular royalism. The husbandmen, traders, and artisans listed must have included people of very varied levels of prosperity—as we have seen, in Dorset a good many were sufficiently impoverished to be able to claim pensions after the Restoration. We should remember, too, that we are dealing with a society with no clear line between the lower rungs of the middling sort and the labouring poor; many of these husbandmen and craftsmen would have been servants or labourers at earlier stages of their lives. But whatever their economic situation, they were independent householders who had to be taken seriously by a government worried about the possibility of another royalist revolt.

The returns confirm the existence of a widespread popular royalism (stronger, as we shall see, in some places than in others), which cannot be dismissed as the mere product of deferential obedience to the élite. Husbandmen, particularly, may still have been vulnerable to pressure from the gentry, but they were likely to be much less so in the circumstances of the 1650s than before the war. 'The landlord', an anonymous observer suggested in 1654, 'not being able to do that he did in former time unto them in feasting and protecting them, hath no power with them.'[53] In the choice between defying a royalist landlord and defying the government it is hard to see the latter as the softer option. It seems even less likely that all the butchers, bakers, and chandlers, the blacksmiths, carpenters, weavers, and the hundred and one other trades that abound in

---

[52] See below, Appendix II, Table 4.
[53] BL Add. MS 4159 (Birch MSS), fo. 236[v].

the lists, can have been Royalists simply because they were told to be by their employers or patrons. Nor is it possible to dismiss the returns as the artificial product of official paranoia. No doubt some of the people listed were unjustly accused, but most of them, for one reason or other, must have been perceived as more dangerous than their more quiescent neighbours who accepted the Protectorate. That popular royalism was a real, not a paper phenomenon is apparent in the striking consistency, within a few percentage points, of the social distribution of the suspects in the three counties: about 10 per cent gentry and clergy, about half that percentage of yeomen, approaching 40 per cent husbandmen, a slightly larger percentage of skilled or semi-skilled traders and craftsmen, and about 7 per cent in unskilled trades. The Royalists, no less than the Parliamentarians, had their following among the middling and industrious sorts of people.

Having reached this stage in the investigation, the next step, ideally, would be a comparative social analysis of different areas. The state of the evidence makes this, alas, a profitless exercise. The discovery that half the royalist suspects in one region are husbandmen compared with only a third in some other area tells us nothing, in the absence of precise data about the social and occupational structures of the two regions in question. What we really need to know is not what percentage of Royalists in a given place were husbandmen, but what percentage of husbandmen (or weavers, or any other group), were Royalists. As this is impossible, all we can do is subject the Major-Generals' lists to the same kind of geographical scrutiny that was applied to the pensions figures.

The incomplete Wiltshire returns can be quickly disposed of. They omit almost the entire cheese country, so it is pointless to attempt to compare different regions within the county. When they are tabulated according to community types, however, the 1656 figures at least do not contradict the picture derived from the county's pensions.[54] Once more the heaviest concentrations of Royalists appear to be in the towns, and this time we know that they are Royalists (or at least believed to be so by the authorities) and not, as was the case with the pensioners, people whose apparent royalism may have been simply a function of their indigence. Similarities between the two sets of statistics appear even at the level of individual places. Of all the small towns in the chalk country, Hindon and Ludgershall had the highest proportions of pensioners: with 24 and 22 per thousand respectively they also have the highest proportions of suspected Royalists. Heytesbury contained few pensioners and correspondingly few suspects, less than 4.5 per thousand. Only at Amesbury, where there were few pensioners but a fairly large number

---

[54] See below, Appendix II, Table 5.

(16.5 per thousand) of suspects, is there any marked discrepancy between the two sets of figures. Royalists, it again seems clear, tended to be thick on the ground in the small towns of the chalk country.

The 1656 returns from Somerset are far more extensive. However, their interpretation presents some serious problems, partly because they appear to be seriously deficient for the western part of the county, and partly because of the uncertainty of available data on the distribution of population.[55] The imprecision of the population figures means not only that the estimates we are using have to be viewed with more than the usual caution, but that the breakdown into geographical regions is less satisfactory. In both Dorset and Wiltshire reasonably adequate parish figures are available and the parishes can be assigned to their respective geographical zones without much trouble. In the absence of such parish figures for most of Somerset the only satisfactory course is to base population estimates on larger units, hundreds in other words. Now hundreds, in Somerset as elsewhere, were often of highly irregular shapes and sizes, and their boundaries did not conform to those of agricultural or other geographical regions: the hundred of Abdick and Bulstone, for example, stretched from villages like Isle Abbots and Isle Brewers on the levels westward into the foothills of the Blackdowns. It should be remembered, therefore, that although every effort has been made to group hundreds in their appropriate geographical zones, the correspondence is not absolute.

For purposes of analysis, Somerset has been divided into five regions: the northern clothing and wood-pasture district; the southern and western Mendip region; the central levels; the south and south-east (the Bruton–Yeovil–Chard area); and the western part of the county.[56] Of these, the only one that demands explanation is the second, composed of the three hundreds of Wells Forum, Whitstone, and Winterstoke. All three cut across geographical zones. Wells Forum includes Mendip villages like Binegar and Priddy, but also Wookey and Westbury-sub-Mendip on the edge of the levels, and the detached parish of Evercreech to the east; Whitstone, centred in Shepton Mallet, contains the Mendip villages of Doulting, Downhead, and Stoke Lane, but also villages on or near the levels like Ditcheat, East Pennard, and Hornblotton; Winterstoke covers the western Mendips from Rodney Stoke to Bleadon and Shipham, but also includes part of the coastal levels around Uphill and Worle. The three hundreds thus have enough in common to justify separate treatment.

[55] For the sources and methods used in estimating the population of Somerset regions see below, Appendix I.

[56] See below, Appendix II, Table 6. The definition of Somerset regions in Michael Havinden, *The Somerset Landscape*, 1982, closely corresponds with mine, apart from my addition of the southern and western Mendip region.

Tabulation of the 1655–6 suspects according to these five regions immediately reveals the second obvious problem: the marked absence of names from many of the western hundreds.[57] Taunton was, we know, a stronghold of Puritanism, yet it seems unlikely that there was not even a single suspected Royalist in the town. None are listed from Minehead, and indeed with the exception of Andersfield and Cannington hundreds the figures for the whole region are far too low to be convincing. It therefore seems safest to leave the western area out of our calculations.[58]

The 1655–6 suspects amount to 10.63 per thousand of the estimated population of the rest of the county. The variations between the four regions are, however, significant, and on the whole confirm the observations made in earlier chapters about the geographical distribution of allegiance within the county. The northern region contains less than half the number of Royalists, in proportion to population, than are to be found in the central levels, and less than a third of the proportion in the south and south-east of the county. We have repeatedly noted the parliamentarianism of the clothing districts, and it is now confirmed statistically. The distribution of suspects also confirms the royalism of the Bruton–Yeovil area, always recognized as the heartland of the King's cause in the county. The levels seem to be somewhere in between, producing a proportion of suspects that is close to the county-wide average. So far there are no surprises.

The area that is surprising is the borderline one, the south Mendip fringe. Of the three hundreds in this region, the most western one—Winterstoke—in fact reported a lower proportion of Royalists than the county-wide average. But the other two—Wells Forum and Whitstone—are substantially above the average, each with almost 20 per thousand. The fairly high figure for the city of Wells, just over 20 per thousand, is perhaps to be expected: the cathedral influence had helped to give the town a strong royalist presence throughout the war. But the rural parishes of the hundred also report some strikingly high figures, most notably in the easternmost one of Evercreech, where Hopton's territorial influence may well have counted for something. In Whitstone Hundred there are some almost equally high figures (over 40 per thousand) for the south Mendip villages of Croscombe and Doulting, and nearly as high a one (32) for the major clothing town of Shepton Mallet.[59]

---

[57] See below, Appendix II, Table 6.

[58] The figures for the western hundreds are as follows. Abdick and Bulstone: 1.82 suspects per thousand. Andersfield: 6.47. Cannington: 10.00. Carhampton: 1.75. North Curry: 0.42. Kingsbury West: 3.82. Milverton: 0.94. Taunton Deane (excluding Taunton): 2.84. Williton and Freemanors: 3.82.

[59] Winterstoke: 8.24 per thousand. Wells Forum: 19.84. Whitstone: 19.61. Wells (city): 20.76. Wells (out-parish): 10.26. Evercreech: 47.54. Croscombe: 41.16. Doulting: 43.89. Shepton Mallet: 32.34.

Shepton Mallet provides a salutary reminder that there is no automatic causal connection between clothworking and support for Parliament. Here is a clothing town with a proportion of royalist suspects higher than any other urban centre we have so far encountered in either Wiltshire or Somerset. Almost two-thirds of the Shepton suspects were clothworkers of one sort or another—49 out of 76—and they are a similar proportion of the suspects at nearby Croscombe. The whole area in fact provides striking confirmation of the importance of local cultural forces. Shepton Mallet and Croscombe lie at the southern edge of the main clothing region, but they also lie very close to the culturally traditional Bruton area, and Croscombe at least had enjoyed a rich tradition of festive pageantry a century earlier. The contrasts between neighbouring parishes in this borderline area are indeed striking. Batcombe and Ditcheat, both exposed to years of Puritan evangelism, produced only three Royalists between them, two of them gentry; Evercreech, with no such Puritan tradition, produced 29 in a population smaller than either. It could be argued that these variations perhaps reflect varying degrees of zeal shown by the parish authorities, but it seems highly unlikely that such people would have been lax in Puritan Batcombe. The whole area clearly reinforces the argument that regional culture was a crucial variable in the determination of allegiance.[60]

This hypothesis is further supported by the large concentrations of suspects in the south-eastern part of the county. Several hundreds in this region reported far more than the average number of suspects: almost 50 per thousand in the rural parts of Bruton Hundred, over 25 per thousand in Horethorne Hundred near the Dorset Border. Two towns in particular stand out: Milborne Port with 70, and Bruton with 77 per thousand. The Berkeleys' influence was undoubtedly a contributing factor at Bruton. The Bruton suspects include the usual range of tradespeople to be found in any market town, and some of them may well have depended on the Berkeleys. Bruton was also an important corn market, and as we have seen at Blandford and Warminster, such places had experienced acute problems of poverty before the war: the Bruton poor may perhaps have followed the Berkeleys out of material necessity. In fact, though, most of the suspects were independent tradesmen, not the very poor, and about a third of them were employed in the cloth industry (eight as master clothiers)—precisely the sort of people who in many north Somerset and Wiltshire towns turned to Parliament and Puritanism. So the Berkeley influence should not be exaggerated. In the circumstances of the 1650s magnate influence was much reduced, for unwilling dependents could turn to the Protectorate authorities for protection against royalist landlords. To be sure, Bruton may have been singled out for special attention

[60] Batcombe: 2.04 per thousand. Ditcheat: 1.52.

by the Cromwellian authorities because of their fear of the Berkeleys, thus exaggerating the proportion of suspects in the town. It would be absurd to suppose that Bruton was in reality six times more royalist than Yeovil, as the figures make it appear. Still, even if the numbers are exaggerated, Bruton was obviously a strongly royalist town in a strongly royalist area, and in neither the town nor the region can that royalism be attributed exclusively to magnate influence. It was, as the Shepton Mallet area demonstrates, the product of a regional culture that was highly traditional in character.[61]

The 1656 returns from Dorset provide further confirmation of this point.[62] They appear to be reasonably complete, with suspects listed from 161 of the county's 271 parishes, and only Blackmore Vale seems to be under-reported, though the under-reporting is not as serious as in west Somerset so the region can still be included in the analysis. Dorset provides one great advantage that is denied us in the other two counties: the possibility of direct comparison between the distribution of suspects in 1656 and of pensioners in the 1660s. If allowance is made for the under-reporting of Blackmore Vale in the former case and of the heathlands in the latter, there are some striking correspondences between the two sets of figures, particularly as they relate to the towns. When the larger Dorset towns are listed in parallel columns, with those showing the highest proportions of pensioners and 1656 suspects at the top, those with the lowest proportions at the bottom, the similarities are obvious. Sherborne easily heads both lists, and the same four towns—Weymouth, Dorchester, Cranborne, and Lyme Regis—are at the bottom, and even in the same order. At the top, after Sherborne, the two lists are less consistent, but the same five towns—Beaminster, Blandford, Gillingham, Shaftesbury, and Sturminster Newton—occupy five of the next six places in both lists, although in a different order.[63]

When we turn to the smaller Dorset towns we find wider discrepancies, scarcely surprisingly given the much less secure statistical base on which they rest. Bere Regis and Milton Abbas both reported almost exactly the same number of suspects as they were later to produce of pensioners. Abbotsbury and Cerne Abbas, on the other hand, show marked differences in the two sets of figures, though they emerge as royalist towns in both.[64] The 1656 returns again confirm the strength of royalist sentiment

---

[61] For Bruton as a market town see J. H. Bettey, 'The Marketing of Agricultural Produce in Dorset during the Seventeenth Century', *DNHP* xcix (1977), 1.

[62] See below, Appendix II, Table 7.

[63] See below, Appendix II, Table 8. The only marked discrepancy is in the case of Wimborne. As already noted, the number of pensioners in the heathlands (the Wimborne area) is probably under-reported, so the 1656 figure is probably a more accurate indicator of the town's royalism.

[64] Bere Regis: 23.71 suspects, 23.17 pensioners per thousand. Milton Abbas: 22.08 (both). Abbotsbury: 33.08 suspects, 14.10 pensioners. Cerne Abbas: 55.71 suspects, 12.86 pensioners.

in the small towns of the chalk country, and indicate a higher level of political consciousness in the towns than in the rural parishes. Comparison between the rural areas is less profitable because of the under-reporting already noted, but it is worth pointing out that pastoral south and west Dorset again seems to have contained a higher proportion of active Royalists than the arable downlands. The chalk country was certainly not parliamentarian, but its royalism, if such it was, seems to have been of a rather passive, neutralist kind. Lacking the larger numbers of marginal, landless poor to be found in the towns and the pasture regions, the chalkland villages seem, until the Club movement, to have played a rather limited part in the civil war.

*

Two completely independent sets of figures, generated by two different authorities for totally different purposes, on the whole corroborate each other. Taken together, the pension lists and the Major-Generals' returns confirm the existence of a widespread popular royalism, and indicate that it was distinctly regional in character. There were, to be sure, striking contrasts in allegiance within quite small areas: between Dorchester and its surrounding villages, for example, and between Batcombe and Bruton. Military circumstances undoubtedly affected the statistics, producing larger numbers of recruits, and thus exaggerating the royalism, in garrison towns such as Devizes, Highworth, and Corfe Castle. The influence of powerful magnates—Digbys at Sherborne, Berkeleys at Bruton—is strikingly apparent in some places. Depressed economic conditions in market towns such as Mere and Warminster may well have increased the number of available royalist recruits. And a few larger towns—Puritan Dorchester is of course the most obvious example—repudiated the generally royalist outlook of their regions.

But when all is said, the significance of regional cultural traditions seems undeniable. Popular royalism was most widespread in areas where the old festive culture had successfully resisted Puritan attack in the forty years before the civil war—Blackmore Vale, south-east Somerset, the chalk country. In the downlands, to be sure, the smaller villages show no impressive indications of active royalism. But the towns in and on the edge of the chalk country include some of the most royalist places in the whole three-county area: Blandford and Shaftesbury among the larger towns; Bere Regis, Cerne Abbas, Hindon, and Ludgershall among the smaller places.

On the other side, as we may perhaps have expected, we have found fewer Royalists in the north Somerset and north-west Wiltshire clothing districts. The one exception to this generalization, the Shepton Mallet area, is further evidence that cultural forces could be stronger than economic ones, suggesting that clothworkers were often Puritan and parliamentarian not just because they were clothworkers, but because they belonged to communities in which Puritan culture was strongly entrenched, as at Shepton Mallet and Croscombe it apparently was not. Clothworkers living in royalist towns like Bruton often took the same line as the rest of their communities. Again the local contrasts are striking, but understandable. Out of thirty-eight 1656 suspects in the parish of Frome, for example, thirty-one came from the ungovernable rural tithings of East and West Woodlands, only seven from the clothing town itself.[65] There were pockets of disorder in the most closely-controlled Puritan regions, and they do not invalidate the conclusion that north Somerset was a parliamentarian stronghold.

How far settlement patterns and the residential structures of communities affected their political behaviour is less clear. The nucleated villages of the downlands displayed a rather tepid royalism until they were aroused by the Clubmen movement, but they were certainly never parliamentarian in sympathy. Blackmore Vale's mixed pattern of settlement at least did not preclude the survival of traditional culture, yet scattered settlement in north-east Wiltshire and west Dorset apparently did not lead to parliamentarianism. And the Somerset levels seem to have been distinctly divided, producing a fairly large number of suspected Royalists, but also displaying parliamentarian sympathies during the Club outbreaks.

We are left, then, with some further valuable reminders of the complexities of the subject—of the numerous, often historically obscure, variables that conditioned the cultures, and hence the politics, of the various regions. But we should remember that the statistical exercise, with all its imperfections, in which we have been engaged tells only half the story. We have useful statistics only for Royalists. If we had them for the other side we might find, for example, even fewer parliamentarian soldiers than royalist ones in downland villages, or signs of deep division in areas like west Dorset and the Somerset levels that would modify the statistical impression of relatively strong royalism. But the historian can only use the evidence available and make the best of it. That evidence surely confirms the significance of regional cultures in the distribution of civil war allegiance.

[65] My estimate of Frome's population (from parish register tabulations kindly supplied by the Cambridge Group) is 3,000. It is impossible to determine its distribution between the town and the tithings.

8

Popular Politics, 1646–1660

A STRIKING feature of the English Revolution is the complete reversal of popular sympathies that it entailed. In 1640 the hopes of an overwhelming majority of the political nation were fixed on the Long Parliament; in 1660 the hopes of a similar majority were fixed on Charles II. Even former Parliamentarians, for the most part, welcomed the Restoration. In this and the following chapter we shall explore some of the reasons for this national change of heart. We shall concentrate first on politics as conventionally defined and then turn to religious and cultural controversies, but it should not be forgotten that the two aspects were in fact inseparable. The widespread alienation from the Long Parliament and its successor regimes occurred because those regimes violated deeply-rooted conceptions of governance, but also because they affronted widely-shared notions about the nature of the community.

The failure of the revolution was in large part the result of its own ambiguities. Parliament's victory in the civil war was followed by a bitter power struggle in which a handful of radical politicians, supported by militant 'Saints' in the Army and the separatist congregations, circumvented Presbyterian hopes of imposing an intolerant church settlement; defeated a resurgence of localist royalism in 1648; purged Parliament of faint-hearted compromisers; executed Charles I; and inaugurated their godly republic in the name of the free people of England. The Rump Parliament which governed that republic until Oliver Cromwell threw it out in 1653 was, however, a curious blend of religious and republican zealots, self-interested time-servers, and erstwhile Presbyterians, many of them as ferociously repressive of radical former friends as of monarchist enemies. The single-person rule of Cromwell between 1653 and 1658 disclosed ever more clearly the revolution's contradictions. The Protectorate wavered uneasily between periods of 'healing and settling' and authoritarian Puritan reform. Within eighteen months of Oliver's death the republic had discredited itself and collapsed.[1]

It is easy to see why the gentry welcomed the Restoration. The New Model and Cromwell's experiment with the Major-Generals had intensified their already deep dislike of military rule. Both nationally and locally, Puritan meddling had undermined their assumed right to govern.

[1] For a general account of Interregnum politics see Ivan Roots, *The Great Rebellion*, 1966.

Fears of renewed experiments by the restored Rump in 1659 were followed by the looming threat of anarchy during the virtual breakdown of government in the following winter. Many former Parliamentarians turned against the republic for the same reasons that moderate Royalists had deserted Parliament in 1642—out of fear of social disorder. Having decided that the revolution would stop short with the execution of the King in 1649 they were forced, in the end, to join with their former enemies to protect the propertied order, though that development could be completed only when the Army, the only solid prop of the successive revolutionary regimes, split in 1659–60.[2]

There is no great mystery about the politics of the élite. But what of the politics of the common people? At the revolutionary end of the spectrum—the Leveller movement and the radical sects of the 1650s—they have received so much historical attention that this book need provide only a brief recapitulation of the subject. For the radicals of 1649 the world had indeed been 'turned upside down'. The execution of Charles I symbolically undermined by the stroke of an axe not only the sanctity of kingship, but also all those familiar related assumptions about patriarchal authority on which social order depended. It was done, to be sure, by a minority, and the success of the King's political testament, the best-selling *Eikon Basilike,* shows how compelling the mystique of monarchy remained. But for those who put their identity as political reformers or members of a godly elect above their identity as members of a cohesive community, the events that began with the emergence of a democratic movement in 1647 and culminated in revolution in 1649 proclaimed the dawn of a new day in which the people, or at least the Saints, would at last be free. For a few brief, intoxicating years Levellers could dream of a democratic, egalitarian society, Diggers of one in which the poison of private property would be eradicated, and a variety of radical sects from Fifth Monarchy Men to Ranters and Quakers could translate the inner light of reason and the spirit into every conceivable kind of liberty of thought and action. Even the doctrine of sin itself was not safe.[3]

But though the radicals had their adherents among the common people, we should not forget that they were indeed a minority. The majority, when all is said, did join in the celebrations of May 1660. It may be that some of the popular rejoicing at the Restoration was artificially contrived, and that many people were either apathetic or downright

---

[2] The most complete account of the events leading to the Restoration is Godfrey Davies, *The Restoration of Charles II 1658–1660*, San Marino, Calif., 1955. See also Austin Woolrych, 'Last Quests for a Settlement 1657–1660', in *The Interregnum: The Quest for Settlement 1646–1660,* ed. G. E. Aylmer, 1972, ch. 8; and for a different view, Christopher Hill, *The Century of Revolution 1603–1714*, Edinburgh, 1961, pp. 141–4.

[3] The ideas of the radical sects are brilliantly discussed by Christopher Hill, *The World Turned Upside Down: Radical Ideas during the English Revolution,* 1972.

hostile.[4] But we ought not to assume without further enquiry that the Restoration concerned only the gentry and the élite, and that the common people had nothing to do with it. When we recall the survival of the old continuities of popular politics during the civil war—the ever-present yearning for the recovery of a just, traditional order—it seems plausible to suppose that they may still have influenced large numbers of people during the war's revolutionary aftermath. It may be, then, that many ordinary Englishmen, for their own reasons, really did welcome the Restoration.

For if in one sense almost everything had changed, in another very little had changed. In spite of the Levellers there were still privileged and unprivileged; in spite of the Diggers still rich and poor; in spite of the Ranters still marriages and families; in spite of the Quakers still parish clergy and tithes. The unquestioning popular acceptance of traditional commonplaces about familial order and social hierarchy ensured that the revolution of 1649 would administer only a fleeting shock to the system. Even the radical sects which admitted women to church membership made no open assault on paternal authority in the family.[5] Parliamentarian, royalist or neutral, most Englishmen's conception of what the war had been about was limited by the conservative vocabulary in which their aspirations were expressed. The Clubmen of both camps shared the same assumptions about good order and governance, the same nostalgia for the good old days of Queen Elizabeth. Even before the fighting ended it was clear that victory for Parliament would simply replace one source of oppression by another. The war generated a massive expansion of the power of the centralized state. Its aftermath, in which a revolutionary minority inevitably had to rely on the support of the military to stay in power, completed the process of popular alienation.

So in the end it was not only the gentry who were able to celebrate the return of Charles II. But popular acquiescence in the Restoration does not mean that the war and revolution had no significant impact on the people of England. The war gave them experiences of community division and disorder which must have long survived in the collective memory, and which could be reawakened by superiors interested in pointing out the calamitous results of resistance to authority. The revolution gave them further experience, if any were needed, of the disruptive impact of Puritan reformation on the ritualized community life of traditional villages. All these matters will be discussed in this and the following chapter. Our first task, however, is to survey the impact of the war on the popular political consciousness.

[4] As argued by Hill, *World Turned Upside Down*, pp. 285–6.
[5] Keith Thomas, 'Women and the Civil War Sects', in *Crisis in Europe 1560–1660: Essays from Past and Present*, ed. Trevor Aston, 1965, pp. 334–5.

*

The civil war had released forces destructive of the very foundations of order: destructive of paternal authority in the family, of neighbourly co-operation in the community, of hierarchal authority in the state. Sons had fought against fathers, tenants against landlords, the people against their king. There were, many feared, renewed signs of female resistance to male dominance. It would be absurd to depict the war as a milestone in the liberation of women, yet it did allow more independence for a few of them, especially in London. Women petitioned Parliament for peace, formed committees to raise funds for local military units, worked on fortifications, and (on rarer occasions) actually took part in the fighting.[6] Women were prominent in Leveller petitioning campaigns: in April 1649 they heckled MPs outside the House of Commons, lectured Cromwell on his oppressive treatment of Lilburne, and had to be dispersed by troops. Some of the religious sects allowed women an unprecedented degree of equality with men, but this was not accompanied by serious demands for female suffrage in the state. Even Leveller women were content to echo their menfolk's political programme. However, a few pamphlets proclaimed somewhat more feminist views, with calls for better educational opportunities for women and denunciations of the subjection of wives to husbands.[7]

Conservatives, as always, were quick to take alarm. There was the familiar resort to derisive stereotypes—denunciations of Billingsgate fishwives and muscular Amazons, indignant reminders that women's proper work was 'to spin or knit, and not to meddle with state affairs'— and pamphlets and ballads appeared on the hilariously unthinkable theme of a 'Parliament of Women'. Even the libertarian Lilburne held conventional assumptions about gender roles, excusing his wife's activism as the product of her 'masculine spirit', while the women petitioners at least professed a consciousness of their 'frail condition' as the weaker sex. The alarm about female militancy was exaggerated, but it contributed to the widespread fear that patriarchal order was endangered.[8]

If familial order was threatened, so even more clearly was that of the state. The spread of democratic ideas, declared William Prynne, was the origin of 'all our late years' confusion'.[9] In their fully-fledged Leveller form, democratic ideas were in fact thin on the ground in Prynne's native Somerset. Still, in 1647 many there, as elsewhere, were sympathetic to the Army's claim to represent the people, even if more would probably have

---

[6] Higgins, 'Reactions of Women', pp. 185–98, 218–21.
[7] Ibid. pp. 199–206. Thomas, 'Women and the Civil War Sects', p. 337.
[8] Higgins, 'Reactions of Women', pp. 179–80, 209–13.
[9] William Prynne, *Brevia Parliamentaria Rediviva*, 1662, p. 324.

shared Prynne's equation of democracy with confusion. All the stock arguments that the state was a union of patriarchal households were endlessly reiterated. The 'new doctrine of the people's sovereignty' was invalid, declared one author, because it gave power 'to all servants and children grown up, as well as to their parents and masters'; the Army, 'the pretended representers of the people', contained 'servants, prentices not yet free, and children unmarried whose parents are yet living'. Henry Ireton's famous interventions at Putney in 1647 stated the obvious: the axiomatic connection between political rights and property. 'See then what antipathy domineers in the veins of the dregs of the people against the gentry'. Marchamont Nedham sneered, reporting the insolence of 'fellows in leather aprons' towards unsympathetic MPs. Establishment opinion of all shades railed against the sinister implications of Leveller democracy.[10]

Much of the revolutionary spirit that was abroad was blamed on the soldiers. There were those, to be sure, who thought that even in the Army Leveller influence was an illusion, promoted by a small 'fraternity of agitators', barrack-room lawyers who had made themselves spokesmen for an apathetic rank-and-file.[11] Not that the rank-and-file were apathetic when they were left unpaid. Mutinies by forces outside the New Model were especially common, of the kind that occurred at Hereford in February 1646 when soldiers besieged committee-men shouting 'Money! Money!' Even in the summer of 1647, when the soldiers' language was becoming more openly political, money was usually a factor in the disorders. With parliamentary tension between Presbyterians and Independents approaching its climax, mutineers seized Hereford Castle and arrested Col. John Birch and his brother as enemies to the Army; but the castle also had £2,000 in its treasury. In November 1647 soldiers imprisoned a Bristol alderman, and the deliberations of the Somerset Committee were interrupted on at least one occasion.[12] In the early days of the war the troops had been more patient—and had plunder to console them—but the longer men served as full-time soldiers the more likely the were to take this kind of action. Disbanded Suffolk soldiers went quietly

[10] BL TT, E. 396 (10): *The Case of the Army Soberly Discussed*, 1647, p. 6.The charge about the Leveller threat to property was made, for example, by Marchamont Nedham in both his royalist and parliamentarian phases. See BL TT, E. 466 (11): *Mercurius Pragmaticus*, no. 28 (3–10 Oct. 1648); and Nedham, *The Case of the Commonwealth of England Stated . . .* , 1650, pp. 71, 78.
[11] The quotation is from BL Add. MS 18979 (Fairfax MSS), fo. 252, Anne Overton to Fairfax, 26 July [1647]. For a modern revision of traditional assumptions about Leveller influence in the Army see Mark Kishlansky, 'The Army and the Levellers: The Roads To Putney', *HJ* xxii (1979), 795–824.
[12] HMC, *Portland*, iii. 145. *Memorials*, ed. Bell, i. 370. *CJ* v. 366. *CCC* ii. 1361. The Dorset Committee was also interrupted: *Memorials of the Great Civil War in England*, ed. Henry Cary, 1842, i. 295–7. For the subject in general see J. S. Morrill, 'Mutiny and Discontent in English Provincial Armies 1645–1647', *P & P* no. 56 (Aug. 1972), 49–74.

home, they said, 'greatly behind hand of our pay'; it took the militant example of others in 1647 to provoke them to belated protest.[13]

Still, the events of 1647 make it clear that there really was a Leveller presence in the Army. Only in London and the home counties, on the other hand, was there any effective civilian movement. In Buckinghamshire and Hertfordshire its appearance was foreshadowed by a vigorous agitation against tithes. In March 1647 a petition from these two counties denounced Parliament's 'arbitrary practices', called for the ending of the judicial authority of the House of Lords, and demanded the release of Lilburne and other imprisoned Levellers. In the autumn there were reports of Leveller agents gathering subscriptions to *The Agreement of the People* further afield, in Nottinghamshire and Rutland. It is not clear how much popular response there was to this, or how far Lilburne's boasts of Leveller cells in Kent and Hertfordshire reflected anything more than wishful thinking.[14] Certainly the Levellers appear to have made little headway in the western counties. There were, to be sure, plenty of radical preachers, lay and clerical, to attract people into various brands of separatism. Petitions inspired by soldiers circulated at Bristol in 1647 and 1648, but apart from this, organized Leveller activity is almost invisible in this region. Only in the spring of 1649, during the eruption in the Army which led to the Levellers' final defeat at Burford, was there even a minor outbreak, in Somerset.[15] The Leveller movement was London based: outside the orbit of the capital it may have aroused sympathy, but little open support.

*

Popular politics in the western counties in the post-war years took more traditional forms. The Leveller programme of sweeping political reform had less immediate relevance than the more pressing threats to customary local rights, the threat even to subsistence itself. The harvests of 1647 and 1648 were among the worst of the century, and the consequent high prices bore heavily on a population already suffering in the trade depression that inevitably followed the war. As usual, the conditions were worst in the clothing districts. In 1647 weavers from Chippenham and other north Wiltshire towns drew attention to the miserable level of unemployment in the area. Early the next year some Westbury petitioners accused the

---

[13] BL Harleian MS 255 (D'Ewes MSS), fo. 97[v].

[14] *The Parliamentary or Constitutional History of England*, 2nd edn., 1761–3, xvi. 399–403. *LJ* ix. 529, 571–3. T. C. Pease, *The Leveller Movement*, Oxford, 1916, pp. 232–3. H. N. Brailsford, *The Levellers and the English Revolution*, ed. Christopher Hill, Stanford, 1961, pp. 313–14. David Underdown, '"Honest" Radicals in the Counties, 1642–1649', in *Puritans and Revolutionaries*, ed. Pennington and Thomas, p. 199.

[15] *Historical Collections*, ed. Rushworth, vii. 798–9. *CJ* v. 289. Underdown, *Somerset*, pp. 152, 156–7. Brailsford, *Levellers*, p. 508.

JPs—'many of your worships being cornmasters'—of having deliberately driven up grain prices by their generosity in granting licences to maltsters. The enraged magistrates promptly summoned the town's officials and received an abject apology. In spite of the usual efforts by the authorities to regulate markets, there were food riots at Warminster and in the Melksham area, and Bristol carriers were reluctant to operate in the neighbourhood because they had so often had corn seized from them 'by a turbulent multitude'. The Wiltshire grand jury asked for a ban on sales of barley to maltsters (the Dorset JPs had already done this), and one of the justices proposed a public meeting 'where the maltsters as well as the poor people might be present . . . for quieting the county'. The Leveller John Wildman heard about the disorders from Wiltshire clothiers in London, but there is no sign that his friends were able to profit from them. During similar outbreaks in Gloucestershire a year later a London newsbook described the rioters as 'clubmen', and their obviously conservative intentions make this an appropriate term.[16]

Grain riots were not the only instances of post-war popular protest. Resistance to landlords who had violated customary rights was almost as common as it had been during the lawless war years, sometimes occurring with the connivance of local officials. Several Lydiard Millicent residents were sentenced to be whipped if they failed to pay fines for throwing down Sir Anthony Ashley Cooper's hedges; the tithingman was arrested for refusing to execute the order.[17] There were no disorders in the Somerset levels to match those still raging in the Lincolnshire and East Anglian fens—the Isle of Axholme men went so far as to enlist the Levellers Lilburne and Wildman in their cause, while in 1653 Norfolk and Cambridgeshire fenlanders helped Dutch prisoners of war, employed on the Earl of Bedford's drainage works, to escape. But Somerset was quiet only because half-hearted efforts to revive earlier projects, as by Sir Cornelius Vermuyden during the Protectorate, were quickly abandoned in the face of local mutterings. Smaller enclosures were still under attack: it took the Seymours at least until 1656 to find a 'sufficient man' to farm their enclosed land in Godney Moor. The tenants, Lord Seymour was told, made 'a great waste and spoil upon it, cutting, hackling the fences and hedges'.[18]

[16] HMC, *Various Collections* i (Wilts QS MSS), 115, 117. *Records of Wilts.*, pp. 180–1, 183, 200, 208. *Western Circuit Assize Orders*, pp. 272–3. DRO B2/16/3 (Dorchester Corporation papers, 1629–94), fo. 36ᵛ. BL TT, E. 527 (3): *Perfect Occurrences*, no. 105 (29 Dec. 1648–5 Jan. 1648/9). Walter and Wrightson, 'Dearth and the Social Order', p. 27. Brailsford, *Levellers*, p. 320. For prices and wages in 1647–8 see Hoskins, 'Harvest Fluctuations 1620–1759', pp. 20, 29; and *Agrarian History*, iv, Appendix, Tables VI, VII, XV, XVI.

[17] WRO, QS Order Book, 1641–54, Michaelmas 1646 and Easter 1647. *Records of Wilts.*, pp. 176–7, where incorrectly assigned to the Epiphany sessions.

[18] *A Collection of State Papers of John Thurloe*, ed. T. Birch, 1742, i. 358. *CSPD*, *1655*, pp. 301–3; *1655–6*, pp. 337–8. BL Add. MS 32324 (Seymour MSS), fo. 32. Williams, *Somerset Levels*, p. 101. For the disorders in Lincolnshire see Holmes, *Lincolnshire*, pp. 208–12.

The most violent disorders occurred in the recently enclosed forests, once again ranging the poorer inhabitants against the former courtiers and their successors and agents. Parliament's authority was quickly enlisted on the side of the absentee owners, sequestered Royalists though they often were. Soon after hostilities had ended the Committee of the West ordered the Dorset Committee and JPs to suppress the 'very great riots' still raging in Gillingham Forest. At about the same time the Earl of Elgin, the principal landowner, tried to divide the opposition by negotiating with the 'ablest' inhabitants of Mere to set aside part of the disputed lands as common, the profits going for relief of the numerous poor of the town. But intermittent violence continued, and not until 1653 did relative peace return to the Gillingham area. Parliament's local officials showed somewhat greater zeal than their pre-war predecessors had done for asserting absentee property rights, mainly because sequestration diverted the profits into their hands. In 1647 the Dorset Committee noted that 'certain closes, parcel of the Lawns within the Liberty of Gillingham', sequestered from the royalist George Kirke, were producing nothing for the state because the fences had been thrown down, and managed to find local tenants who would repair them and farm the property.[19]

Outbreaks also occurred in Neroche and Selwood. Those in Neroche were serious enough for the forest to be still largely unenclosed in 1652; a few years earlier a weaver from the Ilminster area defied repeated orders to desist from throwing down enclosures, announcing that 'he could but lie in the gaol for it'. Efforts to persuade local landowners to inform against those responsible for the lawlessness proved fruitless.[20] In Selwood and Brewham Forests, on the Wiltshire–Somerset border, both royalist and parliamentarian landlords were under attack: the enclosures of the royalist Sir Charles Berkeley at Kilmington and Barnard's Combe and of the absentee parliamentarian Lord Broghil near Maiden Bradley were levelled with equal enthusism. The Berkeleys' experience is another reminder that we cannot attribute the royalism of the nearby Bruton area exclusively to their influence: they obviously had no control over a large segment of the population. Both magnates enlisted the aid of the Council of State between 1653 and 1656, but both also encountered the same kind of foot-dragging by the local justices that had been common a generation earlier. Berkeley and Broghil regularly had their fences restored, and just as regularly local people destroyed them and put in their cattle to graze. But in Broghil the commoners were taking on a formidable adversary, a member of the Protector's Council, who by 1656 could invoke the power of Major-General Disbrowe to overcome local resistance. Recognizing

---

[19] PRO SP 30/24/32/6 (Shaftesbury papers), fo. 7. *Dorset Minute Books*, pp. 292–3. Sharp, *In Contempt*, pp. 237–9.
[20] Sharp, *In Contempt*, p. 246.

that when it came to force Broghil had all the cards in his hands, the inhabitants wisely turned from violence to the courts.[21]

One new form of popular protest made its appearance in these years: the riot against excisemen. It will be recalled that the King's excise had provoked much opposition in wartime Somerset. When Parliament's excise was imposed on the western counties after the war there were similar protests. Dorset people were 'very adverse' to paying it, the Committee reported.[22] By raising prices of commodities such as meat and beer the excise created obvious hardships for the poor. But as a 1650 pamphlet noted, it also hurt producers and retailers, 'thereby utterly disheartening the most ingenious and industrious party'—the very middling sort on whose loyalty Parliament had always relied.[23]

The official mind often tended to dismiss violence against excisemen as royalist-inspired. This was the case, for example, when a 'great company of people' attacked excisemen and their escort of soldiers at Chippenham on New Year's Eve, 1647. Some of the rioters were armed and in disguise, which may suggest the use of skimmington rituals, just as the time of year implies an extension of Christmas merry-making. They were said to have expected help from Gloucestershire and Hampshire as well as from other parts of Wiltshire, where meetings had been held to promote common action. Reports of similar disturbances at Frome, another clothing town, give a different impression. When the excisemen (again with a military escort) were attacked in January 1649 the rioters, it was claimed, were not 'the scum and malignants of the town, but such as have faithfully served the Parliament and kingdom'; people who equated submission to the excise with 'slavery'. This comes from a source favourable to the rioters, and we have no other clue to the quality of the people involved, any more than for similar outbreaks within the next few years at Bruton, Taunton, Poole, Shaftesbury, Somerton, and Norton St. Philip. But historians now know enough about pre-industrial mobs to be very cautious about accepting official descriptions of them as simply the poor and the rabble.[24] The excise, clearly, was hated by all ranks of society, and attacks upon its agents expressed a traditional view of popular rights. Not all excise officers were outsiders to their communities, but they were agents of an innovating, intruding state in its most unpopular guise. John Rogers,

---

[21] *CCC* ii. 1339. *CSPD, 1652–3*, pp. 422–3; *1654*, p. 326; *1655*, pp. 131, 162–3; *1655–6*, p. 94. Sharp, *In Contempt*, pp. 244–5.

[22] Bodleian MS Tanner 53, fo. 45.

[23] Quoted in Margaret James, *Social Problems and Policy during the Puritan Revolution, 1640–1660*, 1930, p. 38.

[24] BL TT, E. 422 (6): *A Declaration Concerning His Majesties Royall Person*, 1647/8; E. 540 (20): *The Moderate*, no. 29 (23–30 Jan. 1648/9). *Western Circuit Assize Orders*, pp. 254, 279–80. Whitelocke, *Memorials*, iii. 162. *CSPD, 1652–3*, p. 301. According to royalist sources, the Poole disorders spread over a wide area of east Dorset. See BL TT, E. 595 (9): *The Royall Diurnall*, no. 4 (11–19 Mar. 1649/50); E. 596 (3): *The Man in the Moon*, no. 48 (13–20 March 1649/50).

exciseman at Cheddar, was beaten up, put in the stocks, and denounced by neighbours as a 'peeping rogue'—and the hostility was expressed by people of many different social levels and shades of political opinion. The village community could make life very uncomfortable for those who violated its norms of good neighbourhood, even if they were backed by the authority of the state.[25]

*

The civil war affected popular politics of this kind only by creating new grievances like the excise and by making it easier to take action because of the weakening of local government. But the war had a more direct impact on popular consciousness. One sign of that impact is the new vocabulary of abuse now available for the conduct of local quarrels. Epithets like 'cavalier rogue' or 'roundhead dog' might be no more accurate as descriptions of their targets' politics than 'cuckoldly knave' or 'whoremaster' were of their morals, but their constant repetition is significant. Religious taunts like 'papist' and 'atheist' retained their currency, but in 'cavalier' and 'roundhead' we encounter a more explicitly political language of abuse, which reflected and may well have strengthened people's perceptions that their communities were politically divided. The stereotypes had appeared before the war, and resort to them became increasingly common as the fighting continued. Robert Janson rode into his native village of Stoke-sub-Hamdon swearing that if he found any roundhead rogues he would cut them in pieces; George Smith, formerly constable of Ilchester, pursued a man from a nearby village and threatened to kill him as a roundheaded rogue: such examples could be endlessly repeated.[26]

Janson and Smith were committed partisans looking for armed enemies. But language of this kind was also used by people outside the context of the war, simply as an extension of their normal repertoire of invective. In counties like Norfolk, which saw little actual fighting, this was less common: the war had not divided village communities as it had in the west.[27] But it was not unknown even in the eastern counties. At Barking, Essex, in 1645 a fisherman's wife caused a 'great tumult' by complaining of a local yeoman that 'it was long of such roundheaded rogues as he was that they were brought into such a condition'. As upstart élites acquired wealth and power from service to Parliament or Protector, it was natural for their less privileged neighbours to denounce them as they had once denounced the agents of a parasitic royal court. These

[25] Patricia E. Croot, 'Aspects of Agrarian Society in Brent March, Somerset, 1500–1700', Ph.D. thesis, University of Leeds, 1981, ch. 7. I am grateful to Dr Croot for permitting me to read her interesting account of events at Cheddar, based on PRO SP 23/66.
[26] These examples are from *Calendar of the Proceedings of the Committee for Advance of Money*, ed. M. A. E. Green, 1888, pp. 1051, 1159.
[27] I am informed by Susan Amussen that such language can rarely be found in Norfolk local records.

outbursts often took on an explicitly royalist colouring. An Essex black-smith in 1655 exploded about genteel passers-by upon the highway: 'These are Parliament rogues, and I am fain to work hard to get money with the sweat of my brows to maintain such Parliament rogues as these are.' Their power, he added, would not last long. The Barking woman had been even less guarded: 'the King is a-coming now, and then we shall have a course taken with you and such as you are'.[28] Outbursts of this kind often came from people who were regarded, for one reason or another, as social outcasts. Robert Willson, already encountered as a notorious ne'er-do-well at Ashwell, Hertfordshire, said that when the Cavaliers came he would direct them to the houses of Roundheads and tell them whom to plunder.[29]

Village rebels were in effect being politicized by the war, albeit at a primitive level—being goaded into seditiously identifying with enemies of the prevailing authority, much as others might be goaded into witchcraft. Joan Walton of Chelwood in north Somerset was a poor, lonely, and embittered woman. In 1650 Thomas Stone suspected her of pilfering his wood. Now Stone's brother Richard was steward to the powerful Alex-ander Popham, the biggest Commonwealth magnate in those parts. Questioned about the wood, Walton denounced Richard Stone as 'a fat gutted rogue', declaring that 'she would make his gut as poor as hers before she had done, and though they now had the power of the country in their hands, yet they should be glad with a bit of bread as well as she, when the King's army did come'. People remembered her threats to 'be revenged on the parish of Chelwood if ever the wind did turn' (she especially singled out the parson), and her boast 'that she had them in the other army that would to it'.[30] A similar case after the Restoration, with the politics reversed, involved a Banwell man, John Woods. Pointing to a picture of Charles II, he said he hoped 'for the turning of the times, and to pull some of his neighbours' mows out of their bartons, and to revenge himself upon some, and that the King could not stand long, he had so many enemies'. When the Bishop gave his customary Easter sixpences to the poor of the parish Woods sneered that 'it was but a small gift given of a gentleman, and that they were a company of Papish rogues'.[31]

Popular responses to the war were thus intensely localist and personal. But the preaching and propaganda to which people had been exposed were not without effect; even quite humble villagers could translate the issues into their own language. A Norfolk woman complained in 1643 that 'now there is no King, no laws, nor no justice'. Asked to explain herself

---

[28] *English History from Essex Sources*, pp. 78–9, 87–8.
[29] *Hertford County Records*, i. 80 (and see also pp. 102, 121).
[30] SRO CQ 3/1/82 (2) (Sessions Rolls, 1650), no. 91. See also *SQSR* iii, intro., pp. xxxv–xxxvi.
[31] SRO CQ 3/1/108 (Session Rolls, 1665), no. 23.

she replied, 'she said so because the King was not where he should be'—that he was not governing as King-in-Parliament, in other words.[32] The war sometimes enabled participants in village quarrels to settle old scores in ways that show that they understood very well what the issues were. At Nunney, for example, the Protestant inhabitants had long resented Richard Prater's colony of recusants in the castle. Before the war they had been unable to 'contradict' them, but when it was over they successfully petitioned to have the Catholics removed and punished.[33]

Local rifts like those that set the two Wrington churchwardens against each other must have taken years to heal. Dr Patricia Croot's reconstruction of events in the parliamentarian village of Cheddar shows how echoes of the war lingered on into the 1650s. Much of the strife arose from the exciseman John Rogers's abrasive Puritanism. Rogers had served the Parliament early in the war, and in 1645, during the siege of Bristol, he appears to have joined the Mendip Clubmen. It did him no good: he came to be perceived as the representative of an oppressive, militarist regime. Most Cheddar people seem to have shared the conservative localism, the typical 'Country' dislike of the military and high taxes, that was repeatedly expressed by Rogers' chief enemy, the constable Henry Bankes. To the extent that men like Bankes identified their enemies in party terms—in 1651 he described the militiamen raised to fight the invading Scots as 'Independent redcoat rogues'—this involved them in a grassroots version of national politics, even though their priorities were ultimately localist and traditional.[34]

Still, it was Rogers, not Bankes, who was on the way up: by 1652 he had moved on from exciseman to collector of sequestrations. The new county bureaucracies were largely staffed by men of his stamp. There was much infighting for jobs, as in the bitter struggle between Pyne and the Gorges brothers in Somerset, which was as much about patronage as policy.[35] After 1649 Puritans such as Rogers naturally felt that as the only reliable servants of the republic they had an automatic right to office. But as early as 1646 the Presbyterian Thomas Edwards was complaining that at Bristol none were 'employed in any service, or put into any place . . . unless they be men of the New Light and New Way'.[36] Anxieties about the dependability of local officials were common both at Westminster and in the provinces. At the top they led to the framing of oaths of loyalty like the Engagement to be 'true and faithful to the Commonwealth of England', and the supervision and replacement of local officials, especially by

[32] NRO C/S 3/34 (Norfolk QS Rolls, 1643–4), Petition of Rachel Merrye, 1643 (I am grateful to Susan Amussen for this reference).
[33] SRO QS 164, Petitions, N.
[34] See n. 25 above.
[35] Underdown, *Somerset*, p. 173.
[36] BL TT, E. 323 (2): Thomas Edwards, *Gangraena* (1645/6), p. [42].

Cromwell's Major-Generals. But the numerous local petitions and complaints indicate that there was corresponding concern from below. Even the most minor village office could be called in question.[37]

Villagers had other priorities besides the political and religious complexion of their officers. In all regions they had of course long since become accustomed to managing their own affairs in vestry and manor court, with or without the direction of parson or squire, and had never been slow to protest when rights were violated. There is therefore nothing new in the fact that some west-country people took advantage of post-war circumstances to defy their landlords. In November 1645 Lord Baltimore made a rare appearance at his manor court at Semley, Wiltshire. According to one of the tenants, he 'threatened such as were absent, that he would re-enter upon their tenements'. A few were brave enough to ask the steward by what right he held court, and to demand to see the order when he said that it was by warrant of the County Committee (Baltimore was under sequestration); at least one copyholder was not satisfied and refused to take the homager's oath.[38] Early in 1647 the Earl of Salisbury's steward encountered trouble at a north Somerset manor, where a tenant 'in a rebellious manner' had abused the Earl's officers 'in a strange way of words'. It would be rash to read these incidents as signs of incipient Leveller feeling, even in the pasture country, for there had been occasional signs of similar tenant independence before the war. In most places manorial custom pursued its placid way. More typical was the attitude of a tenant at Yarlington, in the conservative Bruton area. When the Protector's proclamation about the appointment of local officials was read at the court leet in 1654 he loudly objected, 'We will have no new laws here'.[39]

*

Although the civil war spawned many small groups of religious or political village radicals, English popular politics thus retained its old conservatism. The most significant feature of the post-war period was the continuing alienation of popular opinion by Parliament and its local agents. Even the middling sort of the towns and the clothing districts, Parliament's staunchest adherents during the war, began to turn away, disenchanted by high taxes, military rule, and the overriding of local rights. Before the war they had usually managed to keep their poorer neighbours in line, and even to inspire in some of them their own concern for godly reformation. Some degree of disillusion was inevitable: much of Parliament's appeal in 1642 derived from its defence of 'Country' rights

---

[37] Underdown, 'Problem of Popular Allegiance', p. 90.
[38] BL Add. MS 22084 (Wilts. Sequestrations Register), fo. 132.
[39] HMC, *Salisbury*, xxii. 392–3. *SQSR* iii, intro., p. xxxvii.

against the Court, yet the necessities of war made Parliament an even more vigorously centralizing force than Charles I had ever been. Disillusion came the more swiftly because of the intolerance of Parliament's local officers, especially those employed by such notoriously ruthless committees as those headed by Sir Anthony Weldon in Kent and John Pyne in Somerset. 'Let the well-affected, or more zealous party in the Countries consider', pleaded the influential *Moderate Intelligencer* in October 1645, 'whether they . . . have not taxed beyond and contrary to ordinance, and so exasperated the Country against them and lost their hearts, whom by justice and love they might have held.'[40]

For all its regularity, post-war taxation never produced enough revenue for the armies' needs, so troops continued to have to take free quarter. This remained the most universal grievance in all parts of England. In the autumn of 1645 matters were particularly serious in the north, where the Scots army had provoked the people, the Yorkshire Committee warned, 'to desperate associations'. When the Scots needed anything they were wont to say 'they must go meet with Robin-Hog, meaning . . . country men, saying he shall pay for it'. A man was killed near Haltwistle in one of the numerous outbreaks of violence, and resistance to quartering continued in the Yorkshire dales long after the Scots left. In September 1647 some of Lambert's soldiers had to take refuge in a church to protect themselves.[41] Violence in many other parts of England was provoked by the disorderliness of unpaid troops. In Berkshire in March 1646, an MP reported, the soldiers were 'ranging about the country and breaking and robbing houses and passengers, and driving away sheep and other cattle'. At Woolhampton an honest freeholder of £60 a year, 'a very cordial man for the Parliament', was killed, and there was serious violence when residents combined against soldiers. There were similar complaints in Hampshire about the outrages committed by forces *en route* for Ireland, which led to a riot near Alton in August 1646 because men of Ireton's regiment 'had quartered there more than 24 hours'.[42] In Herefordshire, protests at the 'intolerable charging and oppressing by free quarter' led the Committee to arrest a captain illegally levying money and give him four days to get his troop out of the county. In April 1647 there was a violent affray at Hereford between Birch's soldiers and men of a local troop, and a month later another at Longtown between the inhabitants and soldiers, with fatalities on both sides.[43]

[40] BL TT, E. 306 (3): *Moderate Intelligencer*, no. 34 (16–23 Oct. 1645).
[41] Zachary Grey, *An Impartial Examination of the Third Volume of Mr. Daniel Neal's History of the Puritans*, 1736–9, iii. Appendix, pp. 41–2, 51. *Historical Collections*, ed. Rushworth, vii. 809, 817, 824, 831–2. BL TT, E. 407 (45): *A Fight in the North at the Dales in Richmondshire*, 1647.
[42] Bodleian MS Tanner 60, fo. 491. HMC, *Portland*, i. 319–20. Grey, *Impartial Examination*, iii, App., p. 64. BL TT, E. 350 (21): *Moderate Intelligencer*, no. 76 (13–20 Aug. 1646).
[43] HMC, *Portland*, iii. 152, 154–5, 157–8. BL Loan 29/124 (Harley papers), no. 63. Bodleian MS Tanner 58, fo. 41.

Resentment at the constant military presence was equally fierce in the western counties. The Nunney villagers who had rejoiced at the downfall of the recusant Praters were soon disillusioned. They had to quarter soldiers left behind to demolish the castle; the officer in charge, they complained, 'did press our ploughs, and did send away to Bristol wainloads of beef, bacon, butter and cheese . . . and our parish arms'.[44] The burden on north Somerset was particularly severe when Fairfax's army lay around Bristol during and after the siege. The military authorities issued debentures for quartering, but puzzled villagers often could not remember how long they had quartered Clubmen auxiliaries and how long regular troops. At least the Clubmen were local men and only a temporary nuisance. Far worse was the incessant burden of ill-paid outsiders. The inhabitants of north-west Wiltshire had been promised freedom from quartering in return for their contributions to the Bristol garrison, yet in July 1646 it was still continuing, to their 'great damage and impoverishment'. Promises that quartering would end if the counties paid their full shares of the monthly assessment were worthless. And, as the inhabitants of Westbury pointedly told Fairfax in February 1647, 'whereas the rumour of the soldiers paying for their quarters may appear to the world to be something yet we find it in effect nothing'.[45] It was a far cry from the days before Langport when the New Model had made friends by scrupulously paying for supplies and quarter.

The New Model was bad enough; the less disciplined forces outside its immediate control were intolerable. Troops bound for Ireland were, as we have seen, particularly hated. 'If they lie above a night in a place the country rise', a Long Ashton resident noted in September 1646, 'which has much lessened their numbers'.[46] Another source of trouble was the unpaid and neglected remnant of Massey's brigade, quartered near the Wiltshire–Somerset border. Some of them were apprehended after a highway robbery spree and committed to Ilchester gaol. They immediately escaped, though at least one was recaptured and sent back to prison by Massey's Council of War, which also sentenced another soldier to death for murdering a countryman.[47] In 1647 there were further protests against the 'heavy pressures and burthens by free quartering' from assize and sessions juries, and in May things were so bad that the high sheriff sent out warrants to summon a general rendezvous in north Somerset to round up marauding soldiers. Troops were repeatedly 'broken and

---

[44] PRO SP 28/242 (County Committee papers), fo. 41.

[45] HMC, *Portland*, i. 283. *Records of Wilts.*, pp. 154–5. Morrill, *Revolt*, pp. 173–4.

[46] HMC, *Egmont*, i. 318.

[47] Bodleian MS Dep. c 167 (Nalson papers, xiv), fo. 309. For complaints of the soldiers' outrages see *Diary of John Harington*, p. 31; *CJ* iv. 638; and BL TT, E. 350 (6): *Moderate Intelligencer*, no. 75 (6–13 Aug. 1646).

disbanded' by Clubmen; the reports swelled into rumours of a general insurrection in Somerset and Dorset.[48]

The rumours were exaggerated, but in a region in which vestiges of recent Club organizations still survived, the situation was none the less explosive. In March 1646 impressment of recruits for the New Model provoked a revival of Club activity in the area around Bruton and Castle Cary, places which the investigating constables rightly described as 'always ill-affected to the state'. At about the same time impressment in Dorset caused, the sheriff reported, 'such a distraction and insurrection of the rascality in several parts that it will prove, I fear, little less than another Club business'. He promptly sent for troops from Weymouth and Wareham to restore order.[49] By the summer the Somerset Committee seriously expected a general rising in two of the Clubmen's wartime centres of activity: the Poldens (formerly parliamentarian) and the Castle Cary area (formerly royalist). They arrested the leader of the Polden group, Humphrey Willis, but this did not end the resistance.[50]

The trouble, the Committee professed to believe, was all the fault of the soldiers: the Taunton and Bridgwater garrisons were to blame for 'exasperating the Country against the Committee'.[51] This was a half-truth: the presence of the military was certainly a major factor, but the committees themselves, and not only in Somerset, were largely the architects of their own unpopularity. They had, it is true, performed a vital administrative function in some counties at the end of the war, filling the vacuum caused by the temporary absence of JPs; supervising manor courts, regulating alehouses, and sometimes even dealing with petty crimes. But the misgovernment of which men like Willis repeatedly complained was never reformed. The problem was not confined to the western counties. By 1647 county committees nearly everywhere had become, to quote a typical complaint from Herefordshire, 'contemptible in the eyes of the Country'.[52]

One cause of the committees' unpopularity was the common perception that their members and officers were of lower social origins than their predecessors in county government. The civil war, Clarendon thought, led to the elevation of people 'who were not above the condition of ordinary inferior constables six or seven years before'.[53] This was an exaggeration, for the JPs at least were still drawn from the middle ranks of

[48] *LJ* ix. 172. *SQSR* iii, intro., p. xxix. HMC, *Egmont*, i. 403, 408. *Diary of John Harington*, p. 55.
[49] Bodleian MS Tanner 60, ff. 545–9. Northumberland MS 547 (John Fitzjames' Letter Book, i, 1645–7), fo. 24 (BL Film, no. 330).
[50] Underdown, *Somerset*, pp. 132–3, 135.
[51] Bodleian MS Tanner 59, fo. 353. Underdown, *Somerset*, pp. 135–7.
[52] HMC, *Egmont*, i. 450. For the committees' administrative functions see *Committee at Stafford*, intro., pp. xlvi–li; and Underdown, *Somerset*, p. 128.
[53] Quoted in Hill, *Puritanism and Revolution*, p. 208.

the gentry, even after 1649. But there was still a significant change, as pre-war magnates were either disqualified as Royalists, or withdrew from activity through dislike of Westminster policies and military rule, and such people were particularly likely to refuse to serve as committee-men. Their replacements were often townsmen and minor parish gentry, and there were even a few of Clarendon's upstart constables among them. One such was the Norfolk man Tobias Pedder, who had advanced through the wartime bureaucracy to become a JP by 1653. Sir Hamon L'Estrange was indignant at this violation of old standards of deference: Toby Pedder, he exploded, 'whom I made not chief Constable to repay me with malice and ingratitude for the many favours which he and his predecessors have received from me and mine'.[54] Contemptuous sneers at such upstarts were often expressed by people of much less eminence than L'Estrange. 'Good neighbour Gorges . . .' a Cheddar tailor began with insulting familiarity when summoned before the new JP, John Gorges, who came from the same parish. Gorges was beside himself: he was distantly connected to the Gorges of Wraxall, even if his own claims to gentility were recent indeed.[55]

In spite of the landlords' frequent wartime difficulties, deference was far from dead. County magnates still had, if they chose to exercise it, immense influence. The survival of the old ways can be seen, for example, at Chippenham, where the corporation in the 1650s still routinely ordered gifts and entertainment for visiting notables such as Sir Edward Baynton, Sir John Danvers, and Alexander Popham. When any of the Pophams came to Chippenham the bells were always rung, in gratitude for the family's recent gift of land to the town.[56] But although some magnates of this stamp remained nominally in office, even as committee-men, a good many of them were weeded out in successive purges, and those who remained were usually less active than the more ideologically committed extremists.

'The tail of the gentry, men of ruinous fortunes and despicable estates': so a Dorset petition of June 1648 described that county's committee-men. In fact, even in 1649, the Dorset Committee still contained a nucleus of well-established gentry—men such as William Sydenham, John Browne, and John Bingham. But others such as the Erles and Sir Thomas Trenchard were dropping out, and the committee was increasingly being run by lesser men, several of them townsmen from Dorchester.[57] The

[54] 'L'Estrange Papers', ed. H. L. Styleman, *Norfolk Archaeology*, v (1859), 128. R. W. Ketton-Cremer, *Norfolk in the Civil War*, 1969, p. 354. For a general account of the changes in local government see Underdown, *Pride's Purge*, ch. 10.
[55] PRO SP 23/171 (Committee for Compounding papers), p. 361. I am indebted to Patricia Croot for this reference.
[56] *Records of Chippenham*, pp. 216–23, 303.
[57] Bayley, *Dorset*, p. 352. *Dorset Minute Books, passim*.

committee-men themselves recognized their isolation and unpopularity. In December 1646, noting 'the general grievance of the country and charge of the multiplication of officers', they started reducing the number of sequestration officials. As in other counties, troops often had to be used to enforce the Committee's orders: the sequestrator of the Bridport division in 1645–6 paid out £2.10s. od. 'to troopers at several times for their assistance'.[58] The Wiltshire Committee was no more acceptable, few of its active members being men of much local influence. Of its various regional subcommittees, the one for south Wiltshire, sitting at Falstone House near Salisbury, was particularly resented for its vigorous prosecution of both Royalists and neutrals. In March 1648 its functions were taken over by the parent committee, prompting a Pewsey man to conclude over-optimistically 'that the County Committees are to be dissolved'. By this time Marchamont Nedham was complaining that the republican Edmund Ludlow was in virtual control of the county, 'setting up base fellows to trample down the gentry' by appointing 'one Rede, a serving man, and such other paltry contemptible fellows, all of them sectaries', as militia commissioners.[59]

But it was the Somerset Committee that was the most bitterly resented of the three counties' institutions. Apart from its domineering chairman, John Pyne, and a handful of other reputable gentry, all its active members were townsmen, yeomen's sons, and others on or outside the fringes of gentility. Pyne's bluster set the tone for the behaviour of his underlings. Some of the Committee's agents were men of principle, like Edward Curll from Puritan Batcombe; others were corrupt and brutal thugs who embezzled public money and beat up people who questioned their authority. The murder of the imprisoned Dean of Wells by the Committee's marshal, a Baptist shoemaker, was soon enshrined in royalist martyrology, but people of rank were not the only ones to suffer. In November 1646 there was serious bloodshed at Bridgwater, when the Committee used troops against a crowd of disobedient countrymen. In the spring of 1648, one of their enemies gleefully reported, the Committee's agents could 'hardly pass two miles' without being attacked. On the Committee's own admission, their unpopularity extended beyond the disorderly rabble: a jury, drawn as always from the middling sort, convicted one of their troopers of murder for killing a 'malignant officer' in the course of his duty. If a royalist tract is to be believed, disorders continued in the autumn of 1648, with Clubmen attacking committee

---

[58] *Dorset Minute Books*, pp. 111, 141–2. PRO SP 28/227 (County Committee papers), Dorset.
[59] BL Add. MS 5508 (Committee for Sequestrations papers), ff. 157, 161–70. 'The Falstone Day-Book', ed. J. Waylen, *WAM* xxvi (1892), 388. *Ludlow's Memoirs*, i, intro., pp. xxv–xxvi.

officials and excisemen and being 'miserably butchered' in return.[60]

Plundering soldiers, quartering, impressment, committee misgovernment: all converged between 1646 and 1648 to produce a general mood of alienation from Parliament and its local institutions. 'You had many friends in the county once', Humphrey Willis reminded the Somerset Committee, 'but if they be now taken off from that affection, you may impute it not only to your severe, but to your unequal carriage'—instanced in the illegal imprisonment of Willis himself. Willis's protests reflect the same yearning for normality and the old ways that had inspired the Club movement in 1645. All the traditional clichés of popular politics are repeated, summed up in the demand to be governed by 'the ancient and fundamental laws of the kingdom'. Along with political conservatism naturally went social conservatism. The title-page of one of Willis's attacks on Pyne's Committee neatly captures the essence of a common popular response to the notion of 'The World Turned Upside Down'. An inverted globe is surmounted by a committee-man (obviously Pyne) caught in the act of tyranny, with the legend 'Heu quantum mutatus ab illo!' In this and other pamphlets, Willis's sneers at 'blue-new-made gentlemen mounted', at 'blue apron-blades' whose sole aim was to 'keep the gentry under', express the typical nostalgia of the Clubman for a properly ordered social universe.[61]

*

Hostility to high taxes, quartering, and other military burdens, and to upstart committee-men and sequestrators, surfaced in many different ways in the post-war years. It is occasionally visible in the series of by-elections in which the House of Commons was 'recruited' after the wartime expulsion of Royalists and neutrals. Many of these elections, especially in the smaller boroughs, were of the old kind, with corporations obediently returning their patrons' nominees.[62] This was the case at Minehead, for instance, where the election of Edward Popham is clearly attributable to the Luttrells' interest. The Earls of Pembroke and Salisbury had only to agree for one of their nominees to be returned at decayed Old Sarum. The collapse of the Seymour interest in Wiltshire meant freer choice at Great Bedwyn and Marlborough: the former elected a local gentleman, Henry Hungerford, but also the London merchant Edmund Harvey; the latter the radical Col. Charles Fleetwood.

---

[60] Grey, *Impartial Examination*, iii, App., p. 65. BL TT, E. 435 (12): *Mercurius Pragmaticus*, no. 2 (4–11 Apr. 1648); E. 469 (15): *Mercurius Elencticus*, no. 49 (24–31 Oct. 1648). See also Underdown, *Somerset*, pp. 124–7, 135–7, 147–8, 151–2.

[61] BL TT, E. 345 (3): Humphrey Willis, *The Power of the Committee of the County of Somerset*, 1646; E. 374 (10): Willis, *Times Whirligig*, 1646/7 (title page reproduced in Underdown, *Somerset*, p. 134).

[62] Brunton and Pennington, *Members*, ch. 2. David Underdown, 'Party management in the recruiter elections, 1645–1648', *Eng. H. R.* lxxxiii (1968), 240–1.

Successes by native townsmen like George Skutt at Poole and John Dove at Salisbury require little explanation; Dove, it is worth noting, was one of the Puritan oligarchy against whom the Clubmen had been rebelling.[63] As for Dorset, the return of such prominent gentlemen as William Sydenham at Weymouth and John Bingham at Shaftesbury may have been in part a reflection of their power as local military commanders and committee-men, but they would have been as likely to have been elected in pre-war days, as would the Wiltshire landowner Sir John Danvers at Malmesbury. The competition among the gentry—John Ashe noted at least three or four candidates for every vacant Somerset seat—and the familiar tactics of influence and intrigue are both apparent in the surviving correspondence. Finally, a sheriff determined to manipulate a shire election could still do it. Sir John Horner got his son elected for Somerset in December 1645 by using the old trick of a last-minute adjournment of the County Court from its traditional meeting-place at Ilchester to Queen Camel.[64]

Some of the recruiter elections, however, also reflect the 'new politics' of ideology. It is not clear how much politically-inspired military or committee pressure was needed to elect Fleetwood at Marlborough or Edmund Massey at Wootton Bassett, but both were prominent, partisan outsiders, so there may well have been some. Such pressure was certainly applied, albeit unsuccessfully, on behalf of the radical Henry Henley in the Somerset election. When a second election was held in the summer of 1646 (the first had been invalidated because of Horner's misconduct), the Committee again took a hand, imprisoning Humphrey Willis to prevent him from gathering Clubmen votes against Henley. There was flagrant committee intervention, too, in the borough election at Ilchester, with much bullying of voters and a successful interception of the warrant for the election on the flimsy pretext of a (fictitious) royalist raid. Pyne, the committee boss, was in touch with the radicals' principal manager at Westminster, Edmund Prideaux, and put forward a succession of radical outsiders, including the well-known Major Thomas Harrison. The careful methods of earlier election managers like Ashe, who had been sent from Westminster in the autumn of 1645 to promote the return of 'godly' candidates without regard to party considerations, were supplemented by more violently partisan tactics.[65]

Some of the traditional features of popular politics are obvious in all this: the suspicion of outsiders, the anti-Puritan outlook of many of the

---

[63] Underdown, *Somerset*, p. 131. Keeler, *Long Parliament*, p. 71. Brunton and Pennington, *Members*, pp. 29, 166–7. Dove was also alleged to have an influential patron, Sir John Evelyn: Underdown, *Pride's Purge*, p. 49.

[64] Brunton and Pennington, *Members*, pp. 160–1. Underdown, *Somerset*, pp. 130–1.

[65] Underdown, *Somerset*, pp. 130–3; and 'The Ilchester Election, February 1646', *Somerset Archaeol. and Nat. Hist. Soc. Proceedings*, cx (1966), 40–51.

inhabitants. Pyne's failure to carry Ilchester reflects both features, while the election at Weymouth certainly reflects the first. According to Ashe, a local brewer, Matthew Allin, asserted that by custom only inhabitants should be elected, and there were many speeches against 'strangers and unknown persons'.[66] At Hindon the popular hostility to Puritans is more apparent. Ludlow's uncle was elected by the respectable burgesses, he tells us, 'yet the rabble of the town, many of whom lived upon the alms of one Mr. George How', were enlisted to justify a rival return, which led to the contest being buried indefinitely in the Committee of Privileges.[67]

Radical Parliamentarians could still find support among gentry and middling-sort voters in both counties and boroughs as long as the war was not quite over. There is no recorded opposition to the return of the committee-man John Palmer at Taunton, or to men with local military credentials like Robert Blake at Bridgwater and Thomas Ceeley at Bridport. Nor is there any sign of discontent in Wiltshire at the election of the formidably radical Ludlow, though it followed, to be sure, a deal of the old-fashioned kind in which the Earl of Pembroke was given the other place for his son.[68] Yet as the case of Ilchester shows, even in this early period there were places where opposition to military or committee is visible, and in many other boroughs moderates were returned for one reason or another. At Wells, for example, one of the successful candidates was Clement Walker, soon to reveal himself as a vitriolic 'Country' foe of the Independents. And the two shire elections in Somerset, where the Committee's unpopularity became clear at an earlier date than in other counties, show how quickly the tide of opinion could turn. Other issues affected the Somerset elections—the Horners' influence in north-east Somerset, and the deserved popularity of John Harington, for many years one of the most conscientious of the county magistrates. So for all the shouting at Ilchester Cross, for all Humphrey Willis's boasts of being able to deliver 500 Clubmen votes, the moderate William Strode was defeated even in the apparently less-contrived circumstances of the second election.[69]

*

Popular opinion also had its impact on national politics through petitioning campaigns. As the party strife of Presbyterians and Independents intensified, campaigns were organized by both sides. Many people disliked the practice: it was, a newsbook declared in November 1645,

---

[66] HMC, *Portland*, i. 307.

[67] Brunton and Pennington, *Members*, p. 23. *Ludlow's Memoirs*, i. 132. BL Add. MS 28716 (Notes of Committee of Privileges proceedings), ff. 29–30.

[68] *Ludlow's Memoirs*, i. 133.

[69] Underdown, *Somerset*, pp. 130–3.

'immodest, prejudicial and derogatory to the gravity and majesty of a Parliament'.[70] There were the usual complaints about 'parrot petitions' drafted in London, about spurious signatures, about people being deluded or intimidated into subscribing—sometimes to petitions on opposite sides of the same issue. Still, even allowing for the often bogus claims of mass participation, the petitions of 1647 and 1648 offer some clues to the state of opinion, while their circulation repeatedly brought the issues in dispute at Westminster—religious toleration, church settlement, the disposition of the Army—to the attention of the localities.[71]

The party petitions of 1647 came mainly from the intensely politicized counties around London. Western assize and sessions juries regularly petitioned against quartering and other military abuses, but these were 'Country' petitions, not Presbyterian ones. Some echoes of the party conflict were heard: in March the Wiltshire Committee warned Denzil Holles of a dangerous petition (evidently in support of the Army) being circulated in the county, and asked for authority to suppress it. In September new petitions were said to be on foot in Somerset, including one promoted by the Presbyterian clergy in favour of sending the Army to Ireland, restoring the 'Eleven Members' expelled by the Army from the Commons, and enforcing the Covenant.[72] On the other side there was one from the Bristol neighbourhood, with demands that repeated parts of the Leveller programme (for example, that the laws be reduced 'into a lesser volume, and to speak our language'), as well as the mainstream Independent demand for liberty of conscience. But the grand juries had not yet been politicized, and party issues still seemed remote to many people. A Devon petition echoed radical complaints about the Presbyterians' 'undue election of burgesses' in Cornwall and about oppression of the godly by local magistrates, but still labelled the conflicts between Parliament and Army as 'these outside controversies in the land'.[73]

Majority opinion, both among the gentry and the middling sort, clearly favoured disbandment of the Army, compromise with the King, and a return to traditional, legitimate methods of government. But like the rest of the kingdom, the three western counties were becoming increasingly drawn into the party conflict in 1648, as the second civil war approached. There was no massive uprising in the west that summer to parallel the

[70] BL TT, E. 308 (5): *Mercurius Britannicus*, no. 103 (27 Oct.–3 Nov. 1645).

[71] *Life of Adam Martindale*, ed. R. Parkinson, Chetham Soc. iv, 1845, p. 62. A petition from Harley's regiment in March 1647 was allegedly subscribed by 1,100 men, a number greater than the total strength of the regiment: BL TT, E. 515 (6): *Perfect Diurnall*, no. 192 (29 Mar.–5 Apr. 1647). I am indebted to Mark Kishlansky for this reference.

[72] Bodleian MS Tanner 60, fo. 14. BL TT, E. 406 (9): *Moderate Intelligencer*, no. 129 (2–9 Sept. 1647).

[73] Underdown, 'Honest Radicals', p. 197. *Historical Collections*, ed. Rushworth, vii. 798–9. *CJ* v, 289. A Somerset petition may have been on similar lines, as it was welcomed by the 'Independent'-dominated Commons: Rushworth, vii, 822; *CJ* v. 318.

Essex and Kent revolts, but there were many signs of continuing discontent. Wiltshire was quiet, and Somerset remained firmly in the grip of
Pyne's Committee but the radical machine had clearly lost whatever
popular support it had ever had. This had been apparent early in the year,
when the Somerset radicals joined their counterparts in other counties in
a campaign to endorse the Vote of No Addresses. Puritan-dominated
Taunton led the way with a petition calling also for the more rigorous
imposition of godly reformation, and the full weight of the Committee's
influence was then mobilized behind a county petition on similar lines,
which went on to call for the rooting out of all 'malignants, neutrals, and
apostates'—for the perpetuation rather than the healing of local divisions.
The petition made little headway in the old Puritan strongholds of the
northern clothing districts, and was widely subscribed only in the western
parishes with their heavy sprinkling of neutrals who were more vulnerable
to threats of reprisals. At Chard Assizes, however, a carefully packed
grand jury endorsed the petition as the opinion of the county. The
following summer was marked by more sporadic violence against the
Committee's agents, frequent rumours of plots, and even in the Puritan
northern parishes, a general reluctance to enlist in the new militia being
raised for Parliament.[74]

Dorset, whose Committee lacked both the fanatical determination and
the ties with Westminster radicals that Pyne enjoyed, produced a more
effective protest, even if it was still a long way from the spectacular
rebellion of south-east England. The Committee had been uneasy for a
long time. Royalist Blandford exploded in riot in March 1648 when a
sequestered minister was arrested for using the Book of Common Prayer;
he was rescued by the mob and troops had to be used. Other royalist towns
were anxiously watched. Arms were discovered in the houses of Shaftesbury residents 'vehemently suspected to be enemies to the State', and
the recruiting of men at beat of drum, ostensibly for the service of the
Venetian republic, caused alarm at and around Sherborne. When in the
summer Kent set the example of revolt, the ideological continuity
between the risings of 1645 and 1648 was immediately apparent. The
Dorset petition, which may or may not have obtained the 10,000
signatures its promoters claimed, made the point explicitly. They had
once before engaged themselves 'on the same grounds, under the slighted
and unprosperous notion of Clubmen', and they recalled 'the innocent
blood of the well-meaning countrymen' spilt by the soldiers when they
were suppressed. The petition expressed the familiar platitudes of
defenders of local rights against the centralizing state: ancient laws and
liberties; an account for the money 'cheated or wrested from us by loans,
contributions, taxes, fines, excise or plunder'; government by men 'of

[74] Underdown, *Somerset*, pp. 147–51.

visible estates and of unquestioned repute' instead of committee-men of 'broken condition'.[75] When the rebels in Kent charged Weldon's clique with destroying 'all love and peace in this county', they spoke for 'Country' opinion in all parts of England. It is not surprising that at least one former Clubman, a minor gentleman from Marnhull named William Filliol, rode off from Dorset to join them.[76]

*

But popular risings, however massive, could be no match for Fairfax's army. The Kent and Essex rebellions, along with a few scattered outbreaks in other places, were decisively suppressed. Once again the principal medium of popular politics became the petition, and once again the petitions often do as much to obscure as to illuminate public opinion. This is certainly true of the autumn campaign for 'impartial justice' against the authors of the second civil war (including the King) and against Parliament's last-ditch attempt to patch up a settlement in the Treaty of Newport. The campaign produced a number of county petitions, including one from yet another of Pyne's packed grand juries in Somerset.[77] In November there was a further flood of petitions against the Newport negotiations, and an even more intense campaign after the Army's purge of the Commons on 6 December. Insistent demands for the trial and execution of Charles I came mostly from regiments of the New Model, though in some cases nearby religious and political radicals associated themselves with the soldiers. A petition from the officers and men of Sir Hardress Waller's brigade, for example, was at least nominally supported by the 'well-affected' of Devon and Cornwall. Towns controlled by vigilant Puritan oligarchies, like Rye in Sussex, were the most likely to produce genuinely local petitions—besides expressing support for the Army the Rye petition also complained about taxes, free quarter, and committee misgovernment. Military influence is clear at Bristol, though the 'humble representation of divers honest inhabitants' of Bristol and the adjacent villages sent to Fairfax in December was endorsed by at least some of the local radicals.[78]

Only one petition calling openly for the trial of the King survives with subscribers' names attached: the one from Kent. It appears to have found most support in the towns—Canterbury and small ports like Hythe and Sandwich—and in the clothing parishes of the Weald, where radical

---

[75] Morrill, *Revolt*, pp. 207–8. Bayley, *Dorset*, pp. 351–3.

[76] *CCC* iv. 2847. Everitt, *Community of Kent*, p. 252. Morrill, *Revolt*, p. 206.

[77] Underdown, *Pride's Purge*, pp. 109–10; *Somerset*, p. 151.

[78] BL TT, E. 475 (8): *The Moderate*, no. 21 (28 Nov.–5 Dec. 1648); E. 477 (4): *The Moderate*, no. 23 (12–19 Dec. 1648). Thomas-Stanford, *Sussex in the Civil War*, pp. 214–16. See also Fletcher, *A County Community*, pp. 292–3; and Clark, *Provincial Society*, p. 393.

Puritanism was well entrenched.[79] Of our three western counties, only Somerset produced a similar petition, but not much is known about it. It may have been promoted by Pyne and some of his henchmen, but its author appears to have been the Baptist preacher Thomas Collier of Westbury-sub-Mendip. It reflected the views of only a small minority of sectaries and republicans. Such people were naturally aflame with millenarian excitement in this, the climax of the revolution. Extravagant claims were made about the number of volunteers coming forward to support the Army, and a west Somerset lawyer gloomily expected the Army to endorse the Levellers' *Agreement of the People*, and have it 'sent into every parish for subscriptions'. Surviving correspondence from this period frequently expresses the horrified fascination with which country people viewed the dramatic events unfolding in London.[80]

Popular feeling in the immediate aftermath of the King's death is even more difficult to gauge than usual. From the western counties there are none of the radical petitions that were occasionally forthcoming in other parts of the country—though as these were in many cases the product of well-organized minorities like the one that had for so long ruled Kent, or the one led by Wroth Rogers that had recently taken over in Herefordshire, it is doubtful if they really tell us much about popular opinion.[81] On the other hand there were no openly political disorders in the west like the one at Coventry triggered by the news of Pride's Purge; none of the rumblings of defiance by local militia forces of the kind that kept Lancashire in a state of crisis for months afterwards.[82] But there is no reason to question the received historical wisdom that the situation was of a kind familiar in many later revolutions: a revolutionary minority confronting the sullen opposition of the majority, able to survive only through their control of military power, and because most people preferred conformity even to an unpopular regime to renewed bloodshed and the possibility of social breakdown. Everywhere the Presbyterian clergy preached openly against the Army and the revolution. At Exeter the mayor threw the document proclaiming the Commonwealth into the gutter, and, along with several other corporation members, stayed away from the spring Assizes to avoid recognizing the new regime. Public defiance of this kind was less common than bewilderment and uncertainty of the kind displayed by the corporation of Barnstaple, who in February 1649 sought

---

[79] Bodleian MS Tanner 57, ff. 476–87. Everitt, *Community of Kent*, pp. 271–2, doubts the authenticity of the signatures; but perhaps parts of the list were taken from other copies of the petition, which contained the originals? See also Underdown, 'Honest Radicals', p. 202.

[80] Underdown, *Pride's Purge*, pp. 175–80.

[81] BL TT, E. 541 (15): *The Moderate*, no. 30 (30 Jan.–6 Feb. 1648/9); E. 541 (17): *Kingdomes Weekly Intelligencer*, no. 297 (30 Jan.–6 Feb. 1648/9); E. 542 (11): *The Moderate*, no. 31 (6–13 Feb. 1648/9). Whitelocke, *Memorials*, ii. 518–19. BL Add. MS 11053 (Scudamore MSS), ff. 110–11.

[82] Underdown, *Pride's Purge*, pp. 175–8.

legal advice on 'how to proceed after the death of the King'. At Warminster the new churchwardens refused to serve because of the dangers
of the times.[83]

Hostility to the Commonwealth is impossible to disentangle from the
more traditional attacks on excisemen and resistance to quartering
soldiers. Most of the more graphic complaints about the military come
from the gentry, but there is no doubt that quartering was equally
oppressive to the ordinary householder. Early in 1649 William Prynne
reported strong feeling against Harrison's regiment in the villages near
Bath; when he threatened to 'raise the Country upon them' many people
offered to assist. As a notorious enemy to the Army Prynne was an obvious
target for the soldiers, but he was not the only one to suffer. A Wiltshire JP
feared to leave his home at about this time because of their violence, and a
year later even the influential John Ashe, chairman of the Rump's Committee for Compounding, was the victim of outrages by soldiers at his
house at Freshford.[84] Once again it is worth noting that these incidents
took place in the earlier heartland of Parliament's support, the clothing
parishes. The Wiltshire Committee got an order in January 1649, dis-
banding a troop of horse which had been ravaging the county, but this
made only a minor dent in a much larger problem. In Hampshire,
paradoxically, it was a unit raised in the name of popular liberty—Henry
Marten's regiment of republican enthusiasts—that was, according to the
Committee, responsible for many of the 'insufferable violences and
oppressions this county yet laboureth under'.[85] There was no public
explosion in the south-western counties of the sort that occurred in
Shropshire in June 1649, when troops bound for Ireland were set on by a
mob, reviled as traitors and rebels and deprived of their horses, which
were then sold in local markets.[86] But much simmering resentment
remained.

Middling-sort reluctance to serve the Commonwealth became even
more apparent in 1650, when members of borough corporations, along
with other public officials, were required to take the Engagement 'to be
true and faithful to the Commonwealth of England'. Some corporations
had already been purged of royalist or neutral members: at Weymouth for

---

[83] *Historical Collections*, ed. Rushworth, vii. 1381–2. BL TT, E. 542 (11): *The Moderate*, no. 31 (6–13
Feb. 1648/9); E. 527 (39): *Perfect Occurrences*, no. 116 (16–23 Mar. 1648/9). *Gleanings from the
Municipal and Cathedral Records . . . of the City of Exeter*, ed. W. Cotton and H. Woollcoombe, Exeter,
1877, p. 141. *Memorials of Barnstaple*, ed. Joseph B. Gribble, Barnstaple, 1830, ii. 158. Sir Richard
Colt Hoare, *The Modern History of South Wiltshire*, iii, pt. ii: *Hundred of Warminster*, 1831, p. 27.

[84] Underdown, *Somerset*, p. 156. *Records of Wilts.*, p. 216. *CSPD, 1650*, pp. 126, 206.

[85] Worcester College, Clarke MS 1/5, Order of Committee on Garrisons, 11 Jan. 1648/9. *The
Clarke Papers: Selections from the papers of William Clarke*, ii, ed. C. H. Firth, Camden New Ser. liv,
1894, pp. 212–13.

[86] *CSPD, 1649–50*, p. 282. BL TT, E. 531 (4): *A Perfect Summary of an Exact Dyarie*, no. 23 (18–25
June 1649).

example, several were forced to resign at a meeting attended by the military governor, William Sydenham, in January 1649.[87] But a good many neutrals had survived, and Presbyterians were patently unhappy, so the Engagement led to more extensive purges. At Exeter a succession of mayors refused the oath, and although there was a change of attitude after Cromwell's victory at Dunbar, when the Commonwealth seemed better established, it was still sometimes difficult to get a quorum for council meetings. There was resistance to the Engagement in many other places. The mayor and three other corporation members had to be replaced for refusing it at Bridgwater, while at Dorchester several of the leading burgesses and local clergy took the oath only with reservations which implicitly questioned the Commonwealth's legal basis.[88]

Indications of more widespread dissatisfaction with the republic are visible in the tepid response of Dorchester people to the Rump's official Days of Thanksgiving. The town was remarkable for its inhabitants' charitable contributions, and in the late 1640s, in spite of their wartime sufferings, they were still donating large sums for their own poor and for victims of fires and other disasters elsewhere. The size of church collections varied, naturally, according to the prevailing level of prosperity. Collections in the three Dorchester parishes averaged £4.15s.3d. on the regular monthly Fast Days in 1646 and 1647, collapsed to less than half that amount in the depression of 1648, but then recovered slightly in 1649 and rebounded still further as prosperity returned in 1650. Collections at special Days of Thanksgiving, however, bore no such relation to the state of the economy, and must have been affected by the parishioners' reactions to the events they were being called on to celebrate. Dorchester people still had a clear sense of identification with Parliament's cause in 1648: thanksgivings for victories in the second civil war produced more than double the amount collected on an average Fast Day. But under the Rump it was a different story. Dorchester people were still pouring out large sums for their own poor and for the distressed in other places, yet thanksgivings to celebrate the victories over the Scots at Dunbar and Worcester yielded substantially *less* than the sums routinely contributed on Fast Days. There were few places in England with as much zeal for godly reformation, so Dorchester's lack of enthusiasm for the Commonwealth is particularly striking.[89]

[87] *Weymouth and Melcombe Regis Minute Book 1625–1660*, ed. M. Weinstock, Dorset RS i, 1964, pp. 73, 76.

[88] *Exeter Records*, pp. 143, 146, 154. HMC, *Portland*, i. 523. *CJ* vi. 407. The mayor of Taunton was also removed: Whitelocke, *Memorials*, iii. 185. See also Underdown, *Pride's Purge*, pp. 304–5. The formula used by the Dorchester subscribers reads, 'I will live peaceably under this present power and obey them in lawful things': DRO B2/16/3 (Dorchester Corporation papers, 1629–94), fo. 133.

[89] This analysis is based on figures recorded in *Dorchester Records*, pp. 545–7, 551; and DRO B2/16/6E (Dorchester Accounts of Charitable Collections, 1622–1704).

Dorchester was run by a stable Presbyterian oligarchy, which shows no sign of having been seriously challenged in the early 1650s. In a few west-country towns—Wells is one of them—there appears to have been some broadening of the oligarchy to include people (sometimes radical Puritans) from outside the old governing circles, without serious conflict.[90] Attempts by the military to influence town governments, however, were likely to cause trouble. This was the case at Poole, where the commander, Lt.-Col. John Rede, was a man of extreme views in both religion and politics. The corporation tried to co-operate with him, engaging in April 1649 to assist in preserving the town against enemies of the republic. But Rede, according to his critics, made Poole a refuge for 'exorbitant Levellers and Ranters', installed a Baptist soldier as lecturer in the parish church, cashiered soldiers who would not support him, disarmed the local militia officers, and arrested the mayor when he protested. The townsmen's complaints were seconded by a petition from the surrounding area, recounting Rede's arbitrary levying of assessments and interference with the ordinary course of justice.[91] Eventually Rede was removed: a conservative oligarchy survived because Rede's allies were too few for Whitehall to be able to rely on them. Poole was not unlike other boroughs up and down the land, even after the post-war purges and the weeding out of Presbyterians by the Engagement. In towns as well as villages the old values of custom and neighbourhood could still withstand the onslaught of divisive reforming minorities.

*

Throughout the 1650s, through all the experimental regimes associated with the names of Barebones and Cromwell, the same pattern of popular politics persisted. Much of the conflict in the localities was cultural and religious—a collision between, on the one hand, radical minorities out to impose their version of godly discipline on their less enlightened neighbours, or to separate themselves and seek salvation in their own way; and on the other, people trying to preserve the cultural and religious forms in which more traditional notions of community were expressed. These matters will be considered in the next chapter, but before we embark on them a very brief excursion into Protectorate politics is in order.

It need not be more than that, for the complex divisions within the élite in the 1650s were reflected in the popular political consciousness only in very general and simplified ways. The Barebones experiment; the Protectorate in its various manifestations; the restored Rump of 1659: these were shadowy entities far away in Westminster, remote from the daily realities of provincial life. Commonwealth republicans, Puritan

---

[90] Underdown, 'Case Concerning Bishops' Lands', pp. 30–3.
[91] BL Stowe MS 189 (Civil War papers), ff. 43–4, 52–5, printed in part in Bayley, *Dorset*, pp. 343–6.

Saints, pragmatic Cromwellians, 'Country' Presbyterians, and the still unassimilated Royalists, all had their adherents among the gentry and the middling sort. Among the lower orders there were some who, like John Bunyan, had been awakened to a new vision of a godly community which required political action as well as spiritual grace for its fulfilment. But the majority remained unregenerate. Throughout the decade, in tavern talk, in riotous outbreaks at fairs and revels, in attacks on Quakers and other moral reformers, can be sensed a strong popular nostalgia for the imagined good old days of neighbourliness and fellowship.

This, surely, is an important part of the background to the royalist rebellion in Wiltshire and Dorset in March 1655. The strength of popular royalism in the small towns of the chalk country is very clear, as we have seen, in the 1656 returns of suspected persons. Downland villages are less heavily represented in the returns, yet the rebellion had drawn most of its support from this area. Fifteen of the prisoners taken after the rebels' defeat came from Salisbury, twelve from Blandford, and many more from downland villages, as well as half a dozen from that other notable royalist stronghold, Sherborne. Penruddock, the rising's leader, took a gardener and four servants with him from Compton Chamberlayne; another Wiltshire squire two servants, four husbandmen, a carter, a cordwainer, and a tailor from Enford. The large number of prisoners of low status must in part reflect the strong ties of deference still prevailing in the chalk country. But deference does not as easily account for the turn-out from the towns, and in such villages as Cholderton, Tisbury, and Upavon men of humble station, but no gentry, were among the rebels. Penruddock's rising was part of a wider royalist conspiracy. But like the Club movement and the rumblings of 1648, it was also a protest by the 'Country' against the intrusions of a Puritan central government. One Dorset squire involved in the rising, John St. Loe, had been a 'captain' of the Clubmen, and Robert Hawles, another of the old leaders, attended cavalier meetings that preceded it, though he did not in the end take up arms.[92]

The widespread desire for the revival of ancient law and custom was also demonstrated in less dangerous ways. It is evident, for example, in the behaviour of many county voters in Protectorate elections. There was, to be sure, a sizeable radical minority, especially in the towns, among the lesser tradespeople and artisans. In the hotly contested 1654 election in Bristol the radical candidates polled not far short of 100 votes in spite of the obvious bias of the sheriff and other authorities against them, though they were still beaten by more than two to one. During a long and complicated factional struggle at Colchester the Puritan group could

---

[92] *Thurloe Papers*, iii. 306–8, 309, 372, 630. See also David Underdown, *Royalist Conspiracy in England 1649–1660*, New Haven, 1960, ch. 7; and A. H. Woolrych, *Penruddock's Rising 1655*, Hist. Assn. Pamphlet G. 29, 1955.

obtain over 250 signatures to one of their petitions, many of them by people of substance. Yet the moderate localists clearly had the advantage of numbers—one of their petitions attracted 960 subscriptions—and they were especially strong among the poorer townsmen.[93] In rural constituencies, the preference of Protectorate voters for 'Country' moderates over Puritan or republican reformers is much clearer. Some of the voters newly enfranchised by the Instrument of Government may have preferred republicans, as seems to have been the case in Cheshire in 1656, to the benefit of the regicide John Bradshaw. But much of the enthusiasm for Bradshaw seems to have been aroused by his reputation as a stout opponent of Cromwellian centralization, rather than by his republicanism. Attempts by the Major-Generals in 1656 to ram government candidates down the throats of the voters were widely resisted, and in many places the poll was enlivened by shouts of 'No Swordsman! No Decimator!'[94]

Élite leadership played its customary role in co-ordinating 'Country' electoral activity. Ludlow blamed his defeat in Wiltshire in 1654 on the propaganda efforts of the Presbyterian clergy: he and his republican ally, William Eyre, were assiduously denounced as 'Anabaptists and Levellers'. No doubt the clergy played their part, but it is still worth asking why these terms of abuse should have struck such chords in the minds of the middling-sort voters. On Ludlow's own admission, his defeat was also the result of the effective appropriation of the 'Country' position by Sir Anthony Ashley Cooper. Cooper played a similar role in the 1656 election, and was in touch with his neighbours in Dorset, where a well-organized group of moderate gentry came together to resist (successfully, as it turned out), the Major-Generals' 'tickets'.[95] The most dramatic confirmation of the alignment of middling-sort voters behind 'Country' candidates in 1656 occurred, however, in Somerset. The voters realistically returned the Major-General, John Disbrowe, and his henchman John Gorges, but all the others elected were 'Country' moderates. Their votes ranged from 2,374 down to 1,549 for the lowest successful candidate. Pyne and his republican allies Edward Ceely and Richard Bovett received only 457, 440 and 374 respectively, and their lesser-known underlings did even worse.[96]

[93] *Deposition Books of Bristol*, ii: *1650–54*, ed. H. E. Nott and E. Ralph, Bristol RS xiii, 1948, pp. 179–83. *CSPD, 1654*, pp. 331–3. Samuel R. Gardiner, *History of the Commonwealth and Protectorate 1649–1656*, 2nd edn., 1903, iv. 58–73.

[94] Paul H. Pinckney, 'The Cheshire Election of 1656', *Bulletin of John Rylands Library*, xlix (1967–8), 418–19. Morrill, *Cheshire*, pp. 287–93. HMC, *Portland*, iii. 208.

[95] *Ludlow's Memoirs*, i. 388–9, 545–8. BL TT, E. 808 (9): *An Apology for the Ministers of Wilts.*, 1654. A. G. Matthews, *Calamy Revised*, Oxford, 1934, p. 108. Northumberland MS 551 (Fitzjames Letter Book, v, 1654–6), ff. 89ᵛ–95ᵛ (BL Film, no. 331).

[96] Underdown, *Somerset*, pp. 182–5. *Somerset Assize Orders 1640–1659*, ed. J. S. Cockburn, SRS lxxi, 1971, App. 2.

The 1656 elections occurred at a time when the Major-Generals' rigour had made both godly reformation and centralization particularly obnoxious. The results may also reflect propertied people's fears of the growing militancy of the Quakers. Cromwell made half-hearted efforts to protect them from local persecution, but in other respects the message sent by the voters was taken to heart; the Protectorate retreated from its lurch into military rule and resumed its original course of 'healing and settling'. It was the old Puritan clothier John Ashe who made the first formal motion that Cromwell should take the crown, 'according to the ancient constitution', and although Oliver was prevented from accepting by his republican military colleagues, there is no doubt that Ashe was speaking for a large body of opinion that wanted settlement, not further godly reformation.[97] Soon after Cromwell's death the wheel had come full circle and the revolution (in the seventeenth-century sense of the word) was completed. Popular opinion, which in 1640 had seen the Stuart Court as the greatest threat to an order based on ancient rights, was turning to the exiled Charles II as the only hope of regaining that vanished order.

[97] *Diary of Thomas Burton Esquire, Member in the Parliaments of Oliver and Richard Cromwell*, ed. J. T. Rutt, 1828, i. 362–3.

9

Culture and Politics, 1646–1660

THE civil war brought to power, both at Westminster and in the provinces, men whose outlooks reflected the familiar ambiguities of Puritanism. On the one hand they believed, up to a point, in liberty of conscience (though they argued fiercely about where that point ought to be); on the other hand they believed just as strongly in their duty to enforce on those beneath them the standards of personal and public conduct held by people of 'credit and reputation'. Parliament's victory was inevitably followed by a renewed assault on the idleness and disorderly indiscipline of those who did not accept these standards. It was a moral campaign for public reformation. But it was also a political campaign, for traditional culture was commonly perceived as being (and often was in fact) associated with counter-revolutionary notions about the proper ordering of church and state—with the beliefs and rituals of episcopacy and monarchy.

The impulse to liberty of conscience, the individual's right to interpret God's word without priestly intervention, was always a central strand of Puritan thinking. Its implementation was furthered by the 'long anarchy' which followed the collapse of episcopal authority. The failure of Parliament and its Assembly of Divines to overcome Erastian stonewalling and establish an effective Presbyterian church; the Rump's subsequent paralysis on the question of church government; the bewildering variety of Presbyterian, Independent, covertly episcopalian, and denominationally uncommitted clergy in the parishes; and later, the breadth of Lord Protector Cromwell's tolerationist views: all encouraged the proliferation of sects. Baptists, Fifth Monarchy men, eventually Ranters, Quakers, and a dozen others emerged, all insisting on the individual's right to chart his or her own path to salvation. Their adherents left a permanent mark on English religious and cultural life. But they never overcame the obstinate attachment of the majority of the population to older, deeply-ingrained beliefs and customs. And in separating themselves from their more conservative neighbours they aroused widespread suspicion and hostility, particularly when, as in the case of the Ranters and Quakers, their moral or social teachings were offensive to longstanding community values.[1]

[1] For the radical sects see Hill, *World Turned Upside Down*; and for reasons why they were unpopular, Barry Reay, 'Popular hostility towards Quakers in mid-seventeenth-century England',

The leaders of mainstream Puritan congregations, as well of less extreme sects like the Baptists, were usually respectable pillars of local society. Some of the more plebeian sects, the Ranters especially, were closer to the festive culture of the disorderly poor. But more orthodox separatists were trapped in the inherent contradiction between their aspirations for liberty and for reformation. By expelling the Rump, Herefordshire separatists told Cromwell in 1653, he had made himself God's instrument 'to translate the nation from oppression to liberty, from the hands of corrupt persons to the Saints'.[2] Yet the Saints were soon to discover that the corruption of the majority ensured that the translation to liberty could be achieved only by force—by the same oppressive means earlier visited on the Saints by King, bishops, and Presbyterians.

In the chapter we shall briefly survey the Puritan impact on the western counties. The appearance of socially dangerous opinions among the small minority of separatists was, we shall find, only one of the threats to order which preoccupied the godly and others in authority. More dangerous still was the obstinate survival of those familiar ancient values of neighbourhood and community, and even many of the ritual forms in which they had for centuries been expressed. The connection between traditional popular culture and the cause of the Stuarts was assumed almost automatically by Roundhead and Cavalier alike. Those who haunted taverns or promoted revel feasts were regarded by the authorities as almost certainly disaffected to the Commonwealth. On the other side, people deprived of their simple pleasures and ancient customs looked longingly across the water to the exiled Charles II as the symbol of a vanished sense of community that was perhaps recoverable by his restoration. Popular royalism and traditional culture survived, not surprisingly, in the same conservative areas in which they had flourished before the war. But after 1646 there are also signs of a revival of festive rituals even in the Puritan clothing districts where before 1640 they had been most effectively suppressed. The reaction against godly reformation affected all regions and all social groups, even elements of the reformist middling sort. The resurgence of religious and cultural conservatism explains much of the enthusiasm of the Restoration.

*

Social History, v (1980), 387–407. For the religious conservatism of the majority see John Morrill, 'The Church in England, 1642–9', in *Reactions*, ed. Morrill, ch. 4.

[2] *Original Letters illustrative of English History*, ed. Sir Henry Ellis, 1824–46, 2nd Ser. iii, 368.

The sharpness of the break caused by the civil war should not be exaggerated. Earlier moral reformers had long since developed many of the methods to enforce social discipline that were employed during the Interregnum. Enforcement of the ethic of work and responsibility, for example, had always depended heavily on the operation of the Poor Law. But its functioning was especially crucial during the later 1640s, when the spectre of depression again fell heavily on the clothing districts. The already troubled industry had been further disrupted by the war, and as we have seen, plague and harvest failure produced desperate poverty and unemployment in north-west Wiltshire. The wartime breakdown of government and the painful process of administrative rebuilding in the faction-ridden post-war years added to the difficulties. Stocks for setting the poor to work had been neglected, houses of correction allowed to fail into disrepair, and abuses by trustees and governors of hospitals often left unpunished.[3]

It used to be thought that there was no real recovery from this wartime collapse, and that Interregnum JPs were assiduous only in punishing the undeserving and suppressing idleness and vagrancy. Recent studies have shown that even without the Council's constant breathing down their necks the magistrates of the 1650s were in fact surprisingly innovative and constructive. In Cheshire, for example, they were much more energetic than their Caroline predecessors in controlling grain prices, going beyond the customary methods—the restriction of licenses to dealers and the prevention of forestalling—by appointing commissioners in each parish to ensure that grain was sold freely in the markets and not hoarded for private sale to dealers. They were also distinctly more liberal than earlier JPs had been in enforcement of the act against cottages, accepting a responsibility to provide housing as well as food for the poor.[4]

The efficient response to the depression by Interregnum administrators must be acknowledged, but we should not overstress their humanitarianism. The JPs and the parish notables who implemented their directions were still preoccupied with what was to them a single problem: the enforcement of order and godliness. Dearth and poverty bred disturbance, even riot, but they also bred drunkenness and immorality. The laws might be enforced with some degree of humanity, but enforced they were, in many places more rigorously than ever. The promotion of Puritan justices led to a renewed burst of regulative vigour. In parts of Lancashire hitherto largely immune to Puritan reform, there

---

[3] James, *Social Problems*, pp. 248–54.
[4] For the older interpretation see James, *Social Problems*, pp. 243–301; and E. M. Leonard, *Early History of English Poor Relief*, Cambridge, 1900, pp. 132, 267–76. For more recent views, A. L. Beier, 'Poor Relief in Warwickshire 1630–1660', *P & P* no. 35 (Dec. 1966), 77–100; and Morrill, *Cheshire*, pp. 247–51.

was a massive increase in the suppression of unlicensed alehouses, the enforcement of sabbath observance, and similar measures of social control. The Cheshire magistrates tried to impose a limit of two alehouses to a parish and displayed an even more punitive spirit than usual in the treatment of bastardy cases. This concern for order could be illustrated from the records of towns and counties throughout the land.[5]

It is certainly evident in the western counties. There, as elsewhere, order and godliness were two sides of the same coin. At Dorset's first post-war assizes a grand jury presentment of the excessive number of alehouses (seconded by complaints from the godly of individual parishes) produced a general order for the suppression of unlicensed ones; the court also responded to complaints about lax observance of the sabbath and of Parliament's monthly Fast Days. Over the next few years orders against alehouses and sabbath violations were regularly issued in all three counties, and the justices continued their customary policies of regulating the markets to ensure that grain supplies were not diverted into the brewing trade. The connection between the alleviation of dearth and the reform of morality is especially clear in Somerset. In January 1649 a petition to Quarter Sessions identified unlicensed alehouses, along with 'the many forestallers, ingrossers, hucksters and maltsters swarming in this county', as principal causes of high food prices. At Taunton Assizes in July the grand jury made similar complaints about the excessive number of alehouses; the JPs were ordered to invite the 'ablest men' of each parish to their monthly divisional meetings to obtain their co-operation in the campaign of regulation and reform.[6]

The campaign depended heavily on these 'people of credit' in the villages. Their sense of identity was now even stronger than in pre-war years, often buttressed by memories of having fought and sacrificed for God's cause. Among other signs of this growing self-awareness is the appearance of such terms as 'the honest party' or 'the well affected' in village documents.[7] Leadership to harness the reforming impulses of 'honest' people was now readily available. Edward Curll, sequestrator of Catsash Hundred in Somerset, was as conscientious in his pursuit of moral offenders as of royalist delinquents. In 1648 he got his neighbours in Batcombe and the surrounding villages to petition against the multiplicity of alehouses. Some illegal ale-sellers were convicted, but Curll's

[5] Wrightson, 'Two Concepts of Order', p. 38. Walter and Wrightson, 'Dearth and the Social Order', pp. 38–40. Morrill, *Cheshire*, pp. 244–6.

[6] *Western Circuit Assize Orders*, pp. 238–9, 249–53. *Records of Wilts.*, pp. 182–3, 185–6, 194, 204–5, 215. *SQSR* iii. 25–6, 51, 59, 75, 83. *Somerset Assize Orders 1640–1659*, no. 87. Sharp, *In Contempt*, p. 247.

[7] For example, in a certificate to the Dorset Committee from 'some of the honest part of the inhabitants of Broadwindsor': *Dorset Minute Books*, p. 246. For the term 'honest party' see Underdown, 'Honest Radicals', p. 188.

efforts were hampered by the collusion of other people in authority. Warrants levying penalties were taken from parish officers and, Curll complained, 'enemies of reformation and the good of the county' got licences from other JPs 'by clandestine ways'. One of the worst culprits was the Presbyterian William Strode at Shepton Mallet, who sought popularity by conniving at drunkenness and disorder in the town. At Wells the new mayor allowed alehouses to reopen which his more godly predecessor had suppressed, with predictable results.[8]

Puritan parishes such as Batcombe might rally to the cause of godly reformation, but in many others there was resistance. Interfering outsiders were especially likely to be resented. Eleanor Butt's husband had died in the service of Parliament, leaving her with three children and nothing to maintain them. Her house was destroyed during the war, so she moved to Isle Brewers, her husband's birthplace. She then made the mistake of informing a Commonwealth JP about an unlicensed alehouse-keeper 'who kept much disorder in the said parish'. She was promptly turned out of her house and refused any other accommodation in the village.[9] But outsiders were not the only ones to arouse such hostility. The Cheddar exciseman, John Rogers, was no outsider and he himself kept an alehouse, so he was certainly not against the drink trade on principle. But he was resented both as a divisive Puritan and as a prying agent of authority, a 'peeping rogue'. The constable, Henry Bankes, was required to order local alehouse-keepers to appear before the Excise Commissioners at Axbridge; Bankes sent in only two names, one of them Rogers's, even though there were a score of others in the parish.[10]

Alehouses were not the only targets of moral reformers. The sabbatarian rigour of urban magistrates (at Dorchester, for example) was paralleled in many rural parishes. The royalist John Taylor noted acidly in 1652 that in one Gloucestershire village he visited women had been put in the stocks simply for walking in the fields after church. Many offences hitherto outside their sphere came within the JPs' purview following the abolition of the ecclesiastical courts; after 1653 they were responsible for performing marriages. Interregnum magistrates were just as severe as their predecessors in dealing with sexual lapses, and they may have been somewhat more inclined to punish men as severely as women. When Ann Morgan was put in the stocks as a whore at Wells in 1649 one of her male clients was also sentenced, having to 'ride the wooden horse' in procession to the Palace moat, where he was ritually ducked. Otherwise not much had changed. Scolds and other disorderly women continued to be

[8] SRO QS 164, Petition of E. Curll, [1648]. *SQSR* iii. 63. *Western Circuit Assize Orders*, p. 282.
[9] SRO QS 164, Petitions, I, Petition of Eleanor Butt, [1650?].
[10] Croot, 'Aspects of Agrarian Society', ch. 7.

punished, and there is nothing to suggest that male determination to uphold patriarchal authority had been significantly altered by the war.[11]

Godly reformation reached its climax in 1655 and 1656, with the rule of the Major-Generals. Disbrowe, who presided over the western counties, was a formidable Puritan despot, closely supervising county JPs, insisting that only men of 'honest and blameless conversation' were selected for juries, rounding up vagrants and idle persons and, as we have seen, extracting reasonably complete lists of the disaffected from parish officers. He no doubt inspired the Somerset grand jury's presentment at the 1656 Assizes, which reflected some staple ingredients of earlier campaigns for the reinvigoration of local government: proper regulation of markets for the benefit of the poor; further reduction of 'unnecessary' alehouses; suppression of the 'detestable sins' of swearing, drunkenness, and the 'common profanation of the Lord's day'; with a new demand for measures against 'persons known by the name of Quakers, living often in idleness'. The presentment proclaims the outlook of the Puritan middling sort, continually alive to the threat of property and order from the godless (and probably royalist) poor, and now alarmed by the spread of Quaker opinions among others of the lower orders.

*

The ability of Interregnum authorities to reform the ungodly was impeded by the fact that at both the national and local levels they were so bitterly divided. Among other things, this made it impossible to establish the godly, preaching ministry, incessantly demanded by reformers—instead there was a parochial patchwork, with dedicated Puritans in a few places, quiescent conformists in many other places. Most of the parish clergy, Dr Green concludes, would have been 'content with the Jacobean pattern of church authority and discipline and with the Book of Common Prayer'.[12] Efforts were made to establish Presbyterian classes in all three western counties, but only in Somerset did one even approach real existence. The county committees replaced Laudians and open Royalists, but although some of the replacements were committed reformers, there were well-founded doubts about many others, inevitably so given the shortage of authentically reformist candidates.[13] Committees tended

---

[11] Hill, *Society and Puritanism*, p. 183. Quaife, *Wanton Wenches*, p. 150. Quaife, pp. 228–9, shows that Interregnum JPs generally required fathers of bastards to make larger provision for their maintenance than had been usual before the war. For Commonwealth moral reform legislation and its context see Keith Thomas, 'The Puritans and Adultery: The Act of 1650 Reconsidered', in *Puritans and Revolutionaries*, pp. 257–82.

[12] I. M. Green, 'The Persecution of "scandalous" and "malignant" parish clergy during the English Civil War', *Eng. H.R.* xciv (1979), 530.

[13] For a typical complaint see BL TT, E. 346 (10): *Scotish Dove*, no. 144 (22–31 July 1646). For the Presbyterian classes and intruded ministers see W. A. Shaw, *A History of the English Church during the Civil Wars and under the Commonwealth 1640–1660*, 1900, ii. 31–2, 413–22, 437; Underdown,

naturally to pay special attention to areas where Puritanism had previously been resisted. Two-thirds of the Wiltshire ejections occurred in the southern, downland, part of the county. In Dorset there were vigorous efforts to place reliable ministers in populous and disaffected places such as Sturminster Newton, Blandford, and Shaftesbury.[14] But the Presbyterian intruders, unexceptionable as moral reformers, were often decidedly unsatisfactory as preachers of obedience to republican authority. As we have seen, they frequently ignored official Days of Thanksgiving, observed them only tepidly (as at Dorchester), or preached openly against the Commonwealth.[15]

Some ministers, to be sure, in the west as elsewhere, performed their accustomed roles of predisposing their flocks to obedience. One such was Richard Herring, minister at Drewsteignton, Devon, who preached approvingly on the execution of Charles I and the defeat of his son at Worcester. He also circulated republican newsbooks in his parish with the message, it was said, 'that there would be sad times if ever our king came into England'. Intensive preaching undoubtedly advanced both moral and political reformation in many places after the war, as it had done earlier in such villages as Batcombe and Wrington. The parish of Trent seems to have become an island of Puritanism in the generally traditionalist area on the Somerset–Dorset border, perhaps because of the preaching of the zealous Thomas Elford. Charles II later recalled how, when he was hiding there in Francis Wyndham's house after Worcester, a rumour that he had been captured and killed provoked bells and bonfires, 'most of the village being Fanatics'.[16]

Such transformations were exceptional. In many parishes there were bitter conflicts between intruded ministers and their parishioners. The Dorset Committee had to remove the minister at Silton because of his quarrels with his parishioners, only a year after they had installed him at the 'earnest desire' of some of them. Conflicts often revolved around newcomers' demands for tithes which villagers preferred to pay their sequestered parson. At Compton Abbas in 1646 people were denying tithes to the intruded minister, either fearing that the old rector, the Clubman Thomas Bravell, would sue, or believing that he had the better

Somerset, pp. 143–5; Bayley, *Dorset*, p. 434; Reeves, 'Protestant Nonconformity', p. 101 and n. 23; and Morrill, 'The Church 1642–9', pp. 97, 100–1.

[14] Green, 'Persecution', p. 525 (however, Green's explanation for the preponderance of ejections in south Wilts. is unconvincing: this was in fact the most royalist, least Puritan, part of the county). For Dorset ejections and intrusions see *Dorset Minute Books*, pp. 67, 90, 112–13, 138, 192, 250, 259–60.

[15] Underdown, *Somerset*, pp. 161–2; and above, p. 234.

[16] Bodleian MS J. Walker c. 4, fo. 166. 'The King's Account of His Escape', in *Charles II's Escape from Worcester: A Collection of Narratives assembled by Samuel Pepys*, ed. William Matthews, Berkeley, 1966, pp. 60–1. There was a large nonconformist conventicle at Trent after the Restoration: *Original Records of Early Nonconformity*, ed. G. Lyon Turner, 1911–14, i. 11.

claim. Intruders repeatedly had to invoke the power of the County Committee to get their tithes. It had to be the Committee: the reluctance of JPs to enforce payment gave great encouragement to 'malignant' clergy, the Wiltshire Committee complained. How much of this resistance was simply the age-old game of tithe evasion, and how much the result of the special unpopularity of the incoming Puritans is hard to determine.[17] Certainly in many places the intruders were welcomed by only a handful of the congregation. Occasionally, indeed, they were forcibly resisted, as at Blandford, and the old parsons temporarily restored. In Wiltshire, Adoniram Byfield reported in 1655, few ministers could find people willing 'to join withal in the purer administration of the ordinances of Christ'.[18]

The situation was worst in culturally traditional areas where the intruded reformers were surrounded by less zealous conforming clergy of the old type. The Presbyterian Peter Ince found his flock at Donhead St. Mary as ignorant of 'the plainest principles' of his brand of Christianity 'as if they had never heard of them', even after he had expounded them a hundred times. Yet they could always run 'to some idle drunken fellows' in nearby parishes to get their children baptized and thus avoid subjecting themselves to Ince's stern course of instruction.[19] Even in parishes with stronger Puritan traditions than the Donheads, the divisions of the 1650s seriously hampered the cause of reformation. Disputes about restricting communion to the elect split many parishes and led to long periods with no celebration of communion at all.[20] Sometimes the conflicts were political. At Glastonbury there was a struggle between the radical Puritan JP John Gutch and his local rival, Samuel Austin. Austin disputed the Protector's authority (and cited in support the arguments of the anti-government lawyers in Cony's case) and courted the poorer townsfolk by promising to release imprisoned victims of Gutch's austerity.[21] When in 1659 John Ivie was asked to reinstitute the poor relief system at Salisbury that he and his Puritan friends had created in the 1620s he replied, 'our government was now so divided and our church officers so unruly that I thought it impossible to set up so good a work'.[22]

[17] *Dorset Minute Books*, pp. 108, 234, 364 (with other examples of tithe resistance at pp. 33, 120, 353, 384, 418–19, 422, 442, 453, 486). Bodleian MS Tanner 58, fo. 283. Morrill, 'The Church 1642–9', pp. 110–11, thinks the special unpopularity of the intruded Puritans was indeed responsible for much of the resistance.

[18] *Desiderata Curiosa*, ed. Francis Peck, 2nd edn., 1779, ii. 492. For examples in other counties see Morrill, 'The Church 1642–9', pp. 111–12; and A. Tindal Hart, *The Country Clergy in Elizabethan and Stuart Times*, 1958, pp. 128–9.

[19] Geoffrey F. Nuttall, *Visible Saints: The Congregational Way*, Oxford, 1957, p. 136.

[20] Morrill, 'The Church 1642–9', p. 107.

[21] *SQSR* iii. 316, 346, 350, 361. For Cony's case see Gardiner, *Commonwealth and Protectorate*, iii. 299–301. Austin also questioned the Protector's Declaration of 31 Oct. 1655 (for which see Gardiner, iii. 327). For Gutch, see Underdown, *Somerset*, pp. 153, 169.

[22] *Poverty in Salisbury*, p. 109.

*

A further problem for moral reformers was the fact that those artisans and labourers who had been awakened to an active religious life were often attracted, not to disciplined Presbyterianism, but to the more spiritually adventurous and socially subversive sects. Presbytery was as closely enmeshed with the hierarchical order as episcopacy had been, and was thus at least temporarily acceptable to many propertied conformists who may have been episcopalians at heart. Presbyterian emphasis on election deepened the gulf between the respectable minority and the rest, especially in parishes where only the elect were allowed to receive communion. Some of those excluded formed congregations of their own, which were especially likely to appear in places where soldiers of the New Model were questioning the whole political and ecclesiastical order.[23]

Separatist congregations existed in every part of England, but were particularly numerous in towns and in woodland and pasture regions.[24] There had been a Baptist congregation in Bristol even before the war, but it was only after 1645 that it began to flourish. The arrival of the New Model quickly stimulated the spread of Baptist opinions. The most effective evangelist in the west was Thomas Collier of Westbury-sub-Mendip, a former Army preacher, who helped to establish a congregation at Taunton by 1646; several others took root in places where there had been garrisons—Lyme, Bridgwater, and Plymouth, for example.[25] Outside the towns, the areas of greatest Baptist strength included the Somerset levels and the northern clothing districts. A Baptist was preaching at Middlezoy in 1646, and soon there were other congregations at Wedmore, Mark, Axbridge, and Cheddar. By the time of the Restoration there were Baptist churches in the clothing parishes of Beckington, North Bradley, Trowbridge, and Chippenham, all within the old heartland of Puritanism.[26]

The Baptists attracted a cross-section of society from the middling sort downwards. Their leaders were prosperous tradesmen like the notorious David Barrett at Wells, politically ambitious yeomen like the exciseman

---

[23] Hill, *World Turned Upside Down*, p. 63. For local examples see Holmes, *Lincolnshire*, p. 198; and Underdown, *Somerset*, p. 146.

[24] In Kent separatism was strongest in the towns and clothing villages of the Weald: Everitt, *Community of Kent*, pp. 59–60; Clark, *Provincial Society*, pp. 393–4. In Lincolnshire it was most widespread in the fens: Holmes, *Lincolnshire*, pp. 45–6, 198.

[25] *The Records of a Church of Christ, meeting in Broadmead, Bristol. 1640–1687*, ed. Edward B. Underhill, 1847, pp. 17–41. Geoffrey F. Nuttall, 'The Baptist Western Association, 1653–1658', *Journal of Ecclesiastical History*, xi (1960), 213–15. Underdown, *Somerset*, p. 146. Bayley, *Dorset*, pp. 465–7. R. N. Worth, *History of Plymouth*, 2nd edn., Plymouth, 1890, pp. 249, 266.

[26] Joseph Ivimey, *History of the English Baptists*, 1811–14, ii. 521–8. Croot, 'Aspects of Agrarian Society', ch. 7. BL Add. MS 32324 (Seymour MSS), fo. 108. *Records of Early Nonconformity*, i. 107, 116.

Rogers at Cheddar, clothworkers like Nicholas Elliott of Beckington. A few of the gentry were sympathetic—William King of North Bradley allowed Baptist meetings in his barn and Thomas Hickes of Devizes was a preacher—but it is rare to find adherents above this level of the minor parish gentry. Most congregations were small, and can have attracted only a small minority of the population. The relatively flourishing Wedmore church had no more than fifty members after 1660, though admittedly it may have lost the more fainthearted ones by then. Still, Collier was an effective preacher to large audiences who may have become less amenable to parish discipline after hearing him, even if they did not become Baptists. The presence of preaching soldiers played a large part in bringing new ideas into the villages. Baptists often came to church accompanied by friendly soldiers, as for example at the great debate betwen Collier and the Presbyterian Francis Fullwood at Wiveliscombe in 1652.[27] The Baptists added a major element of division to many parishes in the 1650s, and their military connections made them to a considerable extent an alien presence.

The soldiers were the source of radical ideas that went far beyond the rejection of infant baptism and the congregational separation practised by the Baptists. They were appreciative listeners to the mechanic preachers who began to appear intermittently in west-country pulpits after the war. The preaching of an unordained minister at Radipole attracted great numbers of soldiers from Weymouth, the Dorset Committee complained, 'to the great disturbance and hazard of the garrison'. Countrymen accustomed only to orthodox doctrine and rituals could now hear, if they chose, every conceivable heresy: mortalism, unitarianism, even, the scandalized Thomas Edwards noted, the belief that 'all the earth is the Saints', and there ought to be a community of goods'. People so awakened could have no time for Presbyterian intolerance. Robert Saunders, a Weymouth mariner, announced that 'he fought not against the Papists for their religion, for twas lawful for every man to use his conscience, but . . . he would fight as valiantly against the Presbyterians as ever he did against the Cavaliers'.[28] The religious nihilism which had often lurked below the surface of obedient conformity merged with the new demand for total liberty, total freedom from moral and legal constraints. 'There was no punishment for any man . . . but only in this life', a Somerset man told the woman he was trying to seduce, and 'after this life there was no punishment because there was neither heaven nor hell'.[29]

[27] Underdown, *Somerset*, p. 172.
[28] *Dorset Minute Books*, pp. 130–1. BL TT, E. 323 (2): Edwards, *Gangraena*, pp. 34, 117–18. *Weymouth Documents*, p. 198.
[29] Quoted in Quaife, *Wanton Wenches*, p. 64. Cf. also BL TT, E. 323 (2): Edwards, *Gangraena*, p. 118.

By 1650 alarming ideas of this kind were commonly blamed on the emerging Ranter sect. The Ranters carried the antinomian principle of exemption from the moral law to extreme conclusions, repudiating hell and even sin, and flamboyantly proclaiming that salvation was to be attained by drunken carousing, swearing, free love, and the liberal use of tobacco. Their endorsement of these disreputable aspects of popular culture naturally increased the rage of orthodox Puritans against them. They were never conspicuous for their numbers in the western counties, but a few small groups of them, especially in Wiltshire, achieved notoriety. The two best-known Somerset Ranters were Wells men. One of them, John Robins, proclaimed himself God and gave his followers permission to change their wives or husbands; four of them sold their estates and went off to preach the gospel in the Holy Land. The main centre in Dorset was Poole, which Governor Rede made a refuge for Ranters; in November 1650 a Rump committee against 'obscene, licentious and impious practices' was ordered to consider further information about the sect's activities in Dorset.[30]

Evidence about Ranters in Wiltshire is more plentiful. Among the Puritan clergy occupying cheese country pulpits before the war was Tobias Crisp, vicar of Brinkworth from 1627 to 1642, whose unorthodox views seem to have found ready listeners among the husbandmen and weavers of his and the adjoining parishes. He may have left a legacy on which others were later able to draw, for a few miles away at Langley Burrell another radical vicar, Thomas Webbe, established a small Ranter community in the 1650s. Webbe was popular, an enemy charged, with 'divers of the most ignorant parishioners' because of his refusal to collect tithes. He powdered and frizzled his hair, and combined elements of the old festive culture—music and mixed dancing—with an admiration for radicals like Lilburne and the Ranters Joseph Salmon and Abiezer Coppe. But few of the villagers were tempted to follow Webbe into the life of sexual freedom in which he engaged with his wife and companions. Only two or three families in Langley Burrell actually became Ranters, and most of the group were from outside the parish—soldiers of the Gloucester garrison, a young man from Castle Combe. The godly, and even many of the ungodly of the neighbourhood were outraged: Webbe accused the JPs of prosecuting him for adultery only 'to gain applause amongst the multitude'. He was acquitted but deprived of his living, after which the community broke up. There may have been other small Ranter groups at Bradford-on-Avon and Salisbury, and perhaps one in the clothing village of Lacock. Among statements made there a few years later were assertions that 'there was neither heaven nor hell except in a man's

---

[30] Underdown, *Somerset*, p. 156. Hill, *World Turned Upside Down*, pp. 163, 253–4. BL Stowe MS 189, fo. 53.

conscience', and that 'Tom Lampire of Melksham would make as good Scriptures as the Bible'.[31]

Heresies traceable to Ranter origins thus continued to surface occasionally, but the Ranters were never more than an isolated handful, and by 1653 they had been broken by persecution. By this time a more serious threat to orthodoxy and parish unity came from the Quakers, the most successful of the evangelical movements of the Interregnum. The Quakers were the more threatening to the forces of order because their rejection of ministry and ecclesiastical structure, their emphasis on the equality of all who were guided by the 'inner light', were accompanied by stricter moral rectitude; Ranter doctrines, Thomas Collier sneered, concealed behind 'an outward austere carriage'. They therefore had greater appeal to people of the middling sort alienated from established religion but not from conventional morality. Allegations that the Quakers were the 'dregs of the common people', vagrants 'living often in idleness' have been shown to be the figments of hostile propaganda. However, sociological conclusions drawn from analysis of Quaker leaders present an equally misleading impression, exaggerating the proportion of gentry and wealthy adherents and ignoring the large numbers of temporary supporters and sympathizers who never became members of Quaker societies.[32]

The Quakers made converts in all regions and types of community. Their success in urban centres varied according to local circumstances. At places like Dorchester and Norwich the hold of parochial Puritanism over the population largely defeated them. But at Bristol the conversion of the influential Denis Hollister was followed by mass defections to them from the Broadmead Baptists.[33] In northern and eastern England they were notably successful in the pasturelands, in fen and woodland areas: the Isle of Axholme and the fens of south Lincolnshire, the wood-pasture region along the Norfolk-Suffolk border, and the Chiltern woodlands in Buckinghamshire, for example.[34] In the western counties their distribution was less geographically specific. They were numerous in Wiltshire towns such as Marlborough and Devizes and in the clothing villages around Calne and Chippenham, including Slaughterford, which had a long history of religious radicalism. But there were also Quakers in the

[31] BL TT, E. 669 (5): Edw. Stokes, *The Wiltshire Rant*, 1652, pp. 3, 8, 12–15, 22–6, 30–1, 34, 43–4, 51, 82. Hill, *World Turned Upside Down*, pp. 182–3. Christopher Hill, 'Dr. Tobias Crisp, 1600–1643', in *Balliol Studies*, ed. John Prest (1982), pp. 56, 66–8; I am grateful to the author for this reference.

[32] Richard T. Vann, *The Social Development of English Quakerism 1655–1755*, Cambridge, Mass., 1969, ch. 2. Judith J. Hurwich, 'The Social Origins of the Early Quakers', *P & P* no. 48 (Aug. 1970), 156–61. Alan Cole, 'The Quakers and the English Revolution', in *Crisis in Europe*, pp. 341–8. Hill, *World Turned Upside Down*, ch. 10.

[33] *Records of a Church at Broadmead, Bristol*, pp. 43–4, 50.

[34] Holmes, *Lincolnshire*, pp. 205, 222. Vann, *Social Development of Quakerism*, pp. 13–15.

conservative area around Donhead St. Mary in the south-west of the county. In Dorset Quakers were persecuted at Sherborne and in many villages in the downlands and Blackmore Vale, though there were also some at Weymouth and even a few in Dorchester. In Somerset there were Quakers in the northern Puritan parishes—places like Brislington, Englishcombe, and Nailsea—and they were strong in and around the levels in such villages as Street, Walton, Greinton, Middlezoy, and Moorlinch. But they also attracted a following in the conservative south-east, at Limington, Queen Camel, and Trent.[35]

Quakers were drawn mainly from the middling and lower ranks of society. Many of their local leaders had risen to positions in the service of Parliament. Jasper Batt of Street ('the greatest seducer in all the West', according to a post-Restoration bishop), had been secretary to the Somerset Committee, Christopher Pittard of Martock a committee-man, James Pearce of Keynsham and Robert Wastfield of Brislington both sequestration officers.[36] The number of middling-sort Quakers is clear in the frequent reports of their being punished for refusing to take the oath or give hat honour when appointed to juries or to such local offices (which they often had no objection to performing) as surveyors of highways.[37] But alongside these propertied adherents must be set the large numbers of poor Quakers who were convicted (sometimes as vagrants), or who without becoming members of societies turned out to listen to the sect's egalitarian message at mass meetings. The throngs attending James Nayler's spectacular progress through the west in 1656, or who came to Thomas Budd's orchard in Martock to hear the evangelist Thomas Salthouse, are proof of the Quakers' appeal to a much larger population than the few who submitted to the discipline of formal membership.[38]

*

It is easy to see why members of the élite found the Quakers so threatening. They were, a Somerset JP declared, 'in contempt of government'.[39] Their passionate interruptions of church services, refusal to pay tithes, rejection of oaths and hat honour: all struck, actually or symbolically, at

---

[35] Reeves, 'Protestant Nonconformity', pp. 103–4. *Records of Early Nonconformity*, i. 11–13, 106–18, 124. *CSPD, 1656–7*, pp. 123–4 (actually 1659?). See also [Joseph Besse], *An Abstract of the Sufferings of the People call'd Quakers*, 1733–8, i. 74–81, 210–28, 292–8.

[36] Underdown, *Somerset*, p. 186. G. F. Nuttall, 'Lyon Turner's *Original Records*', *Congregational Historical Soc. Transactions*, xiv (1940–4), 16.

[37] For some examples see [Besse], *Abstract of Sufferings*, i. 216, 297.

[38] BL TT, E. 896 (11): Thomas Collier, *A Looking-Glasse for the Quakers*, 1656, p. 16. John Deacon, 'The Great Imposter Examined' (1656), in *The Harleian Miscellany*, ed. W. Oldys and T. Park, 2nd edn., 1808–13, vi. 425–36. BL TT, E. 926 (6): Robert Wastfeild, *A True Testimony of Faithfull Witnesses recorded*, 1657, pp. 7–8, 27. *SQSR* iii. 339–40. [Besse], *Abstract of Sufferings*, i. 216–23. See also Hill, *World Turned Upside Down*, pp. 200–1.

[39] Underdown, *Somerset*, p. 187.

the foundations of ordered society. But this does not explain why they also aroused such hostility among the lower sort—people who in their different ways, too, were often 'in contempt of government'. Were the mobs who repeatedly beat up Quakers and wrecked their meetings simply the obedient tools of hostile authorities? The Quakers were naturally inclined to blame élite sponsorship for the violence against them, and there was sometimes some truth in this. After Quakers had been 'assaulted and abused by the rabble' at Bath, some of the mob admitted that they had been encouraged by the mayor. Anti-Quaker apprentice riots at Bristol may also have had official sanction. The Dorset JP John Fitzjames, a particularly vindictive persecutor according to the Quakers, was alleged to have stirred up 'the rude people, chiefly Cavaliers', to break up a meeting at Sherborne. Presbyterian ministers were often blamed for the violence. One of the meetings at Martock in 1656 was interrupted by a deputation of five neighbouring clerics leading a crowd of 'wild brutish people' (as a Quaker thought them), armed with cudgels, staves, pitchforks, and other weapons. After arguing with the speaker, Salthouse, the ministers left and the mob immediately attacked the Quakers, throwing 'cow-dung, sticks, and dabs of earth'. At Glastonbury just before the Restoration the Presbyterian Samuel Winney several times called out mobs against the Quakers. Many more incidents of this kind are described in Quaker records.[40]

But we should remember that descriptions of the violence come almost entirely from Quaker sources—from people who could not bring themselves to believe that it was anything but artificially inspired. The truth is that the Quakers, like other separatists, were often perceived as being subversive of a familiar, customary order to which many of the lower orders were as firmly attached as their social superiors: undermining the authority of husbands over wives and children, challenging the comfortably familiar even if inequitable local hierarchy, splitting parish communities. They, and especially their itinerant evangelists, could easily be seen as troublesome outsiders, importing conflict as well as unfamiliar doctrines into the towns and villages they visited. Like pre-war dissenters who went gadding to sermons, Quakers were often prosecuted for travelling to meetings outside their own villages—for violating the old ideal of parochial unity.[41]

Dislike of the Quakers' subversion of familial and parish order needs to be set in the context of popular opposition to other sects on much the same

---

[40] [Besse], *Abstract of Sufferings*, i. 220, 227–8. John Latimer, *Annals of Bristol in the 17th Century*, Bristol, 1900, pp. 256–7, 259. *CSPD, 1656–7*, p. 123. Wastfeild, *True Testimony*, pp. 8–10, 27. On sponsored rioting see Reay, 'Popular hostility', pp. 405–6; but cf. also Hill, *World Turned Upside Down*, p. 188.

[41] There are examples in Wastfeild, *True Testimony*, pp. 52–4.

grounds. On patriarchal authority, for example: the Quakers' challenge was not unique to them, but reflected notions about the spiritual equality of women common in separatist circles for many years. The Brownist exiles in Holland had allowed women who could give the usual proofs of salvation full church membership; London separatist congregations in the 1640s had allowed women to debate, vote, prophesy, and even preach. Alarmed conservatives managed to unearth women preachers in many parts of England, including a Welsh woman named Arabella Thomas in Salisbury, before the war. Not all Baptists were happy about even the limited advances for women that were more common, and the radical Independent Hugh Peter had given a well-known reproof to Anne Hutchinson in pre-war Massachusetts for subverting the 'natural' order of male authority over women. But for the Quakers, as Keith Thomas observes, 'the Inner Light knew no barriers of sex'. Even though the Quakers limited female equality to the religious sphere and continued to uphold male domination in the secular one, it is not surprising that they and other sects attracted women in considerable numbers, as they did male members of other oppressed groups. But it is also not surprising that the great bulk of the population, untouched by the inner light, found these developments distinctly unsettling. The mayor of Chester told a woman Quaker that she deserved to be put in the cucking-stool for her insubordination.[42]

Separatists split parishes as well as families. Again, protests against their divisiveness were widespread. 'None but rogues would put down Common Prayer', the conservative Cheddar constable, Henry Bankes, declared; he hoped to see Thomas Collier and his friends hanged because they were Independents 'and would not go to church'.[43] 'Since toleration and liberty of conscience the Church of England is confounded', an old Herefordshire Puritan wailed, '. . . This cannot be remedied unless the act of Q. Elizabeth that every one keep his parish church be confirmed and upon a greater penalty'.[44] Disruption of parochial unity and contempt for the doctrine and rituals accepted by the majority were particularly likely to be provoked by mechanic preachers. Hostile demonstrations against preaching soldiers or mechanics occurred sporadically in the western counties. At Wimborne Minster members of the Dorset Committee invited a captain to preach in 1646 instead of the locally popular Dr William Stone. There were loud protests bordering on a riot by the congregation and eventually the displaced minister had to be fetched to restore order. In August 1652 at Wookey a preaching soldier was

[42] *A Discoverie of Six Women Preachers*, 1641, pp. 4–5. Thomas, 'Women and the Civil War Sects', pp. 320–35, esp. p. 324. Reay, 'Popular hostility', pp. 389, 396.
[43] Quoted in Croot, 'Aspects of Agrarian Society', ch. 7.
[44] BL Loan 29/177 (Harley papers), fo. 96.

interrupted by parishioners who demanded to see his commission and rang the bells to arouse the village against him.[45]

So it is understandable that Quakers were often abused when they audaciously defied the cherished ideal of parochial harmony. There were many minor riots like the one in Midsomer Norton church in 1657, after a blacksmith had interrupted the preacher, called him a rogue, and told him to come down from the pulpit. Incidents in which Quakers were beaten up by villagers—at Cameley in north Somerset and at Mudford in the south of the county in 1655, for instance—reveal popular perceptions of them as deviants comparable to scolds, witches, or Catholic recusants. Sometimes the connection was explicit. When John Anderson was thrown out of Bridgwater church in 1658 after a disturbance, the parish clerk accused him of having 'been among witches'. Quakers arrested after a meeting at Sherborne were said to have confessed to a compact with the devil, and to have bewitched the town's two ministers. George Fox himself was accused of witchcraft.[46] The natural response to such apparently dangerous people was to shame them into good behaviour or get rid of them. In anti-Quaker demonstrations we therefore encounter some familiar symbols: horns thrown into a meeting of Friends at Evershot in 1656, for instance; the ritual disguise (a bearskin) worn by one of Fox's tormentors in Somerset. More violent riots often contained elements of charivari ritual. When Edward Burroughs was speaking at Glastonbury Cross, a Quaker reports, the mob 'fell to beating their drum, whooping, hallooeing and thrusting the Friends to and fro in a wild and barbarous manner'. At Broad Cerne in May 1660, 'rude people of the baser sort' beat a drum to summon a crowd, fired guns beneath the windows of the house in which Quakers were meeting, and then attacked them as they left the village.[47]

The mobs' choice of Quakers as targets of community disapproval was no more capricious than their selection of unruly women as the objects of skimmington processions. Beliefs that Quakers repudiated conventional views of morality, property, and order were exaggerated. But the movement had its extremists, easily confused with the Ranters, of whom Nayler was the most prominent, and its splinter groups like the 'proud Quakers',

[45] J. M. J. Fletcher, 'A Dorset Worthy, William Stone, Royalist and Divine (1615–1685)', *DNHP* xxxvi (1915), 18–19. *SQSR*, iii, intro., p. xxxix.

[46] *SQSR* iii. 354. [Besse], *Abstract of Sufferings*, i. 79, 220–2, 226. Reay, 'Popular hostility', pp. 369–9. BL TT, E. 1832 (2): [Richard Blome], *The Fanatick History: Or, An Exact Relation and Account of the Old Anabaptists, and new Quakers*, 1660, pp. 117–18. See also William Y. Tindall, *John Bunyan, Mechanick Preacher*, New York, 1934, pp. 218–22.

[47] [Besse], *Abstract of Sufferings*, i. 80, 220. *The Journal of George Fox*, ed. John L. Nickalls, Cambridge, 1952, p. 363. DRO N 10/A 15 (Quaker Sufferings), p. 1 (and pp. 3–4 for other violent assaults). The incidents recorded by Besse and Fox sound suspiciously similar (in both the perpetrator is appropriately attacked by a bull at a bull-baiting shortly afterwards), though in the former a bull-skin rather than a bearskin is said to have been worn.

who permitted drinking, swearing, football-playing, and other moral laxities.[48] In 1659 there was a widespread panic about the Quaker danger, fuelled by rumours of official tolerance and stories of Quakers running naked through the streets 'for a sign' and committing other excesses. Many people who collected arms in preparation for Sir George Booth's royalist-Presbyterian rising against the Rump claimed to have done so to defend their lives and properties against the Quakers. A pretext, no doubt, but its repeated use is significant of the climate of opinion.[49] The sometimes contradictory manifestations of Quakerism explain the hostility shown towards them by very different groups. To responsible, propertied, orthodox Puritans Quakers were threats to order and morality. To many poorer countrymen they were threats to the values of the patriarchal family and the harmonious co-operative community.

We now know enough not to over-stress the unanimity of popular subscription to these traditional values. If tempted to do so we need only remind ourselves of the remarkable effervescence of revolutionary ideas that swept through the countryside when political and ecclesiastical authority was weakened by the civil war. Yet it is also clear that this intellectual eruption touched only a small minority, and that most people continued to accept the still reiterated messages of hierarchical order, and to hanker not for total religious liberty, but for the comfortable certainties of the old religion. Ministerial authority was part of the natural order; so too was the natural authority belonging to rank and birth. In the 1650s the old Clubman Humphrey Willis continued to deplore that the world was turned upside-down. In Willis as in the Clubmen generally, social conservatism—complaints about 'blue apron-blades' taking over from the gentry—is combined with religious conservatism. Willis had no time for the passionate sectarian disputes of his time: 'Religion's made a tennis-ball/For every fool to play withal'.[50]

Attitudes of this sort were widely shared, especially in arable villages where rural capitalism was only just beginning to erode the old community solidarity. The familiar language of the Book of Common Prayer had expressed those old certainties at the weekly gathering of the parish; the austere new Directory was for many people as unsatisfying a substitute as the evangelical spontaneity of the sects. Dr Morrill's analysis of churchwardens' accounts shows that by 1649 few parishes had recorded acquiring copies of the Directory—fewer than those recording continued possession of the outlawed Prayer Book. Somewhat more Dorset parishes may have owned the Directory—the county committee tried to see that

[48] Hill, *World Turned Upside Down*, pp. 199–204.
[49] J. F. Maclear, 'Quakerism and the End of the Interregnum', *Church History*, xix (1950), 240–70. Underdown, *Royalist Conspiracy*, pp. 256–7.
[50] BL TT, E. 988 (16): Humphrey Willis, *England's Changeling*, 1659.

they did—but even in that county ministers still using Common Prayer in 1647 were only warned, not suspended. Parliament's attempt to prohibit observance of the major festivals like Christmas and Easter achieved only limited success. In 1650, at the height of Puritan rule, almost half the parishes surveyed held Easter communions, mostly of the traditional 'open' variety, and the proportion was soon to increase. During the royalist reaction of 1648 ministers were occasionally prosecuted for not using Common Prayer even in Puritan counties such as Norfolk and Cambridgeshire, and local resistance to the Directory continued at a lower level long after that date. Popular attachment to familiar rituals often surfaced in defiance of Puritan order: there were still Rogationtide processions in many parishes, and in Puritan Gloucester one of the town churches was being decorated for Christmas as late as 1650.[51]

How deeply embedded the established religion was in the fabric of popular assumptions about law and society is occasionally revealed by the outbursts of discontented countrymen. In 1646 John Browne of Semley, Wiltshire, saw a connection between Parliament's sequestration policies and the impending religious changes, both threatening the customary rhythms of rural life. Parliament, he declared, 'would take away every man's estate, one after another, and . . . if they did take away Common Prayer, we were as good go to plough upon the Sundays'.[52] Browne was wrong, of course: no Common Prayer did not mean a seven-day working week. But his fears again remind us of the tenacious hold of ancient custom, and of villagers' continuing need for community gatherings—at feasts and revels as well as in the services of the church—at which they could affirm the bonds linking them to kindred and neighbours. The triumph of reforming Puritanism at Westminster and in the county administrations therefore did not end the cultural conflict which had loomed so large in the kingdom's pre-war disputes. To the continuation of that conflict in the years before 1660 we now turn our attention.

*

Parliament's victory inaugurated a new phase in the Puritan attack on the old rituals and symbols. Before and during the war the visual symbols proscribed were principally religious ones: the 'popish' pictures, statues, and ornaments, the altar rails, choirs, and organs of a now outlawed form of worship. Monarchical symbols, although sometimes defaced or removed by over-zealous soldiers, were not before 1648 targets of official censure. The parliamentarian Lord Saye was upset when his troops tore down a royal portrait at New College. But with the establishment of the Commonwealth the royal arms disappeared from parish churches

[51] Morrill, 'The Church 1642–9', pp. 102, 104–8.
[52] BL Add. MS 22084 (Wilts. Sequestrations Register), fo. 128.

throughout the land, their very absence proclaiming that a new political order had been born. In some places there does not seem to have been any great urgency about it. At Tintinhull, for instance, it was not until 1650 that the churchwardens paid a workman 'for striking out the King's arms'.[53] The Rump issued a new coinage and replaced the Great Seal with one bearing the legend, 'In the First Year of Freedom by God's Blessing Restored'. It did not, however, erect reminders of its authority in parish churches, though on other public buildings the royal arms were often replaced with the arms of the Commonwealth. The republic's reliance on verbal means of establishing its legitimacy—declarations, oaths of loyalty, sermons and pamphlets—reflects the characteristic Puritan preference for rational discourse over pictorial modes of communication. The removal of familiar and often colourful monuments must have left a yawning gap in the lives of people accustomed to such pageantry.

So too with public rituals and celebrations. 'Successful religious revolutions', Dr Morrill rightly observes, 'adapt themselves to popular culture': the Puritan revolution failed to do so.[54] Parliament's austere Fast Days and Days of Thanksgiving were pallid substitutes for the religious, monarchical, and local festivals of the old order—more spiritually nourishing for the godly, no doubt, but much less nourishing of neighbourliness and fellowship for the rest. Committed Royalists ignored or defiantly demonstrated against them. At Mundon, Essex, on 1 June 1643, the royalist vicar assembled 'a riotous company to keep a day of profaneness by drinking of healths round a joint-stool, singing of profane songs with hallooeing and roaring'. The date was an appropriate one for a midsummer revel, but it was also deliberately chosen to scandalize the godly, being the day after one of Parliament's Fasts.[55] Roundhead celebrations in royalist communities occasionally led to violence. There was a brawl at Salisbury on one of Parliament's Days of Thanksgiving in September 1646. Citizens discussing the purchase of faggots for a bonfire were loudly denounced as rebels, and when the bonfire was built a gang of men armed with staves came and threw it in the river. A second attempt ended in further disorder.[56]

Military parades were a partial substitute for the vanished spectacles. The disbandment of a regiment might be accompanied by rituals proclaiming the return of civic harmony. When Major Richard Hopton's

[53] *Wood's Life and Times*, i. 64–5. SRO D/P/tin, 4/1/2 (Tintinhull Churchwardens accounts). Sherborne was equally dilatory. Only on 10 Aug. 1650, at the direct command of a parliamentarian captain, did the governors of Sherborne School agree to take down the King's arms: W. B. Wildman, *A Short History of Sherborne*, 2nd edn., Sherborne, 1902, pp. 62–3.
[54] Morrill, 'The Church 1642–9', p. 114.
[55] White, *First Century*, p. 45.
[56] BL Add. MS 22084 (Wilts. Sequestrations Register), fo. 146.

Herefordshire troop was disbanded in March 1648 the soldiers were paraded, 'and then fired every man his pistol on the ground, and so departed unto a place where the Major had very nobly provided for them a hogshead of wine'. Hopton's party then rode into Hereford with a gentleman bearing laurel branches before them as an emblem of peace.[57] More elaborate was the pageantry at Blackheath, Kent, on May day 1645, when Parliament's local commander staged a mock battle between two regiments of foot, playing the parts of Roundheads and Cavaliers respectively. The former 'carried it on with care and love, temperance and order, and as much gravity as might be'. The 'Cavaliers' entered into the spirit of the affair, with much 'drinking and roaring and disorder, and would still be playing with the women, and compass them in, and quarrel, and were exceedingly disorderly'. The spectacle, a newsbook reflected, was an edifying alternative to the customary 'drinking matches, and maypoles, and dancing and idle ways, and sin', which 'gave content to the country people, and satisfied them as well as if they had gone a-maying'.[58]

Puritan authorities were rarely as wise in compensating for the outlawed public ceremonies. Royalists naturally made much of the culturally repressive aspects of parliamentarian rule, often connecting the attack on popular festivals with the concurrent decline of charity and hospitality. Laments for the disappearance of the old habits of good fellowship were widespread. The Isle of Wight, formerly 'the paradise of England', says Sir John Oglander, became like the rest of the country 'a melancholy, dejected, sad place—no company, no resort, no neighbours seeing one of the other'.[59] 'Christmas was killed at Naseby fight', and charity and honesty, too, mourned a popular ballad of 1646, 'The World is Turned Upside Down' (sung, it is worth noting, to the tune of 'When the King Enjoys His Own Again'). The song expresses the spirit of much of the propaganda churned out by royalist scribblers like that inveterate defender of old customs, John Taylor. In 1652 the water poet sneered at the 'hot, zealous brethren' who held 'that Plum-pottage was mere Popery, that a collet of brawn was an abomination, that roast beef was antichristian, that mince pies were relics of the Whore of Babylon, and a goose or a turkey or a capon were marks of the Beast'.[60]

Christmas of course recovered, but some of the old rituals were never to return. 'When I was a child (and so before the civil wars)': looking back years later, John Aubrey saw the Interregnum as a crucial cultural watershed. All kind of local customs, like midsummer bonfires on St.

[57] *Historical Collections*, ed. Rushworth, vii. 1042–3.

[58] BL TT, E. 260 (37): *Perfect Occurrences*, 8–16 May 1645.

[59] *A Royalist's Notebook: The Commonplace Book of Sir John Oglander Kt. of Nunwell*, ed. Francis Bamford, 1936, p. 112.

[60] BL TT, 669 f. 10 (47): 'The World is Turned Upside Down', [1646]; E. 1244 (2): [John Taylor], *Christmas In and Out*, p. 9.

John's Eve, had vanished: 'the civil wars coming on have put all these rites or customs quite out of fashion.'[61] Many of them were vulnerable because of their connection with pagan or popish superstition. Aubrey tells the story of the salt-well at Droitwich, which by custom was annually decorated with greenery and flowers on the day of the well's patron saint. 'In the Presbyterian times in the civil wars' the ceremony was prohibited and the well promptly dried up, 'to the great loss of the town', but the next year the townsmen bravely revived it and the salt water naturally gushed forth again.[62] When John Taylor travelled through Somerset in 1649 he was told the fate of the Glastonbury Thorn: 'the soldiers being over zealous did cut it down in pure devotion; but a vintner dwelling in the town did save a great slip or branch of it, and ... set it in his garden'.[63] The civil war also brought an end to many of the elaborate civic rituals of the urban festive year. The rich pageantry of St. George's Day at Norwich became a memory. At the next feast, an order of the company in 1645 reads, there would be 'no beating of drums or sounds of trumpets; no snap dragon, or fellows dressed up in fools' coats and caps; no standard with the George thereon, nor no hanging of tapestry cloth, nor pictures in any of the streets'.[64]

The rhythm of the working week, in country as well as town, was to be varied by sabbath and Fast Days, by sermons and catechizings, not by festivals and processions. The campaign against rural ales and revels was accordingly resumed after the war. Such customs, always offensive on moral grounds, were now doubly threatening because of their potential use as occasions for royalist sedition. Fears of Cavaliers using football matches, horse-races and cock-fights to organize the disaffected were endemic throughout the 1650s, and a steady stream of official orders called for their suppression. The very first item of the Council's instructions to militia and army officers in July 1659, for example, orders 'diligent inquiries after all horse races, cock matches, bull-baitings, hurlings or other meetings of that kind', and the arrest of the promoters.[65]

Much of the repression was directed primarily against the amusements of the cavalier gentry, and its success should not be exaggerated. There was a lively London culture during the Protectorate, and music and other kinds of entertainment still flourished in country houses. Anthony Wood

---

[61] Aubrey, 'Remaines', p. 207. Anthony Wood (*Life and Times*, i. 140) observed a similar impact by the civil war on undergraduate rituals at Oxford.

[62] Aubrey, 'Remaines', p. 189.

[63] 'John Taylors Wandering to see the Wonders of the West' (1649), pp. 4, 6, in *Occasional Facsimile Reprints*, ed. E. W. Ashbee, viii, 1869. However, Aubrey gives a different version: 'Observations', in *Three Prose Works*, p. 330.

[64] Bolingbroke, 'Players in Norwich', p. 19. This corrects the statement that the dragon survived, in Burke, *Popular Culture*, p. 216. 'Old Snap' returned only after 1660.

[65] Worcester College, Clarke MS 3/3, fo. 78ᵛ. See also, for example, *CSPD*, 1649–50, pp. 335, 337–8; 1655, pp. 53, 296.

found plenty to enjoy in and around Oxford, and Oliver Cromwell himself
was a notable patron of music.[66] Even the cavalier gentry suffered only
sporadically. The exiled Sir Kenelm Digby longed for the 'tabors and
pipes, and dancing ladies' still to be found, he understood, in English
country houses. Actors who rashly tried to revive the London theatre at
Christmas 1648 were promptly arrested, but during the Protectorate there
was greater tolerance. The players occasionally gave private performances in the houses of noblemen and gentlemen, and at Christmas
and during St. Bartholomew's Fair, it was said, bribery enabled them to
act in public. There was always the danger of interruption by more zealous
officials and soldiers, but a tenuous form of theatrical life managed to
survive, and it was in these years that Sir William Davenant produced the
first English opera.[67] In spite of lingering governmental suspicions, by
the later 1650s élite entertainments were returning to normal. There was
much betting at race meetings, and by the winter before the Restoration
both the gentry and wealthy Londoners were keeping Christmas in
something like the old festive way. Samuel Pepys and his wife, for
instance, were entertained by the Strudwicks with a rich cake and the
ceremonial choosing of a Twelfth Night king and queen.[68]

This is looking ahead to a more relaxed period. In the post-war years
the authorities rightly feared that traditional celebrations, with all their
symbolic associations, might provide pretexts for violence. This was
certainly the case at Canterbury at Christmas 1647. Seething resentment
at the harshness of the Kent Committee boiled over when measures to
enforce Parliament's ordinance against 'that darling of rude and licentious persons, called Christmas' were announced. There were 'dangerous
speeches' about 'a course to be taken with the Roundheads'; only a
handful of shopkeepers obeyed the mayor's order to stay open on the day.
Those who did were attacked by the mob, and the signal for further
disorders was given when footballs were thrown in the streets, attracting
'great numbers of rude persons, not only of the city but of country fellows,
strangers from the parts adjacent'. They were soon shouting royalist
slogans, 'crying up King Charles, and crying down the Parliament and
excise', assaulting Roundheads, and consuming the free beer offered by
citizens who set up holly-bushes at their doors. The mayor and his

[66] Arthur Bryant, *Samuel Pepys: The Man in the Making*, 2nd edn., 1947, pp. 10, 41. *Wood's Life and Times*, i. 181, 189–90, 204–6, 208–9, 212. All biographers note Cromwell's love of music: see, for example, Fraser, *Cromwell*, pp. 463–5.

[67] R. T. Peterson, *Sir Kenelm Digby, the Ornament of England, 1603–1665*, Cambridge, Mass., 1956, p. 236. Worcester College, Clarke MS 1/3, fo. 66. James Wright, 'Historia Histrionica: An Historical Account of the English Stage' (1699), in *A Select Collection of Old English Plays*, ed. W. Carew Hazlitt, 4th edn., 1874–6, xv. 408–12. Arthur H. Nethercot, *Sir William D'Avenant*, Chicago, 1938, pp. 309–18.

[68] Underdown, *Somerset*, p. 191. Bryant, *Pepys*, pp. 58, 76. There is a record of betting at a race meeting in 1657 in Hants. RO, 'Catalogue of Kingsmill MSS', no. 1290.

parliamentarian allies were driven into ignominious flight and the Committee had to send troops to restore order.[69]

This was only one among many riots touched off by attempts to suppress popular amusements. There were sporadic outbreaks in London, including an apprentice riot at Christmas 1645, and another in April 1648 when troops broke up a Sunday tip-cat game in Moorfields. At Norwich in 1648, after the apprentices had unsuccessfully petitioned for relaxation of the prohibitions against Christmas, a more permissive mayor allowed the traditional bonfires and feasting on 27 March, the anniversary of the King's accession. When he was summoned to Westminster to explain himself there were massive disorders. The houses of prominent Norwich Puritans were attacked, and serious loss of life occurred when the County Committee's magazine blew up while being looted by rioters in search of arms.[70] These were riots provoked by official repression; in other cases festivities were used as pretexts to initiate royalist risings. In 1648 promoters of a hurling match between teams from Devon and Cornwall were believed to have 'another design'. A minor rising in Norfolk in 1650 was preceded by a great football match near Norwich as well as by numerous genteel hunting parties. Before the more serious revolt in Dorset and Wiltshire in 1655 it was noted that the Cavaliers 'kept great Christmases after the usual time with sets of fiddlers'. In Northumberland in the same year rebels gathered on the excuse of attending a wedding and 'head-washing'; a football match near Gloucester and a race meeting in Northamptonshire were other occasions for assembling royalist plotters.[71]

We shall return again to this tendency for resistance to cultural repression to have political implications. Attempts to preserve ancient sports and festivals, to be sure, were not necessarily royalist-inspired. Ralph Josselin complained of the 500 spectators at a wrestling match in his Essex village in 1646, but does not seem to have been as politically worried as he would assuredly have been two years later when such people were being stirred up by the Royalists.[72] Middling-sort complaints about the unruly behaviour of the poor were more likely to be based on moral than on political considerations. In 1657 the 'principal inhabitants' of High Ongar, Essex, asked for their September fair to be suppressed, as it was 'of no

[69] 'The Parliamentary Diary of John Boys, 1647–8', ed. David Underdown, *BIHR* xxxix (1966), 159–60. Everitt, *Community of Kent*, pp. 230–3.

[70] Underdown, *Pride's Purge*, p. 91. R. W. Ketton-Cremer, *Norfolk Assembly*, 1957, pp. 131–50; *Norfolk in the Civil War*, pp. 331–43.

[71] *The Hamilton Papers . . . 1638–1650*, ed. Samuel R. Gardiner, Camden New Ser. xxvii, 1880, p. 171. BL TT, E. 781 (11): *Perfect Diurnall*, no. 52 (2–9 Dec. 1650). *Thurloe Papers*, iii. 122, 212–13. See also Underdown, *Royalist Conspiracy*, pp. 43–5, 142–4, 151.

[72] *The Diary of Ralph Josselin 1616–1683*, ed. Alan Macfarlane, Records of Social and Economic History, New Ser. iii, 1976, p. 58.

benefit to the county, being only kept and attended by some few pedlars and idle persons', and provoked 'great disorders of quarrelling and drunkenness'.[73]

In spite of official disapproval, now increased by the political fears of successive regimes at Westminster, festive customs survived or recovered in many parts of England. They held up well in arable Oxfordshire: in 1652 Robin Hood games were still being held at Enstone, and Anthony Wood went to Shabbington wake accompanied by a 'mimic and buffoon'; two years later he and a group of Oxford companions disguised themselves as 'country fiddlers' and played at fairs and dances at Kidlington and other villages. There were still lords of misrule in Shropshire and the ancient 'horn dance' at Abbots Bromley was still performed under the Commonwealth.[74] The Sussex JPs had renewed prohibitions against church ales in 1645, following Parliament's strict sabbath-observance ordinance, but in 1652 they had to intervene to stop an ale from being held at Hurstmonceaux.[75] In 1655 the Warwickshire justices were still trying to suppress 'unlawful meetings of idle and vain persons' at Henley-in-Arden 'for erecting of maypoles and may-bushes and for using of morris dances and other heathenish and unlawful customs'.[76] The limited effectiveness of the campaign for godly order is as obvious in the 1650s as in earlier times.

*

In the western counties similar signs of cultural survival can be detected. Christmas was being celebrated most freely, John Taylor thought in 1652, by the 'country farmers' of Devon and Cornwall.[77] Ancient customs retained their vitality in the conservative areas—the downlands, Blackmore Vale, south and west Somerset—where they had been most resilient before 1640. And they were accompanied in the same areas by unmistakable signs of royalist feeling. The reformers struggled hard against the tide of resistance and indifference. By 1655 intruded ministers had been able to establish restricted congregations of the elect in several Wiltshire parishes previously noted for religious and cultural conservatism—at the Donheads and Newton Toney, for example—as well as in other downland parishes such as Aldbourne and Barford, and in episcopal Salisbury.

---

[73] *Essex Quarter Sessions Order Book 1652–1661*, ed. D. H. Allen, Essex RO Publications, lxvi, Chelmsford, 1974, pp. 103–4.

[74] Katherine M. Briggs, *The Folklore of the Cotswolds*, 1974, p. 35. *Wood's Life and Times*, i. 175, 189–90. Chambers, *Mediaeval Stage*, i. 173, n.

[75] *Quarter Sessions Order Book, 1642–1649*, ed. B. C. Redwood, Sussex RS liv, 1954, p. 76. Fletcher *A County Community*, p. 114.

[76] *Warwick County Records*, iii. 271. There may have been similar festivities at Solihull in 1650: Ibid. p. 2.

[77] BL TT, E. 1244 (2): [Taylor], *Christmas In and Out*, p. 15.

Still, this accounts for only a tiny fraction of downland parishes, and as Peter Ince complained, most livings had much less militant occupants, with the rest of the population sunk in ignorance and apathy.[78] Efforts to transform old hotbeds of prelacy and royalism met stubborn resistance. The minister placed at Shaftesbury by the County Committee encountered organized refusal of tithes, while at Blandford, the scene of repeated earlier disorders, there had to be regular round-ups of suspected persons. In January 1650 several Blandford men were arrested for proclaiming Charles II, and in 1653 the town was one of the few places in which a minor royalist plot found much support.[79]

As the 1655 rebellion shows, localist royalism remained deeply rooted in the downlands. The absence of Quarter Sessions records for Interregnum Dorset makes it more difficult to assess the survival of other aspects of traditional society in that county. A few scraps of evidence suggest the continuation of many old traditions. Woodbury Hill Fair was still an annual occasion for merry-making as well as trade: even the Puritan magistrates of Dorchester postponed an official Day of Thanksgiving because it fell 'on Woodbury Fair Eve, at which time most of the town will be from home'. The burgesses of Shaftesbury made their annual Holy Cross Day processions to the springs at Enmore Green well into the 1650s, though how much of the old ceremonial was retained is not clear. On this as on much else the Dorset records are tantalizingly silent.[80]

Arable Wiltshire provides somewhat more information, but only for a few places. The Easter cock-shies at Winterslow survived at least until the end of the civil war, and at Everleigh 'the riotous custom of Christmas ales', as a disapproving rector described it, was still demanded by 'the ruder sort of the parish' throughout the Interregnum.[81] The Vale of Pewsey also seems to have contained a lively festive life. In 1652 a churchwarden at Marden complained about the many 'blind' alehouses open for business on Sundays, the filling of barrels 'under the name of church ales', and the 'warming of houses . . . under the pretence of brewing for Tann Hill Fair'. In the previous year the ale had been sold for at least a month before and after the great midsummer fair on the downs above Devizes, and members of the middling sort as well as the poor were involved: the ale had been 'not sold only by poor people but by those which have good livings and copyholds'. At Woodborough in the same year, a 'lewd company' from neighbouring villages collected and marched in a raucous procession behind a drummer and a fiddler to Pewsey, where they 'very disorderly danced the morris-dance . . . drinking and tippling in

[78] *Desiderata Curiosa*, ii. 492–4.
[79] *Dorset Minute Books*, pp. 80, 169, 384, 412, 448–9, 475–6, 489. Whitelocke, *Memorials*, iii. 138. CCC i. 650. For the Phelips plot see Underdown, *Royalist Conspiracy*, pp. 67–70.
[80] *Dorchester Records*, p. 618. *Shaftesbury Records*, pp. 31–2.
[81] Symonds, 'Winterslow Church Reckonings', p. 43. Whitlock, *Folklore of Wilts.*, p. 76.

the inn and alehouse till many of them were drunk'.[82] Cultural traditions were still strong in this region on the edge of the Wiltshire downs.

In Somerset there is more plentiful evidence of popular resistance to reformation, and as in earlier years, much of it comes from the south and west of the county. There was drinking, dancing, and 'what not' until a late hour at Queen Camel fair in 1647, Sir Humphrey Mildmay records; Edward Curll thought that God was 'much dishonoured' by the excessive drinking in that village.[83] Defiance of official austerity was still sometimes encouraged by parish notables. At Alhampton, near Bruton, in Whitsun week 1653, the tithingman invited people to come 'to make merry with skimmington', promised to provide the beer, and assured them (incorrectly, of course), that the JPs approved of it.[84] In the same summer the tithingman and one of the churchwardens of Holwell, a detached Somerset parish in Blackmore Vale, organized a riotous revel when ordered to attach the goods of an offender. Instead of seizing the goods they put the man in the stocks, it was reported, and played skittles there, 'with great rejoicing and feasting, especially by the said warden and tithingman . . . many people being gathered together of purpose to be merry'. That it was a public Fast Day troubled them not at all, one of them remarking, 'the devil take all the Pope's fasting'.[85]

The JPs made their usual ineffective gestures. In October 1649 they noted 'the great confluence of people of all sorts frequenting meetings in this county commonly called revels or wakes' and the 'general mutinies and contentions' often ensuing, issuing yet another prohibition.[86] But May games and revels continued, especially in the southern and western parishes. At Hillfarrance in May 1650 a brawl erupted at a 'cudgel playing', one of the culprits being a man of some status, a clothier with a reputation for haunting alehouses and frequently disturbing the peace. In 1653 two Charlton Mackrell blacksmiths and a soldier got into a fight on the 'wonted revel or wake day' at Kingweston, the phrase implying that the revel was still an annual event. Two years later an Ashill woman confessed that her pregnancy was the result of an indiscretion after the revel feast at Staple Fitzpaine. And even at the height of the Major-Generals' campaign of reformation in July 1656, a large crowd attended a bull-baiting at Stoke Trister, near Wincanton, and defied orders to disperse.[87]

---

[82] *Records of Wilts.*, pp. 221–2. The village involved in the former incident is identifiable as Marden by the name of the churchwarden, William Holloway, who had also been appointed tithingman in 1644: WRO QS Order Book, 1641–54, Easter 1644.

[83] Ralph, *Mildmay*, p. 139. SRO QS 164, Petition of E. Curll.

[84] SRO CQ 3/1/86 (2) (Sessions Rolls, 1653), fo. 154.

[85] Ibid. fo. 155.

[86] *SQSR* iii. 102.

[87] SRO CQ 3/1/82 (2) (Sessions Rolls, 1650), no. 20. SQSR iii, intro., pp. xxxv–xxvi, and pp. 295, 303–4.

A striking incident of this kind is recorded in the west of the county, at Langford Budville. The revel was still being held there in 1650, in spite of a JP's specific order to the contrary, and it led to serious disorder. As was the custom, the tithingman blamed it all on outsiders. He went to the green with the JP's warrant, he deposed, and found about twenty men from nearby Wellington engaged in cudgel play. When told to disperse one of them shouted, 'we will keep revel in despite of all such tithing calves as thou art, and they were but fools or rogues that have given any order to the contrary', and another that 'they came to fight and fight they would before they went'. Fight they did: the forces of order were badly mauled in the affray that followed.[88] The affair has several interesting aspects. First, even if the Wellington men's guilt was exaggerated by a tithingman anxious to protect his neighbours, it is still clear that their presence was a major cause of the trouble—even as Puritan a town as Wellington still contained people attracted to revelling and violence. But Langford Budville was also a divided community. The tithingman and his assistants tried feebly to suppress the revel, and at about the same time some other village notables petitioned against an unlicensed alehouse kept by a recent arrival from Milverton, who had repeatedly boasted that he would stay open 'in despite of the officers and all opponents'. During the revel week ('an unsavoury term', the petitioners admitted), there had been 'fiddling and dancing and a great rout of people unlawfully assembled' and much ale sold. But although some were trying to put down the festive culture, other influential people at Langford Budville were still protecting or participating in it. Only in 1652 does the 'tray or vessel to brew withal', the tell-tale sign of the holding of church ales, disappear from the churchwardens' inventories.[89]

Cases of this kind, which appear in the record only because there was an unusual amount of disorder, because there were particularly vigilant local officials, or because somebody happened to get pregnant, may well be the tip of a much larger iceberg. These were the most socially and politically conservative parts of the county, where popular rituals had flourished before the war and where the forces of reformation had encountered most resistance. They were, too, the royalist parts of the county, where reformation was likely to be resisted for political as well as cultural reasons. Once again the limits of Puritan rule are apparent.

*

Festive survival in places such as Langford Budville is to be expected. More surprising are the signs of a revival of popular sports and festivities

[88] SRO CQ 3/1/82 (2) (Sessions Rolls, 1650), no. 16. See also *SQSR* iii, intro., pp. xlix–l.
[89] SRO QS 164, Petitions L, Langford Budville petition [1650?]. McDermott, 'Church House at Langford Budville', p. 130.

in a region where they had earlier been successfully restrained: the northern clothing districts. Between 1646 and 1660, indeed, festive disorder by the ungodly is more frequently reported in this area than in the conservative downlands, though not more so than in royalist south and west Somerset. This conclusion may of course be an optical illusion caused by the accidents of record survival. It may also result from the greater likelihood of prosecution in this region for matters which in downland villages would have been tolerated by parish officers. But even allowing for these possibilities, the resurgence of festive disorder in the clothing parishes still deserves to be considered.

Some of the outbreaks were deliberately fostered by local Royalists. This was certainly the case with a series of bull-baitings near Bath in the spring of 1648. Prynne, who was Recorder of the city, tried to arrest the minister of St. James's church, who had been openly using Common Prayer and preaching against the Parliament. Prynne was resisted by a large crowd, some armed with swords, led by a royalist officer named Henry Chapman. Royalist gentry had recently been congregating in the town, it was said, 'many malignants and Cavaliers resorting thither from divers parts, under colour of the bath'. However, Chapman's friends also obtained support from the common people by holding weekly bull-baitings outside the walls, often preceded by noisy processions, 'to which', a report to Parliament stated, 'disaffected people flocked from the adjoining counties'. The episode clearly shows that a segment of the population of the clothing parishes still welcomed bull-baitings and festive processions.[90]

Other rebellious outbreaks in this area after the civil war were also politically inspired, like the riots against the excise—though in some of these too there may have been festive elements. In the 1650s sporting functions were often used as pretexts for assembling the disaffected. In February 1655, for example, royalist plotters, some from as far away as the Poldens, gathered at the house of a sequestered minister near Frome for a 'cock-sparring', which suggests that the sport was still sufficiently common to serve as an innocent cover for a seditious meeting. At Monkton Farleigh, not far away across the Wiltshire border, cock-fighting was certainly continuing at about this time.[91]

Not all the festive outbreaks of the 1650s had explicitly royalist connotations: bull-baiting at Bleadon, at the western tip of the Mendips, or a skimmington at Leigh-on-Mendip in 1655, for instance.[92] The former village lies outside the clothing region, the latter close to its southern edge. But other incidents took place in the very heart of the Puritan area.

[90] BL TT, E. 441 (22): *Perfect Weekly Account*, no. 9 (3–10 May 1648).
[91] *Thurloe Papers*, iii. 181–2. *VCH, Wilts.*, vii. 66.
[92] *SQSR* iii, 350.

In 1656 at Pensford fair the petty constable was 'much ill-treated' by revellers at the inn and in the village street. At Timsbury revel a load of beer was brought from Bristol and 'a great concourse of people' including many from other villages, assembled to watch a cudgel match, at which, the tithingman lamented, many 'disorders and abuses' were committed. Prohibitions against Christmas merry-making were also being ignored. Near Frome, in the lawless tithings of East and West Woodlands, a group of revellers celebrated Christmas in 1657 in the old-fashioned way, with 'drinking, playing cards, and fiddling all day in disguised habits'.[93]

We should not, of course, make too much of these incidents. Other festive outbreaks may have gone unreported, but as in the years before 1640 it seems unlikely that there can have been very many in a region where virtually every parish contained a sufficient sprinkling of the godly for a fuss to be made when the law was broken. Illicit merry-making is more likely to have gone undetected—and the invisible part of the iceberg to be bigger—in more permissive areas such as the downlands and Blackmore Vale. But even if these were the only episodes of this nature in the clothing parishes, they still require explanation. There had always been, to be sure, some survival of festive culture in the region. Puritan reformers had succeeded in disciplining or converting some of their poorer neighbours, but they had never been able to impose absolute control over all of them. But before 1640 the Puritans stood for local liberties against the external forces threatening their communities: against Laudian innovations, against Ship Money and military exactions, against the intrusive policies of an allegedly popish Court. By the 1650s, on the other hand, they themselves were tarred with the brush of centralization, blamed for oppressive assessments, excise, and military rule, especially during the years of the Major-Generals.

It may be, then, that political disillusionment reduced both the numbers and the enthusiasm of the moral reformers, and undermined the acquiescence of the lower orders on which their rule depended.[94] The splintering of parish unity and the divisions that followed the rise of the sects contributed to the breakdown of Puritan discipline. But the turning of the community spirit into anti-Puritan channels was at least as important. These were, to be sure, places very different in character from the downland and more traditional pasture villages. But they were communities none the less. The cultural alienation in which they shared, and the half-submerged, vague, but unmistakably royalist vocabulary in which

[93] *SQSR* iii. 285, 302, 324.
[94] The sense of disillusion is apparent in the behaviour of many members of the élite. Alexander Popham, for example, a committed radical in the 1640s, was in contact with the Royalists long before 1660: Underdown, *Somerset*, pp. 164, 177, 185, 190, 192.

it was coming to be expressed, explain much of the popular rejoicing at the Restoration.

*

Cultural conflict is, then, the thread that links early Stuart popular politics with its Interregnum counterpart, and ultimately with the Restoration. Throughout the period political attitudes could be deduced from external symbols, from fashions of dress and hair styles. Not all Cavaliers emulated the flowing locks of a Prince Rupert, not all Roundheads cut theirs close above the ears. But enough did for eyebrows to be raised if the stereotypes did not fit. When we encounter a Nantwich bricklayer asking why the parliamentarian Earl of Denbigh 'gave offence to good men' by wearing his hair long, we may not be surprised to find that many people also had doubts about Denbigh's political reliability.[95] As Lord Conway reflected in 1650, 'We ought to be very circumspect, for we live in an age where one's looks may make him a traitor'. The Herefordshire committee-man Herbert Perrott appealed to a drinking companion to know 'if he looked like a Roundhead', and then answered his own question: 'God's wounds, I . . . never was, neither ever will be one'. The term was beginning to mean something more than just a supporter of Parliament (which Perrott certainly was), and to signify the stereotypical Puritan bigot, the obsessive moral reformer at odds with his neighbours.[96]

The link between royalism and drinking or other kinds of loose living was always a parliamentarian commonplace. 'Men devoted to sensuality, strong in wine, weak in wisdom, minding more their lusts than their labour, their honour than their honesty': so the well-affected of Devon described the crypto-Royalists returned in the Cornish elections in 1647.[97] The disputes at Hereford in which Perrott was involved began when an officer of the garrison tried to arrest Sir Henry Lingen, a prominent local Royalist, and well illustrate the convergence of cultural and political elements in the rival stereotypes. Roundheads noted the 'admired jollity, and frequent drunken meetings' of cavalier gentlemen like Lingen—their encouragement of resistance to Parliament by the use of hospitality and feasting. On the other side, Lingen's friends denounced the interference with cherished customs typical of Roundheads like the captain of the watch, a 'busy, troublesome, saucy fellow'. Isaac Bromwich, another friend of Lingen on the Committee, was confident that the 'Country' was solidly against the reforming soldiers: 'I have power to raise

[95] BL TT, E. 6 (25): *Mercurius Aulicus*, no. 30 (21–7 July 1644). Denbigh's chaplain assured the bricklayer that there was nothing in the scriptures against long hair, provided that it was a wig.
[96] BL Loan 29/74 (Harley papers), Lord Conway to E. Harley, 3 Sept. 1650. *Military Memoir of Colonel John Birch*, ed. J. and T. W. Webb, Camden New Ser., vii, 1873, p. 142.
[97] *Historical Collections*, ed. Rushworth, vii. 743.

the sheriffs, constables, churchwardens, and other officers . . . to beat you all out of the Country'.[98]

Supporters of Parliament were supposed to be people of absolute moral rectitude; if they were not, their loyalty was automatically in question. John Sheppard of Kilton in west Somerset was regarded as subversive because he allowed drinking and card-playing in his house on the sabbath, rarely attended church, but spent Sunday afternoons gambling and corrupting youths by supplying them with 'bowls, balls, or cudgels'. When nominally in the service of Parliament, his neighbours reported, he had spent a whole summer 'in the furze, living upon robbery and theft'.[99] Local officials were often under fire if they failed to enforce proper standards of behaviour. Residents of West Monkton got their constable and tithingman removed for disaffection to the Protectorate that was proved by their 'countenancing drunkenness, multiplicity of alehouses and profanation of the Sabbath'. At Staplegrove William Pomeroy was appointed registrar by a small group, 'without the approbation' of the rest of the parish, but his opponents got him dismissed as 'a most desperate malignant, a common drunkard, and a man of a most lewd life'. Political and moral rectitude, it was assumed, went together.[100]

Some of these charges, like the frequent accusations of immorality levelled at the royalist clergy, were doubtless exaggerated or invented. But people on both sides shared the same assumptions about the relationship between politics and culture. Festive rituals were often symbolic expressions of opposition to government, as at Oxford on May Day 1648, when soldiers confiscated the garlands and fiddles, or at Bury St. Edmunds in the same year when a maypole was erected. In 1653 the expulsion of the Rump was celebrated at Wolverhampton with another maypole.[101] The licensing laws had obvious political implications. When a Lancashire constable asked some nocturnal carousers if they knew what the laws were, one of them replied that 'he now knew not, they were new model-lised and Cromwellised'.[102] At Stoke St. Mary, Somerset, in 1650, William Mansfield was refused a drink by a woman, she 'knowing him to be a lewd fellow'. Mansfield forced his way into the house, smashed a pot with a billhook and said that 'in like manner he hoped to cut down the Roundhead rogues', making the direct connection between politics and

[98] *Military Memoir of Col. Birch*, pp. 140–3. The document is obviously from Birch or one of his supporters, not (as suggested by the editors) from the Harley-dominated County Committee. For further evidence of the assumed connection between roistering and royalism see the narrative of events at Hereford in 1646 in BL Harleian MS 7189, fo. 248.

[99] *CSPD, 1648–9*, pp. 31–2. *CCC* i. 83. See also Underdown, 'Problem of Popular Allegiance', p. 90.

[100] *SQSR* iii. 239, 271.

[101] Thomas E. Reinhart, 'The Parliamentary Visitation of Oxford University, 1647–50', Ph.D. thesis, Brown University, 1984, p. 441. Hill, *Society and Puritanism*, p. 186.

[102] Wrightson, 'Two Concepts of Order', p. 30.

Puritan repression. Soldiers away from their units were especially tempting targets for insult and provocation. The trouble at Kingweston revel in 1653 was started by efforts to make an unwilling trooper drink the Queen's health.[103]

A large part of the history of the Interregnum lies in the growing identification of the royal cause with freedom from divisive reformers. Older symbols of popular freedom still surfaced occasionally. A reveller at Whitestaunton in 1659 assaulted one of the watchmen and identified himself as Robin Hood before he was taken, still struggling, to the tithingman.[104] But as the 1650s wore on, the exiled Charles II became an evocative symbol for a whole constellation of political, social, and cultural aspirations. It is entirely appropriate that many of the reported expressions of popular royalism should have occurred when tongues had been loosened in taverns. Two days before Christmas 1656 William Higgory led the singing in the Black Boy at Ashcott:[105]

> Let us drink, let us sing
> Here's a health to our King,
> And 'twill never be well
> Till we have one again.

In 1647 the Dorset Committee had noted how countrymen restive at the excise had 'hopes of a better day suddenly', and were attending suspicious football and cudgel matches.[106] Professor Holmes recounts a significant incident in Lincolnshire in 1657. A man took a garland from some children and crowned his companion with it, saying 'he would put him into the power of princely government . . . and desired he would please to take off taxes and excise and other oppressions from the nation'.[107] Here again is the spirit that animated much of the popular politics of the 1650s—the belief that a return to the old order would bring relief from the fiscal and cultural oppressions of the centralizing Puritan state. Only monarchy, it seemed, would guarantee the survival of local liberties and customs, would restore the traditional order of community and good neighbourhood. It was a myth, but it was a powerful one.

---

[103] SRO CQ 3/1/82 (2) (Sessions Rolls, 1650), no. 91. *SQSR* iii. intro., pp. xxxv–xxxvi.
[104] *SQSR* iii. 370.
[105] Ibid. 347. This volume contains many similar instances of 'royalist' outbursts: see, for example, intro., pp. xxxii–xxxviii, and pp. 299, 370–1.
[106] Bayley, *Dorset*, pp. 349–50.
[107] Holmes, *Lincolnshire*, p. 219.

10

The Restoration and English Political Culture

THROUGHOUT the kingdom the proclamation of Charles II was accompanied by jubilant celebrations. Nowhere were the festivities of May 1660 more noisy, or more appropriate, than at Sherborne, the most solidly royalist of all west-country towns. The cross of St. George floated from the abbey tower, for two days the conduit ran with claret, and hogsheads of beer and baskets of white loaves were set out for the poor. George Digby, the Earl of Bristol's son, was followed in tumultuous procession by an array of Dorset gentlemen, their neighbours, and dependents. As they rode through the flower-bedecked streets, old Sir John Strangways was especially loud in his commendations of the cheering townspeople: they had been among the first to take arms for King Charles I, and he now rejoiced to see 'how studious they were to transcend all other places' in welcoming the return of his son. A hundred maids in white marched behind their own drummer; there were 'consorts of music', trumpet fanfares, and volleys of shot. The celebrations reached a fitting climax in an evening of street theatre when some 'witty wags' of the town held a mock High Court of Justice at which effigies of Bradshaw and Cromwell were tried, the crowd's menacing chant of 'Justice! Justice!' recalling the shouts of the soldiers against Charles I in Westminster Hall eleven years before. The 'regicides' were then dragged through the town, hacked to pieces, and burned on a bonfire along with the arms of the Commonwealth. Other great bonfires blazed in the streets and on the surrounding hills.[1]

The wild scenes at Sherborne were paralleled by similar rejoicings up and down the land. They had begun, by happy coincidence, on May Day, when both houses of Parliament had voted 'that, according to the ancient and fundamental laws of this kingdom, the government is, and ought to be, by King, Lords, and Commons'. On the 3rd, when news of this vote reached Somerset, 142 bonfires were counted, blazing within sight of Hinton St. George.[2] The messages conveyed by these rituals, at

[1] BL TT, E. 183 (17): *Mercurius Publicus*, no. 21 (17–24 May 1660). A. M. Broadley, 'The Proclaiming of Charles II at Sherborne', *SDNQ* xiii (1912–13), 179–81.
[2] Davies, *Restoration*, p. 342. Underdown, *Somerset*, p. 193.

Sherborne as elsewhere, were clear enough. The King's return symbolized the recovery of civic harmony and order after twenty years of conflict and confusion, and the restoration of the natural social hierarchy, with the Digbys, Strangways, and all their counterparts in other counties, at its head. But the gentry's relationship with the people was reciprocal: the townsfolk applauded Strangways, but he also applauded (and thus courted) them. The fountains running with wine, the cakes and ale, proclaimed the return of the old customs of hospitality and good neighbourhood; the processional pageantry, the flags, drums, and trumpets, were affirmations of a sense of community that Puritan reformers had tried vainly to suppress. By the execution of Charles I the world had been turned upside-down; by the symbolic (and later, in London, the actual) execution of the regicides it was agreeably turned right-side-up again.

*

We should not exaggerate either the unanimity or the spontaneity of the celebrations. Many a genteel fellow-traveller who had only recently climbed aboard the royalist bandwagon would doubtless have been willing to desert Charles II if ever the times did alter. Both they and people with cavalier credentials of longer standing had good reasons for encouraging their inferiors to put on a show of loyal enthusiasm. And the kingdom's divisions still smouldered not far below the surface. The 'fanatics'—the sectaries and republicans—who were only biding their time and awaiting better days, might be only a small remnant. But many more moderate Puritans who accepted the Restoration were uneasy about it, fearing as did the Warwickshire Presbyterian Thomas Hall, that it was opening the door to 'all licentious practices'. At Lyme Regis the mayor thought it necessary to make special efforts to disperse 'those clouds of fears and doubtings, which perhaps do sadden the spirits of many good people'.[3] It would be absurd to expect the ferment of the Interregnum years to disappear in a mist of boozy conviviality, leaving behind no trace of the aspirations for many different kinds of liberty that had been widely canvassed in two decades of turbulent debate.

Yet neither should we underestimate the sincerity of the popular rejoicing, which surely represented the true, if transitory, feelings of all but the small republican minority. Ever since December 1659, when the Army's attempt to govern by the sword foundered on the soldiers' disunity, the demonstrations that greeted each milestone on the road to returning normality had been enthusiastic and spontaneous. When troops were moved into London early in December they encountered hostile

[3] BL TT, E. 1035 (2): Hall, *Funebria Florae*, 1660, p. 4; E. 1919 (2): Ames Short, *God Save the King. Or, A Sermon preached at Lyme-Regis May 18. 1660*, 1660, Prefatory Letter.

crowds, among whom apprentices threw 'stones, tiles, turnips . . . and rubbish' and kicked footballs among them. Derisive chants of 'A cobbler! A cobbler!' greeted their commander, the erstwhile shoemaker, Col. Hewson. When, soon afterwards, the Committee of Safety collapsed, there were bells and bonfires at Bath, Taunton, and many other places, though not because the old Rumpers who now returned to power were any less unpopular than the soldiers. In February there were shouts of 'Pull out the Rump!' by rioting apprentices at Bristol, while in London Monck's decision to defend the liberties of the City produced a massive eruption of bells, bonfires, and the ceremonial roasting of rumps in the streets. The return of the secluded members to the Commons on 21 February touched off similarly riotous rejoicings.[4]

The ecstatic scenes that marked the King's proclamation, landing at Dover, and triumphant progress to London on 29 May, his birthday, resembled a protracted May-Day celebration. As Charles passed over Blackheath on his way to the capital, country people entertained the cavalcade with long-forbidden morris dances.[5] Though few places could rival Sherborne in the quality of their festivities, they had their counterparts in every town and village. Those at the small Gloucestershire clothing town of Dursley were typical of many, with the usual floral decorations, hogsheads of beer, parades of volunteers, trumpets, and volleys of shot. A royalist cleric threw dozens of spiced loaves to the people from the top of the Market House, 'as an omen of future plenty and prosperity', and the day closed with a bonfire, 'much hindered by the wind', alas, but eventually visible from at least six counties. The next day a crowd of young women took over the place of celebration and spent the day dancing, ordering that 'whosoever should detain either daughter or maid-servant from their solemnity' should be fined a shilling. They then chose a 'captain' and marched in procession, carrying beech boughs, to the top of Stinchcombe Hill, where they drank healths on their knees to the King.[6]

The Restoration had its darker side—the epidemic of mob violence against the Quakers, incidents like the destruction of Kiffin's Baptist meeting-house in London by 'the looser sort of people'—and not all the royalist preachers heeded official calls for tolerance and reconciliation. At East Coker, for example, William Walwyn (not to be confused with his more celebrated Leveller namesake), linked Jesuits, Anabaptists, and Presbyterians as authors of similar doctrines of disobedience, and in

---

[4] Davies, *Restoration*, pp. 181–2, 258, 271, 283–4, 290. Underdown, *Somerset*, pp. 191–2. Bryant, *Pepys*, p. 65.
[5] 'England's Joy, or a Relation of the Most Remarkable passages, from his Majesty's Arrival at Dover, to His entrance at Whitehall' (1660), in *Stuart Tracts*, p. 428. See also Davies, *Restoration*, pp. 342–6, 351–4.
[6] BL TT, E. 183 (21): *Mercurius Publicus*, no. 22 (24–31 May 1660).

effect blamed all Parliamentarians, radical and moderate alike, for th
execution of the King and the recent confusions.[7] In the Dursley cel
ebrations, however, we see a more fitting, and perhaps more common
spirit of national reunion.

Not that the May 1660 rituals were everywhere as unrestrained. At ol
Puritan strongholds such as Lyme and Dorchester the bells were rung
salutes were fired, and young people paraded with banners; but there ar
no reports of fountains running with wine or of other kinds of merry
making. The Dorchester Company of Freemen distributed £2 among th
poor of the town, but they did not provide the free beer that was commo
in other places. Preachers such as Ames Short at Lyme Regis and Gilber
Ironside at the county proclamation ceremony at Dorchester were par
ticularly severe in denouncing the excessive drinking bouts that th
Restoration was provoking.[8] Official celebrations in these places wer
sober and austere, and the rhetoric correspondingly restrained. At th
Dorchester borough proclamation the Town Clerk uttered the conven
tional platitudes about the King's return rescuing them from 'a world o
confusions' and 'unheard of governments', and ended with a prayer tha
his throne might be 'established in righteousness, with peace from th
Lord for ever'. At the subsequent county proclamation Ironside took a
his text the verse from Psalm 85 warning the people not to 'turn again t
folly', identifying as equally serious follies both loose living and sensualit
and the political and religious radicalism of the past twenty years.[9] Th
preachers' denunciations of the drinking of healths suggests that popula
merry-making may have been more widespread even in Puritan town
than the official celebrations allowed for; but it was certainly no
encouraged.

How far things got out of hand at Lyme and Dorchester is not clear; i
other places Puritan authorities were certainly powerless to stem th
festive tide. 'The reins of liberty and licentiousness are let loose',
Newcastle Puritan groaned: 'May-poles and players, and jugglers ... now
pass current'. Maypoles, automatic symbols of release from godly
reformation, were everywhere reappearing, provoking numerou
renewed conflicts between roisterers and moral reformers. In London th
Lord Mayor had one removed when it was set up by 'the rabble' i
Cheapside, but at Deal soldiers in the garrison did not interfere whe
maypoles promptly came out of hiding on May Day. At Oxford th

---

[7] BL TT, E. 183 (12): *Parliamentary Intelligencer*, no. 19 (30 Apr.–7 May 1660); E. 1033 (10)
William Walwyn, *God Save the King, or a Sermon of Thanksgiving ... May* 14, 1660, 1660, pp. 6–11.

[8] BL TT, E. 1919 (2): Short, *God Save the King*, pp. 70–2; E. 1034 (15): Gilbert Ironsyde, *A Sermo
Preached at Dorchester ... at the proclaiming of his Sacred Majesty Charles the II. May* 15. 1660, 1660, pp
29–30. DRO B2/14/1 (Dorchester Company of Freemen, Receivers' Book, 1652–1716), 1660.

[9] BL TT, E. 183 (15): *Mercurius Publicus*, no. 20 (10–17 May 1660); E. 1034 (15): Ironsyde, *Sermo
at Dorchester*, pp. 23–7.

Vice-Chancellor tried to have one of the 'heathenish' symbols cut down, but the mob successfully defied him and by the end of May there were a dozen in the town.[10] There must have been many altercations like the one at King's Norton that Thomas Hall reports. When he resisted the erection of two of the hateful 'ensigns of profaneness' Hall was loudly denounced as 'little better than a Quaker, a preacher of false doctrine, and an enemy to the King'. The parish clerk at Myddle, Shropshire, told revellers that 'it was as great a sin to set up a maypole as it was to cut off the King's head'—words that led to his being fined and dismissed from office.[11] Similar disputes erupted in west-country villages. At Steeple Ashton in the Wiltshire cheese country the godly complained of disorders caused by 'the setting up of summer houses' (arbours for drinking and dancing), while at Ramsbury an officious constable who removed the maypole was told by a villager 'that if he did not set up the pole again he would make him rue it', and received many other 'ill words'.[12]

*

Such disputes were nearly always resolved, sooner or later, in favour of the revellers. But the Restoration was a victory not only for adherents of traditional festive culture, but also of one conception of the social order over another. The civil war was a struggle over something more than the location of political authority, the relative powers of King and Parliament: it was a conflict about the moral basis of English society. Behind the symbolic disputes over maypoles and revel feasts lay contrasting assumptions and aspirations about the nature of the kingdom and the community. Adherents of one set of beliefs stressed the values of good neighbourhood and co-operation; adherents of the other, those of individual piety and sobriety, and the duty of the godly to reform their less enlightened neighbours.

The two polarities had, as we have seen, both social and geographical dimensions. Long before the civil war, especially in towns and pasture regions where clothworking or other industrial pursuits were available, the growing gulf between the people 'of credit and reputation' and their less prosperous neighbours was reflected in the emergence of parish élites who saw it as their duty to discipline the poor into godliness and industriousness, and who found in Puritan teaching (broadly defined) their guide and inspiration. Along with reformist elements of the gentry and clergy, they mounted a campaign against the traditional culture of the

[10] *The Lord's Call to England* (1660), quoted in Hazlitt, *Faiths and Folklore*, ii. 405. BL TT, E. 1035 (2): Hall, *Funebria Florae*, p. 5. *Diary of Samuel Pepys*, ed. Robert Latham and William Matthews, Berkeley, 1970–80, i. 121. *Wood's Life and Times*, i. 314, 317. See also Davies, *Restoration*, p. 345 and n.
[11] BL TT, E. 1035 (2): Hall, *Funebria Florae*, pp. 5, 38. Gough, *Myddle*, pp. 44–5.
[12] WRO QS Order Book, 1654–68, p. 176; QS Rolls, Michaelmas 1660, Examination of John Heath, 17 May 1660.

lower orders—against alehouses, popular sports, and festivals, and all the other disorderly customs of the irreligious poor. The Puritan 'middling sort' provided much of both the popular support and the manpower which enabled Parliament to win the civil war. In the three south-western counties their strength, as we have repeatedly observed, was greatest in the clothing districts of north Somerset and Wiltshire and in towns like Dorchester and Taunton.

But the process of social and cultural differentiation had not occurred at a uniform pace across the country. In rural areas less subject to population pressure and land shortage, both a more paternalist form of society and older habits of good neighbourhood had survived. The Wiltshire and Dorset downlands, Blackmore Vale and pastoral south-east Somerset remained more attached to traditional forms, were less culturally divided and more likely to resist both Puritan and parliamentarian discipline. Many towns in and on the fringes of these 'traditional' areas—places like Sherborne, Bruton, Shaftesbury, and Blandford—had similar characteristics. In such places members of the middling sort were more likely to share with their poorer neighbours important elements of common local culture, to tolerate and on occasions join in, the community's sports and merry-makings.

Many places were divided over issues of moral reformation. Cultural conflict became merged with national politics when the reformers found themselves at odds with the government of the kingdom. After the proclamation of the first Book of Sports in 1618, and more clearly after Charles I's accession, both Court and ecclesiastical hierarchies combined in a counter-offensive on behalf of the older culture, rightly seeing the notions of deference, harmony, and social conservatism it expressed as being more supportive of monarchical and episcopal order than the divisive individualism of their enemies. Laudian ritualism and protection of rural sports and revels infuriated sabbatarian reformers, further inflamed already existing suspicions of a covert Catholic conspiracy, and combined with other grievances to produce the explosion of 1642.

Defence of church ales and rural festivals was not enough to counteract the unpopularity of Ship Money, militia grievances and other oppressions which united gentry, middling sort, and lower orders against the Court. But when civil war came, the distribution of support for the two sides in the western counties shows how strongly Church and King were associated with the old festive culture. Once the war began there was little popular enthusiasm for Parliament outside the towns and the clothing districts; nor in many places for the King either, for localist neutralism was always more pervasive than either cavalier or roundhead zeal. Yet even neutrals can have preferences, as the Clubmen show: those from the downlands and Blackmore Vale in the end took the side more likely to preserve their religious and community traditions. By the end of the war Parliament was as clearly identified with the oppressive forces of centralization as the Court had been in the 1630s. Even the middling sort of the towns and clothing districts, like most of the parliamentarian gentry, began to lose their enthusiasm for the cause, particularly when it lurched into revolution in 1649.

The geographical distribution of allegiance in the civil war confirms that the English people were not simply deferential pawns, doing battle for whichever cause their élite superiors might choose. Deference was, to be sure, an important element in the behaviour of towns and villages subject to a strong aristocratic presence, as at Sherborne and in the Bruton area. It was deeply rooted in the culture of many small downland villages, where resident squires and clerics lived close to their tenants and parishioners. But even in such places élite–plebeian relationships were not totally one-sided: the gentry were as likely to share, or be swept along by, the prevailing mood of their communities, as to impose their authority on an unwilling or apathetic populace. Thomas Bennet of Pythouse may have been exaggerating when he said that he joined the royalist Clubmen because of 'threats from the country people', but it is likely enough that he saw it as his duty to support his neighbours and that like John Somerset at South Brent he shared their sense of outrage at the military oppressions inflicted on them. Later, summoned before Fairfax, Bennet declared that his neighbours 'at his instance' refrained from further resistance to the New Model; again this sounds more like persuasion and a shared perception of the futility of continued conflict than the exercise of tenurial authority.[13] Deference was important in the downlands, but it was not the whole story.

In the pasturelands and clothing parishes of north Somerset and north-west Wiltshire deference has distinctly less explanatory force. Even more than people in other places, the inhabitants of this region had a choice. They could follow Hopton and Dodington into the King's camp, or Hungerford and Popham into the Parliament's. The fact that they opted so heavily for the latter was the result, not of deference, but of the socio-cultural character of their communities. This is not to say that the behaviour of this region can be explained by importing into the period an anachronistic modern conception of class antagonism. There was no 'middle class', no 'working class' in Stuart England, though in every town and village there were people of middle rank, artisans, and labourers. And especially in the towns and clothing districts an early stage of the process out of which the later society of classes was to form can be observed, as the gulf between the respectable and the 'lower sort' widened. The parish élites of clothiers, yeomen and more prosperous husbandmen often

[13] *CCC* ii. 941.

viewed themselves in Calvinist terms—they were the godly, the elect
They played an important part in the campaign for moral reformation an
in advancing the cause of Parliament. They succeeded, temporarily a
least, in conveying some of their urgency for godly discipline to many o
their less affluent neighbours, but the programme was meant to serv
their interests, not those of the poor.

Outside the clothing districts even this primitive kind of class feeling i
absent. In towns such as Sherborne and Bruton and in the surrounding
countryside the middling sort were as likely to be royalist as their counter·
parts in Trowbridge and Chippenham were to be parliamentarian. Even
in the clothing region localism—evident in perceptions of Cavaliers a
outsiders rather than class enemies, and in the reluctance of troops t
serve in distant parts—was usually the strongest motivating force
Localism was common to all regions. But the limited cultural horizons o
many villagers did not mean that broader political divisions had no impac
on their localities, or that their political attitudes were limited to resent·
ment of intruding soldiers and tax-gatherers. The temporary flourishing
of a new vocabulary of abuse—'cavalier rogue', 'roundhead dog' and s
on—shows how far civil war divisions had entered the fabric of village life
Local interests might be paramount, but this did not exclude the possi·
bility that those interests might be better served by the victory of King o
Parliament.

In the end, contrasts in civil war allegiance are best explained as th
product of differences in regional cultures. This hypothesis in effec
assimilates all three of the other explanations we have been considering. I
accepts the primacy of the local community, accepts that popular value
systems were compounds of both specifically local elements and other
common to the wider communities of shire, church, and kingdom. I
suggests that regional cultural variations, including those of politica
culture, were related to different stages of social and economic develop·
ment. This does not imply a reductionist resort to economic determinism
The north Somerset cloth-making region was Puritan and parliamen·
tarian, and Shepton Mallet was a clothing town. But Shepton was als
close to the culturally traditional Bruton area; the social ties resulting
from propinquity help to explain the unusually large royalist presence i
the town and in the surrounding villages.[14] Furthermore, cultural differ·
ences reflected fundamentally divergent beliefs about what a communit
ought to be, beliefs often expressed in ritual or religious forms. In the stil
relatively socially integrated downlands and Blackmore Vale, traditiona

[14] The regional cultural differences are strikingly confirmed by the careful analysis of the geo
graphical distribution of post-Restoration nonconformity in Wiltshire by Donald M. Spaeth
'Parsons and Parishioners: Lay-Clerical Relations and Popular Belief in Wiltshire villages, 1660-
1740', Ph.D. thesis, Brown University, 1985, ch. 5.

notions of the harmonious, co-operative community were still expressed in customs emphasizing the values of neighbourhood and amity. In the clothing districts a more individualistic society, both socially and culturally more polarized, was emerging. The wood-pasture, clothing parishes were still communities, capable of uniting against outsiders, as both the Skimmington riots and the wartime risings of 1642 and 1645 demonstrate. But they allowed more scope for the playing of individual social roles than their downland counterparts: they were stoolball, rather than football communities.

And the cultural conflict had its own dynamic. Villagers might be outraged by the enclosure of their commons, by the imposition of oppressive new taxes. But they might be equally enraged by attempts to prohibit the sports and festivals in which their neighbourly aspirations had been expressed. On the other side, masters and magistrates might wish to ban theatrical performances or convivial revels because they were destructive of the industrious habits required of servants and labourers. But they also did so because popular festivals and the excesses they provoked were in their eyes ungodly, heathenish, and the work of Satan. The cultural conflict impinged on national politics at every stage of the seventeenth-century crisis. Laud and his party saw traditional culture as an essential prop for an ordered, monarchical society, and its Puritan critics as disruptive of that order at the fundamentally important parish level. On the other side we find, of course, the mirror image: Puritan outrage at the manipulative use of revels and rituals to maintain a corrupt episcopal order. The best way to seduce the people into idolatry and superstition, noted the Presbyterian Thomas Hall, was to give them 'feast upon feast (as 'tis in Popery)': 'And this was the practice of the late prelates'.[15]

As in any historical situation, reality was infinitely more complicated than these bald generalizations might imply. The effectiveness of moral reformation in the Puritan parishes, and of resistance to it elsewhere, varied enormously according to local circumstances and personalities: so, consequently, did allegiance in the civil war. Batcombe, after all, is only a few miles from Bruton. In many downland villages by the middle of James I's reign knots of reformers had emerged among the yeomen and husbandmen who were at odds with their neighbours of similar status over such matters as the holding of ales and revels. Again, such variations were likely to affect parish behaviour in the civil war. But these local complications, interesting and important as they may be, should not obscure the broader patterns that are apparent when the regions are viewed from greater distance.

[15] BL TT, E. 1035 (2): Hall, *Funebria Florae*, p. 13.

*

In the long run monarchy was to be little better preservative of the ordered co-operative community and of the rituals in which its values were expressed than the Puritan republic had been. But in 1660 it certainl appeared that the clock had been successfully put back to permit th renewed functioning of an older concept of order. This was strikingly tru at the level of symbol and ritual. We have already noted the immediat reappearance of maypoles at the Restoration, and the festive symbol continued to proliferate in the years that followed. There were two in existence in 1661 at Wells, where they were used for posting libellou verses against local Puritans. In towns across the country other element of the old pageantry were also quickly revived: at Chester, for example where the corporation in 1660 spent £1.16s.0d. for 'making anew th dragon, and for six naked boys to beat at it' in the St. George's Da procession.[16]

Rural wakes and revels, too, enjoyed a notable recovery. Later in th century White Kennett thought that 'by the intermission of them in th late confusions' they had been generally abandoned in 'the east and some western parts' of England, but that they were still common in the north and midlands, and at about the same time Robert Plot could still find many picturesque survivals in both Oxfordshire and Staffordshire.[1] John Aubrey's evidence about Wiltshire customs suggests that there was a strong resurgence of popular festivals in the cheese as well as the chalk country. Aubrey records a good many village feasts in north Wiltshire after 1660: a midsummer revel at Christian Malford; a 'word-ale' around All Saints Day at Midgehall in Lydiard Tregoze; 'Lot-Meads' at Sutton Benger and Wanborough, the latter much frequented by the horse-racing gentry, celebrated with 'great merriment' every year. At Kington Langley the June revel was still 'one of the eminentest feasts in these parts'; at Kington St. Michael the Michaelmas fair was 'much resorted unto by the young people, famous for ale and stubble geese'. Some festivals had been revived, it appears, only in attenuated form. There were no more banquets to accompany the Long Newnton garland ceremony, for instance. The hayward's house, where they had always been held, had been burnt by soldiers during the war, and the recurring violence at the revel—'about 1660 one was killed, striving to take away the garland', Aubrey reports—led to a drastic reduction in the quantity of ale permitted.[18]

[16] SRO CQ 3/1/100 (Sessions Rolls, 1661), no. 23. Fenwick, *Chester*, pp. 370–1.

[17] White Kennett, *Parochial Antiquities attempted in the History of Ambrosden, Burcester, and othe adjacent parts in the Counties of Oxford and Bucks.*, Oxford, 1818, ii. 310. Plot, *Nat. Hist. Oxfordshire*, pp 202–3; *Nat. Hist. Staffs.*, pp. 434–40.

[18] *Top. Coll. John Aubrey*, pp. 125, 139, 146, 185, 198, 273–4. Aubrey, 'Remaines', pp. 194, 212 431–2.

In spite of such occasional restrictions, rural recreations appear to have been more freely practised than ever in the century after the Restoration, as the gentry's desire, and the church's power, to enforce strict sabbath observance declined. Bull-baiting and cock-fighting enjoyed a notable revival, if indeed they had ever been effectively curtailed; traditional sports such as wrestling and cudgel-playing were as popular as ever; and football, especially in the midland and eastern counties, continued to provide a boisterous outlet for feelings of local solidarity. Cricket, before 1660 confined to its original heartland in Kent, Surrey, and Sussex, was spreading to other parts of the country as regional isolation diminished. By the end of the seventeenth century it may have begun to rival stoolball in popularity, even in Wiltshire. Where else, a local clergyman demanded, could 'walking, fishing, bowling, playing at cricket or stopball [stoolball]' be enjoyed with such 'ease, cheapness, and satisfaction' as in that county?[19]

Superficially, then, it might appear that the co-operative world of the vertical community and the festive rituals in which its values were articulated had been restored along with Charles II. A century later in Goldsmith's recollections of 'all the village train from labour free' enjoying their sports 'beneath the spreading tree' we have a nostalgic evocation of that vanished age. Many festive customs were still encouraged by an élite which retained a veneer of paternalist concern for the welfare of its dependents—as long as they behaved themselves, refrained from poaching, and knew their place. The nobility and gentry kept up old traditions of hospitality at harvest dinners, at Christmas, and Whitsuntide. They patronized, participated in, and gambled heavily on sporting events in which even the greatest noblemen might rub shoulders with men of plebeian condition, as did the Dukes of Richmond and Dorset in the 1770s with the yeomen, small farmers, and artisans of the Hambledon Cricket Club.[20]

But the social realities of Georgian England were very different from those of the Restoration era. The cultural divide between the respectable and the poor was deepened and consolidated in the century after 1660: by the continued expansion of commerce, producing a larger, more self-assured and sometimes even gentrified urban middle class; by the further inroads of agricultural capitalism, producing a rural society even more clearly stratified into the three tiers of landlords, tenant farmers, and

[19] Malcolmson, *Popular Recreations*, pp. 17–18, 20–9, 31, and ch. 3. 'A Longford Manuscript', ed. H. C. Brentnall, *WAM* lii (1947–8), 20.

[20] Brookes, *English Cricket*, chs. 4, 5. Many of the subtleties of eighteenth-century class relations are illustrated by the Duke of Dorset's difficulties with the 'little farmer' George Lambert's off-breaks, and the other players' reaction to the bowler's exasperated shout, 'Ah! it was tedious near you, Sir!' when he missed the Duke's leg stump by a hairsbreadth: John Nyren, *The Young Cricketer's Tutor*, ed. F. S. Ashley-Cooper, 1902, pp. 87–8.

labouring poor. Élite patronage of village games and revels had always contained a certain tincture of self-interest, evident in the motives underlying the Book of Sports and Dover's Cotswold Games. But in the eighteenth century the resort to 'theatrical show' to dazzle and divert a grateful tenantry turning out to welcome a returning local magnate, cheer his election triumphs, or gape at his children's weddings, became increasingly openly manipulative.[21]

Popular rituals, however, are (as John Brewer has reminded us), often ambiguous in their meanings, and what might seem to be picturesque quaintness to a patrician observer might express something quite different for the plebeian participant. And traditional festivals could be used by aristocratic party politicians in ways that clearly encouraged the political independence of the lower orders. Guy Fawkes Day, for example, usually served merely as an outlet for the universal desire for feasting and bonfires, pointing the uncontroversial moral of gratitude for the preservation of monarchy and ancient liberties. But during the Exclusion crisis and again after 1715, both Gunpowder Treason and the adjacent anniversary of Queen Elizabeth's accession were appropriated by the Whigs and their anti-Catholic associations directed against the cause of the Stuarts and the Tories. The history of other customary festivals discloses similarly contradictory features. Often tolerated by authority as harmless safety-valves, they were nevertheless affected by the separation between élite and popular cultures. Professor Brewer's account of the mock election at Garret shows the élite at first, before 1760, attending this quaint (but in fact highly subversive) ritual as spectators, but then increasingly attempting to appropriate it and its characters for their own Wilkite or Foxite purposes—or in opposition to those radical groups.[22]

Élite manipulation of popular symbols could be even more undisguised, especially in the years immediately after the Restoration, when the importance of loyalty to the crown needed to be constantly reiterated. Robin Hood, for centuries a symbol of popular independence and resistance to authority, was quickly pressed into service. As part of the Coronation celebrations at Nottingham in 1661 a short play was enacted, in which Robin's traditional loyalty to King Richard was carefully exaggerated to provide the basis for a commentary on the recent confusions. When the messenger arrives in Sherwood offering pardon to the outlaws if they will abandon their evil ways there are a few half-hearted protests. Little John utters some appeals to social levelling—'every brave soul is

---

[21] See E. P. Thompson, 'Patrician Society, Plebeian Culture', *JSH* vii (1973–4), 389.

[22] Malcolmson, *Popular Recreations*, pp. 25–6. David Ogg, *England in the Reign of Charles II*, 2nd edn., Oxford, 1955, ii. 595–6. Nicholas Rogers, 'Popular Protest in Early Hanoverian London', *P & P* no. 79 (May 1978), 76–9. John Brewer, 'Theater and Counter-Theater in Georgian Politics', *Radical History Review*, xxii (1979–80), 7–40.

born a king'—and Robin wistfully recalls 'this gallant attempt we've boldly followed', the Good Old Cause in other words. But like any repentant Roundhead he quickly gives up and leads his men in singing 'health unto our King'.[23]

Coronation Day in 1661 provided many occasions for carefully orchestrated loyal rejoicings on a scale rivalling those of the previous May. At Bath there were two processions to the service at the Abbey. In one the mayor and corporation were escorted by companies of trained bands and volunteers; in the other the mayor's wife led 400 maidens in white and green, carrying 'gilded crowns, crowns made of flowers, and wreaths made of laurel mixed with tulips'. The town was lavishly decorated, the royal arms and the new symbol of loyalty, the royal oak, were displayed on the Guildhall, and there were 'crowns and wreaths on the head of the lion upon the cross in the King's Bath'.[24] In subsequent years the association between May games and monarchy became increasingly obvious, with May Day celebrations being transferred to, or repeated, on the 29th of the month, oak boughs and 'oak-apples' blending with the ancient traditions of garlands, maypoles, and dancing.[25] Charles II may not have been the most appropriate personification of the notion of divinely-ordained monarchy, yet the mystique of royalty was assiduously kept alive throughout his reign and transmitted to the public in numerous ways. The ceremony of 'touching for the King's Evil', for example, reached new heights of popularity during this period.[26]

Even more obviously than before 1640, the old festive culture was being manipulated to reinforce the messages of obedience transmitted in other ways by the church and the law.[27] This does not mean, however, that plebeian culture was totally controlled: throughout the eighteenth century it continued to express, often in disorderly and violent ways, vigorous traditions of popular independence. Fear of disorder joined with other reasons to convince a good many people in authority that the old popular rituals, and the notions of community they represented, were barbarous survivals, unsuited to a disciplined commercial society. Puritanism had been politically defeated in 1660, but much of its social ethos lived on

---

[23] BL TT, E. 1088 (6): *Robin Hood and his crew of Souldiers. A Comedy Acted at Nottingham on the day of his SaCRed Majesties Coronation*, 1661. I am indebted to Jeffrey Singman for this reference.

[24] BL TT, E. 1088 (7): *Of the Celebration of the King's Coronation-Day, In the famous City of Bath, A true Narrative*, 1661. The ceremonies in Bath at the King's proclamation a year earlier are described in Wroughton, *Civil War in Bath*, p. 133.

[25] Malcolmson, *Popular Recreations*, pp. 30–1. However, popular adulation of monarchs, as distinct from monarchy, was not very marked under the Hanoverians until the latter part of George III's reign: Linda Colley, 'The Apotheothis of George III', *P & P* no. 102 (Feb. 1984), 94–129.

[26] Raymond Crawfurd, *The King's Evil*, Oxford, 1911, pp. 105–12. Thomas, *Religion and the Decline of Magic*, p. 193.

[27] For a provocative discussion of this function of the law see Douglas Hay, 'Property, Authority and the Criminal Law', in *Albion's Fatal Tree: Crime and Society in Eighteenth-Century England*, 1975, pp. 17–63.

among the propertied classes (and not only the middling-sort dissenters), and is reflected in the widespread belief that feasting and holiday sports were detrimental to the profits of employers. The temporary lull in the offensive against lower-class culture that began at the Restoration lasted barely a generation. Soon after the Glorious Revolution a new campaign began, carried on into the eighteenth century by the Societies for the Reformation of Manners and the charity school movement, and sustained by a regular drumbeat of propaganda from writers spanning many shades of opinion, in which the virtues of thrift, sobriety, and discipline were assiduously promoted.[28] Backwoods Tory squires might swim against the tide by trying to perpetuate older paternalistic notions of a 'moral economy' requiring the powerful to protect the powerless from the adverse consequeces of a market-oriented economic system. But the whole trend of the century was against them, and long before the publication of *The Wealth of Nations* the intellectual groundwork of the new economic universe had been laid.[29]

Nowhere is this clearer than in the agricultural sector. By the time the great age of parliamentary enclosure began, the erosion of the co-operative, communally-organized open-field village had already passed the point of no return. Individual property rights based on written title replaced ancient custom, removing the barriers which, uneasily and not always effectively, had done something to dilute the disruptive impact of changing agricultural methods. By the 1760s such open-field arrange-ments and rights of common as remained were rapidly disappearing, and Goldsmith could lament the familiar situation in which 'one only master grasps the whole domain'.[30] Enclosure and the logic of the market often destroyed the villager's access not only to land, but also to the commons on which the sports and festivals ritually expressing the neighbourhood's identity had been held. A conception of land as a commodity to be exploited for profit, protected by absolute rights of ownership, had triumphed over an older one under which ancient custom had guaranteed rights of access and use by the community. In that change a process occupying several centuries came close to fruition.[31]

---

[28] Much of this literature is surveyed in Malcolmson, *Popular Recreations*, ch. 6. See also Dudley W. R. Bahlman, *The Moral Revolution of 1688*, New Haven, 1957; and E. P. Thompson, 'Time, Work-Discipline, and Industrial Capitalism', *P & P* no. 38 (Dec. 1967), 56–97.

[29] Thompson, 'Moral Economy'. For the earlier growth of economic individualism see Joyce O. Appleby, *Economic Thought and Ideology in Seventeenth-Century England*, Princeton, 1977.

[30] The contrast between the old and the new is neatly captured in the two Gloucestershire landscapes by an unknown artist of the 1720s, now in the Cheltenham Art Gallery. At Alderton the villagers collectively mow the common field to the accompaniment of singing and morris dancing; at nearby Dixton the squire is greeted on his return to his enclosed manor only by his immediate family and dependents.

[31] The transition is evident in some of the incidents recounted by Malcolmson, *Popular Recreations*, pp. 112–15.

*

We have strayed a long way from Restoration. Let us return to the bells and bonfires of 1660. On the surface a political and social order cemented by the authority of King, Church, aristocracy, and gentry appeared to have been satisfactorily restored. But the Restoration compromise could no more arrest the gradual erosion of the old ideals of paternalism and community than the earlier short-lived Laudian reaction had done. The two revolutionary decades had administered a major shock to the established patriarchal, hierarchial system. Still, many features of that system flourished again in 1660, and were to be undermined only slowly by the long-term social processes that were gradually changing English society.

In many respects the impact of the civil war and revolution on the lives of ordinary English men and women had been distinctly ambiguous. A civil war had been fought. It had been fought by armies which, though small by modern standards, required at least one tenth of the adult male population to leave their homes, sometimes for protracted periods, at one time or another.[32] When they came back to their towns and villages (if they were lucky enough to come back), soldiers brought with them experiences of conflict which must at least temporarily have affected their relationships with other members of the community. The absence of men on military service created temporary fluctuations of the sex ratio, though this seems to have had only an insignificant impact on the birth rate. Illegitimacy rates, too, seem to have been little affected, continuing their long-term decline. Whatever may have been its effect on the élite, for the common people the war led to no obvious change of attitudes towards sexual behaviour. Somerset records contain numerous instances of local girls consorting with the soldiers of both sides, but also reveal the not surprising hostility towards this displayed by other villagers.[33] The scandalized response of Wiltshire country people to the free-loving Ranters at Langley Burrell would certainly have been shared by the inhabitants of many other villages.

[32] The population of Dorset in 1642 was around 84,000, and over 800 indigent former royalist soldiers received pensions after the Restoration: below, Appendix II, Table 3. There would thus have been about 25,000 adult males in 1642, to which must be added another 5,000 or so who would have reached adulthood during the war: altogether some 30,000 possibly eligible recruits. The 800 pensioners were (a) indigent, and (b) Royalists. It does not strain credulity to suppose that at least 3,000 Dorset men served in the war if all those who were not indigent, and all those who served the Parliament, could be counted.

[33] Quaife, *Wanton Wenches*, pp. 49–50, 123. Peter Laslett, *Family Life and Illicit Love in Earlier Generations. Essays in Historical Sociology*, Cambridge, 1977, pp. 113–42. Population estimates for the whole country suggest a slight drop in the birth rate in 1644, but not enough to be conclusive: Wrigley and Schofield, *Population History*, p. 532, Table A 3.3. Of the parishes for which I have received tabulations from the Cambridge Group, Bruton and Yeovil show this decline, but Frome and Milborne Port do not.

Still, a civil war had been fought, and at the end of it the monarch, the ultimate symbol of patriarchal order, had been executed after a quasi-judicial process which asserted *salus populi* above the laws of the kingdom. The power of the hereditary aristocracy had been apparently destroyed, and that of the gentry severely curtailed by the intrusion of men from outside the normal governing circles into county magistracies. Patriarchal order had been further subverted by sects which permitted women to preach, vote as church members, and disobey unconverted husbands. In London at least, women had demonstrated and petitioned on political matters, with or without the consent of their husbands. Urban traders and craftsmen had demanded a more egalitarian political system, broader participation in the government of London companies, and a rational, equitable reform of the law. A few of the poor had gone beyond their customarily limited modes of protest in grain and enclosure rioting to set up co-operative communes like Winstanley's on St George's Hill; many more had found new freedom of expression and association in Baptist, Quaker, and other separatist congregations.

But all these challenges to the old order in the end foundered on the stubborn resilience of traditional culture. The Puritans might have a new conception of marriage, with the wife as the compassionate help-meet sharing more fully in the moral and spiritual as well as the economic life of the family, but only the most radical among them allowed women to preach or otherwise defy the 'natural' system of subordination. They and others might see Parliament rather than King as the best defender of Protestantism and ancient liberties, but few of them wanted a radical restructuring of either the state or the social order. The Protestation of 1641 remained throughout the civil war the basic common denominator of popular aspirations. When the revolution went too far beyond its limited goals, even many of the middling sort of the towns and clothing districts, like most of the moderate Parliamentarians among the gentry, turned against it and in the end acquiesced in the Restoration. For those who retained their Puritan principles, the great cosmic struggle of good and evil, hitherto fought out in the public arenas of church, state, and community, was internalized as a personal struggle within the individual soul.[34]

So the post-Restoration reaction was a continuation of developments that had already begun before 1660. Familial order had been threatened, so it was essential in the interests of social stability to restore and redefine it. It is surely no accident that after the Restoration the frequency of prosecution of both witches and scolds declined. The witch and the scold had risen together as alienated outsiders, casualties of a

[34] Christopher Hill, *Antichrist in Seventeenth-Century England*, 1971, pp. 170–2; and see also his *Milton and the English Revolution*, pp. 418–27.

hanging social order; when a different kind of order was consolidated its defenders found less need to discipline them. The expectations of women, the poor, and the marginal were changing: there was the Poor Law to look after them without complicating residual notions about the duty of private charity whose denial might lead to projections of guilt and the search for scapegoats. The long century of slightly improved economic conditions for the consuming poor also helped to reduce the intensity of this kind of protest. But changing economic conditions are not the sole explanation. The emerging conception of the affective family, making headway in the later seventeenth century in the upper and middle ranks of English society, presented a model of family relationships that was in some ways more humane, in others more oppressive than the system it supplanted. On the one hand, men were a bit less likely to receive community tolerance when they beat their wives; on the other women lost most of the vestiges of economic and personal independence some of them had acquired in the unstable years before 1660. Among the middling sort, growing prosperity made it possible to relegate wives from the work place to the drawing-room, a process greatly assisted by the concurrent revision of patriarchal theory.[35]

After 1688 patriarchy lost much of its credibility as a theory of government, partly as a result of John Locke's redefinition of both family and state in contractual terms. But only the early beginnings of this process can be observed during the civil war period. At that time assumptions about the correspondence between the family and the state were still commonly held by people on both sides of the political divide. Royalists emphasized the parallel between the indissolubility of marriage and the permanence of the obligation of obedience to the King; a few Parliamentarians were driven, for the sake of intellectual consistency, to consider limits to the power of husbands over wives.[36] Restoration arguments for monarchy were naturally still couched in traditional patriarchal language. The most famous such argument was Filmer's *Patriarcha*, written much earlier and published in 1680 when the Exclusion crisis made its message particularly pressing. But Charles II's council had long since recognized the importance of restating the theory. In December 1662 they reprinted Richard Mocket's old tract, *God and the King*, ordering that it should be taught in every school and read by all masters of households and their apprentices. Theory was translated into practice by a governing class constantly fearful of plots by 'fanatics' and republicans. Purges of local officials, especially in the towns under the

---

[35] For this subject see Stone, *Family, Sex and Marriage*, ch. 6; and Alice Clark, *Working Life of Women in the Seventeenth Century*, new edn., 1982.
[36] Mary L. Shanley, 'Marriage Contract and Social Contract in Seventeenth Century English Political Thought', *Western Political Quarterly*, xxxii (1979), 79–91.

Corporation Act (at Dorchester there was almost a clean sweep of the ol
Presbyterian oligarchy) were accompanied by the imposition of oaths o
loyalty on a much wider segment of the population. Whole parishes wer
sometimes required to take the oath of allegiance; the men of Radstoc
and other north Somerset villages did so in April 1661 at their hundre
court.[37]

Throughout Charles II's reign vivid memories of civil war and revol
ution engendered a mood of cautious conservatism on the part of the élite
never again would they carry their political disputes to a point that woul·
require them to put arms into the hands of brewers and draymen. Th·
Whig aristocrats who left Oxford with Shaftesbury after the dissolution o
Parliament in 1681 were clearly influenced by this fear, and seven year
later they made sure that popular support for their revolution on behalf o
'Liberty and Property' was kept firmly under control. Their conservatism
was buttressed not only by political writers like Filmer, but also b·
countless sermons from the Anglican clergy, and by arguments for passiv·
obedience from many of their dissenting counterparts. At Lyme Regis i·
May 1660 the Presbyterian Ames Short set the tone for much Restoratio·
preaching when he urged his listeners to join him in celebrating th·
occasion by 'stopping our ears for ever against the bewitching temptation·
of such as are given to change'.[38]

*

The revolutionary decades of 1640–60 thus had ambiguous and appar·
ently contradictory effects on English society and popular culture. Th·
same is true of popular politics, though we should not exaggerate th·
elements of conservatism and quiescence, for there remained a·
important residue from the civil war in the political consciousness of th·
lower orders. Historians have often stressed the features of stability in th·
years after 1660—aristocratic revival, latitudinarian religion, the rule o·
law—and have regarded the highly visible part political conflict befor·
1714 as superficial and less important, even while recognizing th·
considerable degree of popular participation in elections.[39] Yet we now
know that the common people of England were a lot less submissive an·
deferential than theory required them to be. The civil war was certainl·
one of the factors that encouraged their independence to take somewha·
more political forms.

[37] *CSPD, 1661–2*, p. 583. DRO B2/16/5 (Dorchester Corporation Minutes, 1656–77), 1662
D1/10048 (William Whiteway's Book), p. 19. 'Loyalists of Babington Hundred 1660', *SDNQ* xxiv
(1943–6), 134–5.
[38] BL TT, E. 1919 (2): Short, *God Save the King*, p. 76.
[39] For example, J. H. Plumb, *The Growth of Political Stability in England 1675–1725*
Harmondsworth, 1969; and 'The Growth of the Electorate in England from 1600 to 1715', *P & P* n·
45 (Nov. 1969), 90–116.

The civil war intensified and perpetuated divisions that had long existed in many towns and villages. This is very clear in the religious sphere, with the permanent survival of dissent in countless English communities. But the divisions also persisted, even at the plebeian level, in politics—and it is of course impossible to make a total separation between religion and politics in seventeenth-century England. For much of this the civil war, and the issues it left behind, was responsible. The war had exposed villagers to competing authorities, had required them to make choices about whom to obey, forced some to take sides, and accustomed all to political divisions of a more profound and permanent nature than any they had hitherto experienced. In the process they become accustomed to identifying some at least of their neighbours as Roundheads and Cavaliers.

For years after 1660 memories of the civil war continued to influence the outlook of Englishmen and to be reflected in their vocabulary. 'Roundhead' and 'Cavalier' were soon submerged by other terms—though they lingered for a time in ballads commemorating the war's great events. But even the terms that replaced them were charged with civil war meanings: 'the people of God', the 'honest Protestants' on the one side; 'fanatics', Anabaptists, the 'Presbyterian crew' in the eyes of their enemies.[40] Eventually most of these terms were to be swamped by the more enduring 'Whig' and 'Tory'. This was a slow process: country people in Somerset were already using 'Tory' as a synonym for 'Cavalier' as early as 1655, during Penruddock's rebellion.[41] By the early eighteenth century the transition was virtually complete, enabling party politicians to employ a rhetoric (still, however, with much civil war resonance) comfortingly familiar to their volatile electorates.

So we ought not to telescope the transition from the turbulent conflicts of the civil war era to the deference politics of the following century. The purges of local officials in the 1660s and 1680s, the reappearance of Leveller symbols during the Exclusion crisis, and the regular exposure of popular mutterings against the Stuart monarchy, all reflect the survival of civil war divisions into a later period and the involvement of the common people in them. In some places such divisions were absolutely central to local politics. The 11 May Thanksgiving at Taunton remained for years both an annual reminder of the town's blessed deliverance from the fury of Goring's crew, and an occasion for the 'people of God' to reaffirm their solidarity. The day was still observed 'with great solemnity' in 1671, it was noted, and the celebrations sometimes led to disorder. There were angry scenes when the neighbouring JPs moved troops into the town to keep order in May 1663. People gathering in Fore Street were

---

[40] Peter Earle, *Monmouth's Rebels: The Road to Sedgemoor 1685*, 1977, pp. 5–6, 12, 16, 56.
[41] *CSPD, 1655*, p. 84.

warned that the soldiers would ride them down if they did not disperse
there were scuffles, jeers, and stones were thrown. Later, a trooper left
behind when his horse cast a shoe was surrounded by a menacing crowd
and had his pistols taken away.[42] But Taunton was a deeply divided town.
Residents mindful of the heroic days of 1645 might fondly recall how 'The
cavaliers dispers'd with fear, and forcèd were to run'. But in 1683 the day
of their enemies came, and after the corporation had again been purged a
Tory mayor was able to organize the destruction of both the Presbyterian
and Baptist meeting-houses. Ten cartloads of seats and other woodwork
were consumed in a great bonfire in the market-place, while the bells rang
all night.[43]

These events were part of the deepening crisis in Somerset which
preceded Monmouth's rebellion. Seditious talk became increasingly
common in many parts of England as the prospect of a Catholic king came
close to reality, even in such areas as Norfolk, which did not rebel in
1685.[44] In the region with which this book has been mainly concerned,
the Monmouth rebellion is incontestable evidence of the continued
politicization of the common people. The most striking aspect of the
rebellion is the speed with which thousands of people, without gentry
leadership, took up arms in what was essentially a dispute over national,
not local issues. The west-country artisans who thronged to Monmouth's
standard did so not simply because there was a depression in the cloth
industry, but because in their mental world a Catholic ruler was equated
with a threat to both national and local liberties and to the survival of their
religion. One of the Devonshire rebels, it was said, 'always hated the name
of papist', another felt absolved from the duty of obedience to government, 'the case being between popery and protestantism'.[45]

The traumas of Sedgemoor and the Bloody Assizes, however, are
outside the scope of this study. Like so many other features of late
seventeenth-century England, the events of 1685 suggest many paradoxes
and ambiguities. The Protestant character of the revolt, for example, did
not preclude the expression of beliefs of quite a different kind: John
Aubrey was told of people in Somerset being 'cured of the King's Evil, by
the touch of the Duke of Monmouth'.[46] The rebellion's national

---

[42] SRO CQ 3/1/103 (Sessions Rolls, 1663), nos. 13, 15. Underdown, *Somerset*, pp. 194–5. Earle, *Monmouth's Rebels*, p. 12.

[43] Earle, *Monmouth's Rebels*, p. 14. In spite of the persecution, in the early eighteenth century Taunton could still boast the largest dissenting meeting-house and congregation in the whole of England: Michael R. Watts, *The Dissenters from the Reformation to the French Revolution*, Oxford, 1978, p. 278. For the strength of dissent in north Somerset in the 1660s, see James R. Jacob, *Henry Stubbe*, Cambridge, 1983, pp. 80–1.

[44] Amussen, 'Governors and Governed', p. 307 and n. For other examples of seditious words see Hill, *Some Intellectual Consequences*, p. 15; and *World Turned Upside Down*, p. 286.

[45] Earle, *Monmouth's Rebels*, pp. 19–20.

[46] Aubrey, 'Miscellanies', in *Three Prose Works*, p. 80. See also Crawfurd, *King's Evil*, pp. 137–8.

orientation did not mean that it had no localist component, a fact that is evident in some of the vocabulary used by contemporaries. Monmouth, the rector of Chezdoy observed, expected 'great additions from the Clubmen rising in the marsh country'.[47] And as in civil war days there were marked contrasts in the behaviour of places within only a few miles of each other: Huntspill, for example, remained loyal to James II while nearby Burnham went heavily for Monmouth.

In 1686, the year after the rebellion, there was a riot at Huntspill fair when a group of Monmouth sympathizers from Burnham and other villages went there 'in a tumultuous manner' and assaulted Huntspill people of 'the loyal party'.[48] The incident has many earlier west-country parallels in the 'expressive violence' that so often occurred at fairs, revels, football matches, and disorders like the skimmington riot between the men of Burbage and Wilton. But in the course of the seventeenth century some at least of the participants in these outbreaks had become politicized. The Monmouth episode reignited local divisions whose roots lay in the 1640s, for the civil war had begun a process that enabled even ordinary villagers to make judgements about matters of government. Throughout that process popular politics, whether in 1685 or during the civil war, drew heavily on the rituals and traditions—often regionally contrasting ones—of popular culture.

[47] C. D. Curtis, 'Battle of Sedgemoor', *SDNQ* xxviii (1961–7), 16; but see also Earle, *Monmouth's Rebels*, p. 103. For the social composition of the rebel army see Earle, pp. 16–21, 201–5. Earle also notes the high proportion of rebels from towns and large villages (pp. 198–201), confirming the evidence in ch. 7, above, that such places were more highly politicized than were the smaller villages.

[48] Earle, *Monmouth's Rebels*, p. 189.

APPENDIX I

Population Estimates

MY estimates of population for the towns and regions of Wiltshire and Dorset are based on the Protestation returns of 1641–2 and the Compton Census of 1676. The methods used to translate these figures into population estimates are explained in my article, 'The Problem of Popular Allegiance in the English Civil War' and therefore need not be repeated here.[1] For Somerset the sources are less plentiful and do not permit even the degree of confidence that is possible for the other two counties. Protestation returns survive for parts of only 14 of Somerset's 42 hundreds.[2] They provide, however, a base from which estimates for other parts of the county can be made. Neither parochial nor decanal returns survive from Somerset in the Compton Census: all we have are totals of conformists, nonconformists, and recusants for the whole diocese of Bath and Wells. These together add up to a total of 151,496, but the figure is not of much help to us because of the notorious inconsistency of the parochial returns in the 1676 census: in other parts of the country they are sometimes the numbers of adults, sometimes estimates of the whole population.[3] For reasons that will become clear below, 151,496 is too low to be an estimate of the total population of Somerset, too high to be an estimate of adults only. I suspect that as in other dioceses the Bath and Wells parochial returns contained a mixture of both.[4]

To obtain rough estimates of the population of regions of Somerset not covered by the Protestation returns we thus have to use back-projection from the 1801 census, a method whose validity for the country as a whole has recently been established by E. A. Wrigley and R. S. Schofield's definitive *Population History*.[5] Now it would obviously be absurd to assume uniform growth between 1642 and

---

[1] *TRHS* 5th Ser. xxxi (1981), 93–4.

[2] Printed in *Somerset Protestation Returns and Lay Subsidy Rolls 1641/2*, ed. A. J. Howard and T. L. Stoate, Almondsbury, 1975. The hundreds from which Protestation returns survive are: Abdick and Bulstone (most); Carhampton (all); Crewkerne (most); North Curry (all); Glaston Twelve Hides (all); Kingsbury East (most); Kingsbury West (all); Milverton (all); North Petherton (Bridgwater only); South Petherton (most); Taunton Deane (most); Whitstone (most); Williton and Freemanors (all).

[3] For this problem see my 'Problem of Popular Allegiance', p. 94. The Compton Census totals are listed in T. H. Hollingsworth, *Historical Demography*, Ithaca, 1969, p. 83, mis-dated 1688; that these are in fact Compton Census figures is made clear by Wrigley and Schofield, *Population History*, p. 570. I am grateful to Mr D. V. Fourkes for confirming the Bath and Wells figure from the MS in the Staffordshire Record Office.

[4] It might be noted that the dangers of using the Protestation and Compton Census figures interchangeably, as I did in working out the Dorset and Wiltshire population estimates, are much reduced by the discovery that the population of England was almost exactly the same in 1676 as it had been in 1641: Wrigley and Schofield, *Population History*, p. 528.

[5] Wrigley and Schofield, *Population History*, pp. 192–9. The 1801 census figures are listed in *VCH, Somerset*, ii. 340–52.

1801 in different towns and regions, so some estimate of variations from the national norm has to be made. This has been done by comparing the 1801 figure with estimates based on the Protestation returns in those parishes that possess the latter, and in other cases with estimates for the 1640s derived from parish register material kindly supplied by the Cambridge Group.[6] From these sources it appears that the population of Somerset's rural parishes in 1642 was about 80 per cent of the 1801 figure, except in the central levels, where it was about 75 per cent. In the towns, on the other hand, population growth varied dramatically. Bath in 1642 had less than 10 per cent of its 1801 population, Frome only 34 per cent, Taunton 45 per cent, Shepton Mallet 46 per cent, and Bridgwater 59 per cent. Other places, however, show much less striking growth: in 1642 Glastonbury had 75 per cent of its 1801 population, Yeovil 86 per cent, and Bruton 92 per cent, while Wells suffered a slight decline during this period (though not if the out-parish of St. Cuthbert is included).[7]

The regional estimates in Appendix II, Table 6 thus rest on a combination of information from the Protestation returns, parish registers, and back-projection from 1801. It would be rash to put too much confidence in them. Nevertheless they may not be totally useless. My estimate from these sources of the total population of Somerset in 1642 is 196,000. This is within 5 per cent of the figure of 204,800 that would be reached by back-projection from 1801, using the formula (1641 = 58 per cent of 1801) applied by Wrigley and Schofield to the whole country. The 196,000 estimate is also supported by the estimates of the number of houses in each county made by John Houghton later in the seventeenth century, using Hearth Tax returns.[8] Houghton gives the following distribution of houses in the three western counties: Dorset, 21,944; Wiltshire, 27,093; Somerset, 49,808. This conforms very closely to the distribution of population between the three counties indicated by my own estimates: 84,000; 113,500; and 196,000 respectively. Thus Dorset has 22.12 per cent of the houses in the three-county area and 21.35 per cent of the population. Wiltshire has 27.6 per cent of the houses, 28.84 per cent of the population. Somerset has 50.28 per cent of the houses, 49.80 per cent of the population. The rough correspondence of the figure for the whole county with those derived from both the back-projection method and from Houghton's work provides some grounds for supposing that the estimates for the Somerset regions are not totally without validity.

---

[6] For the parishes of Bruton, Frome, Milborne Port, and Yeovil. I am grateful to Dr Richard Wall for this information.

[7] This accounts for most of the major Somerset towns. My estimates for 1642 are as follows: Bath 2,000 (R. S. Neale, *Bath 1680–1850: A Social History*, 1981, p. 44); Frome, 3,000 (parish registers); Taunton, 2,600 (Protestation); Shepton Mallet, 2,350 (Protestation); Bridgwater, 2,100 (Protestation); Glastonbury, 1,575 (Protestation); Yeovil, 2,400 (parish registers); Bruton, 1,500 (parish registers); Wells, 2,900, plus 1,275 in the out-parish (Protestation). Other towns for which 1642 estimates can be derived from the Protestation returns are Crewkerne, 1,500; Dunster, 1,000; Ilminster, 1,950; Milverton, 1,400; Minehead, 1,050; Watchet, 1,300; Wellington, 2,175; and Wiveliscombe, 1,425.

[8] John Houghton, *A Collection for the improvement of husbandry and Trade*, 1727 (originally published weekly, 1692–1703), i. 74.

APPENDIX II

Tables

TABLE I

Wiltshire Pensioners. See above, pp. 192–5

	Estimated Population	Royalist Pensioners	Pensioners per 1,000 population
1. Cheese country			
Rural	18,000	44	2.44
Towns under 1,000	2,000	16	8.00
Towns and villages over 1,000	17,000	20	1.18
Total	37,000	80	2.16
2. Intermediate parishes			
Rural	12,300	36	2.93
Towns under 1,000	450	0	0.00
Towns and villages over 1,000	8,000	55	6.88
Total	20,750	91	4.39
3. Chalk Country			
Rural	36,000	89	2.47
Towns under 1,000	4,250	21	4.94
Towns and villages over 1,000	15,500	46	2.97
Total	55,750	156	2.80
Total Wiltshire	113,500	327	2.88

TABLE 2

Occupations of Dorset Pensioners. See above, pp. 195–6

	Gentry, Yeomen	Trades, Crafts	Husbandmen	Unskilled	Total
Towns	4	91	32	12	139
Chalk Country	2	11	11	2	26
Heathlands	—	1	—	1	2
S. and W. Dorset	2	7	14	1	24
Blackmore Vale	1	7	13	—	21
Totals	9	117	71	15	212
Percentages	4	55	33	7	

TABLE 3
Dorset Pensioners. See above, pp. 192, 196–8

	Estimated Population	Royalist Pensioners	Pensioners per 1,000 population
1. Chalk Country			
Rural	29,700	146	4.92
Towns under 1,000	3,300	64	19.39
Towns and villages over 1,000	7,000	98	14.00
Total	40,000	308	7.70
2. South and West Dorset			
Rural	12,700	87	6.85
Towns under 1,000	—	—	—
Towns and villages over 1,000	7,500	68	9.07
Total	20,200	155	7.67
3. Heathlands			
Rural	4,250	10	2.35
Towns under 1,000	—	—	—
Towns and villages over 1,000	3,500	27	7.71
Total	7,750	37	4.77
4. Blackmore Vale			
Rural	10,500	110	10.48
Towns under 1,000	850	9	10.59
Towns and villages over 1,000	4,800	196	40.83
Total	16,150	315	18.89
Total, Dorset	84,100	815	9.69

TABLE 4

Status and Occupations of 1656 Suspects. See above, pp. 199–201. (The first figure given is the percentage of all those of known status or occupation. Actual numbers are given in parentheses.)

	Wilts.	Dorset	Somerset	Total
Peers, Knights, Gentry	10.1 (38)	8.2 (121)	9.8 (165)	9.2 (324)
Clergy, professions	0.56 (2)	0.47 (7)	0.66 (11)	0.57 (20)
Yeomen	4.0 (15)	4.5 (66)	5.1 (86)	4.7 (167)
Husbandmen	40.6 (152)	34.4 (508)	36.9 (619)	36.2 (1,279)
Skilled and semi-skilled trades	38.1 (143)	44.2 (652)	40.6 (681)	41.8 (1,476)
Unskilled trades	6.7 (25)	8.3 (123)	6.9 (115)	7.5 (263)
Unknown	(9)	(30)	(36)	(75)
Totals	(384)	(1,507)	(1,713)	(3,604)

TABLE 5

Wiltshire Suspects. See above, pp. 201–2

	No. of parishes making returns	Est. Pop.	Suspects (number)	Suspects per 1,000
Villages under 1,000	63	17,600	216	12
Towns under 1,000	4	2,550	40	16
Towns and villages over 1,000	6	13,600	128	9
Total, Wiltshire	73	33,750	384	11

TABLE 6

Somerset Suspects. See above, pp. 202–5

Region*	Est. Pop.	Suspects	Suspects per 1,000
North	56,700	288	4.94
S. & W. Mendips	23,250	354	15.23
Central (levels)	25,300	264	10.43
South & South-east	40,150	639	15.96
[West]	[50,700]	[151]	[3.14]
[Unidentifiable places]		[17]	
Totals (omitting West)	145,400	1,545	10.63

* The regions as defined include the following hundreds:
North: Bath Forum; Chew; Chewton; Frome; Hampton and Claverton; Hartcliffe and Bedminster; Keynsham; Kilmersdon; Portbury; Wellow.
South and West Mendips: Wells Forum; Whitstone; Winterstoke.
Central (levels): Bempstone; Brent; Glaston Twelve Hides; Huntspill; North Petherton; Pitney; Somerton; Whitley.
South and South-east: Bruton; Catsash; Crewkerne; Horethorne; Houndsborough; Barwick and Coker; Kingsbury East; Martock; Norton Ferris; South Petherton; Stone; Tintinhull.
West: Abdick and Bulstone; Andersfield; Cannington; Carhampton; North Curry; Kingsbury West; Milverton; Taunton Deane; Williton and Freemanors.

TABLE 7

Dorset Suspects. See above, pp. 205–6

	Estimated Population	1656 Suspects	Suspect per 1,000 population
1. Chalk Country			
Rural	29,700	338	11.38
Towns under 1,000	3,300	108	32.73
Towns and villages over 1,000	7,000	81	11.57
Total	40,000	527	13.18
2. South and West Dorset			
Rural	12,700	208	16.22
Towns under 1,000	—	—	—
Towns and villages over 1,000	7,500	87	11.60
Total	20,200	295	14.60
3. Heathlands			
Rural	4,250	44	10.35
Towns under 1,000	—	—	—
Towns and villages over 1,000	3,500	89	25.43
Total	7,750	133	17.16
4. Blackmore Vale			
Rural	10,500	120	11.43
Towns under 1,000	850	32	37.65
Towns and villages over 1,000	4,800	400	83.33
Total	16,150	552	34.18
Total, Dorset	84,100	1,507	17.92

TABLE 8

Royalists in Dorset Towns. See above, p. 205

	Pensioners per 1,000		1656 suspects per 1,000
1. Sherborne	57.72	1. Sherborne	135.90
2. Shaftesbury	30.86	2. Gillingham	40.85
3. Blandford	29.10	3. Wimborne	30.84
4. Sturminster Newton	25.00	4. Beaminster	25.71
5. Gillingham	22.00	5. Blandford	23.44
6. Bridport	16.00	6. Shaftesbury	19.22
7. Beaminster	14.29	7. Sturminster Newton	16.67
8. Netherbury	13.42	8. Wareham	15.83
9. Wareham	10.00	9. Bridport	14.67
10. Wimborne	6.61	10. Netherbury	11.84
11. Weymouth	4.74	11. Weymouth	9.47
12. Dorchester	2.94	12. Dorchester	5.15
13. Cranborne	0.87	13. Cranborne	4.36
14. Lyme Regis	0.83	14. Lyme Regis	1.67

Bibliography

THIS bibliography lists all manuscript collections cited, and all printed works cited more than once in the footnotes to this book. Newspapers and pamphlets in the Thomason Tracts, however, are not listed, but their British Library press-marks are given in the footnotes. For all TT references, see G. Fortescue's *Catalogue of the Pamphlets, Newspapers, and Manuscripts relating to the Civil War, the Commonwealth, and Restoration, collected by George Thomason*, 2 vols., 1908.

As in the footnotes, the place of publication of printed books is London unless otherwise stated.

I. MANUSCRIPTS

Bodleian Library
  Aubrey 12
  Dep. c. 167 (Nalson papers, xiv)
  J. Walker c. 4, 6 (Eastern Association, Committee for Scandalous Ministers)
  Oxf. Archd. papers: Berks. c. 61, 155 (Deposition books, 1616–20, 1594–1600)
  Tanner 53, 57–60, 62 (Nalson collections)
British Library
  Additional Charters 28283 (Stawell manors)
  Additional MS   4159 (Birch papers)
              5508 (Committee for Sequestrations papers)
              11044, 11053 (Scudamore papers)
              15570 (Miscellaneous papers, 16th-17th centuries)
              18979 (Fairfax correspondence)
              18980–2 (Rupert correspondence)
              22084–5 (Wilts. Sequestrations Register)
              22836 (Maton collection)
              23150 (Compton Abdale Court Book)
              23151 (Nettleton Court Book)
              28716 (Committee of Privileges proceedings)
              29975–6 (Pitt correspondence)
              32324 (Seymour correspondence)
              34012 (Major-Generals' returns)
              34566 (Jackson collection)
  Egerton MS 2533 (Nicholas papers)
  Film 330–1 (Northumberland MSS 547, 551: Fitzjames letter books)
  Harleian MS   255 (D'Ewes papers)
             6802, 6804 (Sir Edward Walker papers)
  Lansdowne MS 620 (Notes on Star Chamber cases)

Loan 29/50, 74, 121, 124, 177 (Harley papers)
Stowe MS 184 (Dering correspondence)
         189 (Civil War papers)
Dorset Record Office, Dorchester
  Borough Records
    Dorchester: B 2/8/1 (Court Book, 1629–37)
               B 2/14/1 (Company of Freemen, Receivers' Book, 1652–
               1716)
               B 2/16/3 (Corporation papers, 1629–94)
               B 2/16/5 (Corporation minutes, 1656–77)
               B 2/16/6E (Accounts of charitable collections, 1622–1704)
               D 1/10048 (William Whiteway's book)
    Lyme Regis: B 7/1/8 (Court Book, 1613–27)
               B 7/D1/1 (Corporation orders, 1594–1671)
  Churchwardens accounts
    P 9, CW/1 (Charlton Marshall)
    P 11, CW/1, 2 (Corfe Castle)
    P 22, CW/1 (Cerne Abbas)
    P 155, CW/72, 73 (Sherborne)
    P 173, CW/1 (Dorchester, Holy Trinity)
    P 213, CW/1–3 (Bere Regis)
    P 241, CW/3 (Motcombe)
  Ecclesiastical Court records: Wimborne Peculiar
    P 204, CP/10 (Act Book, 1601–3)
    P 204, CP/13 (Court papers, 1619–40)
    P 204, CP/32 (Catalogue of presentments)
  Nonconformist records
    N 10/A15 (Quaker Sufferings)
  Quarter Sessions records
    Order Books, 1625–37; 1663–74
Gloucestershire Record Office, Gloucester
  Churchwardens accounts
    P 34, CW/2/1 (Barnsley)
    P 63, CW/2/1 (Bromsberrow)
    P 107, CW/2/1 (Daglingworth)
    P 124, CW/2/4 (Dursley)
    P 230, CW/2/1 (North Nibley)
    P 328, CW/2/1 (Stroud)
    P 329, CW/2/1 (Tewkesbury)
  Diocesan Court records
    GDR 108 (Office cases, 1609–10)
    GDR 111 (Detections, 1610)
    GDR 114 (Depositions, 1611–13)
    GDR 148 (Depositions, 1622–5)
Norfolk Record Office, Norwich
    DEP/25, 35 (Consistory Court Deposition Books, 1590–1, 1608)
    C/S 3/12, 12A, 15, 34 (Sessions Rolls, 1594–6, 1597, 1605–6, 1643–4)

Oxfordshire VCH Office, Oxford
  Glympton papers
Public Record Office
  E 179 (Assessments, 1642)
  REQ 2 (Court of Requests)
  SP 16/131–2, 491 (State Papers, Charles I)
  SP 23/171 (Committee for Compounding papers)
  SP 28/128 (Military accounts)
  SP 28/227 (County Committee papers)
  SP 28/242 (Committee of Accounts papers)
  SP 28/249 (County Committee papers)
  SP 30/24/7 (Shaftesbury papers)
  SP 46/83 (Warner papers)
  STAC 5 (Star Chamber cases, Elizabeth I)
  STAC 8 (Star Chamber cases, James I)
Somerset Record Office, Taunton
  Churchwardens accounts
    D/P/ax, 4/1/1 (Axbridge)
    D/P/bur, 4/1/1 (Burrington)
    D/P/cas, 4/1/1 (Castle Cary)
    D/P/tin, 4/1/2 (Tintinhull)
  Diocesan Court records
    D/D/Ca 187 (Act Book, 1615–16)
    D/D/Ca 191, 194 (Comperta, 1615)
    D/D/Ca 220 (Comperta, 1620)
    D/D/Cd 28 (Depositions, 1599); 35 (1604); 37 (1606); 65 (1628–30); 71
      (1631–5); 76 (1633–4); 81 (1635)
  Family papers
    DD/L/48 (Luttrell papers)
  Quarter Sessions records
    CQ 3/1/23 (Sessions Rolls, 1616); 25 (1616); 70 (1633); 82 (1650); 86
      (1653); 98 (1658–9); 99 (1660–1); 103 (1663); 108 (1665)
    QS 164 (Petitions)
Wiltshire Record Office, Trowbridge
  Diocesan Court records
    AS/ABO 11–15 (Act Books, 1612–40)
    AW/ABO 5 (Act Book, 1616–22)
    B/ABO 5–11 (Act Books, 1600–33)
    D/ABO 28 (Act Book, 1622–7)
    Bishops' Deposition Books 22a (1602–3); 22b (1603–4); 42 (1627–8)
    Dean's Deposition Book 6 (1608)
    Dean's Peculiar, Presentments, 1606–8; 1609; 1613; 1616; 1620; 1625; 1635
    Precentor's Peculiar, Presentments, 1614–40
    Treasurer's Peculiar, Presentments, 1633
  Quarter Sessions records
    Order Books, 1641–54, 1654–68
    Sessions Rolls, 1617, 1620, 1660, 1662

Worcester College, Oxford
Clarke MSS 1/3, 1/5, 3/3, 4/2

2. PRINTED SOURCES

[Ashe, John], *A Perfect Relation of All the Passages and Proceedings of the Marquesse Hartford*, 1642.
The Case Book of Sir Francis Ashley J.P. Recorder of Dorchester 1614–1635, ed. J. H. Bettey, Dorset RS vii, 1981.
Aubrey, John, *The Natural History of Wiltshire*, ed. John Britton, 1847.
—— 'Remaines of Gentilisme and Judaisme', in Aubrey, *Three Prose Works*, pp. 129–304.
—— *Three Prose Works*, ed. John Buchanan-Brown, Carbondale, Illinois, 1972.
—— *Wiltshire. The Topographical Collections of John Aubrey*, ed. J. E. Jackson, Devizes, 1862.
Reliquiae Baxterianae: Or, Mr. Richard Baxter's Narrative of the most Memorable Passages of His Life and Times, ed. M. Sylvester, 1696.
Beard, Thomas, *The Theatre of Gods Judgements: wherein is represented the admirable justice of God against all notorious sinners*, 4th edn., 1648.
Memorials of the Civil War: Comprising the Correspondence of the Fairfax Family, ed. Robert Bell, 2 vols., 1849.
Military Memoir of Colonel John Birch . . . written by Roe his Secretary, ed. J. and T. W. Webb, Camden New Ser., vii, 1873.
Breton, Nicholas, 'The Court and Country' (1618), in *The Works in Verse and Prose of Nicholas Breton*, ed. A. B. Grosart, 1879, vol. ii.
The Records of a Church of Christ, meeting in Broadmead, Bristol, 1640–1687, ed. Edward B. Underhill, 1847.
British Library, Thomason Tracts.
Burton, Henry, *A Divine Tragedie Lately Acted, or A Collection of Sundrie Memorable Examples of Gods Judgements upon Sabbath-breakers*, 1641.
Calendar of the Proceedings of the Committee for Compounding, ed. M. A. E. Green, 5 vols., 1889–92.
Calendar of State Papers, Domestic, 1619–62, 40 vols., 1858–93.
Carew, Richard, *The Survey of Cornwall*, ed. F. E. Halliday, 1953.
Records of Early English Drama: Chester, ed. Lawrence Clopper, Toronto, 1979.
Records of Chippenham relating to the Borough . . . 1554, to 1889, ed. Frederick H. Goldney, 1889.
Clarendon, Edward, Earl of, *The History of the Rebellion and Civil Wars in England begun in the year 1641*, ed. W. D. Macray, 6 vols., Oxford, 1888.
Commons Debates 1628, ed. Robert C. Johnson, Mary F. Keeler, Maija J. Cole, and William B. Bidwell, 4 vols., New Haven, 1977–8.
Journals of the House of Commons, vols. ii–vii.
Corbet, John, 'A True and impartial History of the Military Government of the Citie of Gloucester', in *A Collection of scarce and valuable Tracts . . . Selected from . . . libraries, particularly that of the late Lord Somers*, ed. Sir Walter Scott, v (1811), 296–374.

The Court and Times of Charles the First, ed. Thomas Birch and [R. F. Williams], 2 vols., 1849.

Church-Wardens' Accounts of Croscombe, Pilton, Yatton . . . 1349 to 1560, ed. Bishop Hobhouse, SRS iv, 1890.

Some Annals of the Borough of Devizes, ed. B. H. Cunnington, 2 vols., Devizes, 1925–6.

The Journal of Sir Simonds D'Ewes from the Beginning of the Long Parliament to the Opening of the Trial of the Earl of Strafford, ed. Wallace Notestein, New Haven, 1923.

The Municipal Records of the Borough of Dorchester, ed. C. H. Mayo, Exeter, 1908.

The Minute Books of the Dorset Standing Committee, 23rd Sept., 1646, to 8th May, 1650, ed. Charles H. Mayo, Exeter, 1902.

English History from Essex Sources 1550–1750, ed. A. C. Edwards, Chelmsford, 1952.

Gleanings from the Municipal and Cathedral Records . . . of the City of Exeter, ed. W. Cotton and H. Woollcombe, Exeter, 1877.

[Fennor, William], *Pasquil's Palinodia, and His progresse to the Taverne,* 1619.

The Constitutional Documents of the Puritan Revolution 1625–1660, ed. Samuel R. Gardiner, 3rd edn., Oxford, 1906.

Gough, Richard, *The History of Myddle,* ed. David Hey, Harmondsworth, 1981.

Grey, Zachary, *An Impartial Examination of the Third Volume of Mr. Daniel Neal's History of the Puritans,* 1736.

The Diary of John Harington, M.P. 1646–53, ed. Margaret F. Stieg, SRS lxxiv, 1977.

Letters of the Lady Brilliana Harley, ed. T. T. Lewis, Camden 1st Ser., lviii, 1854.

Harrison, William, *The Description of England,* ed. Georges Edelen, Folger Documents of Tudor and Stuart Civilization, Ithaca, 1968.

The Works of George Herbert, ed. F. E. Hutchinson, Oxford, 1941.

Hertford County Records, i: *Notes and Extracts from the Sessions Rolls, 1581 to 1698,* ed. W. J. Hardy, Hertford, 1905.

Hinde, William, *A Faithfull Remonstrance of the Holy Life and Happy Death of John Bruen of Bruen Stapleford,* 1641.

Historical Manuscripts Commission, *Reports:*
 Fourth Report (1874): House of Lords and De La Warr MSS
 Fifth Report (1876): House of Lords MSS
 Sixth Report (1877): House of Lords MSS
 Eleventh Report, vii (1888): Bridgewater MSS
 Twelfth Report, ix (1891): Southwell MSS
 Bath, iv (1968)
 Egmont, i (1905)
 Portland, i, iii (1891, 1894)
 Salisbury, xxii (1971)
 Various Collections, i (1901): Wiltshire QS MSS
 Wells Dean and Chapter, ii (1914)

Epistolae Ho-Elianae. The Familiar Letters of James Howell, Historiographer Royal to Charles II, ed. Joseph Jacobs, 2 vols., 1892.

Kethe, William, *A Sermon made at Blandford Forum, in the Countie of Dorset*, 1571.
'Letters from a Subaltern Officer of the Earl of Essex's Army, written in the Summer and Autumn of 1642', ed. Sir Henry Ellis, *Archaeologia*, xxxv (1853), 310–34.
Journals of the House of Lords, vols. iv–x.
The Memoirs of Edmund Ludlow, Lieutenant-General of the Horse in the army of the Commonwealth of England, ed. C. H. Firth, 2 vols., Oxford, 1894.
The Letter Books 1644–45 of Sir Samuel Luke, ed. H. G. Tibbutt, 1963.
Probate Inventories and Manorial Excepts of Chetnole, Leigh and Yetminster, ed. R. Machin, Bristol, 1976.
'Extracts from Accounts of the Churchwardens of Minchinhampton, in the County of Gloucester', ed. John Bruce, *Archaeologia*, xxxv (1853), 409–52.
Minutes of the Norwich Court of Mayoralty 1632–1635, ed. William L. Sachse, Norfolk RS xxxvi, 1967.
Overbury, Sir Thomas, 'Characters' (1614–16), in *The "Conceited Newes" of Sir Thomas Overbury And His Friends*, ed. James E. Savage, Gainesville, Florida, 1968, pp. 63–217.
Desiderata Curiosa: or, a Collection of divers scarce and curious pieces, relating chiefly to matters of English History, ed. Francis Peck, 2nd edn., 2 vols., 1779.
Plot, Robert, *The Natural History of Oxfordshire*, Oxford, 1677.
—— *The Natural History of Staffordshire*, Oxford, 1686.
Prynne, William, *Canterburies Doome. Or the first part of a compleat History of the Commitment, Charge, Tryall, Condemnation, Execution of William Laud late Archbishop of Canterbury*, 1646.
Historical Collections of Private Passages of State, ed. John Rushworth, 2nd edn., 8 vols., 1721–2.
Poverty in Early Stuart Salisbury, ed. Paul Slack, Wilts. RS xxxi, 1975.
Sanderson, William, *A Compleat History of the Life and Raigne of King Charles*, 1658.
The Municipal Records of the Borough of Shaftesbury, ed. C. H. Mayo, Sherborne, 1889.
The Diary of Sir Henry Slingsby, of Scriven, Bart., ed. Daniel Parsons, 1836.
Smith, Sir Thomas, *De Republica Anglorum: a Discourse on the Commonwealth of England*, ed. L. Alston, Cambridge, 1906.
Calendar of the Correspondence of the Smyth Family of Ashton Court 1548–1642, ed. J. H. Bettey, Bristol RS xxxv, 1982.
Snell, George, *The Right Teaching of Useful Knowledge*, 1649.
Somerset Assize Orders 1629–1640, ed. Thomas G. Barnes, SRS lxv, 1959.
Somerset Assize Orders 1640–1659, ed. J. S. Cockburn, SRS lxxi, 1971.
Quarter Sessions Records for the County of Somerset (1603–60), ed. E. H. Bates [Harbin], 3 vols., SRS xxiii, xxiv, xxviii, 1907–12.
The Assembly Books of Southampton, i: *1602–1608*, ed. J. W. Horrocks, Southampton RS xix, 1917.
[*Southampton*] *Court Leet Records*, i: *1550–1624*, ed. F. J. C. and D. M. Hearnshaw, Southampton RS, 1905–8.
The Southampton Mayor's Book of 1606–1608, ed. W. J. Connor, Southampton Record Series xxi, 1978.

The Committee at Stafford 1643–1645, ed. D. H. Pennington and I. A. Roots, Manchester, 1957.

Stuart Tracts, 1603–1693, ed. C. H. Firth, Westminster, 1903.

Suffolk and the Great Rebellion, 1640–1660, ed. Alan Everitt, Suffolk RS iii, 1960.

[Taylor, John], *Divers Crabtree Lectures, Expressing the Severall Languages that Shrews read to their Husbands*, 1639.

A Collection of State Papers of John Thurloe, ed. T. Birch, 7 vols., 1742.

Original Records of Early Nonconformity under Persecution and Indulgence, ed. G. Lyon Turner, 3 vols., 1911–14.

Visitation Articles and Injunctions of the Period of the Reformation, ed. W. H. Frere and W. M. Kennedy, 3 vols., Alcuin Club Collections, xiv–xvi, 1910.

Walker, Sir Edward, *Historical Discourses upon Several Occasions*, 1705.

Warwick County Records, iii: *Quarter Sessions Order Book, Easter, 1650, to Epiphany, 1657*, ed. S. C. Ratcliff and H. C. Johnson, Warwick, 1937.

Wastfeild, Robert, *A True Testimony of Faithfull Witnesses recorded*, 1657.

Westcote, Thomas, *A View of Devonshire in MDCXXX*, ed. G. Oliver and P. Jones, Exeter, 1845.

Western Circuit Assize Orders 1629–1648, ed. J. S. Cockburn, Camden 4th Ser., xvii, 1976.

Descriptive Catalogue of the Charters, Minute Books and other Documents of the Borough of Weymouth and Melcombe Regis, ed. H. J. Moule, Weymouth, 1883.

White, John, *The First Century of Scandalous Malignant Priests*, 1643.

Whitelocke, Bulstrode, *Memorials of the English Affairs from the beginning of the reign of Charles the First to the happy Restoration of King Charles the Second*, 4 vols., Oxford, 1853.

'Extracts from the Records of the Wiltshire Quarter Sessions: Reign of King James the First', ed. R. W. Merriman, *WAM* xxii (1885), 1–38, 212–31.

Records of the County of Wilts: being Extracts from the Quarter Sessions Great Rolls of the seventeenth century, ed. B. H. Cunnington, Devizes, 1932.

The Life and Times of Anthony Wood, i: *1632–1663*, ed. Andrew Clark, Oxford Historical Society, xix, 1891.

Diary of Walter Yonge . . . 1604 to 1628, ed. George Roberts, Camden 1st Ser., xli, 1848.

Records of Early English Drama: York, ed. Alexandra F. Johnston and Margaret Rogerson, 2 vols., Toronto, 1979.

3. PRINTED SECONDARY WORKS

Allan, D. G. C. 'The Rising in the West, 1628–1631', *Ec. H.R.* 2nd Ser., v (1952–3), 76–85.

Andriette, Eugene A., *Devon and Exeter in the Civil War*, Newton Abbot, 1971.

Ashton, Robert, *The English Civil War: Conservatism and Revolution 1603–1649*, 1978.

Aston, Trevor (ed.), *Crisis in Europe 1560–1660: Essays from Past and Present*, 1965.

Atkyns, Sir Robert, *The Ancient and Present State of Glostershire*, 1712.

Barnes, Thomas G., 'County Politics and a Puritan Cause Célèbre: Somerset Churchales, 1633', *TRHS* 5th Ser., ix (1959), 103–22.
—— *Somerset 1625–1640: A County's Government During the "Personal Rule"*, Cambridge, Mass., 1961.
B[artelot], R. G., 'Dorset Royalist Roll of Honour, 1662', *SDNQ* xviii (1924–6), 89–93, 165–7, 200–3; xix (1927–9), 43–6, 139–42.
Bayley, A. R., *The Great Civil War in Dorset 1642–1660*, Taunton, 1910.
Beer, Barrett L., *Rebellion and Riot: Popular Disorder in England during the reign of Edward VI*, [Kent, Ohio], 1982.
[Besse, Joseph], *An Abstract of the Sufferings of the People call'd Quakers*, 3 vols., 1733–8.
Bettey, J. H., *Dorset*, Newton Abbot, 1974.
—— 'The Revolts over the Enclosure of the Royal Forest at Gillingham 1626–1630', *DNHP* xcvii (1975), 21–4.
—— 'Sheep, Enclosures and Watermeadows in Dorset agriculture in the Sixteenth and Seventeenth Centuries', in *Husbandry and Marketing in the South-west 1500–1800*, ed. Michael Havinden, Exeter, 1973, pp. 9–18.
Bindoff, S. T., 'Parliamentary History 1529–1688', *VCH, Wilts.*, v, 111–69.
Bolingbroke, L. G., 'Players in Norwich, from the Accession of Queen Elizabeth until their Suppression in 1642', *Norfolk Archaeology*, xiii (1898), 1–20.
Brailsford, H. N., *The Levellers and the English Revolution*, ed. Christopher Hill, Stanford, 1961.
Brewer, John, and Styles, John (eds), *An Ungovernable People: The English and their law in the seventeenth and eighteenth centuries*, 1980.
Broad, John, 'Gentry Finances and the Civil War: The Case of the Buckinghamshire Verneys', *Ec. H.R.* 2nd Ser., xxxii (1979), 183–200.
Brookes, Christopher, *English Cricket: The Game and its Players through the Ages*, 1978.
Brunton, D., and Pennington, D. H., *Members of the Long Parliament*, 1954.
Bryant, Arthur, *Samuel Pepys: The Man in the Making*, 2nd edn., 1947.
Burke, Peter, *Popular Culture in Early Modern Europe*, 1978.
Campbell, Mildred, *The English Yeoman Under Elizabeth and The Early Stuarts*, 2nd edn., New York, 1960.
Chambers, E. K., *The Mediaeval Stage*, 2 vols., Oxford, 1903.
Chambers, R., *The Book of Days: A Miscellany of Popular Antiquities*, 2 vols., 1863–4.
Christie, W. D., *A Life of Anthony Ashley Cooper, First Earl of Shaftesbury, 1621–1683*, 2 vols., 1871.
Clark, Peter, *English Provincial Society from the Reformation to the Revolution: Religion, Politics and Society in Kent 1500–1640*, Hassocks, Sussex, 1977.
—— 'Popular Protest and Disturbance in Kent, 1558–1640', *Ec. H.R.* 2nd Ser., xxix (1976), 365–81.
—— '"The Ramoth-Gilead of the Good": Urban Change and Political Radicalism at Gloucester 1540–1640', in *English Commonwealth*, ed. Clark, Smith, and Tyacke, pp. 167–87.
—— and Slack, Paul (eds), *Crisis and Order in English Towns 1500–1700: Essays in urban history*, 1972.

Clark, Peter, and Smith, Alan, G. R., Tyacke, Nicholas (eds), *The English Commonwealth 1547–1640: Essays in Politics and Society*, Leicester, 1979.

Clifton, Robin, 'The Popular Fear of Catholics during the English Revolution', *P & P* no. 52 (Aug. 1971), 23–55.

Cockburn, J. S. (ed.), *Crime in England 1550–1800*, Princeton, 1977.

Cox, J. Charles, *Churchwardens Accounts from the Fourteenth Century to the Close of the Seventeenth Century*, 1913.

Crawfurd, Raymond, *The King's Evil*, Oxford, 1911.

Cressy, David, *Literacy and the Social Order: Reading and writing in Tudor and Stuart England*, Cambridge, 1980.

Cust, Richard, and Lake, Peter G., 'Sir Richard Grosvenor and the Rhetoric of Magistracy', *BIHR* liv (1981), 40–53.

Davies, Godfrey, *The Restoration of Charles II 1658–1660*, San Marino, Calif., 1955.

Davies, Maud F., *Life in an English Village: An Economic and Historical Survey of the Parish of Corsley in Wiltshire*, 1909.

Dawson, John P., *A History of Lay Judges*, Cambridge, Mass, 1960.

Dictionary of National Biography.

Robert Dover and the Cotswold Games: Annalia Dubrensis, ed. Christopher Whitfield, 1962.

Earle, Peter, *Monmouth's Rebels: The Road to Sedgemoor 1685*, 1977.

Everitt, Alan, *The Community of Kent and the Great Rebellion 1640–1660*, Leicester, 1966.

——— 'Farm Labourers', in *Agrarian History*, iv, ed. Thirsk, pp. 396–465.

——— *The Local Community and the Great Rebellion*, Historical Association Pamphlet G. 70, 1969.

Farnham, Edith, 'The Somerset Election of 1614', *Eng. H.R.* xlvi (1931), 579–99.

Fenwick, George L., *A History of the Ancient City of Chester from the earliest times*, Chester, 1896.

Ferris, J. P., 'The Gentry of Dorset on the Eve of the Civil War', *Genealogists' Magazine*, xv (1965), 104–16.

Firth, C. H., *Cromwell's Army: A History of the English Soldier during the Civil Wars, the Commonwealth and the Protectorate*, 1902.

Fletcher, Anthony, *A County Community in Peace and War: Sussex 1600–1660*, 1975.

——— 'Factionalism in Town and Countryside: the Significance of Puritanism and Arminianism', *Studies in Church History*, xvi (1979), 291–300.

——— *The Outbreak of the English Civil War*, 1981.

——— *Tudor Rebellions*, 2nd edn., 1973.

Fraser, Antonia, *Cromwell The Lord Protector*, 1973.

Gardiner, Samuel R., *History of England from the Accession of James I to the outbreak of the Civil War, 1603–1642*, 10 vols., 1883–6.

——— *History of the Commonwealth and Protectorate 1649–1656*, 2nd edn., 4 vols., 1903.

——— *History of the Great Civil War 1642–1649*, 3 vols., 1886–91.

Gay, Edwin F., 'The Midland Revolt and the Inquisitions of Depopulation of 1607', *TRHS* New Ser., xviii (1904), 195–244.

Green, I. M., 'The Persecution of "scandalous" and "malignant" parish clergy during the English Civil War', *Eng. H.R.* xciv (1979), 507–31.

Hazlitt, W. Carew, *Faiths and Folklore of the British Isles: A Descriptive and Historical Dictionary*, 2 vols., New York, 1965.

Higgins, Patricia, 'The Reactions of Women, with special reference to women petitioners', in *Politics, Religion and The English Civil War*, ed. Brian Manning, 1973, pp. 177–222.

Hill, Christopher, *Economic Problems of the Church From Archbishop Whitgift to the Long Parliament*, Oxford, 1956.

—— *Milton and the English Revolution*, New York, 1977.

—— *Puritanism and Revolution: Studies in Interpretation of the English Revolution of the 17th Century*, 1958.

—— *Society and Puritanism in Pre-Revolutionary England*, 1964.

—— *Some Intellectual Consequences of the English Revolution*, Madison, 1980.

—— *The World Turned Upside Down: Radical Ideas during the English Revolution*, 1972.

Hirst, Derek, *The Representative of the People? Voters and Voting in England under the Early Stuarts*, Cambridge, 1975.

Hole, Christina, *English Sports and Pastimes*, 1949.

Holmes, Clive, 'The County Community in Stuart Historiography', *JBS* xix, no. 2 (1980), 54–73.

—— *The Eastern Association in the English Civil War*, Cambridge, 1974.

—— *Seventeenth-Century Lincolnshire*, History of Lincolnshire, vii, Lincoln, 1980.

Hone, William, *The Every Day Book, or a guide to the Year: describing the Popular Amusements, Sports, Ceremonies, Manners, Customs, and Events . . . in past and present times*, 2 vols., 1888–9.

Hoskins, W. G., *Essays in Leicestershire History*, Liverpool, 1950.

—— 'Harvest Fluctuations and English Economic History, 1620–1759', *Agricultural History Review*, xvi (1968), 15–31.

—— *The Midland Peasant: the Economic and Social History of a Leicestershire village*, 1957.

—— *Provincial England: Essays in social and economic history*, 1963.

Hunt, William, *The Puritan Moment: The Coming of Revolution in an English County*, Cambridge, Mass., 1983.

Hutchins, John, *The History and Antiquities of the County of Dorset*, 3rd edn., ed. W. Shipp and J. W. Hodson, 4 vols., Westminster, 1861–73.

Ingram, M. J., 'Communities and Courts: Law and Disorder in Early Seventeenth-Century Wiltshire', in *Crime in England*, ed. Cockburn, pp. 110–34.

——'Le charivari dans L'Angleterre du XVIᵉ et du XVIIᵉ siècle', in *Le Charivari*, ed. Jacques le Goff and Jean-Claud Schmitt, Paris, 1981 pp. 251–64.

James, E. O., *Seasonal Feasts and Festivals*, 1961.

James, Margaret, *Social Problems and Policy during the Puritan Revolution, 1640–1660*, 1930.

Keeler, Mary F., *The Long Parliament, 1640–1641: A Biographical Study of its Members*, American Philosophical Society Memoirs, xxxvi, Philadelphia, 1954.

Kent, Joan, 'Attitudes of Members of the House of Commons to the Regulation of "Personal Conduct" in Late Elizabethan and Early Stuart England', *BIHR* xlvi (1973), 41–71.

—— 'The English Village Constable, 1580–1642: The Nature and Dilemmas of the Office', *JBS* xx, no. 2 (1981), 26–49.

Kerridge, Eric, *The Agricultural Revolution*, 1967.

—— 'Agriculture c.1500–c.1793', *VCH, Wilts.*, iv, 43–64.

—— 'The Revolts in Wiltshire against Charles I', *WAM* lvii (1958–60), 64–75.

Ketton-Cremer, R. W., *Forty Norfolk Essays*, Norwich, 1961.

—— *Norfolk in the Civil War: A Portrait of a Society in Conflict*, 1969.

Laslett, Peter, *The World We Have Lost*, 2nd edn., 1973.

Lindley, Keith, *Fenland Riots and the English Revolution*, 1982.

MacCulloch, Diarmaid, 'Kett's Rebellion in Context', *P & P* no. 84 (Aug. 1979), 36–59.

McDermott, M. B., 'Church House at Langford Budville', *SDNQ* xxix (1968–73), 127–31.

Malcolm, Joyce L., *Caesar's Due: Loyalty and King Charles 1642–1646*, Royal Hist. Soc. Studies in History, xxxviii, 1983.

Malcolmson, Robert W., *Popular Recreations in English Society 1700–1850*, Cambridge, 1973.

Manning, Brian, *The English People and the English Revolution 1640–1649*, 1976.

Matthews, A. G., *Walker Revised: Being a Revision of John Walker's Sufferings of the Clergy during the Grand Rebellion 1642–60*, Oxford, 1948.

Minchinton, W. E. (ed.), *Essays in Agrarian History*, 2 vols., Newton Abbot, 1968.

Morrill, J. S., *Cheshire 1630–1660: County Government and Society during the English Revolution*, Oxford, 1974.

—— 'The Church in England, 1642–9', in *Reactions*, ed. Morrill, pp. 89–114.

—— (ed.), *Reactions to the English Civil War 1642–1649*, 1982.

—— *The Revolt of the Provinces: Conservatives and Radicals in the English Civil War 1630–1650*, 1976.

Murray, John T., *English Dramatic Companies 1588–1642*, 2 vols., 1910.

Nicholas, Donald, *Mr. Secretary Nicholas (1593–1669) His Life and Letters*, 1955.

Pennington, D. H., 'County and Country: Staffordshire in Civil War Politics', *North Staffs. Journal of Field Studies*, vi (1966), 12–25.

—— and Thomas, Keith (eds), *Puritans and Revolutionaries: Essays in Seventeenth-Century History presented to Christopher Hill*, Oxford, 1978.

Phythian-Adams, Charles, 'Ceremony and the Citizen: The communal year at Coventry 1450–1550', in *Crisis and Order*, ed. Clark and Slack, pp. 57–85.

Pope, F. J., 'Sidelights on the Civil War in Dorset', *SDNQ* xii (1910–11), 52–5.

Quaife, G. R., *Wanton Wenches and Wayward Wives: Peasants and Illicit Sex in Early Seventeenth Century England*, 1979.

Ralph, Philip L., *Sir Humphrey Mildmay: Royalist Gentleman*, New Brunswick, NJ, 1947.

Ramsay, G. D., *The Wiltshire Woollen Industry in the Sixteenth and Seventeenth Centuries*, Oxford, 1943.

Reay, Barry, 'Popular hostility towards Quakers in mid-seventeenth-century England', *Social History*, v (1980), 387–407.

Reeves, Marjorie E., 'Protestant Nonconformity', *VCH, Wilts.*, iii, 99–149.
Roy, Ian, 'England Turned Germany? The Aftermath of the Civil War in its European Context', *TRHS* 5th Ser., xxviii (1978), 127–44.
—— 'The English Civil War and English Society', in *War and Society: A Yearbook of Military History*, ed. B. Bond and I. Roy, 1975, pp. 24–43.
Russell, Conrad (ed.), *The Origins of the English Civil War*, 1973.
—— *Parliaments and English Politics 1621–1629*, Oxford, 1979.
Salerno, Anthony, 'The Social Background of Seventeenth-Century Emigration to America', *JBS* xix, no. 1 (1979), 31–52.
Samaha, J., 'Gleanings from Local Criminal-Court Records: Sedition Amongst the "Inarticulate" in Elizabethan Essex', *JSH* viii, no. 4 (1975), 61–79.
Schochet, Gordon J., *Patriarchalism in Political Thought: The Authoritarian Family and Political Speculation and Attitudes Especially in Seventeenth-Century England*, New York, 1975.
Scrope, G. P., *History of the Manor and Ancient Baronage of Castle Combe*, 1852.
Sharp, Buchanan, *In Contempt of All Authority: Rural Artisans and Riot in the West of England, 1586–1660*, Berkeley and Los Angeles, 1980.
Sisson, C. J., *Lost Plays of Shakespeare's Age*, Cambridge, 1936.
Slack, Paul, 'Poverty and Politics in Salisbury 1597–1666', in *Crisis and Order*, ed. Clark and Slack, pp. 164–203.
—— 'Vagrants and Vagrancy in England, 1598–1664', *Ec. H.R.* 2nd Ser., xxvii (1974), 360–79.
Somerset and Dorset Notes and Queries.
Spufford, Margaret, *Contrasting Communities: English Villagers in the Sixteenth and Seventeenth Centuries*, Cambridge, 1974.
Stieg, Margaret, *Laud's Laboratory: The Diocese of Bath and Wells in the Early Seventeenth Century*, Lewisburg, Pennsylvania, 1982.
Stone, Lawrence, *The Causes of the English Revolution 1529–1642*, 1972.
—— *Family and Fortune: Studies in Aristocratic Finance in the Sixteenth and Seventeenth Centuries*, Oxford, 1973.
—— *The Family, Sex and Marriage In England 1500–1800*, abridged edn., Harmondsworth, 1979.
Symonds, W, 'Winterslow Church Reckonings, 1542–1661', *WAM* xxxvi (1909–10), 27–49.
Tait, James, 'The Declaration of Sports for Lancashire (1617)', *Eng. H.R.* xxxii (1917), 561–8.
Taylor, Christopher, *The Making of the English Landscape: Dorset*, 1970.
Thirsk, Joan (ed.), *The Agrarian History of England and Wales*, iv: *1500–1640*, Cambridge, 1967.
—— 'Enclosing and Engrossing', in *Agrarian History*, iv, ed. Thirsk, pp. 200–55.
—— *English Peasant Farming. The Agrarian History of Lincolnshire from Tudor to Recent Times*, 1957.
—— 'The Farming Regions of England', in *Agrarian History*, iv, ed. Thirsk, pp. 1–112.
Thomas, Keith, *Religion and the Decline of Magic*, New York, 1971.
—— 'Women and the Civil War Sects', in *Crisis in Europe*, ed. Aston, pp. 317–40.

Thomas-Stanford, Charles, *Sussex in the Great Civil War and the Interregnum 1642–1660*, 1910.

Thompson, E. P., 'The Moral Economy of the English Crowd in the Eighteenth Century', *P & P* no. 50 (Feb. 1971), 76–136.

Tyacke, Nicholas, 'Popular Puritan Mentality in late Elizabethan England', in *English Commonwealth*, ed. Clark, Smith, and Tyacke, pp. 77–92.

—— 'Puritanism, Arminianism and Counter-Revolution', in *Origins of the English Civil War*, ed. Russell, pp. 119–43.

Underdown, David, 'A Case Concerning Bishops' Lands: Cornelius Burges and the Corporation of Wells', *Eng. H.R.* lxxviii (1963) 18–48.

—— 'The Chalk and the Cheese: Contrasts among the English Clubmen', *P & P* no. 85 (Nov. 1979), 25–48.

—— '"Honest" Radicals in the Counties, 1642–1649', in *Puritans and Revolutionaries*, ed. Pennington and Thomas, pp. 186–205.

—— *Pride's Purge: Politics in the Puritan Revolution*, Oxford, 1971.

—— 'The Problem of Popular Allegiance in the English Civil War', *TRHS* 5th Ser., xxxi (1981), 69–94.

—— *Royalist Conspiracy in England 1649–1660*, New Haven, 1960.

—— *Somerset in the Civil War and Interregnum*, Newton Abbot, 1973.

—— 'The Taming of the Scold: The Enforcement of Patriarchal Authority in Early Modern England', in *Order and Disorder in Early Modern England*, ed. Anthony Fletcher and John Stevenson, Cambridge (1985), ch. 4.

Vann, Richard T., *The Social Development of English Quakerism 1655–1755*, Cambridge, Mass., 1969.

Vayda, Andrew P. (ed.), *Environment and Cultural Behavior: Ecological Studies in Cultural Anthropology*, Austin, 1969.

Victoria County History, Somerset, vols. ii–iv,

Victoria County History, Wiltshire, vols, iii–v, vii–xii, 1953–83.

Walter, John, 'Grain Riots and Popular Attitudes to the Law: Maldon and the Crisis of 1629', in *An Ungovernable People*, ed. Brewer and Styles, pp. 47–84.

—— and Wrightson, Keith, 'Dearth and the Social Order in Early Modern England', *P & P* no. 71 (May 1976), 22–42.

Ware, Sedley L., 'The Elizabethan Parish in its Ecclesiastical and Financial Aspects', *Johns Hopkins University Studies in Historical and Political Science*, Ser. xxvi, nos. 7–8, Baltimore, 1908.

Whiteman, Anne, 'The Church of England 1542–1837', *VCH, Wilts.*, iii, 28–56.

Whitlock, Ralph, *The Folklore of Wiltshire*, 1976.

Willcox, William B., *Gloucestershire: A Study in Local Government, 1590–1640*, New Haven, 1940.

Williams, J. Anthony, *Catholic Recusancy in Wiltshire 1660–1791*, Catholic Record Society, 1968.

Williams, Michael, *The Draining of the Somerset Levels*, Cambridge, 1970.

Wiltshire Notes and Queries.

Wright, A. R., *British Calendar Customs: England*, ed. T. E. Lones, 3 vols., 1936–40.

Wrightson, Keith, 'Aspects of Social Differentiation in rural England, c.1580–1660', *Journal of Peasant Studies*, v (1977–8), 33–47.

Wrightson, Keith, *English Society 1580–1680*, 1982.
—— 'Two Concepts of Order: Justices, Constables and Jurymen in Seventeenth-Century England', in *An Ungovernable People*, ed. Brewer and Styles, pp. 21–46.
—— and Levine, David, *Poverty and Piety in an English Village: Terling, 1525–1700*, 1979.
Wrigley, E. A., and Schofield, R. S., *The Population History of England 1541–1871*, 1981.
Wroughton, John, *The Civil War in Bath and North Somerset (1642–1650)*, Bath, 1973.
Young, Peter, and Emberton, Wilfred, *The Cavalier Army: Its Organization and Everday Life*, 1974.

4. UNPUBLISHED PAPERS AND THESES

Amussen, Susan D., 'Governors and Governed: Class and Gender Relations in English Villages, 1590–1725', Ph.D. thesis, Brown University, 1982.
Anderson, Jay Allan, '"A Solid Sufficiency": An Ethnography of Yeoman Foodways in Stuart England', Ph.D. thesis, University of Pennsylvania, 1973.
Bettey, J. H., 'Agriculture and Rural Society in Dorset, 1570–1670', Ph.D. thesis, University of Bristol, 1977.
Croot, Patricia E., 'Aspects of Agrarian Society in Brent Marsh, Somerset, 1500–1700', Ph.D. thesis, University of Leeds, 1981.
Cust, Richard, 'The Forced Loan and English Politics 1626–1628', Ph.D. thesis, University of London, 1984.
Harrison, G. A., 'Royalist Organisation in Wiltshire, 1642–1646', Ph.D. thesis, University of London, 1963.
Hill, Christopher, 'The Poor and the People in Seventeenth-Century England', William F. Church Memorial Lecture, Brown University, 1981.
Ingram, M. J., 'Ecclesiastical Justice in Wiltshire 1600–1640', D.Phil. thesis, University of Oxford, 1976.
Manning, B. S., 'Neutrals and Neutralism in the English Civil War 1642–1646', D.Phil. thesis, University of Oxford, 1957.
Reinhart, Thomas E., 'The Parliamentary Visitation of Oxford University, 1647–50', Ph.D. thesis, Brown University, 1984.
Spaeth, Donald M., 'Parsons and Parishioners: Lay-Clerical Relations and Popular Belief in Wiltshire villages, 1660–1740', Ph.D. thesis, Brown University, 1985.
Wrightson, Keith, 'The Puritan Reformation of Manners with special reference to the counties of Lancashire and Essex', Ph.D. thesis, University of Cambridge, 1973.

Index

Note: Names of places in Dorset, Somerset, and Wiltshire are followed in parentheses by the initial letter of the county in which they were situated in the seventeenth century.

Abbotsbury (D) 146, 205
Abbotts Bromley, Staffs. 46, 262
Adber (S) 98
Aldbourne (W) 160, 194, 262
alehouses, regulation of 48, 84, 241–3
ales 94, 263; clerk 83, 98; Cobb (Lyme Regis) 57–8. *See also* church ales
Alhampton (S) 264
Allein, Richard 77, 83
Allington (W) 92
Alton Pancras (D) 75
Amesbury (W) 131, 194, 201
Arden, Forest of 34
armies, civil war 183–4, 285. *See also* impressment, pensions, plundering, quartering, recruiting
army, of Parliament 147–8, 150–3, 160–1, 175, 177–8, 185–7, 190, 209; and politics 211–12, 231; and religion 247–8; hostility to 221–3, 229, 233, 272–3
army, royalist 147–8, 150–3, 160, 165, 188–9
Arne (D) 91
Arundell family 122, 129, 160
Arundell, Thomas, 1st Baron Arundell of Wardour 89
Arundell, Thomas, 2nd Baron Arundell of Wardour 141
Ashcott (S) 270
Ashe family 25, 181
Ashe, John 135, 153, 170, 173, 227–8, 233, 238
Ashill (S) 109
Ashley Cooper, Sir Anthony 22, 148, 156 n., 214, 237
Ashton Keynes (W) 60, 83
Ashwell, Herts. 35, 218
Aubrey, John 17, 46, 82, 103, 153; quoted 7, 14–15, 45, 52, 73, 75, 76, 80, 88, 258–9, 280, 290
Austin, Samuel 246
Axbridge (S) 81, 247
Axholme, Isle of 74, 159–60, 214, 250

Badbury (D) 157
Baltimore, Lord. *See* Calvert
Bankes family 172
Bankes, Henry 219, 243, 253

Banwell (S) 218
Baptists 239–40, 247–8, 250, 253, 286
Barford St. Martin (W) 93, 262
Barrington, Sir Francis 48
Basing House, Hants 175, 186
Batcombe (S) 77–8, 84, 104, 225, 242–3, 245; in civil war 147, 174, 180; Royalists in 204, 206
Bath (S) 77, 127, 252, 266, 273, 283, 294; Archdeaconry of 86
Bathampton (S) 27, 79
Batheaston (S) 85
Bathford (S) 77
Baxter, Richard 3, 169, 178; quoted 1, 131, 143–4, 177
Baynton family 77, 173
Baynton, Sir Edward 134, 224
Beach, William 175
Beaminster (D) 15, 131, 197, 205, 299
bear-baiting 47, 67, 69, 98
Beard, Thomas 9, 51
Beckington (S) 78, 126, 130, 135, 137, 247–8
Bedford, Earl of. *See* Russell
Bedfordshire 76, 138
Bedwyn, Great (W) 226
Beer Crowcombe (S) 99
Bemerton (W) 90
Bennet, Thomas 277
Bere Regis (D) 91, 197, 205–6
Berkeley family 180, 198, 204–6, 215
Berkeley, Sir Charles 181, 215
Berkley (S) 101
Berkshire 91, 221; places in 60, 61, 81, 101
Biddestone (W) 83
Bingham, John 224, 227
Birch, John 212; soldiers of 221
Bisley, Glos. 60
Blackheath, Kent 258, 273
Blackmore Vale (D) 7, 25, 104–5; culture of 96–7, 180, 207, 262, 264, 276; religion in 140–1; in civil war 165, 167–8, 171–2, 181, 276; Royalists in 197–8, 199, 205–6, 295–6, 298
Blagdon (S) 83
Blake, Robert 228
Blandford (D) 47, 123, 230, 245–6, 276; in civil war 153, 171, 179; Royalists in 196, 205–6, 236, 263, 299

Index

Bleadon (S) 85, 266
Booth, Sir George, rising of 255
Box (W) 79
Boyle, Roger, Baron Broghil 215–16
Brabazon, Wallop 142
Bradford-on-Avon (W) 79, 84, 85, 194, 249
Bradley, North (W) 83, 247–8
Bradshaw, John 237, 271
Bravell, Thomas 245
Braydon Forest (W) 7, 108–9, 111–12, 160–1
Brent, South (S) 83, 157
Breton, Nicholas 64
Brewham Forest (S) 215
Bridgwater (S) 32, 223, 225, 228, 234, 247, 255, 294; in civil war 148, 149, 165
Bridport (D) 54, 100, 166, 197, 225, 228, 299
Brinkworth (W) 249
Brislington (S) 79, 251
Bristol 213, 219, 231, 236, 247, 250, 252, 273; in civil war 147–8, 152, 154, 165, 169–70, 186, 222
Broghil, Lord. *See* Boyle
Bromham (W) 85
Bromwich, Isaac 268
Broughton Gifford (W) 77–8
Browne, John 224
Bruce, Thomas, Lord Bruce and 1st Earl of Elgin 108, 161–2, 215
Bruen, John 59
Bruton (S) 104, 215–16, 221, 276–8, 285 n., 294; in civil war 146, 168, 180–1; Royalists in 204–7
Buckingham, Duke of. *See* Villiers
Buckinghamshire 145, 150, 156, 159, 250
Buckland, West (S) 22, 98
bull-baiting 47, 63, 69, 98, 259, 264, 266, 281
Bunyan, John 236
Burbage (W) 110, 163, 291
Burford, Oxon. 46, 213
Burnham (S) 291
Burrington (S) 79
Burroughs, Edward 254
Burton, Henry 67–8, 95
Burton, Long (D) 81
Bury St. Edmunds 269
Byfield, Adoniram 246

Cadbury, North (S) 97, 104, 181
Cadbury, South (S) 97, 104
Calne (W) 83, 84, 189, 194, 250
Calvert, Cecil, 2nd Baron Baltimore 220
Cambridgeshire 256; places in 21, 24
Camel, Queen (S) 251, 264
Camel, West (S) 155, 181
Cameley (S) 85, 102, 254
Cannings, All (W) 46, 71

Cannings, Bishops (W) 75
Canterbury 177, 231, 260
Castle Cary (S) 104, 157, 181, 223
Castle Combe (W) 13, 77, 79, 249
Castle Eaton (W) 96
Castlehaven, Earl of. *See* Touchet
Catholics 89, 122, 145; and popular festivals 47, 65, 279; in civil war 146, 164–; hostility to 70, 128–9, 133–4, 140–1, 217–;
Cavaliers 156, 259; in civil war 146–8, 157–; 162, 166, 174, 178, 188–9; stereotype 142–3, 164, 258, 268; as term of abuse 21; 278, 289–90
Cavendish, William, Marquis of Newcastle 17
Cecil, William, 2nd Earl of Salisbury 23, 16; 172–3, 220, 226
Ceeley, Thomas 228
Cerne Abbas (D) 37, 92, 196, 197, 205–6
Cerne, Broad (D) 254
chalk country, the 295–6, 298; culture of 7; 75–6, 88, 90–5, 263–4, 280; religion in 89–90, 180; in civil war 167, 179, 20; Royalists in 194, 196–7, 201–2, 205–6, 23; 295–6, 298
Chalke, Bower (W) 95
Chalke, Broad (W) 95, 171, 189
Chambers, Humphrey 77
Chapman, Henry 266
Chard (S) 147, 165, 230
Chardstock (D) 32
charivari 39, 55, 100–1, 178, 254. *See* al; Skimmingtons
Charles I, King 71, 113, 121, 125, 135, 13; 142; in civil war 147, 155, 165; execution 208–9, 245
Charles II, King 238, 240, 245, 270, 273, 28; *See also* Restoration
Charlton (W) 76
Charlton Horethorne (S) 97
Charminster (D) 58, 101
Cheddar (S) 34, 137, 216–17, 219, 243, 247–;
cheese country, the 7, 25; culture of 73, 76–; 82–3, 100, 102–3, 280; religion in 78–9, 10; 140, 249; in civil war 170; Royalists in 19; 295–6. *See also* clothing districts
Chelmsford 50, 139
Chelwood (S) 79, 218
Cheselbourne (D) 75
Cheshire 67, 154, 156, 180, 236, 241–2
Chester 45, 69, 253, 280
Cheverell, Great (W) 12
Chew Stoke (S) 77
Chilmark (W) 92
Chippenham (W) 29, 36, 121, 123, 134, 21; 216, 224, 247, 250; in civil war 150–1, 27; Royalists in 194; Forest 7, 108
Cholderton (W) 236
Christian Malford (W) 280

Christmas 14, 46, 60, 216, 256, 258, 260–1, 262–3, 267, 281

Christmas, Richard 60, 89

Chubb, Matthew 57

church ales 45, 46, 47–8, 55, 63, 68, 86, 92–3, 95–6, 97–9, 178, 263; abandonment of 60–1, 82–3, 91–2, 97–8, 265; prohibition of 49, 66, 98, 262

Church of England; Book of Common Prayer 230, 244, 253, 255–6; calendar of 14; clergy of 29, 31, 90, 179–81, 296 (*See also* Laudians, Presbyterians); in Interregnum 244–6. *See also* churches, courts, parish

churches, parish; altars 78, 97, 126, 130; bell-ringing 47, 71, 94; cock-fighting in 94; organs 56, 78, 97, 181; rates for 31, 53, 60, 83, 91–3, 97; seats in 14, 22, 29–33, 91; as social centre 14

churchwardens 10, 27, 31, 33, 60, 78, 94, 98, 130, 131

Clarendon, Earl of. *See* Hyde

classes, conflict of 2, 3, 21, 108, 110, 114–15, 117–18, 168–71, 277

classes, polarization between 20, 24–8, 30, 32–3, 40, 48, 80, 277, 281–2

clergy. *See* Church of England; clergy of

Cley Hill (W) 82, 109

clothing districts 7, 202, 240, 266–8, 278–9; depression in 25, 34, 116–17, 137, 195, 213–14, 241; Puritans in 62, 77–9, 82, 104, 207, 247, 276; in civil war 150, 165–6, 169–70, 190–1, 277; Royalists in 191, 194, 203–4

Clubmen 150, 162, 166, 170, 175, 207, 214, 219, 222, 230–1, 245, 291; risings of (1645) 148, 152, 156–9, 167–8, 189, 276–7; (1646) 189, 223; (1648) 225; and Royalists 172, 174; conservatism of 178, 180, 210, 226, 255

cock-fighting 94, 99, 259, 266, 281

cock-shying 93, 263

Coker, East (S) 30, 32, 99, 104, 273

Colchester 236–7

Coleford (S) 67–8, 86

Colerne Down (W) 76

Collier, Thomas 232, 247–8, 250, 253

Collingbourne Down (W) 76

Commonwealth, the 240, 257; Engagement to 221, 233–4. *See also* Rump

community, local 168, 240; values of 11–12, 15–17, 106–7, 174; culture of 41, 64–5, 66–7, 72; Puritans and 42. *See also* custom, parish

Compton Abbas (D) 245

Compton Chamberlayne (W) 236

conservatism, popular 14–15, 110, 118–19, 162, 219, 226. *See also* Clubmen, custom

Constantine, William 155

Conway, Edward, 2nd Viscount Conway 268

Copley, Christopher 190

Corbet, John 169–70, 175

Corfe Castle (D) 91, 134, 146, 148, 167, 172, 187, 197, 206

Cornwall 45, 74, 188, 231, 261, 262

Corscombe (D) 129

Corsham (W) 86

Corsley (W) 32

Cotswolds, the 7, 96; Games 64, 282

Cottington, James 27

Cotton, John 54

county committees 147, 153, 221, 224–6, 246

Court, the, hostility to 108, 119–20, 125, 127–8, 136

courts, ecclesiastical 27, 32, 130

courts, manor 10, 12–14, 220

Coventry 45, 71, 177, 232

craftsmen 10, 192, 196, 200–1

Cranborne (D) 23, 160, 172, 197, 205, 299

Creech St. Michael (S) 27

Crewkerne (S) 97, 294 n.

cricket 74–5, 281

Crisp, Tobias 249

Crockerton (W) 93

Cromwell, Oliver 113, 136, 148, 157, 208, 211, 234, 238, 239–40, 260, 271. *See also* Major-Generals, Protectorate

Crooke, Samuel 77, 79, 182

Croscombe (S) 45, 203–4

Crowland, Lincs. 160

Crudwell (W) 29

cucking-stools 16, 39, 100, 253

Curll, Edward 225, 242–3, 264

custom 15, 107, 120, 124–5. *See also* conservatism

Cutcombe (S) 97

dancing 46, 48, 60, 62, 64, 84, 88, 93–5, 98. *See also* morris dancing

Danvers family 77

Danvers, Sir John 138, 224, 227

Davenant, Sir William 260

Dean, Forest of 106, 108–10, 137, 159

deference 1–2, 4, 22, 121–2, 171–4, 277

Denbigh, Earl of. *See* Feilding

Derby, Earls of. *See* Stanley

Devereux, Robert, 3rd Earl of Essex 147, 165, 175, 180

Deverill, Hill (W) 114

Deverill, Kingston (W) 76, 94

Deverill, Longbridge (W) 93

Devizes (W) 16, 29, 36, 39, 51, 100, 250; in civil war 146, 148, 158, 167, 188, 194, 206

Devonshire 49, 74, 139, 152, 154, 229, 231, 261, 262, 268; places in 47, 63, 141, 178, 232

D'Ewes, Sir Simonds 132

Digby family 141, 146, 171–2, 198, 206, 272

Digby, George 271

Digby, George, Lord 137–8
Digby, Sir Kenelm 260
Diggers 115, 209–10
Dinton (W) 91, 171
Disbrowe, John 199, 215, 237, 244
Ditcheat (S) 77, 84, 102, 104, 204
Dodington, Sir Francis 173, 188, 277
Donhead St. Mary (W) 89, 246, 251, 262
Dorchester (D) 32, 36, 100, 117, 119, 128, 234, 243, 245, 263, 276; Puritans in 51–2, 56–7, 71, 89, 140, 179, 250; in civil war 165, 166–7, 170, 187, 205, 206, 224; Royalists in 191, 196, 205, 299; and Restoration 274, 288
Dorset 108, 109, 129, 214, 216, 242, 270; agricultural regions 5–8; enclosures in 19, 114 (*see also* Gillingham Forest); petitions from 139, 141, 224, 230; politics in 120, 124, 133, 134–5, 141, 227, 237; popular festivals in 47, 49, 93, 263; population of 285 n., 293–4, 296, 298; in civil war 146–8, 153–5, 157–62, 165–8, 170–4, 188–9, 190–1; Royalists in 191, 192, 195–8, 199–200, 205–6, 296–9; County Committee of 215–16, 224–5, 230, 253, 255; 1655 rebellion in 236, 261; and Restoration 274
Doulting (S) 203
Dove, John 227
Dover, Robert 64, 72
downlands. *See* chalk country
Downton (W) 194–5
Droitwich 259
Dundry (S) 68, 86–8
Dunster (S) 148, 294 n.
Dursley, Glos. 79, 83, 273–4

Easter 14, 256
Easton Royal (W) 60
Eburne, Richard 34
Edington (W) 91, 193
Edwards, Thomas 219, 248
Elford, Thomas 245
Elgin, Earl of. *See* Bruce
Ely, Isle of 160
enclosures 14, 18–19, 26, 61, 80–1, 107, 113–14, 284; riots against 107–12, 114–16, 136–7, 159–62, 214
Enford (W) 93, 236
Engagement, the. *See* Commonwealth
Englishcombe (S) 251
Erbury, William 79
Erle family 224
Erle, Sir Walter 124, 167, 190–1
Essex 36, 49, 50, 116, 125, 132, 171, 218, 230, 261; places in 29, 139, 217–18, 257
Essex, Earl of. *See* Devereux
Evercreech (S) 203–4
Everleigh (W) 70, 263

Evershot (D) 254
excise; Commissioners 243; resistance to 14, 216, 270
Exeter 50, 154, 232, 234

Fairfax, Sir Thomas 148, 151, 157, 166, 16, 222, 231, 277
fairs 85, 88, 261, 264, 267. *See also* Tann H Fair, Woodbury Hill Fair
Falstone House (W) 225
family, the. *See* patriarchal authority
Farrington Gurney (S) 78
Feilding, Basil, 2nd Earl of Denbigh 156, 268
Fennor, William 54, 64
fens, the 75, 112–13, 136, 159–60, 214, 25 drainage of 19, 24. *See also* Axholme, Isle of
festivals, popular, campaigns against 47–53–9, 276, 279, 283–4. *See also* Christma church ales, Easter, Gunpowder Treaso Day, Hallowe'en, harvest homes, Ploug Monday, revels, Whitsun
Fiennes, William, 1st Viscount Saye an Sele 180, 256
Fifth Monarchy Men 209, 239
Filliol, William 231
Filmer, Sir Robert 10, 287
Fisherton Anger (W) 94
Fitzjames, John 252
football 67, 69, 75–6, 94, 259, 261, 270, 281
Fordington (D) 56, 197 n.
forests 19, 34, 136. *See also* Arden, Braydo Brewham, Dean, Gillingham, Melkshan Neroche, Selwood
Forthampton, Glos. 160
Fox, George 254
Fraunceis, Thomas 22
Freshford (S) 191, 233
Frome (S) 37, 85, 207, 216, 285 n., 294
Fuller, Thomas 19
Fullwood, Francis 248
Fussell, John 172

Geare, John 57–8, 81
gentry 10, 20–3, 63, 125–6, 281, 296; in civ war 169, 172–4, 184, 200–1. *See also* Justice of the Peace
Gerard, Thomas 26
Gilbert, Maurice 23, 60, 97
Gillingham (D) 15, 93, 161, 198, 205, 299 Forest 108–10, 112, 161–2, 196, 215
Glastonbury (S) 83, 246, 252, 254, 259, 294
Gloucester 51, 68, 123, 128, 144, 170, 256
Gloucestershire 25, 79, 82–3, 109, 117, 214 216, 243; in civil war 146, 151–2, 166, 169 188
Godmanstone (D) 157
Godney Moor (S) 137, 214

orges, John 224, 237
oring, George, army of 148, 151–2, 157–8, 167, 189, 289
ough, Richard 30, 31, 183, 196
reinton (S) 251
rey, Henry, 1st Earl of Stamford 188
rosvenor, Sir Richard 48, 123, 126
uise, Christopher 153
unpowder Treason Day 68, 70–1, 129, 139, 282
ussage Corner (D) 157
utch, John 246

all, Thomas 272, 275, 279
allowe'en 70
alstock (D) 90, 97
alton (S) 97
ambledon, Hants 281
ambledon Hill (D) 148, 158, 168
ampshire 88, 175, 185–6, 216, 221, 233
anley (D) 93
annington (W) 60, 96
arington family 77
arington, John 140, 228
arley, Sir Robert 138–40
arrison, Thomas 227; regiment of 233
arrison, William 5, 9, 49
arvest homes 14, 46
astings, Francis 48, 97
astings, Henry 22–3
atch (W) 92
axey Hood game 74
enley, Henry 227
enley-in-Arden 34, 262
enstridge (S) 163
erbert family 134, 171
erbert, George 29, 65
erbert, Philip, 4th Earl of Pembroke 134, 160, 171, 226, 228
erbert, William, 3rd Earl of Pembroke 110, 113, 123
ereford 177–8, 187, 212, 221, 258, 268
erefordshire 75, 139, 140, 142, 221, 223, 232, 240, 253, 268
ertford, Earl of. *See* Seymour
ertford, Marquis of. *See* Seymour
ertfordshire 76, 213
eytesbury (W) 31, 194, 201
ighworth (W) 194, 206
illfarrance (S) 264
indon (W) 194, 228
inton, Broad (W) 76
obbes, Thomas 1
ole, John 55
olles, Denzil 128, 229
olwell (S) 264
opton family 20

Hopton, Sir Ralph 147, 152, 166, 173, 174, 188, 198, 203, 277
Hopton, Richard 257–8
Horner family 20, 77, 170, 173, 228
Horner, Sir John 113, 227
Horningsham (W) 160
horns, symbolic use of 100–1, 178, 254
horse-racing 64, 69, 259, 261
Howell, James 52, 136
Hungerford, Berks. 155–6
Hungerford family 77, 121, 173
Hungerford, Sir Edward 150, 160, 161, 181, 277
Hungerford, Henry 226
Hunstrete (S) 173
Huntspill (S) 291
hurling 74, 259, 261
husbandmen 10, 28, 192, 196, 200–1, 296
Hyde, Edward, 1st Earl of Clarendon 2–3, 164, 166, 223–4

iconoclasm by Puritans 51, 78, 139–40, 177–8, 181
Ilchester (S) 81, 98, 227–8
Ilminster (S) 294 n.
Ilton (S) 98
impressment of soldiers 184, 187–9, 223
Ince, Peter 246, 263
Independents; in politics 212, 219, 228; in religion 239, 253
Ireton, Henry 212
Ironside, Gilbert 274
Isle Brewers (S) 243
Ivie, Sir George 22
Ivie, John 51, 57, 246
Iwerne Courtney (D) 114

James I and VI, King 65, 120
Jonson, Ben 64
Josselin, Ralph 261
Justices of the Peace 10, 23, 109–10, 161, 191–3, 213–14; and moral reformation 48–9, 241–3; and civil war 147, 149, 152, 223–4

Keevil (W) 66, 83, 84
Kemble (W) 96
Kennett, White 280
Kent 68, 74, 75, 118, 133, 213, 221, 231–2, 260–1, 281; in civil wars 4, 149, 178, 230–1; places in 67, 274
Kethe, William 47, 89, 91
Keynsham (S) 86
Kidderminster 143–4
Kilmington (S) 215
Kilton (S) 269
Kingsdon (S) 98
King's Evil, touching for the 283, 290

King's Norton, Warwickshire 275
Kington Langley (W) 280
Kington St. Michael (W) 45, 280
Kington, West (W) 22
Kingweston (S) 264, 270

labourers 10, 106, 196, 200
Lacock (W) 37, 148, 249
Lancashire 49, 65, 76, 169, 171, 173, 232, 241–2, 269
Langford Budville (S) 99, 265
Langley Burrell (W) 249, 285
Langport, battle of (S) 148, 157
Lansdown, battle of (S) 147
Laud, William, Archbishop 66, 129–30, 140
Laudians (Laudianism) 66–8, 77–8, 90, 129–31, 139–40, 244, 276, 279
Lavington, Market (W) 93, 194
lectureships 77, 130
Leicestershire 18, 35, 49, 67, 75, 138
Leigh-on-Mendip (S) 102, 266
L'Estrange, Sir Hamon 224
Levellers 114, 115, 209–13, 229, 232, 235
levels, Somerset 26, 137, 202, 247, 251; agriculture in 7–8, 12; drainage of 19, 113, 214; in civil war 157, 166, 207; Royalists in 203, 207
Lilburne, John 211, 213–14, 249
Limington (S) 251
Lincolnshire 54, 113, 133, 136, 214, 270
Lingen, Sir Henry 268
Litton Cheney (D) 93
Loan, Forced (1626–7) 121, 125–6, 128
localism 2, 4, 107, 124, 174–6
Locke, John 287
Loder, Robert 24
London 128, 211, 213, 253, 260, 274, 286; riots in 140, 261, 272–3; street demonstrations in 136, 138, 145, 154; regiments from 185–6
Longborough, Glos. 31
Longford House (W) 148, 188
Longleat (W) 160
Ludgershall (W) 94, 194, 201
Ludlow family 114
Ludlow, Edmund 161, 169, 175, 179, 192, 225, 228, 237
Ludlow, Sir Henry 22
Ludlow, Shropshire 138, 177
Luke, Sir Samuel 171, 179
Lullington (S) 22
Luttrell family 226
Luttrell, Alexander 134
Lydiard Millicent (W) 214
Lydiard Tregoze (W) 280
Lyme Regis (D) 57–8, 81, 100, 128, 247; in civil war 146, 153, 167; Royalists in 197, 299; and Restoration 272, 274, 288

Lyneham (W) 120

Maddington (W) 46
Maiden Bradley (W) 22, 192
Major-Generals 220, 237–8, 244, 264; Royalists listed by 185, 195, 199–206, 296–9
Malmesbury (W) 53, 123, 146–8, 150, 227
Manningford Abbas (W) 93
Maperton (S) 97, 181
Marden (W) 102, 263
Mark (S) 247
Markham, Gervase 15, 19
Marlborough (W) 39, 46, 66, 146, 148, 171, 17, 226–7
Marten, Henry, regiment of 233
Martock (S) 26, 160, 251–2
Massey, Edward 150, 227; brigade of 222
masterless people 11, 36–7. *See also* vagrants
Maurice, Prince 147, 150, 160
May Day celebrations 46, 56, 59, 64, 258, 26, 269, 273, 274, 283
May Games. *See* May Day
maypoles 56, 60, 68, 86–8, 90, 260, 282; defen of 64; demolition of 54, 92; denunciatio of 77, 83, 178; as royalist symbols 177, 26, 274–5
Melcombe Regis (D) 81, 197
Melksham (W) 78, 194, 214; Forest 7, 108
Mells (S) 78, 130, 137, 173, 191
Mendips, the 8, 146, 173, 174, 202–4
Mere (W) 37, 93, 104, 157, 161–2, 194, 206, 21
Merriott (S) 98
Middlezoy (S) 247, 251
middling sort 3; and civil war 169–70, 276–8 and politics 123, 126, 216, 220; and popul festivals 85, 90–1; and Puritanism 42, 7 130, 275–6
Midsomer Norton (S) 254
Milborne Port (S) 97, 204, 285 n.
Milborne St. Andrew (D) 90, 94
Mildenhall (W) 76
militia 109, 144, 166–7, 184
Milton Abbas (D) 197, 205
Milverton (S) 294 n.
Minchinhampton, Glos. 82
Minehead (S) 134, 141, 165, 203, 226, 294 n.
Mocket, Richard 128, 287
Mompesson, Sir Giles 108, 110
monarchy 10, 63–4, 69; symbols of 256–7, 28
Monkton Combe (S) 78
Monkton Farleigh (W) 266
Monkton, West (S) 269
Monmouth's rebellion 290–1
Montacute (S) 99, 102
Moorlinch (S) 251
moral reformation 48, 51–2, 239, 241–4, 275–6 *See also* Puritans

Morgan, Robert 163, 176
morris dancing 46, 54, 56–7, 59, 63, 68, 96, 262, 263, 273
Motcombe (D) 97, 161, 198
Mudford (S) 254
Myddle, Shropshire 30, 31, 275

Nailsea (S) 251
Nayler, James 190, 251, 254
Nedham, Marchamont 212, 225
Neroche Forest (S) 108–9, 122, 136, 137, 161, 173, 215
Netherbury (D) 81, 197, 299
Nettleton (W) 13, 16–17, 37, 58, 100
neutralism 2, 144, 153–4, 156, 163, 276. *See also* Clubmen
New Model Army. *See* army, of Parliament
Newcastle, Marquis of. *See* Cavendish
Newland, Glos. 106, 110, 112
Newnton, Long (W) 96, 280
Newton Toney (W) 76, 94, 179, 262
Nibley, North, Glos. 79
Nicholas, Sir Edward 161, 171
Norfolk 19, 76, 116, 214, 217, 218, 250, 256, 261, 290; places in 21, 46, 67
Northamptonshire 115, 133, 177, 261
Northbrooke, John 48
Northumberland 261
Norton Bavant (W) 95
Norton St. Philip (S) 216
Norwich 46, 50, 70, 71, 100, 250, 259, 261
Nottingham 282
Nottinghamshire 213
Noyes, John 26
Nunney (S) 219, 222

Osborne (D) 99
Oglander, Sir John 258
Okeford, Childe (D) 47, 89
Okeford Fitzpaine (D) 196
Oldmixon, John 151, 176
Oliver, Samuel 77
Osmington (D) 61
Overbury, Sir Thomas 17, 64, 127
Oxford 177–8, 260, 269, 274–5
Oxfordshire 61, 88, 114, 137, 262, 280

Palmer, John 228
Parham, Sir Edward 63, 97
parish, the 14, 27; Puritans and 65, 78–80; separatists and 252–4
Parker, John 61–3
Parliament 126; elections to 10, 123, 127, 132–3, 135–6, 236–8; Members of 120; of 1628–9 121 (*see also* Petition of Right); of 1640 (Short) 132–3, 140; of 1653 (Barebones) 235. *See also* Parliament, Long

Parliament, Long (1640) 132, 136, 137–8, 149, 208, 213, 220–1, 229, 239, 256; elections to 132–5, 226–8; purged 1648 231; supporters of 268–9 (*see also* Parliamentarians, Roundheads). *See also* Commonwealth, Rump
Parliamentarians 156, 208–9. *See also* Roundheads
paternalism 23, 281, 284
patriarchal authority 9–11, 145; Puritans and 42–3, 67, 99; revolution and 210–11, 212, 244, 286; separatists and 252–3; after 1660 287; threats to 38–40, 48, 99–100
Paulton (S) 84
Peacham, Edmond 120
peers, influence of 171–2, 184, 281, 296
Pembroke, Earls of. *See* Herbert
Penruddock's rising 236, 289
Pensford (S) 267
pensions 184–5, 191–8, 295–6, 299
Pepys, Samuel 260
perambulation of bounds 14, 46, 81, 91. *See also* Rogationtide
Perrott, Herbert 268
Peter, Hugh 165, 253
Petherton, South (S) 181
Petition of Right 71, 121, 128
petitions 137, 138–9, 147, 154–6, 159, 211, 213, 228–32
Pewsey (W) 263
Phelips family 20, 135
Phelips, Edward 135
Phelips, Sir Robert 113, 120, 122, 124, 127
Piddlehinton (D) 114
Piers, William, Bishop 66, 77–8, 126, 130, 137
Pitcombe (S) 98
players, plays 45, 50, 52–3, 57, 69, 260
Plot, Robert 46, 61, 88, 280
Plough Monday 14, 45, 47
plundering 151, 152–3
Plymouth 46, 141, 188, 247
Poldens, the 8, 157, 223
Poole (D) 147, 166, 216, 227, 235, 249
Popham family 77, 121, 170, 173, 224
Popham, Alexander 135, 170, 181, 218, 224, 277
Popham, Edward 226
Popham, Sir Francis 79
Portland (D) 146, 148
Poulett family 20, 135–6
Poulett, John, 1st Baron Poulett 109, 122–3, 127, 135, 164, 173
Poyntington (S) 63
Presbyterians; in politics 212, 228–9, 236; in religion 208, 239, 247; clergy 232, 237, 244–6; Directory for Worship 255–6
Prideaux, Edmund 227
processions 45, 69, 115, 271, 273. *See also* charivari

propaganda 138, 147, 164–5, 180
Protectorate, the 208, 220, 235–8; Council of 215. *See also* Major-Generals
Protestation, the (1641–2) 144–5, 158–9, 174, 286
Prynne, William 211–12, 233, 266
Puddletown (D) 14, 22–3, 93, 107
Purbeck, Isle of (D) 167, 172
Puritans (Puritanism) 36, 41–2, 52, 67, 72, 112, 239–40, 257, 278, 287; and marriage 42–3, 99–100; and politics 128, 133, 135, 219, 267; and popular festivals 47–8, 53–60, 70, 279; and civil war 143, 166, 177, 179–80; and Restoration 272, 274–5; regional distribution of 73–4, 77–80, 89, 130; hostility to 54–7, 60, 62, 64, 89, 131. *See also* lectureships, moral reformation
Putney, debates at 212
Pym, John 140, 143, 180
Pyne, Arthur 112
Pyne, Hugh 120
Pyne, John 219, 221, 225–7, 230, 232, 237

Quakers 209–10, 236, 238, 239–40, 244, 250–5, 273, 286
quartering 150–1, 222
Quemerford (W) 102

Radipole (D) 248
Radstock (S) 288
Ramsbury (W) 107, 275
Rangeworthy, Glos. 61–3, 83
Ranters 209–10, 235, 239–40, 249–50, 254, 285
Reading, Berks. 30
recruiting, military 183–4, 186–7, 190–1. *See also* impressment
regions, agricultural 4–5, 73–4, 103–4; arable 5, 12, 16, 18, 22, 26, 28, 40–1 (*see also* chalk country); pasture 7–8, 18, 19, 24–6, 28, 35, 80–1, 99–101, 107, 111, 130, 250 (*see also* cheese country)
Restoration, the 208–10, 240, 271–5, 280, 282, 285, 288
revels, village 45–6, 66, 67–8, 82, 84–5, 93, 95, 143–4, 240, 262, 264–5, 280; campaigns against 47, 49, 61–2, 98, 259, 264
Rich, Robert, 2nd Earl of Warwick 132, 171
Rimpton (S) 81
riots; in fens 113, 132, 136–7, 214; at festivals 69, 85, 96, 110, 264, 291; in forests 106–12, 160–2, 215; grain 116–19, 214; in London 132, 136, 140, 272–3; against Parliament 230, 261, 272–3; against Quakers 252, 254, 173; against soldiers 157, 221, 225. *See also* enclosures, excise, rituals

rituals 44, 101, 177, 257, 259; civic 68–9; riots 115, 137. *See also* charivari, hor[n] Skimmingtons
Robin Hood 110–11, 135, 270; in plays a[nd] processions 45, 55, 57, 98, 262, 282–3; Sc[ots] version of 221
Robins, John 249
Rogationtide 45, 47, 90, 97, 115, 256. *See a[lso]* perambulation of bounds
Rogers, John 216, 219, 243
Rogers, Richard 167, 172
Roundheads 177; in civil war 146–8, 158, 16[6] 170, 188; stereotype of 143–5, 164, 258, 26[6] as term of abuse 217–18, 278, 289
Roundway, battle of (W) 147, 162
royalism, popular 4, 179–81, 200–7
Royalists 149, 169–70, 177, 185, 263; a[nd] festive culture 258–9, 266; pensioners 19[4–] 8, 295–6, 299; suspected (1655–6) *see* Majo[r-] Generals. *See also* Cavaliers
Rump, the 208–9, 234, 235, 239–40, 249, 26[8,] 273
Rupert, Prince 147–8, 152, 268
Russell, Francis, 4th Earl of Bedford 19
Russell, William, 5th Earl of Bedford 166, 21[?]
Rye, Sussex 231

sabbath observance 47–8, 68, 103, 242–4
Salisbury (W) 30, 35, 134, 227, 249; Purita[n] in 36, 51, 57, 78, 246, 253, 262; in ci[vil] war 154–5, 170, 179; Royalists in 236, 257
Salisbury, Earl of. *See* Cecil
Salisbury Plain (W) 5, 167
Saltford (S) 86
Salthouse, Thomas 251–2
Samborne, Sir Barnaby 121
Sanderson, Robert 54
Sandys, Sir Samuel 22
Sanger, Gabriel 89
Sarum, Old (W) 226
Saye, Lord. *See* Fiennes
scolds 16–17, 38–40, 243, 286
Sedgemoor (S) 113, 157; battle of 290
Sedgwick, Obadiah 89
Seend (W) 84
Selwood Forest (S and W) 7, 34, 108, 109, 16[0,] 215
Semley (W) 220, 256
separatists 42, 79, 140, 239–40, 246–7, 286. *S[ee]* *also* Baptists, Fifth Monarchy Men, Quaker[s,] Ranters
Seymour family 134, 171, 173, 214, 226
Seymour, William, 2nd Earl and 1st Marquis [of] Hertford 60, 137, 146–7, 150, 164, 166–[7,] 170–1

haftesbury (D) 37, 89, 109, 123, 196, 216, 227, 245, 263, 276; in civil war 171, 187; Royalists in 196, 205–6, 230, 236, 299

hepton Mallet (S) 203–4, 206–7, 243, 278, 294

herborne (D) 30, 46, 53, 97–8, 230, 251–2, 254, 257 n., 276, 277–8; Digbys' influence at 171, 206; in civil war 146–8, 166–8, 172; Royalists in 197–8, 205, 299; and Restoration 271–2

herfield, Henry 51, 78

herfield, Richard 23, 172

herston Magna (W) 31, 32, 77, 80

hip Money 122, 124–5, 133–4

hort, Ames 274, 288

hrewsbury 39

hrewton (W) 76, 94

hropshire 233, 262

hute, Nathaniel 12

ilton (D) 245

kimmingtons 102–3, 106, 110–11, 279; rituals of 100, 216, 264

kutt, George 227

laughterford (W) 77, 79, 250

lingsby, Sir Henry 125, 136

mith, Sir Thomas 9–10

myth, Thomas 135, 173

omerset 20, 21, 25, 102, 116, 117, 119, 141, 211, 213, 222; agricultural regions 7–8; petitions from 139, 141, 155, 229–32; politics in 122–3, 124–5, 133, 135–6, 219, 227–8, 237; popular festivals in 49, 83–4, 85–6, 97–8, 264, 266–7; population of 293–4, 297; religion in 77–9, 130, 140, 242–4, 251; in civil war 4, 146–8, 151–3, 155–7, 164–6, 167–8, 170, 172–3, 174, 176, 178, 180–1, 189, 191, 285; Royalists in 192, 199–200, 202–5, 296–7; County Committee of 212, 221, 223, 225–7, 230, 251; and Restoration 271; and Monmouth's rebellion 290–1

omerset, Henry, 5th Earl of Worcester 171

omerset, John 157

omerton (S) 216

outhampton 36–7, 39, 51, 70, 116, 117

paxton (S) 30–2

ports 64, 85–8, 93, 99; restrictions on 47, 51, 259; first Book of (1617–18) 65–6, 84, 276; second Book of (1633) 49, 66–8, 77, 86, 95, 130, 177, 282. See also cricket, football, horse-racing, hurling, stoolball

tafford 54–5

taffordshire 46, 154, 156, 280; places in 46, 269

talbridge (D) 163

tamford, Earl of. See Grey

tanley, James, 7th Earl of Derby 171, 173

tanley, William, 6th Earl of Derby 65

tanton Drew (S) 79

Staple Fitzpaine (S) 264

Staplegrove (S) 269

Stawell, Sir John 113, 127, 147, 155–6, 172

Steeple Ashton (W) 83, 275

Steeple Langford (W) 94–5

Stoke St. Gregory (S) 98

Stoke St. Mary (S) 269

Stoke-sub-Hamdon (S) 217

Stoke Trister (S) 264

Stone, William 253

stoolball 75, 76–7, 106, 111, 281

Stour Valley 154, 169

Stourton family 122, 129, 141

Strangways, Sir John 172, 271–2

Stratford-on-Avon 54, 56, 66

Stratton-on-the-Fosse (S) 78

Stratton St. Margaret (W) 80

Street (S) 251

Strode, William 113, 124, 135, 161, 228, 243

Stroud, Glos. 71, 81

Stubbes, Philip 48

Sturminster Newton (D) 98, 158, 205, 245, 299

Suffolk 50, 173, 212, 250

Sussex 74, 152, 158, 173, 262, 281

Sutton Benger (W) 280

Sydenham, William 224, 227, 234

Sydling, Broad (D) 89

Symondsbury (D) 86

Tann Hill Fair (W) 85, 263

Tarrant Crawford (D) 32

Taunton (S) 99, 127, 216, 223, 228, 230, 234 n., 247, 273, 276, 289–90, 294; in civil war 148, 165–7, 170, 187, 191, 203

taxation, opposition to 149–50. See also excise, Loan, Ship Money

Taylor, John 39, 243, 258–9

Terling, Essex 21, 24, 26

Tetbury, Glos. 76

Tewkesbury, Glos. 46, 52–3

Thomas, William 77

Thornbury, Glos. 61–2, 123

Timsbury (S) 267

Tintinhull (S) 98, 181, 257

Tisbury (W) 33, 76, 91, 236

Tockenham Wick (W) 84–5

Tolpuddle (D) 95

Tories 282, 289

Touchet, Mervyn, 2nd Earl of Castlehaven 122

trained bands. See militia

Trenchard, Sir Thomas 224

Trent (S) 98–9, 245, 251

Trowbridge (W) 85, 194, 247, 278

Uley, Glos. 83

Upavon (W) 157, 236

Upton Lovell (W) 164

Upwey (D) 93
Uxbridge, treaty of 156

vagrants 11, 28, 34–6, 244
Vicars, John 54
Villiers family 108
Villiers, George, 1st Duke of Buckingham 121, 127–8

wakes. *See* revels
Walker, Clement 228
Waller, Sir William 150, 157, 166, 176, 185–6, 188
Walton (S) 251
Wanborough (W) 280
Wardour Castle (W) 146–7, 170, 188
Wareham (D) 147, 171, 191, 223, 299
Warminster (W) 104, 117, 193, 194–5, 206, 214
Warwick, Earl of. *See* Rich
Warwickshire 262
Wastfield, Robert 251
Watchet (S) 294 n.
Waterman, Peter 90, 180
Webbe, Thomas 249
Wedmore (S) 247–8
Weldon, Sir Anthony 221
Wellington (S) 70, 99, 133, 191, 265, 294 n.
Wellow, hundred of (S) 150
Wells (S) 55–6, 68, 140, 228, 235, 243, 247, 249, 280, 294; in civil war 146, 149, 155, 163, 165, 170–1, 178; Royalists in 203; Dean of 225
West, William 163
Westbury (W) 95, 104, 122, 193, 194–5, 213–14, 222
Westbury-on-Severn, Glos. 58–9
Westcote, Thomas 10, 28
Westmorland 36
Weston Bampfylde (S) 81, 97
Weymouth (D) 36, 56, 66, 100, 117, 223, 227–8, 234–5, 248, 251; in civil war 153, 165, 167; Royalists in 197, 205, 299
Wharton, Nehemiah 177–8, 185–6
Wheate, William 35
Whigs 282, 288, 289
White, John 51, 57, 139
Whiteparish (W) 157
Whitestaunton (S) 270
Whitsun (-tide) 14, 45, 46, 51, 57, 61–2, 63–4, 69, 84, 93, 281
Whitsun ales. *See* church ales
Wight, Isle of 171, 258
Wigston Magna, Leics. 13, 15, 18, 21
Wildman, John 214

Williams, John 106, 108, 110–11
Willis, Humphrey 223, 226–8, 255
Wilton in Vale of Pewsey (W) 110, 291
Wiltshire 25, 49, 102, 109, 116, 119, 129, 13 216, 222, 241, 281; agricultural regions 5– 73 (*see also* chalk country, cheese country enclosures in 19, 114 (*see also* forest petitions from 141, 229; politics in 122 ı 134, 226–8, 237; popular festivals in 46, 8 92–3, 280; population of 293–5; religi in 78–9, 140, 245–6, 249–50, 262–3; in ci war 146–8, 150–1, 152, 154–5, 157–60, 16 7, 170–1, 173–4, 175–6, 179–80, 188–9, 1 198; Royalists in 192–5, 199, 201–2, 295 County Committee of 225, 233; 16 rebellion in 236, 261
Wimborne Minster (D) 56, 58, 196, 205 n., 25 299
Wincanton (S) 168
Winchester 56, 151, 177
Winney, Samuel 252
Winsham (S) 27
Winsley (W) 59
Winstanley, Gerrard 26, 286
Winterbourne Earls (W) 150
Winterbourne Monkton (D) 93
Winterslow (W) 91, 93, 263
Wintour, Sir John 137, 159
Wishford, Great (W) 114
witchcraft 35, 38, 40, 254, 286
Wiveliscombe (S) 248, 294 n.
women; status of 11, 287; independence of 38 40, 48, 67, 99–100; masterless 36– preachers 140, 253; and church seats 30, 32 3; and civil war 154, 200, 211, 286
Wood, Anthony 64, 259, 261
Woodborough (W) 263
Woodbury Hill Fair (D) 85, 263
Woodlands, East and West (S) 207, 267
Wookey (S) 253
Wootton Bassett (W) 85, 194, 227
Wootton Rivers (W) 90
Worcester, Earl of. *See* Somerset
Worcestershire, places in 59, 68, 76
Wrington (S) 77, 155, 184, 219, 245
Wylye (W) 66, 94–5, 171

Yarlington (S) 180, 220
yeomen 10, 21, 24, 26–7, 64, 108–9, 201, 296
Yeovil (S) 46, 98, 285 n., 294
Yeovilton (S) 98
Yonge, Walter 127
York 45, 69
Yorkshire 126, 137, 138, 154, 169, 221